Postcolonial America

Postcolonial America

Edited by C. Richard King

University of Illinois Press

Urbana and Chicago

Chapter 4, "Is the United States Postcolonial? Transnationalism,
Immigration, and Race," originally appeared in *Diaspora* 4 (2):
181–200, © 1995 by Oxford University Press, and is reprinted by
permission of the University of Toronto Press, Ltd.

Library of Congress Cataloging-in-Publication Data
Postcolonial America / edited by C. Richard King.
p.   cm.
Includes bibliographical references and index.
ISBN 0-252-02531-8 (cloth)
ISBN 0-252-06852-1 (paper)
1. United States—Civilization—1945–   . 2. Postcolonialism—
United States. 3. Imperialism—United States—History—20th
century. 4. Civilization—American influences. 5. Nationalism—
United States—History—20th century. 6. Culture conflict—
United States. 7. Minorities—United States. 8. United States—
Relations—Developing countries. 9. Developing countries—
Relations—United States. I. King, C. Richard, 1968–
E169.12.P647   2000
973.92—dc21   99-6692
CIP

1 2 3 4 5 C P 5 4 3 2 1

Contents

Acknowledgments

The efforts of diverse individuals and institutions have made this volume possible. I am most grateful to my friends, family, and colleagues for their assistance, advice, and encouragement.

The editors and staff of the University of Illinois Press helped me realize the promise of the collection. Veronica Scrol's initial enthusiasm pushed it forward, and later Richard Martin ably guided it to completion. And the diligence of Bruce Bethell, our copyeditor, improved both its content and its form. The review process greatly enhanced the collection. The comments of the anonymous reviewers were quite helpful. The thoughts of Donald Pease merit special recognition for their quality and vision.

A grant from the Humanities Center at Drake University defrayed the expensive costs of securing copyright permissions. It proved crucial to publishing the volume.

The contributors deserve high praise for both their brilliant intellectual endeavors assembled here and their patience during the publication process. Countless other individuals knowingly and unknowingly ensured the success of the volume. They offered support, shared their ideas, gave invaluable counsel, directed me to sources, and read drafts. I wish to thank in particular Nancy Abelmann, Marsha Brofka, Edward M. Bruner, Rosa de Jurio, Ida Fadzillah, Sandra Hamid, Bill Kelleher, Charles R. King, Walter Little, Alejandro Lugo, David Prochaska, Joseph Schneider, Carol Stabile, and Bill Wood. Over the life of this project, Chuck Springwood has distinguished himself as a colleague. His kind friendship has been priceless.

Above all others, my family deserve recognition for their support and sacrifices. My partner, Marcie Gilliland, has been a constant source of joy and inspiration. Glimmering as the rare jewel she is, she has given me more than she can imagine. Throughout, our daughters, Abigail and Ellory, have reminded me of what matters.

Postcolonial America

Introduction: Dislocating Postcoloniality, Relocating American Empire

C. Richard King

At the end of December 1954, *Time* magazine ran a feature story on Walt Disney. The article did not begin with a preview of Disneyland, which was to open the following summer, or with a celebratory review of the then popular Davey Crockett films. Instead, it introduced the famed artist-entrepreneur by traveling to Africa, highlighting the global circulation and transcultural appropriations of Disney's imaginative creations. In the Belgian Congo, the magazine related, "a district officer peacefully cycled on his rounds. All at once he heard shrieks of terror, and a horde of natives plunged past him screaming a word he had never heard before. 'Mikimus!' they cried in horror, 'Mikimus!' Drawing his revolver, the officer went forward on foot to investigate. At the entrance to the village he staggered back, as out of the depths of the equatorial forest, 2,000 miles from civilization, came shambling toward him the nightmare figure of a shaggy, gigantic Mickey Mouse." Happily, the startled colonial agent discovered, "it was only the local witch doctor, up to his innocent tricks. His usual voo had lost its do, and in the emergency he had invoked, by making a few passes with needle and thread, the familiar spirit of that infinitely greater magician who has cast his spell upon the entire world—Walt Disney."

   This passage ostensibly oscillates between mocking African mimicry of white "magical arts" and celebrating the universal appeal and supernatural qualities of Disney's narratives and characters. Read over forty years later, however, the story's offensive, ethnocentric, and even racist elements over-shadow its seemingly innocent, humorous, and celebratory aspects. This discursive fragment, like journalistic texts more generally, reproduces catego-ries central to colonial discourse as it represents a colonial situation (Spurr 1993). It pivots around a series of binary oppositions, such as civilization/ savagery, America/Africa, self/other, and disciplined officer/superstitious native, reinforcing and reinscribing the hierarchical relations central to daily life in the Belgian Congo. Of equal significance, it demonstrates the inter-penetration of a decaying (European) imperialism aimed at territorial colo-nization and at the exploitation of natural and human resources and an as-cendant (American) imperialism primarily concerned with political control without colonization and the circulation of cultural commodities. Impor-tantly, as the formerly taken-for-granted, naturalized aspects of this account become unfamiliar and even awkward, this passage affords an opportunity to outline the intersections and contradictions of postcoloniality and or in American culture, not as an exemplary instance of a fully formed cultural condition, but as a transitional moment illuminating its emergent, uneven, and distinctive contours. I want to use this discursive fragment, then, to tease out some of the fundamental features of postcolonial America. To briefly foreshadow what follows, *Postcolonial America* is a complex, often conflicted, and ultimately uncomfortable strategic reframing of the specific, shifting, and contradictory conditions and structures of cultures of U.S. imperialism as well as of postcolonial studies' preoccupations and presuppositions.

* * *

The complexities of imperial cultures and their intersections animate this rendering of Mickey Mouse in colonial Africa. Even the most cursory criti-cal interpretation cannot ignore its enactments of colonial discourse or the significant, if ambivalent, role of mimicry. In fact, my earlier brief exegesis highlighted these features. Colonial discourse, mimicry, and even my account direct attention to the first sense in which the term *postcolonial* applies to the United States—namely, as it refers to postcolonial studies, a range of perspec-tives, intellectual interventions, and academic fields that engage empires and their alterations. Homi Bhabha usefully condenses some of the fundamen-tal features:

> Postcolonial criticism bears witness to the unequal and uneven forces of cul-tural representation involved in the contest for political and social authority ... Postcolonial perspectives emerge from the colonial testimony of Third World countries and the discourses of "minorities" within the geopolitical

divisions of East and West, North and South. They intervene in those ideological discourses of modernity that attempt to give a hegemonic "normality" to the uneven development and the differential, often disadvantaged, histories of nations, races, communities, peoples. They formulate their critical revisions around issues of cultural difference, social authority, and political discrimination in order to reveal the antagonistic and ambivalent moments within the rationalizations of modernity. (1994, 171)

Surely this rendering of postcolonial studies resonates in the contemporary United States. Unfortunately postcolonial studies has rapidly established a fairly stable canon, one anchored within select thinkers and texts, devoted to Europe and its former colonies, delimited by decolonization, and overly committed to literary and historical perspectives (see Ashcroft, Griffiths, and Tiffin 1995; Barker, Hulme, and Iversen 1994; Tiffin and Lawson 1994; Williams and Chrisman 1994). These orthodoxies, whatever their other problems, deflect attention from American culture.

Indeed, postcolonial studies are Eurocentric, focusing almost exclusively on Europe and its former colonies, primarily on British and to a lesser extent French endeavors in Africa and Asia, especially India. In their "scramble for post-colonialism" (Slemon 1994), theorists have all but ignored American empire, accepting the public, popular, and professional assumptions that (1) colonialism has never occurred within the United States; (2) imperialism and its aftermath have had little or nothing to do with the formation of distinctly American identities, institutions, and idioms (see Kaplan 1993); and (3) postcoloniality cannot refer to American culture. On the contrary, with few exceptions, their scholarship has emphasized that colonialism happened elsewhere and that the articulations of empire and American culture ended with the close of the Revolutionary War.

Contributing unique understandings of postcolonialism, culture, and America, all the essays in this collection undermine this central characteristic of postcolonial studies. They advance fundamental critiques of postcolonial studies' central tendencies, offering important correctives to the emerging field (see also Kaplan 1993; McClintock 1992; Parry 1987; Shohat 1992; Thomas 1994). Indeed, although some contributors (e.g., San Juan and Martin) explicitly challenge the appropriateness of using postcolonial perspectives to describe the contemporary United States, all of them problematize the prevailing assumptions of postcolonial studies.

* * *

In retrospect, an impending decolonization weighs down any reading of this passage. Less than six years after this episode, Zaire emerged as an independent nation-state, shattering the tyrannical hold Belgium formerly exercised within the Congo. For many, postcoloniality demands this sort of progressive, linear account of liberation and self-determination through which the margins break free from the center. Such versions foreground the "after colonialism" implied by the term *postcolonialism* as a tangible break or temporal shift. Amy Kaplan (1993, 17) highlights this framework's implications for postcolonial studies: "Most current studies of imperial and postcolonial culture, however, tend to omit discussions of the United States. . . . The history of American imperialism strains the definition of the postcolonial, which implies a temporal development (from 'colonial' to 'post') that relies heavily on the spatial coordinates of European empires, in their formal acquisition of territories, and the subsequent history of decolonization." Thus, postcolonial studies maintains its limited scholarly domain, and these misreadings of American empire, by explicitly or implicitly distinguishing postcoloniality with reference to decolonization.

Importantly, decolonization as a model of postcoloniality can offer important insights into the American experience. Popular readings of American history have suggested that formative features of the American character and of the United States as a unique nation-state derive from the colonies' struggle for independence from Great Britain and the subsequent establishment of a sovereign republic. Numerous myths and monuments attest to the significance of decolonization and postcoloniality to American identities and institutions. Mirroring these accounts with a critical twist, some scholars have proposed that the United States be read in postcolonial terms. In their by now classic assessment, Bill Ashcroft, Gareth Griffiths, and Helen Tiffin (1989, 16) have positioned the United States as "the first post-colonial society to develop a 'national' literature." Not only is it first, but according to Ashcroft, Griffiths, and Tiffin, it exemplifies postcoloniality: "In many ways the American experience and its attempts to produce a new kind of literature can be seen to be the model for all later post-colonial writing" (1989, 16). Despite their conviction, they do not engage or analyze American literature or American culture further. More recently others have more fully examined the postcolonial emergence of American culture. Lawrence Buell (1992), Laura Murray (1996), and Jon Stratton (this volume), for instance, have stressed the centrality of decolonization, the importance of America's dependent relationship with Europe, and its efforts to locate a distinct national tradition, identity, or culture. Of course, as valid as such assertion are, they provoke unease in many cultural critics, a point to which I return later and one that Stratton addresses in his afterword, precisely because the imaginaries and imagined communities central to the United States emerged not simply through a break with

European imperialism but through the establishment and elaboration of its own imperial cultures.

As significant as decolonization may be, however, it is problematic, if not inadequate (see Pieterse and Parekh 1995). A number of scholars have proposed more fluid, dynamic notions of postcoloniality. Sally Keenan (1993, 45) emphasizes the continuity and change inscribed within the term *postcolonial*: "In the United States, as elsewhere, the *post* of that term should not be regarded as a sign that the processes of colonialism have ended; rather their legacy continues to exist as a lived reality for many citizens." Likewise Peter Hulme (1995, 120) underscores the processual qualities of postcoloniality, noting, "If 'postcolonial' is a useful word, then it refers to a *process* of disengagement from the whole colonial syndrome, which takes many forms and probably is inescapable for all of those whose worlds have been marked by that set of phenomena: 'postcolonial' is (or should be) a descriptive, not an evaluative, term." A more processual rendering of the postcolonial turns attention away from happy endings, tidy temporal schemes, and progressive, irreversible ruptures to stress emergent formations shaped by social struggles, persistent asymmetries, and novel arrangements. Indeed, framing the United States as postcolonial, as emergent through its changing relations both with European imperialism and with its own imperial endeavors, directs attention to its production as an imperial nation-state. It foregrounds, as the essays in the first section do, the narratives, discourses, and myths that center the formation of America as an imagined community and nation.

* * *

The encounter between an African appropriating and reconfiguring American cultural commodities and a Belgian colonial agent foreshadows an emergent world-system. Surely in 1954 it was clear that European empires were not what they used to be, that American imperial endeavors had entered a new phase, and that the contours of global culture were rapidly shifting. Increasingly American media, public policies, and military interests intruded on and reshaped local contexts in the then still emergent Third and Fourth Worlds. As American activists and intellectuals would begin to recognize not more than a decade later—largely as a result of U.S. involvement in Vietnam and the proliferation of a range of new social movements—the global restructuring of the world-system produced by the Cold War, the emergence of global or transnational capitalism, and decolonization had important implications for the connections between colonialisms and cultures.

In the most general sense, this restructuring might be read as the postcolonial condition. That is, postcoloniality also refers to a global condition emergent after World War II. In *Orientalism and the Postcolonial Predicament*, Carol Breckenridge and Peter van der Veer (1993, 1) argue for such a general periodization: "We can therefore speak of the postcolonial period as a framing device to characterize the second half of the twentieth century. The term 'postcolonial' displaces the focus on 'postwar' as a historical marker for the past fifty years." Breckenridge and Van der Veer no doubt capture the transparent condition of the past half-century. This formulation is useful because it reframes the present, emphasizing not simply the importance of World War II and the reconfigurations discernible in its wake but also the centrality of colonial cultures and changes apparent within them. As such, Breckenridge and Van der Veer use postcoloniality in a way that deflects attention from decolonization exclusively, clearing space for a more complex understanding of the former concept.

Despite its importance, their definition remains overly general. A more specific definition is needed, one that counters or even refuses easy correlations and overly general assessments. Such a definition must begin, as Breckenridge and Van der Veer recognize, to address the world-system and the manner in which shifting forms of colonialism have reconfigured it. The essays in the second section of this volume explicitly struggle to formulate a working understanding of the global networks of inequality that have displaced systems of neocolonialism and modern imperial domination (conquest, exploitation, and occupation). Although they do not share a single sense of the transnational formation of postcolonial America, they begin at a crucial intersection highlighted by Jenny Sharpe (this volume), who usefully reinterprets postcoloniality with reference to the United States, characterizing it as "the point at which internal social relations intersect with global capitalism and the international division of labor"; Sharpe thus seeks "to define the 'after' to colonialism as the neocolonial relations the United States entered into with decolonized nations."

* * *

The wonderful world of Disney is no longer what it was in 1954. To be sure, Mickey Mouse has gone global in much more disturbing and direct ways, including the international circulation of theme parks, films, characters, and commodities. To concentrate on the transnational production and consumption of Disney exclusively, however, misses a fundamental set of alterations that characterize postcolonial America. In the 1950s, as the encounter described in *Time* unfolded, Disney celebrated American empire. In the various films devoted to Davey Crockett, the media giant reinscribed the conquest of North America as a heroic struggle of Euro-American masculinity against nature and savagery, championing Crockett as "the king of the wild frontier" for, among other things, pacifying Native Americans and making the margins safe for white settlement. At Disneyland similar narratives punctuated visitors' sojourns in the magic kingdom. In a section of the theme park known as Frontierland, visitors could witness "full-blooded Indians from seventeen tribes perform authentic and symbolic dances" and attack, or at least threaten to attack, Euro-American settlers and audience members themselves (Wiener 1994, 133). Much has changed over the past four decades. In place of Davey Crockett and Manifest Destiny, Pocahontas and the ambiguities of cross-cultural relations now confront audiences. "Hostile" Native Americans have been replaced by dancing bears in Frontierland, and Walt Disney World even includes such tragic historical figures as Chief Joseph the animatron. I do not want to deny the manner in which stereotypes persist here, perhaps even legitimating the same values and actions they did forty years before; instead, I want to draw attention to the discernible changes. To my mind, this schematic outline suggests that postcoloniality might be reimagined in terms of change, decentering, and displacement. In the contemporary United States, this ongoing process entails a shift from the celebration, comfortable acceptance, and largely unquestioned appropriateness of conquest and colonization to the predicaments associated with living through the illegitimate, uncomfortable, conflicted aftermath of an irreversible conquest.

Such a rereading of postcoloniality and the American experience has powerful implications, as the essays in the final section of this text clarify more fully. At the risk of overstating and generalizing this reframing of American empire, let me touch on some of the central structures of a decentered or postcolonial America. First, postcoloniality highlights the profound alterations in American culture, rearticulations of signifying practices, semantic fields, and power relations. Second, the displacements structured by and structuring postcolonial America turn on the decentering of Euro-American culture and history. Third, postcoloniality is marked by the emergence of novel discourses, by "a search for alternatives to the discourses of the colonial era" (Spurr 1993, 6), ranging from Black Power to multiculturalism. These narratives and practices tend to counter and reproduce imperial relations, categories, and hierarchies. As such, postcoloniality entails the "reaccentuation of colonial and anti-colonial languages" (Thomas 1994, 7). Fourth, the centrality of counterhegemonic, anticolonial practices to struggles within public culture distinguishes postcolonial America. Oppositional strategies, including the civil rights movement, protests against the Vietnam War, and Native American demands for sovereignty, have opened novel sites of resistance, contexts "of contesting and contested stories attempting to account for, to recount, the asymmetry and inequality of relations between peoples, races, languages" (Niranjana 1992, 1). Fifth, reactionary projects and recuperative effects maintain and reinstate colonial clichés and imperial cultures.

* * *

Throughout this collection, postcolonial America is examined as the intersections of local, national, and transnational formations, as specific articulations of histories, processes, and relations. Reformulating postcoloniality and American empire in this manner demands a sensitivity to the contradictions of "the American experience" and a willingness to accept the difficulties and discomfort associated with engaging these contradictions.

For many, the production of American institutions and identities through decolonization and colonization provokes unease. Sangeeta Ray and Henry Schwarz (1995, 165n3) nicely encapsulated this tension: "Interestingly enough, it is the US, of all the 'postcolonial' societies around the world, in which we find perhaps the most dramatic example of turning the colonial relationship on its head. Post-colonies are obviously capable of becoming oppressor-states, but none has been quite so successful at this as the US." Clearly, as Gesa Mackenthun (1996, 264) has observed, "the United States cannot be called 'postcolonial' in any easy sense." Nevertheless, accepting this dis-ease and interrogating the conflicted aspects of postcolonial America should energize rather than paralyze critical scholarship. In fact, such a repositioning contrasts with the righteous declarations that so easily dismiss the significance of thinking about the United States in postcolonial terms. Anne McClintock (1992, 87), for instance, finds the notion of postcolonial America to be offensive: "By what fiat of historical amnesia can the United States of America, in particular, qualify as 'postcolonial'—a term which can only be a monumental affront to the Native American peoples currently opposing the confetti triumphalism of 1992."

Others have gone further. Ruth Frankenberg and Lata Mani (1993, 293) suggest, "Here, the term 'postcolonial' sticks in our throats." Its application to the histories and conditions of the United States should make us uneasy. To overcome the difficulties and discomforts associated with thinking about postcoloniality in American culture, they propose an alternative characterization and periodization of the present: "Post–Civil Rights" America. Such a move nicely encapsulates "the serious calling into question of white/Western dominance by the groundswell of movements of resistance, and the emergence of struggles for collective self-determination" increasingly characteristic of American culture after 1945 (1993, 293). It does not, unfortunately, confront or theorize a set of equally important features: recuperative practices, discursive inertia, reactionary spaces, and imperial practices.

Instead, their notion of post–civil rights America focuses so narrowly on race, resistance, identity, and juridical structures that it threatens to erase the complex connections of colonialism and culture in the contemporary United States.

Unlike numerous cultural critiques exemplified by the work of McClintock, Frankenberg, and Mani, the essays in this collection do not excise the uneasiness associated with theorizing and examining postcoloniality in American culture. Thus, their usage remains strategic, even provisional, designed to intervene within current debates about colonialism and culture and disrupt prevailing understandings of America while describing a constellation of relations, structures, and conditions. Retaining postcoloniality, moreover, captures many of the present complexities of American empire. For all its awkwardness, for all the tensions and troubles, postcoloniality describes specific sociohistorical relations between colonialism and culture in the contemporary United States. Although perhaps inadequate, postcoloniality permits us to speak of the forms of power, fields of discourses, and conditions of possibilities germane to the present.

* * *

This collection describes, theorizes, and debates postcolonial America. The essays undertake an initial mapping of the patterns, connections, and histories characteristic of postcoloniality in the United States. Examining local, national, and transnational formations, as well as the articulations of and tensions among them, they seek to open discussion of and encourage reflection on the problems and possibilities of explicitly inserting American culture within postcolonial studies. As a consequence, the assembled essays simultaneously clarify and challenge prevailing conceptions of postcolonialism and accepted understandings of American culture. Significantly, they initiate crucial discussions about the material conditions, social relations, cultural contours, and discursive formations particular to postcolonial America. Thus, they make novel contributions to postcolonial studies and American studies, problematizing and refining these fields' theories, foci, and findings.

Three intertwined concerns unite the interpretations of postcolonial America advanced in this volume. First, they engage postcolonial theory, alternatively interrogating its utility and validity, applying it to highlight the peculiarities of American culture, or offering important alternatives suggested by the specificities of American empire. Second, the essays trace the emergence, novelty, and significance of postcolonial patterns, practices, and precepts in the United States. Third, they detail the manner in which the unique sites and uneven relations central to the crystallization of postcoloniality have informed, imprinted, and reinvented American identities and institutions.

These shared concerns derive from diverse foundations. The collection is interdisciplinary, containing approaches and strategies associated with American studies, anthropology, cultural studies, history, literary criticism, religious studies, and women's studies. The volume manifests important theoretical differences as well. Contributors employ techniques and perspectives derived from poststructuralism, postmodernism, feminism, Marxism, psychoanalysis, and of course postcolonialism. Substantively, the essays focus on an equally wide range of topics, including narratives and discourses, law and public policy, immigration and tourism, academic disciplines, musical subcultures, and virtual communities. Finally, they locate postcolonial America in diverse spaces and communities, mapping specific local, regional, national, and transnational variations on postcoloniality. Beyond making a shared effort to expose and challenge the social privileges and cultural patterns associated with Euro-Americans—the transparent center, as it were—various essays consider African American, Asian American, Native American, immigrant, and multicultural communities inside the United States; postcolonial formations in the American West, Southwest, and Hawai'i; and the complex circuits uniting Asia, the Caribbean, and Latin America with the United States.

As a consequence of this diversity, the volume advances multiple, perhaps even conflicted, visions of the shape of postcolonial America, its connections with postcoloniality as some sort of global condition, and its implications for prevailing understandings of cultures of U.S. imperialism. Although readers desiring a solitary position or single definition will be frustrated, the diverse interpretations presented here fashion a richly textured account of the specificity and historicity of the central and shifting structures of postcolonial America.

* * *

Although this collection reconceptualizes U.S. cultures of imperialism, neither American empire nor its implications are particularly new subjects. In the United States, despite early critiques of American imperial endeavors, empire emerges as a subject of wider concern and scholarly debate largely in the wake of the civil rights movement and the New Left critique of the Vietnam War. In fact, for the past thirty years, academicians and activists alike have struggled to map the colonial contours of the United States. Early accounts of American empire interpreted the imperial structures of American foreign policy or multinational capitalism, in the limiting and limited perspectives associated with vulgar materialist and Marxist frameworks, as neoimperialism (Fann and Hodges 1971; Tomlinson 1991; Woddis 1969; Zeitlin 1972) and internal colonization (Bailey and Flores 1973; Barrera 1979; Barrera, Muñoz, and Ornelas 1972; Blauner 1972; Liu 1976). These earlier efforts concentrated almost exclusively on the economic and sociopolitical aspects of American empire, however, disregarding the crucial intersections of colonialism and culture. Only after American scholars reconfigured poststructuralism, a theoretical framework developed largely in response to French decolonization (Young 1990; see also Ross 1995), did they begin to take seriously the cultural aspects of American empire. This revitalized appreciation of the intersections of colonialism and culture is best manifested in *Cultures of United States Imperialism* (Kaplan and Pease 1993; but see also Lutz and Collins 1993; Mitchell 1988; Rogin 1990). Both early attention to neocolonial networks of power and more recent poststructural approaches to colonial cultures inform this collection, energizing its efforts to examine and theorize postcolonial America. As the following essays demonstrate, postcoloniality affords a more flexible, specific, and insightful conceptualization of prevailing articulations of colonialism and culture in the contemporary United States.

* * *

The following essays each engage postcolonial America, remapping the shape of American culture while also challenging postcolonial studies. Inserting the United States within a postcolonial framework, they speak of the specific, multiple, historical, and changing contours of American empire. Their discussions cluster around three deeply imbricated themes: national narratives, transnational formations, and local elaborations of postcoloniality in American culture. The organization of the text corresponds to these overlapping thematic units.

The essays in the first section examine the discourses and stories through which America takes shape as an imperial nation. The contributors to this section offer sophisticated rereadings of the American experience and the public and professional perspectives that have materialized it.

Jon Stratton directs attention to the manner in which a series of interconnected myths in literature, film, and music structured the formation and alteration of the United States as the first postcolonial state. He concerns himself with the dominant mythology of the apocalypse and the related fictions of the frontier, the promised land, and the road. His readings of these national narratives highlight the preoccupation with identity and the sense of displacement so crucial to the American experience. In his afterword he returns to these themes in an effort to clarify the unique qualities of postcoloniality in American culture (such as its particular relationships with race, civil rights, and multiculturalism) and the importance of speaking of the United States in postcolonial terms.

Of late the national narratives at the center of Stratton's analysis have troubled many scholars, particularly those working in American studies who have recognized the role the field played in advancing such grand narratives in the latter half of the twentieth century. Attempting to replace these myths and coming-of-age stories, some have sought postnational narratives as an alternative, dubbing themselves the "New Americanists." Despite their good intentions, Susie O'Brien argues, their efforts too often advance teleological frameworks rooted in an emancipatory rhetoric of progress. Through a close reading of Jamaica Kincaid's *Lucy,* she problematizes the postnational turn, suggesting that it relies on the same narrative structure as do more conventional formulations of America and Americanism. In conclusion, she traces the intersections of national, postnational, and postcolonial narratives.

Shifting the focus from myths, stories, and fictions, Donna Maeda traces the formation of postcolonial America within legal discourse. She deconstructs the "cultural defense" and its application in legal cases involving Asian immigrants in an effort to locate the production of the nation and its subjects. The cultural defense, she argues, dependent as it is on essentialized, static conceptions of culture and difference, marginalizes the foreign, traditional beliefs and behaviors it purports to defend while devaluing women and legitimating "male-gendered behaviors" by placing them at the center of culture. Drawing on the work of Homi Bhabha, Gayatri Spivak, and Trihn T. Minh-ha, she offers a meaningful reinterpretation of cultural difference as dynamic, strategic, structured, and hybrid.

Extending these efforts to deconstruct national narratives, the essays in the second section, "Unsettling the American Experience," examine the ways in which transnationalism, immigration, and global capital reshape the articulations of American empire, imagined communities, and international networks. They interrogate the intertwined, asymmetrical transcultural flows through which peoples, ideologies, and commodities shuttle, using these circulations to isolate the globalization of American empire, its restructuring of local contexts within "the core" and "the periphery," and asking how individuals and collectives have responded to these ascendant structures of the world order.

Jenny Sharpe frames the key issues taken up in this section. Placing race, transcultural processes, and differential power at the center of her discussion, she offers a powerful critique of existing models of postcolonial studies that reduce them to discussions about marginality and oppression. Against these more orthodox formulations of postcolonialism, she argues that this important interdisciplinary field should be reconstituted as the study of differential power and transnationalism.

Examining the debates over federal Indian and immigration policy between 1945 and 1965, Rachel Buff asks difficult questions about the transnational production of America as an imperial nation. She analyzes the internal and external colonies of the United States from the standpoint of postcolonial theories of nation and narration, arguing that federal policies and public discussions of these policies constituted a culturally charged "national romance" that selected immigrants and Native Americans for assimilation into a highly administered body of the national family. These policies, which compelled both groups to migrate to cities, created a racialized context against which these "new immigrants" would come to define politicized identities in the 1960s and 1970s.

Accentuating the structures of transnational capitalism undergirding the arguments advanced by Sharpe and Buff, Elena Glasberg examines novel forms of American imperialism made possible by shifting global flows of information and capital. To isolate these ascendant articulations and their relations with American empire, she plugs into the Internet, examining its use by both multinational corporations, such as Chrysler, and new social movements, such as Greenpeace, to consolidate and challenge the virtual and actual hegemonies of American imperialism. Throughout, she argues that the only way to make sense of postcolonial America in a global frame is in terms of postnationalism.

Part 2 closes as it began, with a powerful critique of postcolonial studies. E. San Juan Jr. challenges established understandings of postcolonialism and their connections with postmodernism and poststructuralism. He argues that these critical theories tend to be complicit with global networks of inequality, obfuscating the workings of American neocolonialism, post-Fordist capitalism, and local cultures of terror. Setting aside postcolonial theory, he locates alternative and meaningful forms of counterhegemonic struggle within the work and writings of Maria Lorena Barro, C. L. R. James, and Rigoberta Menchú.

The final section, "Postcolonial Formations: Complicity, Opposition, and Possibility," addresses the unique forms of postcolonialism discernible within American culture. Individual contributors explore the ways in which diverse localities and lives reconfigure, reinstate, reinvent, and resist postcoloniality in American culture.

Laura Donaldson initiates the effort to specify, multiply, and problematize postcolonial America through a nuanced rereading of the life and works of William Apess, the nineteenth-century Pequot writer, preacher, and activist, that reclaims him as an oppositional postcolonial intellectual. To formulate this interpretation, she proposes a useful distinction between complicit postcolonialism and oppositional postcolonialism: "the former designates eras of political decolonization that repeat many colonial tendencies; the latter, the potentially insurgent underside of any colonial context." Concerned as it is with "the colonized in the newly decolonized United States," her argument pluralizes postcoloniality, stressing the postcolonial emergence of America, its imperial endeavors, and the counterhegemonic interventions enacted by the colonized. In the process she also encapsulates the critical project defining this section, namely, how to distinguish between postcolonialities, between those forms of postcoloniality that collude with and stabilize imperial hegemony and those forms that challenge and undermine it.

For Arthur Martin, the public culture and daily lives of middle-class migrants in Taos, New Mexico, perpetuate the central structures of modern colonization. He is particularly interested in documenting "the will to alterity," or the desire to be different, to transcend the mundane, and its connections with commodification, experience, and place. At root he argues that the lives and lifestyles of middle-class migrants hinge on a contradiction: rather than open the alternative, transcendent, or oppositional spaces they envision, they collude with and reproduce privileges and positions rooted in colonial categories and capitalist relations. As such, he isolates an important instance of complicit postcoloniality and the difficulties associated with formulating alternative formations.

Engaging scholarship's complicity with the differential power structures and imperial idioms central to American hegemony, Russell McCutcheon reinterprets religious studies. He concentrates on the ahistorical and essentialist qualities of its representations, which tend to conceptualize religion as sui generis, as unique, autonomous, and free from the constraints of cultural, historical, or socioeconomic factors. This disavowal and mystification, he asserts, is best exemplified by the accounts of the first instance of Vietnamese "self-immolation" within religious studies, which disconnects religion from imperial geopolitics. In conclusion, he calls for postcolonial religious studies to counter the regnant discourse and imagine alternative, oppositional practices.

In contrast with Martin and McCutcheon, who document more or less complicit, recuperative variations of postcoloniality in American culture, Brij Lunine details the counterhegemonic force emergent from particular spaces within hip-hop culture. Discussing the cultural productions of the rap group the Coup, he elucidates the postcolonial themes and practices made possible in and through rap music. For Lunine, hip-hop culture is meaningful as it reframes, inverts, and challenges dominant constructions of race, culture, and power. Stressing the Afro-diasporic foundations of rap, he highlights its ability to materialize a postcolonial consciousness among African Americans while simultaneously disrupting hegemonic relations and categories. As such, he nicely outlines the oppositional possibilities of subcultural and even marginal sites, such as hip-hop culture, and, as does McCutcheon, the subversive potential of postcolonial studies.

Exploring the recent and ongoing struggles over Devils Tower National Monument, John Dorst addresses the conflicts and contradictions arising as

Native Americans and Euro-Americans struggle for control of the spiritually significant yet recreationally defined tourist site. He maps out the complex political, perceptual, and discursive contours of postcolonial America. Stressing the intersections of narrativity and visuality, he documents the breakdown of colonial networks of power and their resuscitation in a postcolonial guise. That is, changing narrative forms and visual norms expose the manner in which strategies of containment and control have shifted from coercion and subjugation to incorporation and inclusion. Thus, he outlines the interplay of oppositional politics and liberal, multicultural absorption at the heart of postcoloniality in American culture.

The volume closes hopefully with David Prochaska's effort to map alternate engagements with postcoloniality. Prochaska proposes a museum exhibit designed to deconstruct the exotic fabrications of Hawai'i through postcards and the fetishization of postcards that all too frequently makes their effects transparent. Through his playfully serious reworking of museum culture, an institutional site central to American and European imperialisms, he highlights the potential to use postcolonial theories to open American empire to public scrutiny and discussion while re-creating the shape and significance of images, identities, and imagined communities.

Works Cited

Ashcroft, Bill, Gareth Griffiths, and Helen Tiffin. 1989. *The Empire Writes Back: Theory and Practice in Post-Colonial Literatures.* New York: Routledge.

————, eds. 1995. *The Post-Colonial Studies Reader.* New York: Routledge.

Bailey, Ronald, and Guillermo Flores. 1973. "Internal Colonialism and Racial Minorities in the U.S." In *Structures of Dependency,* ed. Frank Bonilla and Robert Girling, 149–60. Stanford, Calif.: Stanford Institute of Politics.

Barker, Francis, Peter Hulme, and Margaret Iversen, eds. 1994. *Colonial Discourse/Postcolonial Theory.* Manchester, U.K.: Manchester University Press.

Barrera, Mario. 1979. *Race and Class in the Southwest: A Theory of Racial Inequality.* South Bend, Ind.: Notre Dame University Press.

Barrera, Mario, Carlos Muñoz, and Charles Ornelas. 1972. "The Barrio as an Internal Colony." In *Peoples and Politics in Urban Society,* ed. Harlan Hahn, 465–98. Beverly Hills, Calif.: Sage.

Bhabha, Homi. 1994. "The Postcolonial and the Postmodern: The Question of Agency." *The Location of Culture,* 171–97. London: Routledge.

Blauner, Robert. 1972. "Internal Colonialism and Ghetto Revolt." *Racial Oppression in America,* 82–110. New York: Harper and Row.

Breckenridge, Carol, and Peter van der Veer, eds. 1993. *Orientalism and the Postcolonial Predicament.* Philadelphia: University of Pennslyvania Press.

Buell, Lawrence. 1992. "American Literary Emergence as a Postcolonial Phenomenon." *American Literary History* 4:411–42.

Fann, K. T., and Donald C. Hodges, eds. 1971. *Readings in U.S. Imperialism.* Boston: Porter Sargent.

Frankenberg, Ruth, and Lata Mani. 1993. "Crosscurrents, Crosstalk: Race, 'Postcoloniality,' and the Politics of Location." *Cultural Studies* 7:292–310.

Hulme, Peter. 1995. "Including America." *Ariel* 26, no. 1:116–23.

Kaplan, Amy. 1993. "'Left Alone with America': The Absence of Empire in the Study of American Culture." In *Cultures of United States Imperialism,* ed. Amy Kaplan and Donald E. Pease, 3–21. Durham, N.C.: Duke Univerity Press.

Kaplan, Amy, and Donald E. Pease, eds. 1993. *Cultures of United States Imperialism.* Durham, N.C.: Duke University Press.

Keenan, Sally. 1993. "'Four Hundred Years of Silence': Myth, History, and Motherhood in Toni Morrison's *Beloved.*" In *Recasting the World: Writing Colonialism,* ed. Jonathan White, 45–81. Baltimore: Johns Hopkins University Press.

Liu, John. 1976. "Towards an Understanding of the Internal Colonial Model." In *Counterpoint: Perspectives on Asian America,* ed. Emma Gee, 160–68. Los Angeles: Asian American Studies Center, University of California.

Lutz, Catherine, and Jane L. Collins. 1993. *Reading National Geographic.* Chicago: University of Chicago Press.

Mackenthun, Gesa. 1996. "Adding Empire to the Study of American Culture." *Journal of American Studies* 30:263–69.

McClintock, Anne. 1992. "The Angel of Progress: Pitfalls of the Term 'Post-colonialism.'" *Social Text* 31–32:84–98.

Mitchell, Timothy. 1988. *Colonising Egypt.* Cambridge: Cambridge University Press.

Murray, Laura J. 1996. "The Aesthetic of Dispossession: Washington Irving and Ideologies of (De)Colonization in the Early Republic." *American Literary History* 8:205–31.

Niranjana, Tejaswini. 1992. *Siting Translation: History, Post-Structuralism, and the Colonial Context.* Berkeley: University of California Press.

Parry, Benita. 1987. "Problems in Current Theories of Colonial Discourse." *Oxford Literary Review* 9, nos. 1–2:27–58.

Pieterse, Jan Nederveen, and Bhikhu Parekh, eds. 1995. *The Decolonization of the Imagination: Culture, Knowledge, and Power.* London: Zed.

Ray, Sangeeta, and Henry Schwarz. 1995. "Postcolonial Discourse: The Raw and the Cooked." *Ariel* 26, no. 1:147–66.

Rogin, Michael. 1990. "'Make My Day': Spectacle as Amnesia in Imperial Politics." *Representations* 29:99–123.

Ross, Kristin. 1995. *Fast Cars, Clean Bodies: Decolonization and the Recoding of French Culture.* Cambridge: MIT Press.

Shohat, Ella. 1992. "Notes on the 'Post-Colonial.'" *Social Text* 31–31:99–113.

Slemon, Stephen. 1994. "The Scramble for Postcolonialism." In *De-Scribing Empire: Post-Colonialism and Textuality,* ed. Chris Tiffin and Alan Lawson, 15–32. New York: Routledge.

Spurr, David. 1993. *The Rhetoric of Empire: Colonial Discourse in Journalism, Travel Writing, and Imperial Administration.* Durham, N.C.: Duke University Press.

Thomas, Nicholas. 1994. *Colonialism's Culture: Anthropology, Travel, and Government.* Princeton, N.J.: Princeton University Press.

Tiffin, Chris, and Alan Lawson, eds. 1994. *De-Scribing Empire: Post-Colonialism and Textuality.* New York: Routledge.

Tomlinson, John. 1991. *Cultural Imperialism: A Critical Introduction.* Baltimore: Johns Hopkins University Press.

Wiener, Jon. 1994. "Tall Tales and True." *The Nation* 31 (Jan.): 133–35.

Williams, Patrick, and Laura Chrisman, eds. 1994. *Colonial Discourse and Post-Colonial Studies: A Reader.* New York: Columbia University Press.
Woddis, Jack. 1969. *An Introduction to Neo-Colonialism.* New York: International.
Young, Robert. 1990. *White Mythologies: Writing History and the West.* New York: Routledge.
Zeitlin, Irving M. 1972. *Capitalism and Imperialism.* Chicago: Markham.

PART I

(Post)National Narratives

I   The Beast of the Apocalypse: The Postcolonial Experience of the United States

Jon Stratton

> But the funniest thing was
> When I was leavin' the bay,
> I saw three ships a-sailin'
> They were all heading my way
> I asked the captain what his name was
> And how come he didn't drive a truck
> He said his name was Columbus
> I just said, "Good Luck."
>
> — Bob Dylan, "Bob Dylan's 115th Dream"

This essay discusses the American structure of culture in the post–World War II period. I use the term *structure of culture* to echo Raymond Williams's (1977) analytical term *structure of feeling* while emphasizing the importance of cultural specificity (Stratton 1986). In this essay I take the United States of America as a specific cultural entity. I briefly examine a number of inter-related American myths as they have been articulated in literature, music, and film and discuss their relation to the specific experience of the United States as the first postcolonial state. I am using the term *postcolonial* here to refer to the complex of concerns surrounding the problem of identity that characterizes the experience of states—particularly settler states—that have their origins in the European practice of colonization. Over the last half-century or so, it has become clear that independence from the colonizing state does not solve the problem of identity for such new states. It is equally clear that a sense of place is a fundamental constituent in the formation of the identity of the modern state. Despite the fact that the United States gained its independence as long ago as 1782, it is still a postcolonial state in terms of its sense of displacement and its preoccupation with identity (Ashcroft, Griffiths, and Tiffin 1989). Perhaps the most important way in which a settler state expresses this experience of displacement is in its construction of the indigenous inhabitants of the land (Stratton 1989). The myths with which I will be concerned are characteristically utilized by the American white, Anglo-Irish, male middle class, for this group has dominated the nation's power structure. Nevertheless, other groups within the United States can and do use the same myths for their own purposes.

The myths with which I am concerned can be grouped in the context of the dominant mythology of the apocalypse. I will argue that the idea of the apocalypse has informed a fundamental myth in the American experience. There are three other significant myths that operate in relation to the myth of apocalypse: those of the frontier, the promised land, and the road. In general these myths relate to the myth of apocalypse in the following way. The American myth of apocalypse is ultimately based in the Christian story of apocalypse described in the New Testament book of the Revelation of St. John the Divine. As it has become a part of the American structure of culture, the myth of apocalypse refers to the period during which the United States, or the world, undergoes a series of extraordinary upheavals and cataclysms. It is during this time that the beast of the apocalypse rules. The associated chaos and decimation cleanse the population, out of which only the chosen survive. The chosen are then able to live in the promised land. The temporal moment between the time of the last days and the time of the promised land is materialized as the geographic moment of the frontier. The road takes on significance as the time of travel toward the salvation of the promised land. I have been deliberately vague in this outline because one of my main points is that because the myth of apocalypse has been articulated differently at different times in American experience, the term's referents have varied considerably. This essay is taken up with precisely this issue.

Those people familiar with the Christian story of the apocalypse will note that I have left out what is usually considered to be the most important topos in this story, the day of judgment. This is because in the secular American myth of apocalypse, the day of judgment is always already present in the American experience. The United States stands in judgment on itself. Throughout the transformations in the American myth of apocalypse, this condition has remained stable. It provides what I will go on to describe, following Baudrillard, as the moral perspective that binds the United States together. Whether the United States has found itself wanting has depended on the particular myth of apocalypse in place at the time the judgment was being made.

The Beast of the Apocalypse

As I have already noted, the American experience of the myt
lypse has not remained the same. As a consequence the America
of the frontier, the promised land, and the road has also changed ov‿.
This essay will concentrate mainly on one period, from the development oı
the atomic bomb to the end of the cold war. To explain what was special about
this period, however, I will refer to earlier times. I will also begin an examination of the transformation in the American experience of apocalypse, and
some of the implications of this transformation, in the wake of the cold war.
It is becoming common to describe the period of intensified hostility that
coincided roughly with Ronald Reagan's presidency as the "second cold war."
I am taking the period around 1989–90, which includes Gorbachev's reforms
and the beginning of the breakup of the Eastern Bloc, as the main historical
marker for the end of the period with which I am concerned. The final end
of the cold war around 1989–90 marks a critical moment in the American
experience of the apocalypse and its associated myths.

The myths of the frontier, the promised land, and the road all operate
within the general myth of the apocalypse. Nevertheless, these myths began
to be transformed rather earlier. One marker of this shift can be found in the
assassination of President Kennedy in 1963; another is the moral crisis over
the waging of the Vietnam War. A third is the final loss of that war in 1975.
These events provoked a reconstruction of the three subordinate myths.
Nevertheless, these myths did not receive the final blow to their post–World
War II significance until the end of the second cold war forced a more general reconstruction in the articulation of the myth of apocalypse itself.

President Bush's deployment of the rhetoric of a "New World Order," a
global promised land, marked one attempt to reconstitute the apocalypse
myth. It depended on a conviction that the apocalypse has already happened
and that the whole world has been led to a postapocalyptic new world by the
United States. President Clinton's much more inward-looking and isolationist
rhetoric draws on post–World War II images of the United States as the promised land,but his preoccupation is fundamentally nostalgic. It is common
knowledge that Clinton has modeled himself on John F. Kennedy. Clinton's
speeches look backward to the promised land of 1960s American prosperity.
Neither Bush nor Clinton has a way of understanding the internal problems
of the United States through the apocalypse myth. Whereas Bush looked
outward to the world, Clinton looks backward to the past. The problem is this:
if the United States thinks of itself as living in a postapocalyptic world, can it
sustain an identity and meaning for itself when it can no longer view itself as
the specially constituted promised land? Clinton's rhetoric of nostalgia cannot be strong enough to sustain American identity given that Americans now
experience themselves as living in a postapocalyptic world. In this claimed

postapocalyptic global promised land, the United States loses its ability to judge itself from a special moral perspective. As a consequence, the United States is increasingly unsure of the grounds that might justify its attempt to impose that same moral perspective on the world. Simultaneously, the generalization of the American moral perspective in terms of an achieved global promised land means that the United States can no longer, as it did in the post–World War II period, present itself to itself and to the world as an exemplary promised land. The moral crisis that began in the mid-1960s has begun to take on a new dimension.

The United States is a unique ex-colony. It is the only settler state to have developed an industrial and financial capitalism powerful enough to dominate the global order. The end of World War II, when an intact American economy was able to expand into the devastated countries of Europe and Europe's old markets, inaugurated this period. It ended around 1974 when, in the wake of the oil crisis, it became increasingly apparent that the global economic order could no longer be controlled by one country, no matter how much military control that nation could exercise. In the United States this crisis was reinforced by the loss of the Vietnam War. The reconstruction of Eastern Europe and the breakup of the USSR in the late 1980s and early 1990s mark the high point of the transitional period that began around 1974. During this period the United States' position in the global order changed considerably. At the same time that it became impossible for the United States to dominate the world economically, the cold war was ending. The effect of these developments has been to problematize the position of the United States as the defender of the Free World. After all, it is now more problematic as to who constitutes the Free World and more problematic as to the threats from which it might be being defended. Meanwhile, in the aftermath of the Vietnam War and the failed attempt to rescue the Iranian hostages, absolute confidence in the combination of military power and moral right that characterized the post–World War II American martial experience was put into question both in the United States and in the countries that viewed themselves as a part of the Free World. For the United States, these changes signal a crisis in the way it has come to terms with the postcolonial experience.

European Fantasy and the American Dream

It has become a theoretical commonplace to describe the United States as part of the core of the world-system (Wallerstein 1974). This assumes that the United States and the old colonialist states of Europe share interests and capitalist power. In broad rhetorical terms, it is the United States and Europe, along with the rest of the settler states, that make up "the West." In the post–

World War II period, this construct was legitimated by U.S. opposition to the USSR. The Free World of the West was opposed to the Other of the communist world, with the rest of the world's countries bit players classified since the mid-1950s as the Third World. This classification, itself constructed by the Western First World, sought to incorporate the diversity of the non-Western world in terms of an evolutionary development/underdevelopment model.

From a European perspective at the end of the modern period—that is, the era of state-based production capitalism—the world was dominated by two peripheral powers, two non-European states. Russia and the United States acted out modernist European myths of utopia. The Russian Revolution provided a temporally mythic moment for the Leninist attempt to materialize the Hegelian and Marxist narrative of an end to history. Russia was colonized by European ideas just as surely as Europe physically colonized the American continents (which, of course, it also named). Both states emulated the European states by becoming colonizers in their own right. The similarities between the two unions of states are remarkable, but I do not want to extend the comparison here. My purpose is to suggest that from a European perspective, the cold war was fought out between two versions of the utopian myth that underlay the experience of European modernity. If the communist version "lost," it did so because it was fundamentally contradictory. On the one hand, it wanted to live out the European bourgeois fantasy of reason's connection to unlimited industrial power. On the other hand, it attempted to do this from within a theoretical critique of the capitalist free market and in terms of an attempt to create a "workers' paradise," a communist utopia that had its ideological origins in the same nineteenth-century bourgeois thought that dominated European constructions of the United States. My point, which I develop in this essay, is that the construction of the cold war enabled the United States to transpose the experience of its identity crisis as a settler colony of displaced people from a relation with the indigenous people of the country—the aggressively misnamed Indians—to a state beyond the United States.

With the collapse of the Soviet Union, the United States will have to find a different way to deal with the problem of displacement and identity. The development of the Western film genre in the post–World War II period is worth examining in this context. As the Western developed through the 1950s, Native Americans—the Indians—were represented less as people who occupied land and more as existing as "part-civilized" people in urban settings associated with white American "civilization." Gradually Westerns became primarily concerned with "good" and "bad" cowboys. Finally, at the height of the cold war in the late 1960s, Westerns themselves declined as a genre. The increasing invisibility of Native Americans corresponded to the American certainty of its mission to defend the Free World. In this light it is possible that *Dances with Wolves* signals the return of the Native American to the settler consciousness as the end of the cold war returns the United States to the experience of its own insecurity as a settler state.

Whereas colonialist Europe has constituted itself in terms of self-identity, troped by the idea of home, the settler colonies have always experienced themselves in terms of displacement. The point of contact between the American colonial experience and the European experience of the United States has been the myth of apocalypse and particularly the subordinate myth of the promised land. The American construction of the United States as the promised land is a reworking, in terms of the apocalypse myth, of the European fantasy of a forthcoming utopia (as exemplified in Marx's work), which itself has a heritage in Judeo-Christian myths of apocalypse. The promised land/utopia myth forms the basis for both the European construction of the United States and the United States' experience of itself. The connection between the two aspects of the myth is explicit in the idea of America as the New World. The United States' appropriation of the colonizing continental name signals its simultaneous appropriation of the myth of the promised land/utopia. The United States as the New World is a rhetorical turn that has informed the American image throughout this century. It colludes with the European preoccupation with the United States. In American rhetoric there is a complex relation between the terms *America* and *United States*. The use of the term *United States* was established at independence, though it began earlier. It has become a marker of the "real," literally postcolonial, state of the United States. *America,* on the other hand, collapses the United States into the mythic order of the New World. The adjective *American,* used for both terms, conflates both sets of connotations.

From Toqueville to Eco and Baudrillard, writers have constructed the United States as a mythic Other that has, for better or for worse, attempted to realize the fantastic hopes and fears of bourgeois Europe. Baudrillard's (1989) book on the United States is called *America.* The name signifies the mythic heterotopian experience of the European visitor. From a European perspective, life in the United States is experienced as a European fantasy. At the same time, the idea of the American experience as the realization of European bourgeois fantasy pervades the American structure of culture and forces the question of the status of American reality. This is why the myth of apocalypse is fundamental to the American structure of culture. Robinson has argued that "the American Dream as European Dream was fundamentally a Protestant dream of historical apocalypse—a dream of a transformation *of* history *in* history that would consummate and so give meaning *to* history" (Robinson 1990, 2). I will go on to describe how this dream of an historical apocalypse informs the American postcolonial experience.

In Alexandre Kojève's discussion of Hegel's *Phenomenology of Mind,* which Raymond Queneau assembled from Kojève's lectures, Kojève claims: "One can even say that, from a certain point of view, the United States has attained the final stage of Marxist 'communism.' . . . I was led to conclude that the 'American way of life' was the type of life specific to the post-historical period, the actual presence of the United States in the world prefiguring the 'eternal present' future of all humanity" (in Pefanis 1991, 2). Baudrillard's *America* echoes this position, albeit with a likely touch of Baudrillardian irony, in a section entitled "Utopia Achieved." Kojève ignores the colonial background to the American experience. As a consequence the United States becomes the culminating moment in the Hegelian and Marxist grand narrative of history. The United States realizes the world about which bourgeois Europe dreams. Baudrillard (1989, 78) comments on this idea: "For the Old World [colonization] represents the unique experience of an idealised substitution of values, almost as you find in science fiction novels (the tone of which it often reflects as in the U.S.), a substitution which at a stroke short-circuited the destiny of these values in their countries of origin." One of Baudrillard's points is that the process of colonization allows the colonizer to impose his fantasy on a land unencumbered by his own country's historical tradition.[1] It has become traditional to take the bourgeois French Revolution of 1789 as one marker of the beginning of modernity. The French Revolution is the clearest case in which a European bourgeoisie attempted to construct a European bourgeois state. American independence from its colonial power was achieved seven years before that revolution. In its aftermath Toqueville traveled the United States to see what democracy held in store for France. Already secular Europe saw the United States as prefiguring the bourgeois modern experience. In this sense Europe already viewed the United States as being "ahead" of European history.

The experience of America was the prototypical colonizing experience. The distinction between the Old World and the New articulates the apocalyptic representation of European fantasy in the realization of the United States. In this sense the United States acts out the European bourgeois fantasy. There are two main aspects to this fantasy. One is best described in terms of the French sociological tradition. In this tradition, whose major thinkers are Comte and Durkheim, we have the bourgeois myth of the social as the governing interpretive term. The social is the theorization of the lived experience described as "society." Society is claimed to be founded on the nuclear family and hegemonically articulated through a shared moral order. The other aspect of the fantasy is psychoanalysis. Perhaps when Freud remarked to Jung as they traveled to the United States that they were bringing the plague, Freud had an inkling of the importance Americans would find in psychoanalysis. In reference to this pairing of functionalism and psychoanalysis, it is suggestive to think that the success of the ideology of the nuclear family as a privatized entity in the United States has led, in turn, to the conservative success of Freudian psychoanalysis as a way of dealing with the problems of the nuclear family.

In commenting on the importance of morality to the American experience, Baudrillard (1989, 91) notes that "if America were to lose this moral perspective on itself, it would collapse." Whereas American reality is constructed in terms of bourgeois European fantasy, sociological functionalism and psychoanalysis are the theoretical gifts of Europe that discursively articulate the American experience. The sociological development of American functionalism (epitomized in the work of Talcott Parsons) and the spread of psychoanalysis both occur in the postwar period. Together they provided a bourgeois theoretical structure that incorporated, legitimated, and expressed the American moral perspective during the cold war, when the United States viewed itself as the promised land.

There is one more context for the American post–World War II articulation of the myths of apocalypse and the promised land. It was during this period that the United States expanded into the world economy as the major purveyor of consumption goods. This occurred in the context of a shift in capitalism generally from an emphasis on production to an emphasis on consumption. With the spread of a fetishistic concern with commodities, the utopian European experience of the United States was transformed. The United States was reconstructed as the site of apparently limitless consumer goods at a time when Europe was suffering a scarcity even of staples. This reworking of the myth of utopia enabled the United States to be constructed as the place of materialization for the nexus of concerns that articulated the commodity fetishism of consumption capitalism: primarily, youth, sexual desire, female beauty, and leisure.

The United States, for its part, attempted to transform itself into the bourgeois fantasy it had inherited from Europe. Ewen and Ewen (1982) have described how the United States forged itself into a homogeneous society early in this century by means of Hollywood films and commodities. In "The Meaning of Memory" Lipsitz (1990) demonstrated how this homogenizing strategy was continued using television. The image offered for realization was again that put forward in functionalism and psychoanalysis: a society with a unified moral order based on the nuclear family. This image was both the way Americans experienced themselves (European fantasy as American reality) and the way Americans and Europeans aspired to be (the American Dream as European fantasy) inflected through the desire articulated in the American-originated consumption capitalism first deployed in the United

States. Ethnic differences, languages, moral precepts, extended families, and working-class experience and culture were all subjugated to a bourgeois American experience of a society in which identification through consumption formed the basis for social order.

American Apocalypses

In postwar American capitalism, consumption articulated the moral order. At the same time apocalypse became the medium of commentary. Understanding this requires a closer look at the place of apocalypse in the American structure of culture. Robinson (1990, 2–3) argues that "the whole question of the apocalyptic ideology, of the transformation of space and time from old to new, from corruption to new innocence, from death to rebirth, is fundamental to American literature." He goes on to argue that American literary criticism has nevertheless consistently devalued authors who work in the apocalyptic mode. This is understandable when we remember that American literary criticism developed in the colonial shadow of a British literary criticism that privileged a bourgeois patrolled realism. In naming writers who have attempted to come to grips with "the problems raised by the apocalyptic thrust of the American Dream" (1990, 3), Robinson lists Emerson, Poe, Hawthorne, Melville, Twain, Henry James, Faulkner, West, Ellison, and Barth, as well as Coover, Pynchon, and Vonnegut.[2]

From a European perspective, the apocalypse marks the transition from Old World to New. In the American experience it suggests the problem of the status of American reality. In the pre–World War II period the American apocalypse was always imagined as taking place within the United States itself. Robinson (1990, 62) argues: "One of the most obsessive concerns for American apocalypses in the centuries since Wigglesworth [*The Day of Doom*, 1662] has been the task of infusing the biblical revelation with the visionary force of locality, the *American* power of dream. American apocalypses, to the extent that they are American, *are* American dreams—and dream becomes the characteristic American revision of the apocalypse." Although when viewed from a European perspective the United States, located in the New World, has always had a postapocalyptic hyperreal quality to it, this is not the case in the American experience of itself. Here the image of apocalypse traces the insecurity of displacement. It is the coming apocalypse that will invest the American experience with a sense of presence it requires to be reality. This is the importance of the dream in American apocalyptic rhetoric. The burden of the oneiric prophesy is that, like the psychoanalytic experience of the dream, it expresses a reality of greater substance than that of everyday life. In American rhetoric, then, the dream foretells the postapocalyptic reality. This is the reason for the signifying power of the myth of the Great American Dream. The postapocalyptic dreamworld will be the world of American fulfillment and identity. Dylan's songs of the 1960s, such as "The Gates of Eden" and "The Times They Are a-Changin'," are suffused with apocalyptic imagery. "Bob Dylan's 115th Dream," in which the narrator visits North America before Columbus has discovered it, leaving just as the explorer arrives, can be read as a commentary on the American experience of displacement. Perhaps the most well-known use of the dream metaphor during this period was that of Martin Luther King. King's "I Have a Dream" speech, made in 1963, shows how nondominant groups within a culture can rework dominant cultural myths for their own purposes.

As the United States became the world's leading capitalist country and was forced into a leading international political role through its need to develop export markets, the American experience of apocalypse was transformed. Whereas previously the apocalypse had signaled the settler state's insecurity with its own identity and sense of place, it now began to be used to assert that identity and sense of place. We can best understand this by going back to Robinson's insight that the Protestant apocalypse was a transformation in history that would give meaning to history. In this view, the United States will have achieved its identity once the apocalypse has happened, or possibly has begun to happen. To put this more simply, the moment of the apocalypse is the key marker in the American construction of identity. If the apocalypse is still in the future, then so is the achievement of American identity. After the apocalypse has occurred, however, the United States will have achieved its identity. It would then be able to take a secure place as a part of the core, those European nation-states certain of their identities from which capitalist modernity, including colonialism, emanated. The cultural moment in this transition was the American production of the atomic bomb.

In American military and political rhetoric, the explosion of the atomic bomb marked the beginning of a new era. From this moment on American rhetoric divided the world into those who had "the Bomb" and those who did not. After the first test of the atomic bomb in July 1945, Robert Oppenheimer, the scientist in charge of work on the bomb, made the religious connection explicit. He said that after the explosion he thought of a line from the *Bhagavad Gita*, "I am become death, the shatterer of worlds." The previous lines of the *Bhagavad Gita* compare the radiance of a thousand suns bursting in the sky to the splendor of God. The simile could easily have come from the Christian book of the Revelation. The atomic bomb was constructed as the beginning of a secular apocalypse, an apocalypse produced by the United States. The exploding of the atomic bomb marked the rhetorical beginning of the last days. World events could now be constructed and interpreted apocalyptically. The end of the eschatological period would be the moment of Armageddon, the final battle. Armageddon was rhetorically constructed in terms of global nuclear destruction.

Many of Dylan's songs are, in the first place, American apocalypses looking toward a better, more realized postapocalyptic United States. In several of his songs, however, as in many other uses of the image of apocalypse during the post–World War II period, the United States is not specified and is merged rhetorically with the rest of the world. In Dylan's 1963 song "A Hard Rain's Gonna Fall," the traditional local American apocalypse is connected with the new global apocalypse. In Dylan's oeuvre there is a marked decline in the usage of the apocalypse myth after the late 1960s. Dylan stopped using the apocalypse myth as a medium to describe and critique the United States around the time the United States lost its postwar certainty of itself as the promised land. The concomitant shift to a concern with personal salvation, which, as I will show, is a theme of the road movie genre, is reflected in Dylan's biography in his own religious conversion.

As late as 1989, in their song "Wake Up," from their *Yellow Moon* album, the Neville Brothers sing:

> We're living in the times
> the Bible calls Revelation
> It seems keeping peace on Earth
> is man's greatest tribulation
> But you know the greatest crime of all
> the greatest sin
> The next war will be the final conflict
> and no one's gonna win.

By transforming the American experience of apocalypse into a global eschatology, the Americans were able to change the quality of their reality. In doing this they were able to give themselves an identity and a sense of place in the global order. In other words, by externalizing the themes through which it articulated its insecurity and displacement as a settler society, the United States was able to claim security and identity for itself.

From within this eschatology came the rhetoric of the cold war, the period of the last days. Inglis (1988, 35) has described the cold war as "the supreme fiction of our epoch." He argues that the narrative began with George Kennan's article "The Sources of Soviet Conduct" published in *Foreign Affairs* in 1947. Inglis (1988, 36) describes this article as announcing "the advent of the Cold War as America's historic and unrefusable opportunity to assume leadership of the free world." Previously the United States had been concerned with an American apocalypse; now the apocalypse was constructed as global, and the United States identified itself as the savior of the world or, in more pedestrian rhetoric, as the global policeman.

It was in this eschatological context that the construction of the myth of the cold war enabled the United States to act out the Manichaean battle between God and the Devil, good and evil, as the battle between the Free World, epitomized in and defended by the United States, and communism, materialized in the demonized Soviet Union. In 1959 Albert Wohlstetter published "The Delicate Balance of Terror" in *Foreign Affairs*. This article articulated the theory of nuclear deterrence. In a capitalist order newly dominated by spectacular consumption, we have a theory of the cold war in terms of display. The nuclear warheads must be produced and displayed so that the other side can see their spectacular existence, but they must not be used.

Throughout the 1950s and into the 1970s, the final battle between good and evil was represented allegorically in countless films until, near the end of the narrative, Reagan was able to draw on *Star Wars* for his Manichaean description of the USSR as the Evil Empire. Around the same time, Reagan's Strategic Defense Initiative became popularly known in the United States as "Star Wars," suggesting the extent to which the *Star Wars* film trilogy enacted on an apocalyptic scale—that of a galaxy—the American eschatological experience of the cold war. *Star Wars* was released in 1977, shortly before the easing of tensions that led to the "end" of the first cold war. As the ideological narrative of the cold war weakened, the experience of it became more obviously fictionalized and spectacular. *Star Wars* was perhaps the most successful representation of cold war mythology. Whereas earlier cold war films had tended to construct a metaphorical or literal communist threat to a real United States, *Star Wars* constructed an eschatology of galactic dimensions. It provided an interpretation of the cold war narrative that was itself eschatological. The second cold war can be understood as a spectacular attempt to recapitulate the narrative of the first cold war using *Star Wars* as a mythic touchstone.

Star Wars forms a pair with the made-for-television film *The Day After* (1983). Whereas other post–World War II apocalypse films used the nuclear apocalypse strategically to construct an "Other" world, *The Day After* was an attempt to realize the nuclear apocalypse itself. It was only around 1980, when changes in the USSR were rendering the myth of the cold war unsustainable, that a film concentrating on the nuclear Armageddon itself became a possibility.[3] This change occurred because the construction of the post–World War II period in terms of the last days left no space for thinking about an actual postapocalyptic world. Indeed, the idea of an actual world of revelation was a contradiction in terms. Real nuclear Armageddon was constructed as the end of the world rather than as the cleansing moment of transition to a revealed hyperreal world. The idea of nuclear war as being unthinkable, not only morally but literally, reinforced the idea of the last days as being in themselves endless. It was in this context that nuclear war could become a fictional trope for the construction of other Americas in which aspects of life in the United States could be discussed. This is the mythic basis for the use of apocalypse as a means of social commentary on post–World War II American life.

I have explained that the American transformation of the myth of apocalypse allowed a new experience of American life as complete, as real. The apocalypse movies use the topos of apocalypse to comment on that experience by presenting a secular postapocalyptic future that is defined by lack. The postapocalyptic future is constructed as lacking everything from consumer goods to security, all of which can be generalized as a lack of society. (Note here how remarkably similar these postapocalyptic worlds are to Thomas Hobbes's image of the state of nature, as outlined in *Leviathan* [1651]. C. B. McPherson, in *The Political Theory of Possessive Individualism* [1962] has argued that this image is a representation of the ideology of possessive individualism when there are no imposed constraints, when there is no state.) To use a trope to which I will return, as the present is reconstructed as the promised land of plenitude, so the postapocalyptic future becomes a site for commentary on the present.

The Day the Earth Stood Still was released in 1951. In this apocalyptic scenario an alien named Klaatu arrives in Washington in a flying saucer. Klaatu explains his mission. The other civilized planets are concerned about the combination of aggression and atomic capability that they see on Earth. Although they do not mind Earth destroying itself, they do not want to have Earth disrupting their peaceful coexistence. To this end Klaatu leaves behind a robotic policeman who will enforce the wishes of the other planets. The robot seems to have much the same sort of role as the United States imagined for itself in the postwar period. Klaatu is a messianic figure. He heralds the last days, which are the days of atomic capacity. In terms of the American narrative of apocalypse, it is inevitable that Klaatu's flying saucer should land in Washington. Although Klaatu wishes to speak to all the world leaders, his speaking position is literally from Washington. Klaatu connects Washington with a higher authority, the civilized planets/God, but he also articulates the role of the postwar United States as the global policeman. This was one of the first of a genre of films I call apocalypse movies.

The common theme in this genre is the end of civilization—for which we should read American middle-class society—usually by nuclear destruction. This apocalyptic scenario surrounding the atom bomb is signaled in the title of a 1947 dramatized documentary about the development of the bomb, *The Beginning or the End*. Early films of the genre tended to concentrate on the threat and the destruction. A good example is *The Beast from Twenty Thousand Fathoms* (1953), in which, after nuclear tests melt the Arctic ice that traps it, a prehistoric animal attacks New York. In this film, as in many of the 1950s films using nuclear capacity as a motif, the destruction is not caused directly by nuclear explosions but rather is an indirect effect. The late 1950s saw the first of the films dealing with nuclear destruction and life afterward. *Beyond the Time Barrier* is mostly set in 2024, when people live underground to avoid nuclear contamination. The 1962 film *Panic in Year Zero* describes the effects of a nuclear attack on Los Angeles. Later films that show life after the apocalypse include *The Omega Man* (1971), *The Ultimate Warrior* (1975), and *Damnation Alley* (1977).[4] *The Terminator* (1984) describes a future in which the defense computers of both the United States and the USSR have united to set off a nuclear war intended not only to destroy civilization but to wipe out humanity. There is also the more recent *Cyborg* (1987).

All these films imagine a dystopian postapocalyptic future that provides a contrast to an American present idealized by that very contrast. In this way they reinforce the experience of living in the last days, which was the fundamental experience of the cold war. The gradual end of the cold war, despite the best efforts of the U.S. political and military-industrial complex, led, on the one hand, to an ability to conceptualize the American experience of global apocalypse in *Star Wars* and, on the other hand, to an ability to think and realize—that is, to remythologize as a conceivable experience—nuclear war. The very title of *The Day After* shows a new ability to conceptualize nuclear war as an event in history rather than an inconceivable end to it. *Terminator 2* was released in 1990. Its subtitle was *Day of Judgment.* Interestingly, given what I have been suggesting about the transformation in the myth of apocalypse around 1990, the narrative is dominated by the attempt to eradicate from history the nuclear war precipitated in the future by the machines. At the end of the film we are led to believe that the attempt to change the future has been successful. There will now no longer be the war that led to the terminators' being sent back in time. The apocalypse will now not occur. In this development the film erases its own narratival reason for existence. This erasure occurs at the same time that the American post–World War II construction of apocalypse was being transformed, with the apocalypse itself being eliminated.

Postcolonial Insecurities

The problem with the post–World War II transformation of the apocalypse myth is that it meant that the United States could never be thought of as being the losing side. The certainty of the United States as the chosen country in a global order living through the last days had to come from its success in defending the Free World. By the early 1960s this reconstruction of the United States as the postapocalyptic promised land led to the messianic overtones associated with John F. Kennedy and the idea of the United States as Camelot. After her husband's assassination, Jaqueline Bouvier Kennedy remembered that Kennedy had loved listening to the record of the musical *Camelot*. The lines he loved most were "Don't let it be forgot, that once there was a spot, for one brief shining moment that was known as Camelot." It was Jaqueline Kennedy who went on to describe the period of Kennedy's presidency as a Camelot lost at his assassination. In his speech on his adoption as the Democratic candidate in 1960, Kennedy said, "We stand today on the edge of a new frontier." Martin Luther King's 1963 "Promised Land" speech echoed this idea, although, as I noted earlier, he used it in relation to the position of black Americans. In 1964 Lyndon Johnson described his policy for a "Great Society." During a speech at the University of Maryland he said: "The challenge of the next half-century is whether we have the wisdom to use wealth to enrich and elevate our national life—and to advance the quality of American civilization—for in your time we have the opportunity to move not only toward the rich society and the powerful society, but upward to the Great Society." Any major political, economic, or military loss would cast doubt on this reconstruction of the apocalypse myth and, with it, the United States' sense of identity and purpose.

There is no need here to document the traumatic effects of America's loss of the Vietnam War or the strenuous attempts in films such as *Rambo* to reconstruct history to fit American eschatological reality. Nonetheless, I want to look briefly at *Apocalypse Now* as an American postcolonial film. *Apocalypse Now* can be categorized within a genre of postcolonial fiction that can be briefly described as a supplementary writing back. Typical of such works are J. M. Coetzee's *Foe* (1986), which reworks Defoe's *Robinson Crusoe,* and Jean Rhys's *Wide Sargasso Sea* (1966), which traces the life of Bertha Mason, Rochester's "mad" wife whom he keeps locked in the attic in Charlotte Brontë's *Jane Eyre.* In these works the colonialist assumptions of the earlier English novels are challenged and unsettled by the new point of view (see Tiffin 1987).

Apocalypse Now is a reworking of Conrad's *Heart of Darkness.* Although it is not a self-conscious writing back, it nevertheless operates as a postcolonial reworking of a novel from the core, inflicting it with distinctively American concerns. By virtue of reworking a core text concerned with colonialism, it becomes itself a commentary. The change of concern is apparent in the film's title. Whereas Conrad's book located its narrative in the movement from English civilization to African savagery, *Apocalypse Now* locates its concern in the American postwar experience of apocalypse. It belongs in the genre of apocalypse movies but features no nuclear holocaust. Because of the connection between nuclear warfare and the apocalypse, the Vietnam War could not be for the American experience the final battle between good and evil, the mythical nuclear-war ending to the eschatological cold war. The Vietnam War was thought of as only one battle within the cold war.

Still, the loss of the Vietnam War seriously called into question the postwar mythic structuring of the global apocalypse with the United States as the savior. The title of *Apocalypse Now* can be understood as a commentary on this crisis. The film examines the postwar American experience of apocalypse from an awareness that the crisis in the experience of the myth is itself apocalyptic. *Heart of Darkness* offers a reading guaranteed by the certainty of the colonial order. Its narrative traces the voyage from an English certainty of place. *Apocalypse Now* describes a doubled colonial experience. In literal terms the film shows an independent settler society fighting a colonial war. In *Heart of Darkness* Marlow returns to Europe unable to articulate what he has experienced. In spite of this, his new knowledge is made safe by the certainty of place in England. In *Apocalypse Now* there is no certainty to make safe the horror of the lost colonial adventure for a country where the loss itself unsettles the myth on which it has, as an ex-settler colony, attempted to construct its own identity, its presence in and to the world.

Apocalypse Now was made in the mid-1970s and opened in 1979. Released two years after *Star Wars, Apocalypse Now* connected the American crisis of identity that resulted from the loss of the Vietnam War with the deeper crisis associated with the end of the cold war narrative itself. In *Apocalypse Now* we have a clear expression of the United States' renewed uncertainty about its own identity, epitomized in its uncertainty over place. In *Heart of Darkness* the story is told from England. Marlow's story is narrated from the core. Within the narrative Marlow tells his story of leaving England for Africa and of his eventual return to Europe, culminating in his visit to Kurtz's fiancée. In *Apocalypse Now* we never see the United States. The film's entire narrative is set in Vietnam and Cambodia. Early in the narrative Willard, the rewritten figure of Marlow, muses on his inability to live in the United States. At one point he comments, "I'd been back and it just didn't exist anymore." The United States was no longer the promised land of America.

There are three different versions of the film's end. In none of them does Willard return to the United States. In *Heart of Darkness* Marlow returns to Belgium and lies to Kurtz's fiancée about his final words. In *Apocalypse Now* it seems unlikely that Willard will return to the United States to tell Colonel Kurtz's story to his son, as Kurtz has asked him to do. Unlike that of *Heart of Darkness,* the narrative of *Apocalypse Now* does not supplant Kurtz's final expression of his feelings, "The horror, the horror." Marlow was able to reconstruct Kurtz's experience for his fiancée from within the certainty of place and identity of the core. For Willard, however, there is no place from which to understand and reinterpret his experience. He would have grown up in the post–World War II United States. His ideal is to kill without judgment. Ironically this apocalyptic loss of vision is precisely the loss of moral perspective that Baudrillard argues would be so disastrous for the United States. The loss of the promised land implies this loss of vision. Willard, a member of the next generation, does not have to struggle to be like Kurtz. Coming from a settler society that now has no certain identity or moral perspective, Willard is already like Kurtz.

Heart of Darkness is narrated from the colonizing core's certainty of place and morality. *Apocalypse Now* is narrated in colonial uncertainty. The established reading of the relation between the two texts understands *Apocalypse Now* as radicalizing *Heart of Darkness* in a strategy for clarifying and critiquing the American involvement in Vietnam as a colonial enterprise. While accepting this reading, I am suggesting something further. Made after the Vietnam War, after the oil crisis, and toward the end of the cold war narrative, *Apocalypse Now* articulates the renewed uncertainty of the United States as a settler society.

Apocalypse Now constructs the Vietnam War itself as an apocalyptic moment in post–World War II American experience. The film opens with an American helicopter air strike. On the soundtrack the Doors sing "The End." My earlier discussion of the Great American Dream suggests that the Vietnam War marked the apocalyptic end to the living of that dream as real. Within the film Willard's journey up the river to Kurtz is a movement toward the apocalyptic moment. In this sense Willard's journey is a transformation of the journey in American road movies, which I discuss later. When Willard reaches Kurtz's camp, there is a whitewashed sign on a wall that reads "Apocalypse Now." The code for the air strike that Willard is supposed to call up is "Almighty." In one ending Willard calls up the air strike and the film closes in an apocalyptic conflagration. In another ending Willard kills Kurtz and returns to his boat. On looking through Kurtz's typescript, Willard, along with the viewer, sees that Kurtz has scrawled across one page, "Drop the Bomb, Exterminate them all." In *Heart of Darkness* Marlow's visit to Kurtz is crucial, but it is not apocalyptic. In *Apocalypse Now* the failed American colonial adventure marks the loss of moral certainty. In this apocalyptic moment the United States loses its eschatological claim to being the chosen country and returns to being a settler society searching for its own identity.

I have argued that Dylan always invoked the apocalypse topos within its traditional American formulation, using the apocalypse to condemn aspects of American life. In 1983 he recorded "Blind Willie McTell," which went unreleased until 1991. This is perhaps the only Dylan song since "All Along the Watchtower," recorded in 1968, to make significant reference to the apocalypse mythology. In "Blind Willie McTell" Dylan describes a corrupt "world"—he means in the first place the United States—which is condemned "all the way from New Orleans to Jerusalem." The purpose of the song, however, is not to describe this condemned world as such. The song is a blues lamenting the lack of any present-day singer, such as the dead Blind Willie McTell, who can adequately describe the present state of affairs. In this song, then, Dylan's apocalypse relates not to the state of the United States but to the loss of an apocalyptic vision appropriate to the subject matter. In this way "Blind Willie McTell" takes up and develops the same concerns as *Apocalypse Now*.

Both these texts suggest that the real American apocalypse is the one indicated by Baudrillard: if the United States—the mythic America—loses its moral perspective on itself, it will collapse. There is, however, a more profound possibility. Although both *Apocalypse Now* and "Blind Willie McTell" articulate the experience of apocalypse in the post–Vietnam War United States, the late 1980s saw the collapse of the Evil Empire not in a global nuclear Armageddon but in a loss of totalitarian communist political control. This end to the myth of the cold war entails also an end to the secular eschatology that has secured the identity of the United States since the end of World War II. It is in this context that the United States has been forced back into a postcolonial search for its own sense of presence, its place in the world. The American postwar transformation of the myth of apocalypse can no longer be sustained. If Bush's New World Order is indeed postapocalyptic, the question becomes how the United States can sustain its sense of identity in a world without apocalypse. One answer is to be found in the American rhetoric of the promised land, a reworking of the European modernist idea of utopia.

The Promised Land, Won and Lost

The postapocalyptic New World Order is being constructed in terms of a utopian myth of a world concert of democratic states all operating within an endlessly dynamic global capitalism. The phrase itself is intriguingly ambiguous. Is it a new order of the world or an order of the New World? From an American point of view, it is both.[5] In the idea of the New World Order we have another externalization of an American myth internalized from the colonial period. This myth is most succinctly summed up in the title of a late 1950s Chuck Berry song, "The Promised Land." The myth developed as an inflection of the colonial Christian understanding of apocalypse. For the Puritans who settled New England, the New World was the promised land. When John Winthrop's group founded Boston, Winthrop was not only looking for a new site for Zion; he was extending the frontier. In this millenarian view, the frontier literalizes the moment of transition from an earthly world of imperfect reality to a heavenly world of perfection. In colonial America the displacement of the settler society, characterized in the name New England and in the insistent mimetic naming of places such as Plymouth, Portsmouth, and New London , was compensated by the Puritan millenarian project of creating America as the promised land. In this way the frontier took on a transcendental liminal quality.

Understanding the myth of the promised land requires a prior understanding of the myth of the frontier, for the former depends on the latter. The utopian promised land always existed in the mythical space of the frontier. With settlement came the loss of transcendence, as the settled area became incorporated into earthly reality. As the frontier moved west, New England became just a settler colony struggling to define its identity against the presence of Old England. When Frederick Jackson Turner read his paper "The Significance of the Frontier in American History" to the American History Association in 1893, the mainland geographic frontier had been closed since the United States had acquired California from Mexico in the peace treaty of 1848, but Turner was not primarily concerned with national frontiers. He began his paper by quoting from an 1890 bulletin of the superintendent of the census. This quotation describes the end of the frontier in terms of the end of a line of settlement.

What Turner's thesis did was to secularize the productive quality of the myth of the frontier. Whereas previously the frontier had marked the millenarian moment of heaven on earth, now the frontier was to be understood retrospectively as the site that produced all the distinguishing features of life in the United States. It is worth quoting the last two sentences of Turner's paper: "What the Mediterranean Sea was to the Greeks, breaking the bond of custom, offering new experiences, calling out new institutions and activities, that, and more, the ever retreating frontier has been to the United States directly, and to the nations of Europe more remotely. And now, four centuries from the discovery of America, at the end of a hundred years of life under the Constitution, the frontier has gone, and with its going has closed the first period of American history" (Turner 1950, 38). Here, again, we have Puritan millenarian rhetoric. The closing of the frontier has led, Turner tells us, to an end of history in history. The questionable comparison to the role of the Mediterranean for the ancient Greeks—it was after all a means of communication, not a frontier— shows the need to reinforce the United States' identity through a comparison with the mythic historical founding nation of modern Europe. What is most interesting for my purposes, however, is that Turner describes the frontier as retreating, not advancing.

Turner's paper constructs the secular importance of the frontier in opposition to the importance of Europe. In this way he asserts an identity for the United States outside a mimetic relationship with Europe. At the same time he situates his paper within a United States from which the frontier retreats. In this reworking of the myth, it is the moving frontier itself that creates the identity of the United States. The rhetorical slippage from the United States to America, although contextually justified, still prepares the way for the apocalyptic conclusion that, with the end of the frontier, the United States has been transformed into a country of place and identity.

It was the closing of the geographical frontier that gave rise to the secular construction of the last-acquired part of the mainland as the promised land. It is this reconstruction that is echoed and legitimated in Turner's thesis. From then on the transcendental power of the frontier would flow inward to the United States rather than outward. Whereas the pioneers sought the promised land beyond the frontier, the closure of the frontier signaled an end to a spatial promised land beyond the kairotic frontier.[6] Instead the promised land began to be constructed within the frontier of the United States. In the context of the secular myth of American capitalism, California acquired meaning as a land of unparalleled and easily accessible wealth. The discovery of gold at Sutter's Mill at the same time that the U.S. Senate ratified the treaty with Mexico gave the myth a strong shove. With California constructed as the promised land, journeying within the United States gained its own transcendental quality as a journey to a postapocalyptic world of wealth. In Chuck Berry's song "The Promised Land," the poor boy starts on the East Coast in Norfolk, Virginia. He starts from a town bearing the name of an English county in the first state to be settled by the English. He travels by a variety of means of transport across the United States to Los Angeles, California. He ends up, then, in a city founded by the Spanish in a state named after a mythical land said to be close to the terrestrial paradise. For the American traveler it is the promised land.

In the post–World War II United States, the movement from the East Coast to the West was a movement away from an imperfect mundane reality that lacked the quality of identity into the more real world of the dream. It was also a movement away from the historically colonial land to the territory incorporated into the United States after the settler state became independent. The description of Hollywood as the dream factory signals the spatial and temporal movement away from the colonial northern East Coast to a southern West Coast closer to the last geographical frontier and to the greater reality of the dream. The fantasy of the dream's realization is the fantasy of colonial transcendence, the acquisition of a certainty of place in a promised land. In Berry's narrative the journey (with its historical Christian overtones of pilgrimage) leads to a secular redemption in a promised land within the now unmoving frontier. This secular redemption is manifested in wealth. In the post–World War II period the externalization of the apocalypse and the narrative of the last days enabled not just California but the whole United States to take on the status of the promised land. This was the mythic inflection of the American attempt to construct a certainty of place and identity.

In his 1984 song "Born in the U.S.A.," Bruce Springsteen articulates the same postcolonial crisis of identity I have remarked in *Apocalypse Now* and Dylan's "Blind Willie McTell." In "Born in the U.S.A." the working-class narrator describes how he was born "in a dead man's town" and how he has ended up "like a dog that's been beat too much." He describes how he and his brother fought in Vietnam and how his brother died there. For the narrator, the mythic America has become the real United States. In the postapocalyptic aftermath of the Vietnam War, there is no longer a promised land—not even in California:

> Down in the shadow of the penitentiary
> Out by the gas fires of the refinery
> I'm ten years burning down the road
> Nowhere to run ain't got nowhere to go.

In this new reality there is no redemption. For the narrator, there is no longer a future because, in this postapocalyptic demythologized world, there is no longer a dream of a promised land, let alone a realized promised land in California.

On his 1978 album *Darkness on the Edge of Town,* Springsteen included a song called "The Promised Land." This song forms a bitter commentary on Chuck Berry's earlier song. In Springsteen's song the worker now has a desperate belief in a promised land beyond the depressing mundanity of his life. The last line of the chorus is "And I believe in a promised land," a line repeated without the *and* at the end of the song. This narrator's image is of an apocalypse that will bring the promised land:

> There's a dark cloud rising from the desert floor
> I packed my bags and I'm heading straight into the storm
> Gonna be a twister to blow everything down
> That ain't got the faith to stand its ground
> Blow away the dreams that tear you apart
> Blow away the dreams that break your heart
> Blow away the lies that leave you nothing but lost and
>   brokenhearted.

Whereas in Chuck Berry's song the promised land exists, in Springsteen's song it requires an American apocalypse to bring it into being. In the later

"Born in the U.S.A." there is no longer a belief in a promised land. The narrator was born in the United States (not in the mythical America) but now has "nowhere to run ain't got nowhere to go." The moral perspective that Baudrillard writes about as so necessary to the United States is to be found in the dream of a promised land. The loss of that dream is the loss of a unifying moral perspective and a return to the existential uncertainty that marks the experience of a settler society.

The Road (to Nowhere)

Allied to the apocalyptic myth of the promised land is the myth of the road. The American road provides the site for the journey to identity. The road articulates the temporal movement to the apocalypse and the promised land as a spatial movement. When the frontier was moving, the mythic road led to the frontier. When the frontier stopped and the border was closed, the road led West, ultimately to California. The road movie of the late 1960s onward has a prehistory in the wagon train Westerns of the 1940s and 1950s. These latter films restate the colonial experience of displacement in terms of a narratival journey to the unsettled land of the frontier. Constructed within the postwar eschatological myth of good versus evil, the settlers' righteousness is always already undermined by the preexisting aboriginal presence of the Native Americans. In a seemingly endless retelling of the same story, the wagon train Western attempted to instate a right of place through an apocalyptic story of a journey to the promised land at the frontier. By contrast, the road movies of the late 1960s and after increasingly described a personal redemptive journey through a diminished land of failed dreams, a world without an American promised land.

The first film to make clear the relation between the road and the promised land, and certainly the prewar precursor of the late-1960s road movies, was *The Wizard of Oz*. Made in 1939, it was based on a book published forty years earlier, in the same decade that Frederick Jackson Turner helped to reconstruct the myth of the frontier. In this pre–"the Bomb" period the search is for a sense of place within the United States. Dorothy lives in rural Kansas with her aunt and uncle. She is thus already displaced, not living with her parents.

Dorothy runs away from her home that is not quite home and has just returned to it when a twister hits. As in Springsteen's song, the twister is used as an apocalyptic trope. The twister takes Dorothy's house, along with Dorothy and her dog, Toto, and moves it to Oz. The narrative in Oz concerns Dorothy's attempts to return to Kansas. The scenes of Kansas at the film's beginning and end are shot in black and white, whereas the bulk of the film, showing the land of Oz, is shot in color using hues much brighter than normal. In this way we are led to accept that Kansas, the United States, is lacking while Oz is more real than real, having a postapocalyptic superplenitude of identity.

At this point it is instructive to compare *The Wizard of Oz* with Lewis Carroll's *Alice in Wonderland*. In important ways the narratives are similar. Both involve young girls visiting societies beyond their own where strange things happen. *The Wizard of Oz* can be read as a colonial rewriting of Carroll's story. Elsewhere I have analyzed *Alice in Wonderland* as a colonialist story (Stratton 1990). In general it is the story of a young English girl who visits Wonderland, behaves extremely rudely to the local people, and attempts to impose her English morals on them. It is a story written from the core. Like Marlow in *Heart of Darkness,* Alice knows who she is and where she has come from and lives in Wonderland with the absolute knowledge of her superiority over the locals.

The narrative of Dorothy in Oz is quite different. The film is preoccupied with the problem of home. The film's irony is that when Dorothy is presented with a world more real than her own, she can not accept it as home. At the end of the film, when Dorothy has finally made it back to Kansas, all she can talk about is being home. The concern is so constant that the film betrays its insecurity about home precisely through Dorothy's claim that she is home. Alice would never have worried so much about being home. When Dorothy is talking with her aunt and uncle, she insists, "It wasn't a dream; it was a place. . . . Some of it wasn't very nice, but most of it was beautiful. Just the same, all I kept saying to everybody was that I wanted to go home." In this statement Dorothy brings together the American apocalyptic trope of the dream with the American concern over place.

The film sets out to reassert home as being Dorothy's aunt and uncle's house, Kansas, the United States. As a film from a settler society, however, it constantly undermines this claim. What Dorothy discovers is that the postapocalyptic world of the American Dream is not home either. As a fantasy Oz serves to give meaning and a moral perspective to American experience, but as a reality it turns out to be more alien than the world Dorothy has left behind. Dorothy is doomed always to experience her lack of a home. As if recognizing this, she reconstructs her fundamental experience of lack, the lesson she has learned from her experience of Oz. Asked by the Good Witch of the North what she has learned from her experience, Dorothy says: "If I ever go looking for my heart's desire again, I'll never look further than my own backyard, because if it isn't there, I never lost it in the first place." If what Dorothy lacks most is a sense of place, a feeling of being home, then this must be her heart's nameless desire. Unlike Alice, who enjoys her colonial adventuring, Dorothy is so insecure about place that she never wants to leave her aunt and uncle's farm again.

To send Dorothy back to the Kansas farm, the Good Witch instructs her to repeat, "There's no place like home." Dorothy keeps repeating the sentence as if to persuade herself that she really is home even after she has returned to her aunt and uncle's house.

In the promised land of Oz Dorothy has to travel the entire length of the Yellow Brick Road, from Munchkinland to the Emerald City, to meet the Wizard of Oz, who she hopes will get her back to Kansas. Along the road Dorothy meets the Scarecrow, the Tin Man, and the Cowardly Lion. All three are transfigured characters from Dorothy's life in Kansas, as is the Wicked Witch of the West. The three all lack something—a brain, a heart, and courage, respectively—in this most complete of countries. Dorothy is lacking her home. In this road movie the road itself is already in the promised land. The journey to the Emerald City is the journey back to the lacking black-and-white world of Kansas. It turns out that the wizard is another displaced person from Kansas, but he is quite happy with his lot, having become a highly respected member of the community by tricking the local population into believing that he is a wizard. Here we have a version of the colonial experience quite different from that of Alice. The Wizard has used his American-learned trickery to attain a powerful position in Oz for his own benefit. In Kansas he was a traveling salesman and entertainer. It seems as if he has learned to accept the experience of displacement and make the most of his opportunities wherever he is. Dorothy and the revealed wizard are the only human beings in Oz. In the end it is not the Kansas charlatan but the Good Witch who sends Dorothy back to Kansas. The Good Witch is the only main character in Oz who has no counterpart in Kansas. She is, then, "other" in a way the other main characters are not. She is a magical person with religious overtones who enables Dorothy to pass back through the frontier, over the rainbow, to Kansas.

The end of The Wizard of Oz is an attempt to invert the pre–"the Bomb" myth of apocalypse and of the promised land, to assert that the lived world of a displaced settler society is really home. In this case the journey down the road (with the Christian echoes of Pilgrim's Progress) leads to the revelation that Dorothy should never have tried to leave the reality of the Kansas farm, even if that meant accepting the killing of her dog. With all the insecurity of a settler society, the film attempts to assert the farm as home. Perhaps this reading helps us to understand the parochialism of small-town values in the United States more generally.

In the 1950s and 1960s the prehistory of road movies involves films in which people travel to the promised land of California. In the main these films concentrate not on the journey but on life in the secular and realized promised land, something easy to do given that the Hollywood dream factory was built in the promised land. The song "Route 66," popularized by the Rolling

Stones on their first album (1964), but written by Bobby Troup in 1946, is a postwar celebration of a road that led from Chicago to Los Angeles, listing the towns and cities on the way as if they are points on the journey to the promised land. Troup wrote the song having driven to California with the hope of making it big in the music business. As I have shown, by the early 1960s—by the time of Kennedy—the whole of the United States was coming to be thought of as the promised land.

Kerouac's *On the Road* was published in 1955. It chronicles the period from 1947 to 1955. The hero and narrator is named Sal Paradise, and his first journey takes him from New York to San Francisco. Paradise does not find his promised land in California, however. He writes, "Here I was at the end of America—no more land—and now there was nowhere to go but back." *On the Road* signals the early beginning of disillusionment with California as the promised land. The ironically named Paradise cannot find his promised land, and the rest of the novel chronicles his constant journeying. In *On The Road* the search is a male concern. Women, in the main, remain fixed to place and, in traditional American colonial terms, operate as a metaphor of the male experience of the land itself. It is not only the geographical end of the United States but the end of the myth of California as the promised land that is being suggested. At the conclusion of the novel, Paradise is back in New York. He watches the sun go down. As he does so, he sits "on the old broken-down river pier watching the long, long skies over New Jersey and sense[s] all that raw land that rolls in one unbelievable huge bulge over to the West Coast, and all that road going, all that dreaming in the immensity of it." The sentence goes on. The sun is setting on American dreams. The popularity of *On The Road* reflects the change in the American experience of the promised land and the road in the postwar period. Looking at its reprintings we see they pick up after 1965. The book was reprinted twice in 1968 and again in 1971 and 1972. Even though *On the Road* was published in 1955, the American experience it expresses was that of the late 1960s and 1970s.

Another example of the new concern with the road in the early 1960s was the television series *Route 66,* which began in October 1960 and finished in September 1964, spanning Kennedy's presidency. The series was based on the idea of two men traveling the United States in a car. Each episode recounts one adventure on their journey. The intended effect was a celebration of traveling in the United States, but the program's mood began to change toward the end of the series. One of the lead actors left in March 1963. His replacement played a Vietnam War hero who had returned to the United States unsure of what he wanted from life. For him the road became a search for personal salvation.[7]

The late-1960s' loss of the promised land led to a fundamental transformation in the American experience of the road. As California, and the United States more generally, lost its eschatological claim to a sense of place, the road itself, the revelatory journey, was increasingly all that was left. On the 1968 Simon and Garfunkel album *Bookends*, Paul Simon has a song called "America," in which the narrator has gone traveling across the United States "to look for America." At one point in the song he describes his sense of directionlessness to his traveling companion:

> "Kathy, I'm lost," I said,
> Though I knew she was sleeping.
> "I'm empty and aching and
> I don't know why."

From the late 1960s onward the United States began to lose its claim to being the promised land, just as the narrative of the global last days began to falter. Without an apocalypse the United States has no special history, no future, and, worst for a settler society, no sense of identity. The narrator is metaphorically lost in both space and time.

Also in 1968 Dylan released "The Ballad of Frankie Lee and Judas Priest" on his *John Wesley Hardin* album. In this ballad Judas Priest offers to lend Frankie Lee money. Judas Priest then goes to leave. When Frankie Lee asks him where he'll be,

> Judas pointed down the road
> And said, "Eternity!"
> "Eternity?" said Frankie Lee,
> With a voice as cold as ice.
> "That's right," said Judas Priest, "Eternity,
> Though you might call it 'Paradise.'"

In this verse the promised land is troped as the postkairotic timeless place of eternity, also known as paradise. The road leads there. Frankie Lee follows Judas down the road and finds Judas Priest in a house. When he asks Judas Priest about the house, he is told, "It's not a house . . . [;] it's a home." In this song the connection between the promised land and home is clearly made.

Judas, as we know from the New Testament, is a deceiver. For Frankie Lee this house turns out not to be home. He dies of thirst, and Dylan ends the song with a moral:

> Well, the moral of this story,
> The moral of this song,
> Is simply that one should never be
> Where one does not belong.
> So when you see your neighbor carryin' somethin',
> Help him with his load,

And don't go mistaking Paradise
For that home across the road.

This song, as well as the Paul Simon song, expresses a lack of certainty in home. This parallels the increasing loss of moral certainty that is a part of the crisis in the experience of the United States as the promised land. In the Dylan song the moral connects home with paradise and suggests a further connection with Vietnam, the "home across the road." This further connection involves a conflation of Vietnam with the promised land, something made possible by the American postwar mission to save the Free World. The song implicitly signals the experience of the Vietnam War as an apocalyptic event and provides a commentary on it. Dylan's ballad articulates a search for home just as "America" does, but my reading of "The Ballad of Frankie Lee and Judas Priest" has a further implication: it suggests that the song makes a connection between the American search for identity and the Vietnam War as a colonial war.

Midnight Cowboy (1969), with its narrative of a journey to Florida through a threatening United States, formed a transition between the view of the United States as the promised land and the new view of the United States as a mundane, imperfect reality. In *Easy Rider* (1969) the two main characters ride their Harleys through a threatening southern United States. They are traveling to New Orleans to see Mardi Gras, but when they get there, they spend the bulk of their time in a brothel and tripping on LSD in a cemetery with two prostitutes. At the end of this journey the promised land is debased, reduced from an ecstatic celebration of community and identity to a concern with carnality and capitalism. The American term for an LSD experience, a trip, signals the idea of a mental journey. After the two leave New Orleans, Peter Fonda says, "We blew it." He does not explain. The film ends with both characters being shot by rednecks. There is nowhere left to go. The journey of revelation reveals the loss of a future as it reveals the loss of a moral perspective.

Two films released in 1971 articulated the new understanding of the road: *Two Lane Blacktop,* which focuses on a race between two cars across the American Southwest, and *Vanishing Point.* In both films the driving is what is important. With the loss of the United States as the promised land, the road no longer leads anywhere. Rather, the road becomes the site for a journey through a fallen world. The traveling itself becomes a narrative of personal salvation that often ends in death. The outlaw as hero, as in *Bonnie and Clyde* (1967) and *Badlands* (1973), is set against the experience of the United States as a fallen world. In addition to films, a number of popular road songs, such as Steppenwolf's "Born to be Wild" and Canned Heat's "On the Road Again," celebrated the

ideas of traveling and, often, of the outlaw who was wiser—and in a way morally superior—to the fallen world that had outlawed him.

In Springsteen's lyrics the road becomes increasingly bleak. On the 1975
album *Born to Run,* the title track is a celebration of the road. The last verse
begins:

> The highways jammed with broken heroes
> On a last chance power drive

and ends:

> Someday girl, I don't know when,
> we're gonna get to that place
> Where we really want to go
> And we'll walk in the sun
> But till then tramps like us
> Baby we were born to run

The road here still operates as a site of redemption. The American dream may
be failing (in the first verse Springsteen sings about the "runaway American
dream"), and Americans may now be broken heroes, but the road still leads
to the promised land. It is because the road still leads to the promised land
that it is a site of redemption. The song does not celebrate traveling to the
promised land, however; it celebrates running. The only redemption possible
is now to be found in the driving itself. The promised land of the American
Dream will never be reached. By *The River* (1980) the road is a place of rain,
isolation, and wrecks.

In 1985 Talking Heads released *Little Creatures.* The cover of the album is
a primitivist painting, an apocalyptic vision. One of the most popular tracks
on the album is "Road to Nowhere":

> We're on a road to nowhere
> Come on inside
> Takin' that road to nowhere
> We'll take that ride
> I'm feelin' okay this mornin'
> And you know,
> We're on the road to paradise
> Here we go, here we go

Here nowhere and paradise are the same place. The lyrics work as a double
vision. One part describes the road to paradise and the city of paradise that
is approaching. The other part, which opens and closes the song, describes
the road as going nowhere. Americans are being told that they have to get
on the road, but the place to which the road leads does not exist.

Against this background, it is instructive to compare *Wild at Heart* (1989) with *The Wizard of Oz*. *Wild at Heart* recognizes *The Wizard of Oz* as a road movie and makes constant allusions to it. In *The Wizard of Oz* Dorothy travels the Yellow Brick Road of Oz to return to her home in Kansas. In *Wild at Heart* Oz and the United States are conflated. The Wicked Witch and the Good Witch appear in the United States. Sailor and Lula are traveling from Cape Fear, near the border of North and South Carolina, to California. They never reach the promised land. The road they travel tropes the Yellow Brick Road. The United States has become Oz, but in doing so, it has lost its moral perspective. This is the United States of Springsteen's "Born in the U.S.A." It is also not home. At one point in the film Lula clicks her red shoes together, just as Dorothy did, and intones "I want to go home." But Lula goes nowhere. She is home, but home is not home. The United States is once again, and this time in a more profound way, not home to the settler society. The end of *Wild at Heart* displays a desperation similar to that at the end of *The Wizard of Oz*. The Good Witch visits Sailor and tells him, "If you're truly wild at heart, you won't turn away from your dreams. Don't turn away from love." The only salvation the film can offer is an assertion of the personal myth of romantic love. Sailor returns to Lula and their son, and the film ends with a celebration of the nuclear family as home. They are, however, in a car stuck in a traffic jam.

The same point made in *Easy Rider* is also made in the 1991 film *Thelma and Louise*. Thelma and Louise find that outside American patriarchal reality there is nowhere to go. They cannot even leave the United States. The narrative closure of *Thelma and Louise* echoes that of *Easy Rider* and many other road movies. In *Thelma and Louise* the pair literally run out of road. Having been finally trapped by the patriarchal police of the Law of the Father at the end of a dirt track by the Grand Canyon, the two drive over the edge. The major difference between *Thelma and Louise* and earlier road movies is that, for the first time, the outlaws are women. Previously, as in both *Bonnie and Clyde* and *Badlands,* women outlaws were secondary to their male associates. As it was prefigured in *On the Road,* the road movie has been a white male genre, like the Western out of which it developed. *Thelma and Louise* appropriates the myth of the road, and the road movie, to make a point about the situation of women in patriarchy. The transformation of the myth that the film appropriates is that of the 1970s onward.

Beyond the Myth of the Apocalypse

It seems that at the same time that the United States is articulating the postapocalyptic utopian myth of global capitalism's New World Order, it is itself returned to a postcolonial search for identity. The myth of a global utopia is the externalized myth of the promised land. It is in this context that there can be an American claim to an end to history. The apocalyptic transformation of history in history leads to the claim that in the global promised land of global capitalism, there is no more history. At this point there is a complex relation between the European myth of America, and subsequently the United States, as the promised land and the American myth of a global promised land. In 1960 (the year Kennedy was elected; his inauguration was in January 1961) Daniel Bell published a book entitled *The End of Ideology,* which became important in academic circles and precipitated what became known as the "end-of-ideology" debate (Bell 1960). The book's key idea was that political ideologies had lost all worth. The underlying assumption was that American politics was not ideological. At the end of the book Bell (1960, 406) summed up his argument:

> The problems which confront us at home and in the world are resistant to the old terms of ideological debate between "left" and "right," and if "ideology" by now, and with good reason, is an irretrievably fallen word, it is not necessary that "utopia" suffer the same fate. But it will if those who now call loudest for new utopias begin to justify degrading *means* in the name of some utopian or revolutionary *end,* and forget the simple lessons that if the old debates are meaningless, some old verities are not—the verities of free speech, free press, the right of opposition and of free inquiry.

Here we can see clearly the claim that idealistic ideological utopianism is giving way to the real utopian society based on American liberal pluralism. The promised land is nigh. Bell's view, popularly held in the 1960s in the United States, was another articulation of the construction of the United States as the postapocalyptic promised land.

In the 1990s the "end-of-history" debate precipitated by Francis Fukuyama's book *The End of History and the Last Man* (Fukuyama 1992) is one articulation of the claim to a postapocalyptic New World Order. Fukuyama's work is self-consciously Hegelian. He makes use of Hegel's idea of recognition, arguing that "in particular, Man [sic] wants to be recognised as a *human being,* that is, as a being with a certain worth or dignity" (1992, xvi). Fukuyama couples this interpretation of Hegel with Hegel's evolutionism to argue that the global spread of liberal democracy, which he claims best expresses the human need for recognition in political practice, represents the end of history. Producing a telling image, Fukuyama writes that "while modern natural science guides us to the gates of the Promised Land of liberal democracy, it does not deliver us to the Promised Land itself." For Fukuyama, the drive for this deliverance is an effect of the human need for recognition. In this image Fukuyama equates the promised land with the end of history. He further equates both these terms with the institution of liberal democracy first in the United States and subsequently across the globe. Once more the United States takes on itself the burden of the European utopian fantasy. It is enlightening to note, given what was said about Kojève at the beginning of this essay, that of all the commentators on Hegel he mentions, Fukuyama most often cites Kojève. Given the similarities of their concerns, the one claiming the United States as the promised land and the other claiming the world as the promised land, it is intriguing to note that Fukuyama does not reference Daniel Bell's *End of Ideology*. What Fukuyama does is to appropriate the European modernist idea of an end to history, epitomized in Hegel's work, and conflate it with the American idea of an apocalyptic consummation of history to produce an understanding of the New World Order. This too illustrates Douglas Robinson's point that the American dream is of a historical apocalypse, "of a transformation *of* history *in* history that would consummate and so give meaning *to* history."

In the post–World War II period, while the Americans deployed eschatological rhetoric, the Europeans reworked the myth of the American promised land and fetishized the United States as the promised land of unlimited consumption possibilities. By the late 1980s the American myth of the apocalypse and its associated myths had undergone a fundamental transformation. From an American point of view, the paradox of the American myth of a global utopia is that it places all countries on the same metaphysical footing. The effect of this is that the United States must lose its claim to having a special quality, a special status and therefore a special claim to identity. Most important, it loses its apocalyptic claim to a unifying moral perspective. The United States is thus forced to confront its own history as a settler society and to deal with the same problems of displacement, identity, and the experience of living in an Other's land that are a part of the histories of other English-speaking settler societies, including Canada, New Zealand, South Africa, and Australia. It may be that within the next fifty years, we will begin to see the beginning of the political end for the last of the two superpowers produced from European modernity.

Afterword: Postcoloniality, Race, and the Land of Promise

Postcoloniality and the United States

There has been an anxiety about describing the United States as postcolonial. In their watershed text *The Empire Writes Back*, Ashcroft, Griffiths, and Tiffin (1989, 2) write: "So the literatures of African countries, Australia, Bangladesh, Canada, Caribbean countries, India, Malaysia, Malta, New Zealand, Pakistan, Singapore, South Pacific Island countries, and Sri Lanka are all post-colonial literatures. The literature of the USA should also be placed in this category. Perhaps because of its current position of power, and the neo-colonizing role it has played, its post-colonial nature has not been generally recognised." They go on to argue that the United States is not just another postcolonial society; rather, "its relationship with the metropolitan centre has been paradigmatic for post-colonial literatures everywhere" (2). Unfortunately, having made this claim, Ashcroft, Griffiths, and Tiffin do not back it up with an examination of American literary texts. This omission paves the way for McClintock (1992, 87) to ask rhetorically, "By what fiat of historical amnesia can the United States of America, in particular, qualify as 'postcolonial'—a term which can only be a monumental affront to the Native American peoples currently opposing the confetti triumphalism of 1992." In addition, it allows Ahmad to critique both Ashcroft, Griffiths, and Tiffin and McClintock for what he calls the "inflation" of the term *postcolonial*—he refers to its historical application beyond the specific effects of decolonization and the independence of previously colonized countries in the post–World War II period. Ahmad (1995, 14) writes: "The sort of inflation that has come about in literary theory with the publication of such books as *The Empire Writes Back* were [*sic*] also not available at the time [in the 1970s, when Marxist critics were using the term]. It has now become quite common to push the moment of postcolonialism back to the American Revolution, the decolonization of Latin America, the founding of Australia; indeed, according to some, postcolonialism begins with colonialism itself, with the earliest practices of resistance, perhaps as early as 1492." The point of Ahmad's critique is his worry over the loss of historical specificity for the term *postcolonial*, a specificity that, he argues, is an effect of the particular conditions and consequences of capitalism in the post–World War II period, the time of the development of the postcolonial state. Clearly, from this point of view, the United States could not be described as a postcolonial state. Not only did its independence come about in a time of quite different capitalist organization, but, during the post–World War II period, it has been a part of the economic core driving the decolonizing project and the associated forms of economic and cultural neocolonialism.

Having more in common with his position than Ahmad perhaps recognizes, McClintock criticizes the authors of *The Empire Writes Back* for deciding, "idiosyncratically to say the least, that the term 'postcolonialism' should not be understood as everything that has happened *since* European colonialism, but rather everything that has happened from the very beginning of colonialism, which means turning back the clocks and unrolling the maps of 'postcolonialism' to 1492, and earlier" (1992, 87). McClintock is arguing two points here. She claims, first, that the historical referent for the term *postcolonial* should be the independence of those countries previously colonized and, second, that the complexities and divergences in the economic and cultural processes and practices that have taken place around postindependence situations render the use of the term limited and questionable, contrary to the tendency to homogenize under its rubric.

Within this formulation the United States certainly occupies an ambivalent position. It is most definitely a part of the global capitalist core—indeed, the dominant country in the systems of economic, political, and cultural domination that (dis)order global capitalism. At the same time, however, we must recognize that the United States is a settler state and was once a British-ruled settler colony. In McClintock and Ahmad's terms, the problem with classifying the United States as postcolonial concerns the qualitative differences between its history of postcoloniality and the histories of the countries that gained independence after World War II. Note that both McClintock and Ahmad use 1492, the date of Columbus's "discovery" of the New World, to suggest the point from which Ashcroft, Griffiths, and Tiffin might date postcolonial practices. The date is significant for two reasons. First, it suggests a historical limiting of the postcolonial to British colonization—a questionable move that nevertheless allows recognition of the specificities of British/English colonial practice; second, and more important, it implies that the postcolonial is associated with capitalist colonialism. The year 1492 connects the European finding of America with the exploratory period associated with mercantile capitalism. If we crudely distinguish three phases of capitalism—mercantile, colonial, and global—then we can argue that the independence of what became the United States roughly correlates with the expansionary period of colonialism. It is clear, then, that the history of the United States marks it as out of synch with, and therefore as distinct from, other British colonies and settler colonies.

One site of agreement between McClintock and Ahmad is their periodization of the postcolonial. McClintock and Ahmad are right to assert the importance of post–World War II global capitalism's effects on the independence of British colonies and on the resulting state forms, politics, and cultures. Nevertheless, these manifestations of postcoloniality must be articulated with a "postcolonial experience" that evolves from the process of colonization itself. In this sense, I want to argue that the *post* in *postcolonial* does not signal "after," in the sense that colonization as direct imposition of colonial power ceases. Rather, it refers to the reactive processes of colonized and colonizers enmeshed in the practice of colonization. It is to this understanding that Ashcroft, Griffiths, and Tiffin subscribe. They argue that what postcolonial literatures have in common is "that they emerged in their present form out of the experience of colonisation and asserted themselves by foregrounding the tension with the imperial power, and by emphasizing their differences from the assumptions of the imperial centre" (1989, 2).

The key to the divergence between Ashcroft, Griffiths, and Tiffin and both McClintock and Ahmad lies in the object of their interest. Whereas McClintock and Ahmad focus, in the first instance, on economic structures and effects and those institutions, power effects, and systems of domination associated with them, Ashcroft, Griffiths, and Tiffin "use the word 'post-colonial' to cover all the culture affected by the imperial process from the moment of colonisation to the present day" (1989, 2). In particular, they are concerned with literature and literary texts. This concern distracts them from something central to the production of the literary texts they describe, that is, the formation of a *postcolonial imaginary* specific to particular postcolonial circumstances but expressing the experience of the capitalist processes of exploration, colonialism, and the independence of the colonies. In this essay I have sought to elaborate some aspects of the postcolonial imaginary of the United States.

Race and Ex-British Settler Colonies

The discussion of McClintock and Ahmad provides a context for talking about Frankenberg and Mani's intervention in the question of the applicability of the term *postcolonial* to the United States. Their position is clear: "USA: Here, the term 'postcolonial' sticks in our throats" (1993, 293). They are placing India, Britain, and the United States side by side. Frankenberg and Mani, like McClintock and Ahmad, want to associate the postcolonial with the ending of colonial rule. In addition, however, they want to describe the process of the postcolonial as decisive rather than definitive, as pertaining to "the shift effected by decolonization without claiming either a complete rupture in social, economic and political relations and forms of knowledge . . . or its opposite, admittedly argued by few, that the present is nothing more than a mere repetition of the past" (300). It is in this context that they can describe Britain as postcolonial, as a colonizer deeply affected by the loss of its colonies and by the diasporic influxes to Britain from many of those former colonies.

It is clear from their thumbnail sketch that Frankenberg and Mani associate the United States with Britain rather than with India; that is, they see it in terms of a colonizer rather than the colonized. Nevertheless, they feel that the two nations occupy quite different positions: "The particular relation of past territorial domination and current racial composition that is discernible in Britain and which lends a particular meaning to the term 'postcolonial' does not, we feel, obtain here" (1993, 293). Absent here is any trace of the United States' commonality with Canada, New Zealand, Australia, and South Africa as British settler colonies, though its circumstance as a "White settler colony" is mentioned (293).

In the context of this claim to difference, if not uniqueness, of the United States, Frankenberg and Mani still want to argue for a similarity of transformation in social experience for the United States in the post–World War II period. This similarity is located in "the serious calling into question of white/

Western dominance by the groundswell of movements of resistance, and the emergence of struggles for collective self-determination most frequently articulated in nationalist terms" (1993, 293). It is this development in the United States, which has not undergone the post–World War II decolonizing experience of either colonizer or colonized (e.g., Britain and India, respectively), that leads Frankenberg and Mani to coin the term *post–civil rights* for the United States. Here they are thinking not only of the African American experience but also of the struggles of Native Americans, La Raza, and Asian American groups, as well as those groups of "recent immigrants/refugees borne here on the trails of US imperialist adventures" (293) who are also a part of the post–civil rights United States. At this point it should be recognized, as McClintock implies in her reference to Native American peoples quoted earlier, that the struggles for recognition and rights of indigenous peoples in settler states formerly colonized by Britain and other European nations are, in an important sense, of a different order from those of racialized and ethnicized groups within the state.

This shift in attitude to race, and the attempt to reconstitute the nation-state on a multiracial basis, is not unique to the United States—though its specific circumstances and ways of dealing with it are (see, e.g., Hollinger 1995). The new concerns are to be found in all the British settler states listed earlier, and "multiculturalism," meaning something more or less different in each country, has come to be the preferred solution for managing the situation (see Stratton 1997a). In Canada multiculturalism was adopted as official government policy in 1971. In Australia the White Australia policy was gradually done away with during the post–World War II period, and multiculturalism was adopted as government policy in 1973–74. In New Zealand multiculturalism was taken on board in the late 1970s, and it became government policy in South Africa when the Interim Constitution was put into place in 1993.[8] All these countries have experienced changes in more than just migrant intake patterns and expectations about how migrants might be expected to fit in. There has also been a change in the status of indigenous peoples and—except for South Africa, where political developments made this unnecessary—a debate over whether the indigenous people should be incorporated under the umbrella of multiculturalism or have their special situation acknowledged.

If this change in the United States during the post–World War II period was structurally equivalent to developments in the other independent British settler states, then we need to consider whether this event might be contextualized as a part of the general postcolonial historical experience of that particular group of colonies that can be defined as British settler states, all of which were, more or less, independent of Britain by the start of World War II. If it can be, then it would be worthwhile briefly to adumbrate some of the possible causes of this change, something Frankenberg and Mani fail to do in their argument for the use of *post–civil rights* as a descriptor for the United States. We must first acknowledge, though, that *post–civil rights* does refer to a uniquely American circumstance: the presence within the nation-state of a very large community of nonindigenous people who, from before the formation of that nation-state, were identified as racially distinct, whose ancestors were brought to the American colonies as slaves, and who, although incorporated as citizens within the nation-state, were nevertheless deprived of their civil rights, discriminated against, and actively excluded from marriage to members of the white population, sometimes by force of law (two relevant books here are Roediger 1991 and Allen 1994). I want to discuss the specifically American situation later.

The first point to make about the general shift in the British-originated independent settler states is that the post–World War II period saw a transformation in the discourse of race, something that had begun earlier. Saul Dubow writes:

> Robert Miles has pointed out that the word "racism" was coined only in the 1930s, reflecting both a rejection of the rise of Nazism in Germany and a concomitant realisation that the concept of race was deeply suspect on scientific grounds. Prior to this period, terms such as "race hatred" were in use. In America the scientific challenge to the validity of "race" was pioneered by the anthropologist Franz Boas and his circle of followers. By the 1930s Boas enjoyed widespread influence, though by no means all scientists were in agreement with him. In Britain a systematic anti-racist position also began to coalesce by the mid-1930s. (1995, 190)

In the post–World War II period, the turn from scientific racialism was reinforced by an awareness of the Nazis' use of race theory in their genocidal attacks on Jews, Gypsies, and Slavs. The move away from the use of race as an exclusivist paradigm articulated with the spread of mass-consumption capitalism. By the 1950s and 1960s this was being reinforced by a restructuring of global capitalism in which the old core/periphery, white/Other model no longer obtained. The increasing economic power of the oil-rich Arab countries and Nigeria, the new industrial strength of Japan, and the rapid industrialization of South Korea and Taiwan all entailed a gradual reformation in understandings of and practices around race that culminated in the 1970s and 1980s.

At this point we need to backtrack. In "What is Post(-)Colonialism?" Mishra and Hodge argue against what they describe as the "homogenizing drive" of *The Empire Writes Back*. In particular, they assert, "it is especially important to recognize the different histories of the White settler colonies which, as fragments of the metropolitan centre, were treated very differently by Britain, which, in turn, for these settler colonies, was not the imperial centre but the Mother Country" (1991, 428). Although the tenor of Mishra and Hodge's argument suggests that they were not including the United States here, the point is applicable, although not in the same way that it is to the other British-originated settler states I have listed.

For Mishra and Hodge, the key to what they see as "the unbridgeable chasms that existed between White and non-White colonies" (1991, 428) is race. They write: "Race is not part of an unproblematic continuum alongside discursive categories such as linguistic rupture, syncretism, hybridity, and so on. In all kinds of oppositional postcolonialism (within settler countries themselves and without) race was part of a larger struggle for self-respect" (428). This complication resulted from the fact that, as the modern Western nation-state developed in the nineteenth century and in coordination with the establishment of full-fledged capitalist colonialism, the discourse of race became the crucial means for distinguishing who could and could not be a member of the nation.[9] It was this irreducible fault line, rather than migration per se, that distinguished the two forms of British colony—and that returned to haunt Britain from the 1950s and 1960s with movements of people from the Caribbean and South Asia to the old imperial core.

In an article comparing the modes of construction of national identity and multiculturalism in Australia and the United States, Ang and I argue that there are two ways in which national community is produced, by emphasizing either ideology or culture (Stratton and Ang 1994). The latter is the most common and was used in Australia and other British-originated settler states until the advent of multiculturalist rhetoric. With the War of Independence, however (the United States was the only British settler colony to achieve independence by war), there was, in what was becoming the United States, "a shift away from the concern with 'natural' (British) national culture as the site for identification, and towards a messianic espousal of ideology as the basis for forging an identity for the new nation" (Stratton and Ang 1994, 134). It was in this context that the moral values of the Enlightenment became inextricably linked with the eschatology of Puritan fundamentalism to form the basis for the American postcolonial national imaginary.

At the same time, "In US history, the key exclusionary category is that of 'race'" (Stratton and Ang 1994, 139). Although race could not be used to distinguish Americans from British—both were definable as white—it was used to place limits on access to American national identity. Hence, most important, African Americans were made members of the American state, especially after the Civil War, but remained excluded from membership in the nation (see, e.g., Conzen et al. 1992). From this point of view, what Frankenberg and Mani describe as the post–civil rights United States is a country in which those people identified as nonwhite, as African American, Hispanic, Asian, and so forth, are asserting their moral right, in the terms of the American moral vision, to be members of the American nation. Put simply, this is the claim of the American version of multiculturalism.

The Land of New Promise

A shared moral vision, not a shared culture, is what has incorporated the American nation. As I outlined in the main body of this essay, this vision has been expressed in an eschatology whose elements have been mythically identified with the United States in different ways at different times. Between the closing of the frontier and the mid-1970s, the dominant discourse about the United States was that it was the promised land. This discourse became increasingly assertive in what was experienced as the consumerist utopia of the 1950s and 1960s. This is the same period that Frankenberg and Mani associate with the post–civil rights United States. In this period, when the dominant American myth assured Americans that they lived in the plenitude of the promised land, the claims of the racially excluded could be made, and dealt with for better or worse, within the uplifting certainty of a utopian moral vision—most notably that of Lyndon Johnson's "Great Society." In the 1990s, as I previously suggested, things are not so easy. The loss of moral vision in the United States, connected with the staging and loss of the Vietnam War and more generally with the effects of the loss of hegemonic global economic power, has been associated with a loss of the certainty that the United States is the promised land.

In this context the racial fractures that are such a central part of the American experience, especially the fracture between white and African American, are perceived to threaten the fabric of the nation-state. An analysis of Bill Clinton's second inaugural address, on 20 January 1997, shows how the Clinton White House is attempting to reassert a moral vision through a reworking of the national myth of eschatology that has been central to American understanding of itself and its history. In particular, I will focus on the way the problem of race is refigured through the reformation of the myth as an attempt to deal with the fracturing effects of racialized division.

The first thing to notice is the crucially important shift from identifying the United States with the promised land to placing the promised land in the future. Clinton said: "Guided by the ancient vision of the promised land, let us set our sights upon a land of new promise."[10] The metaphor here is one of traveling to the promised land, with traveling given a temporal connotation. Later in the speech Clinton made the connection with migration and settlement clearer when he asserted, "The promise we sought in a new land we will find again in a land of new promise." Here, somewhat awkwardly, the land of the United States is being connected with its migrant, promised land past, and then the promise is moved to the future. The purpose of the speech is rhetorically to reconstitute the United States as the land of new promise. Accepting that the United States in the present is not the promised land, the speech places the promised land in the future, providing a moral vision of a time of fulfillment when the injustices of the present will have been rectified.

Within this image the apocalypse is figured not negatively, as a time of cleansing destruction, but positively, within the topos of the Enlightenment idea of historical progress through science. The speech alludes in positive terms to the rapid spread of the Internet. American rhetoric around the Internet is heavily influenced by eschatological thinking. For example, it is thought of as a new frontier—witness the libertarian Electronic Frontier Foundation (for a discussion of the Internet as the new frontier, see Healy 1997). In contrast to the perceived degradation of today's American life, where the promised land has been lost, the Internet is thought to lead to a new utopian land of community. This is the theme of Howard Rheingold's book *The Virtual Community: Homesteading on the Electronic Frontier* (1993), as epitomized in the book's title (I discuss the American application of the myth of community to the Internet in Stratton 1997b). Even the image of the information superhighway conjures up the connotations of the road as I have discussed them earlier in this essay. In this revision the Internet as information superhighway is the road that leads to the land of new promise.

As we approach this new utopia, Clinton says, "scientists now are decoding the blueprint of human life. Cures for our most feared illnesses seem close at hand." We are then offered an image of what this land of new promise will be like when Americans arrive there: "In this new land, education will be every citizen's most prized possession"; "Our streets will echo again with the laughter of our children, because no-one will try to shoot them or sell them drugs anymore." There will be work for everybody and upward mobility for the underclass. The new medical cures will be available to everybody. This image of the future land of new promise sounds remarkably like the old promised land of the 1950s and 1960s that white, middle-class Americans thought they lived in, and that was, seemingly, available for all Americans. The bourgeois utopia, with its democratic and distributive moral vision, has not changed. Only now it is positioned in the future. Implicit here is the myth of community. Community, a term rich in meaning for Americans, has been the concept in terms of which life in the promised land has been imagined. The loss of the promised land is expressed

through the experience of the loss of community. The land of new promise is a place where community will be reinstated. The moral renewal extends to American world leadership also. When the United States is (in) the
land of new promise, "We will stand mighty for peace and freedom, and
maintain a strong defense against terror and destruction."

It is within this context of future moral and material renewal that the
speech deals with the problem of race, particularly with African Americans.
The speech asserts: "The challenge of our past remains the challenge of the
future—will we be one nation, one people, with one common destiny, or not?
Will we all come together, or come apart?" Here the speech makes clear how
in the United States race still functions to limit membership in the nation.
The speech goes on: "The divide of race has been America's curse." The
speech was made on Martin Luther King Day, incorporating the celebration
of the African American struggle for civil rights into the unitary national
American struggle for the future land of new promise. The incorporation
does not stop there. In what is perhaps the most extraordinary paragraph of
the speech, King's own use of eschatological rhetoric laying out a future
promised land when African Americans would be treated equally is appropriated into the new national rhetoric for a future land of new promise. It is
worth quoting the paragraph in full:

> Thirty-four years ago, the man whose life we celebrate today spoke to us down
> there, at the other end of this Mall, in words that moved the conscience of a
> nation. Like a prophet of old, he told of his dream that one day America would
> rise up and treat all its citizens as equals before the law and in the heart. Mar-
> tin Luther King's dream was the American Dream. This quest is our quest: the
> ceaseless striving to live out our true creed. Our history has been built on such
> dreams and labors. And by our dreams and labors we will redeem the promise
> of America in the 21st century.

Here the fracture of race in the American nation-state, which has become the
most divisive national issue over the past twenty years,[11] since the loss of the
understanding of the United States as the promised land, has been reworked
in the terms of the new eschatological formation in such a way that claims
for equality are placed on a par with the other utopian expectations for the
land of new promise. In this way African Americans, and by implication the
other, unnamed minorities mentioned earlier in the speech—presumably the
other racialized groupings, Hispanics, Asians, and Native Americans—are
assimilated into a new unitary version of the national eschatological imaginary. The reformulation of the eschatology places the United States as heading toward the land of new promise when all racial(ized) groups will be
equally a part of the American nation. By this means the Clinton White House

is seeking to neutralize the present racial threat to national unity. This is the utopian, American version of multiculturalism.

Conclusion

I started this afterword by discussing the applicability of the term *postcolonial* to the United States. Because of its early date of colonization, but even more because of its early date of independence and its subsequent economic, political, and cultural power, the United States is anomalous among British colonies. Although its state formation is plainly not postcolonial in the same way that, for example, India's or Pakistan's is, the historical construction of the American state, and perhaps especially the American constitution, is nevertheless marked by the trace of the United States' complex transaction with Britain.

I have argued for the applicability of the term *postcolonial* to the consequences of the experience of colonization, including those that occur during colonization. It is in this period that there begins to evolve what I have called a postcolonial imaginary, which is inflected differently according to the diverse circumstances of the colonies. The postcolonial imaginary becomes a foundational element in the formation of a national imaginary.

I wanted to take up Mishra and Hodge's important distinction between British colonies and British settler colonies, recognizing the blurring of this distinction in the case of colonies such as Kenya and Zimbabwe. Mishra and Hodge's recognition of the different ways in which the discourse of race was mobilized in the different kinds of colony is an important insight, one that, when connected with Frankenberg and Mani's claim that the term *post–civil rights* applies to the United States better than *postcolonial* does, allows us to appreciate both the specificity of the American experience and its commonality with other British-originated settler states. In these states race has held a central position in the identification of who has been considered eligible for membership in the national imagined community and who has not.

In the final section of this essay I took up the vexed issue of race, and in particular of African Americans, within the context of the formation of the American nation. Using Clinton's second inaugural speech, I showed how the eschatology myth important in the United States' postcolonial imaginary was being reworked once more and how, in the context of the ideological production of a future "land of new promise," a claim was being made that the racial fracture would be healed at this time. Although the speech suggests that the healing will be a result of all Americans sharing the same (white and Enlightenment-originated) dream, one that will lead to the utopian access to plenty in the land of new promise, the ideological work of the speech was to diminish the salience of race in the United States by assimilating all racial divergence of interests to a single hegemonic dream. The success of the United States in avoiding increasing racial conflict, and that conflict's consequent threat to the integrity of the national community and the unity of the American state, may well depend on the extent to which Americans accept the Clinton White House's reformulation of the postcolonial national imaginary.

Notes

I would like to thank Ien Ang for her help in editing the original extremely dense essay—and for her suggestions, which have helped to make it even denser. An earlier version of this essay, up to the afterword, appeared in *New Formations* 21 (1994): 35–63.

The lyrics to "The Ballad of Frankie Lee and Judas Priest," written and composed by Bob Dylan, "Bob Dylan's 115th Dream," written and composed by Bob Dylan, and "Wake Up," written and composed by Stoltz, Neville, Hall, and Green, are all reprinted by kind permission of Sony/ATV Music Publishing.

The lyrics to "Wake Up," written and composed by Stoltz, Neville, Hall, and Green, are reproduced by kind permission of Rondor Music (Australia) Ltd.

The lyrics to "America," written and composed by Paul Simon, are reprinted by kind permission of Music Sales.

The lyrics to "Born in the U.S.A.," written and composed by Bruce Springsteen, "The Promised Land," written and composed by Bruce Springsteen, "Born to Run," written and composed by Bruce Springsteen, and "Road to Nowhere," written and composed by David Byrne, are reprinted by kind permission of Warner/Chappell Music Australia, Ltd.

1. The characteristic gendering of the colonizing situation marks the European colonizing power as male and the colonized as female.

2. There is another minor but significant American myth, that of the "Great American Novel." The term *novel* here can be extended to include film or, indeed, any medium that allows for extensive fictional development. There is no myth of the "Great British Novel" or "Great French Novel," however, although there is a myth of the "Great Australian Novel." The idea of the great novel, the one that will encapsulate and articulate the American—or Australian—experience is an idea born of the experience of settler colonies. In the British tradition the canon is realist. In the empiricist, representational terms in which the discourse of realism was articulated, the quality of the (British) novelistic representation was ultimately determined by certainty about the pregiven existence of the place being represented. The novel represents a sense of place. The meaning of the novel, born of its ability to represent, is guaranteed by the British sense of place. To put it simply, the presence of Britain allows for the confidence in its imitation. The settler colony has, by definition, no such sense of place. The settler colony is always already displaced. The myth of the Great American/Australian Novel signals the attempt to recuperate that displacement in a totalized representation that will give the sense of place lacking in the United States/Australia being represented. The myth inscribes its own impossibility. Since the canon is realist, the novel must always be less than what it represents. Its meaning—its truth in the traditional representational assumptions of the correspondence theory of truth—depends on the conflation of place and presence. The myth of the Great American/Australian Novel requires that the novel is greater than what it represents. Neverthe-

less, the excessive novel cannot be the Great Novel. The myth of the Great Novel is a part of the colonial baggage of the settler colony.

3. In 1965, while working for the BBC, Peter Watkins made a British made-for-television film about nuclear apocalypse entitled *The War Game*. It was banned from television. Around the time of *The Day After*, the British made *Threads*. Whereas *The Day After*, as its name suggests, concentrated on the immediate effects of the nuclear apocalypse, *Threads* emphasized the continuities and differences in people's lives before and after a nuclear war.

4. For films I have not seen, information comes from Leslie Halliwell 1979.

5. Thanks to Karl Neuenfeldt for pointing out this ambiguity to me.

6. Frank Kermode, in *The Sense of an Ending* (1966, 47) discusses two different understandings of time, which he distinguishes by use of the Greek words *chronos* and *kairos*: "*chronos* is 'passing time' or 'waiting time'—that which, according to Revelation, 'shall be no more'—and kairos is the season, a point in time filled with significance, charged with a meaning derived from its relation to the end."

7. This information comes from Brooks and Marsh 1981.

8. Section 31, chapter 3, of the Republic of South Africa's Interim Constitution, entitled "Language and Culture," asserts that "every person shall have the right to use the language and to participate in the cultural life of his or her choice."

9. The mimicry that Homi Bhabha (1994) describes in the context of Indian colonial history stemmed from the British practice of providing Indians with a British education while using race as a means of denying them equality with Britons.

10. I am using the version of the speech placed on the White House website.

11. For their mythic encapsulation of the relations between race, nation, and state in the United States as these are played out in the American national imaginary of the 1990s, one can cite the Rodney King case and the two trials of O. J. Simpson with their opposite verdicts.

Works Cited

Ahmad, Aijaz. 1995. "Postcolonialism: What's in a Name?" In *Late Imperial Culture*, ed. Roman de la Campa, E. Ann Kaplan, and Michael Sprinker, 11–32. London: Verso.

Allen, Theodore. 1994. *The Invention of the White Race*. London: Verso.

Ashcroft, Bill, Gareth Griffiths, and Helen Tiffin. 1989. *The Empire Writes Back: Theory and Practice in Post-Colonial Literatures*. London: Routledge.

Baudrillard, Jean. 1989. *America*. London: Verso.

Bell, Daniel. 1960. *The End of Ideology*. New York: Free Press.

Bhabha, Homi. 1994. "Of Mimicry and Man." *The Location of Culture*. London: Routledge.

Brooks, Tim, and Earle Marsh. 1981. *The Complete Directory of Prime Time Network T.V. Shows*. New York: Ballantine Books.

Conzen, Kathleen Neils, D. A. Gerber, E. Morawska, G. E. Pozzetta, and R. J. Vecoli. 1992. "The Invention of Ethnicity: A Perspective from the USA." *Journal of American Ethnic History* 12, no. 1:3–41.

Dubow, Saul. 1995. *Illicit Union: Scientific Racism in Modern South Africa*. Cambridge: Cambridge University Press.

Ewen, Stuart, and Elizabeth Ewen. 1982. *Channels of Desire: Mass Images and the Shaping of American Consumerism*. Minneapolis: University of Minnesota Press.

Frankenberg, Ruth, and Lata Mani. 1993. "Crosscurrents, Crosstalk: Race, 'Postcoloniality,' and the Politics of Location." *Cultural Studies* 7:292–310.

Fukuyama, Francis. 1992. *The End of History and the Last Man.* New York: Free Press.

Halliwell, Leslie. 1979. *Halliwell's Film Guide.* 2d ed. London: Granda.

Healy, Dave. 1997. "Cyberspace and Place: The Internet as Middle Landscape on the Electronic Frontier." In *Internet Culture,* ed. David Porter, 55–68. New York: Routledge.

Hollinger, David. 1995. *Postethnic America: Beyond Multiculturalism.* New York: Basic Books.

Inglis, Fred. 1988. *Popular Culture and Political Power.* Hemel Hempstead, U.K.: Harvester-Wheatsheaf.

Kermode, Frank. 1966. *The Sense of an Ending.* Oxford: Oxford University Press.

Lipsitz, George. 1990. *Time Passages: Collective Memory and American Popular Culture.* Minneapolis: Unviversity of Minnesota Press.

McClintock, Anne. 1992. "The Angel of Progress: Pitfalls of the Term 'Post-colonialism.'" *Social Text* 31–32:84–98.

McPherson, C. B. 1962. *The Political Theory of Possessive Individualism: From Hobbes to Locke.* Oxford: Clarendon.

Mishra, Vijay, and Bob Hodge. 1991. "What is Post(-)Colonialism?" *Textual Practice* 5, no. 3:421–47.

Pefanis, Julian. 1991. *Heterology and the Postmodern: Bataille, Baudrillard, and Lyotard.* Sydney: Allen and Unwin.

Rheingold, Howard. 1993. *The Virtual Community: Homesteading on the Electronic Frontier.* Reading, Mass.: Addison-Wesley.

Robinson, Douglas. 1990. *American Apocalypses: The Image of the End of the World in American Literature.* Baltimore: Johns Hopkins University Press.

Roediger, David. 1991. *The Wages of Whiteness: Race and the Making of the American Working Class.* London: Verso.

Stratton, Jon. 1986. "Australia—This Sporting Life." In *Power Play,* ed. Geoffrey Lawrence and David Rowe, 85–114. Sydney: Hale and Iremonger.

———. 1989. "A Question of Origins." *Arena* 89:133–51.

———. 1990. *Writing Sites: A Genealogy of the Postmodern World.* Hemel Hempstead, U.K.: Harvester-Wheatsheaf.

———. 1997a. "The Impossible Ethnic: Jews, Ethnicity and Multiculturalism in Australia." *Diaspora: A Journal of Transnational Studies* 5, no. 3:330–73.

———. 1997b. "Cyberspace and the Globalization of Culture." In *Internet Culture,* ed. David Porter, 253–75. New York: Routledge.

Stratton, Jon, and Ien Ang. 1994. "Multicultural Imagined Communities: Cultural Difference and National Identity in Australia and the USA." *Continuum* 8, no. 2:124–58.

Tiffin, Helen. 1987. "Comparative Literature and Post-colonial Counter-discourse." *Kunapipi* 9, no. 3:17–34.

Turner, Fredrick Jackson. 1950. "The Significance of the Frontier in American History." In *The Frontier in American History,* 1–35. New York: Holt and Winston.

Wallerstein, Immanuel. 1974. *The Modern World-System.* New York: Academic.

Williams, Raymond. 1977. *Marxism and Literature.* Oxford: Oxford University Press.

2 New Postnational Narratives, Old American Dreams; or, The Problem with Coming-of-Age Stories

Susie O'Brien

In his introduction to the second volume of a special issue of *boundary 2,* titled *New Americanists 2: National Identities and Postnational Narratives,* Donald Pease heralds a revolution in the field of American studies, the primary agents of which, he suggests, are the critics whose essays are contained in the collection.[1] These critics—the "New Americanists"—depart radically from the tradition to which they are nominally bound in their determination to expose the contradictions that animate the liberal myth of the national subject, a subject whose abstract universalism is produced by bracketing off the markers of difference (race, class, and gender) that are at once constitutive of the narrative of national subjecthood and unrepresentable within it. Exposing the exclusivist terms of this narrative, New Americanists also resist identification with the specters of integrity offered by countermythologies, maintaining instead a precarious position "at the intersection between interpellation and exclusion" (Pease 1992, 9), an intersection that, Pease suggests, offers strategic possibilities for the articulation of a new, *post*national narrative.

Although this boundary-straddling assertion of identity seems to offer a plausible, even an inspirational, means of overcoming the limitations of national narratives, on close examination the borderland occupied by the "postnational" subject—the New Americanist—turns out to be less promising than its would-be developers have claimed. As this essay seeks to demonstrate, not only is the frontier territory staked out by the postnational narrative already well worn by the tracks of other liberationist expeditions, most notably those grouped under the banner of "postcolonial," but these expeditions have a funny way of always arriving back at the same place—the mythological landscape of America. Before optimistically setting out on yet another quest to establish yet another western frontier, it seems logical, at this point, to take a more critical look at the area in which all these new "posts" are being planted and to examine the history of earlier claims to the territory.

The ground that the New Americanists seek to contest is currently occupied, Pease suggests, by the work of contemporary scholars such as Frederick Crews, whose *New York Review of Books* article "Whose American Renaissance?" (Crews 1988; the article coined the pejorative label "New Americanist") exemplifies the "Americanism" that defines the cultural parameters of the American nation. The narrative of national culture clearly has a much earlier provenance, however, in texts such as Emerson's "American Scholar," which itself, as Sacvan Bercovitch (1975) and others have pointed out, contains echoes of the Puritan tradition of exempla. Frequently read as a kind of mission statement for the development of a uniquely American subjectivity realized in the person of the scholar, Emerson's text contains a number of the ingredients whose reconstitution Pease identifies in Crews—most notably, a defense of romantic individualism against the constraints of political ideologies and the invocation of a universal/American subject—what R. W. B. Lewis later termed "American Adam"—in whom might be read the distillation of the qualities of life and liberty that animate the unfolding truth of America.

Carrying the Puritan stamp of millennial promise, this narrative of progress, in which the redemption of a nation is figured allegorically through the development of an exemplary individual, gained secular authority in the eighteenth and nineteenth centuries through its scientistic representation as the fruition of a natural growth process. By citing "natural law," Albert K. Weinberg (1958, 218) points out, it was possible to argue throughout the nineteenth century that expansion "was demanded by America's very entrance upon unconfined manhood." This representation of American masculinity is strengthened by its contrast to images of England as, in Emerson's words, "an old and exhausted island, [that] must one day be contented, like other parents to be strong only in her children" (1903a, 275). Locating the exemplary identity of America within the extended structure of the imperial family, Emerson's metaphor represents a shift in register from the biological to the psychosexual, a shift that also finds expression in James Russell Lowell's "Fable for Critics" (1894). Written a half-century before Freud conceived what was to become the dominant narrative of identity formation, Lowell's poem deploys an explicitly Oedipal trope in its advice to the young American critic:

No matter what John [Bull] says, don't try to outcrow him,
'Tis enough to go quietly on and outgrow him;
Like most fathers, Bull hates to see Number One
Displacing himself in the mind of his son
. . . .
To love one another you're too like by half;
If he is a bull, you're a pretty stout calf,
And tear your own pasture for nought but to show
What a nice pair of horns you're beginning to grow.

Thus America—or at least the American critic—assumes the role of the ar-
chetypal child who, in symbolically displacing his father, provides what Emerson says the earth awaits: "exalted manhood" (1903b, 535). For his Puritan
forefathers, this quality was embodied most perfectly in the figure of the religious leader; for Emerson as for Lowell, it resides in the figure of the scholar
or the critic. In and through these exemplary figures, the emergence of a national culture could be traced.

From a contemporary perspective, the mythology of national identity
formation just outlined represents a vision breathtaking in its arrogant simplicity. The image of individual development, extended to the nation via the
popular notion that ontogeny recapitulates phylogeny, gave rise to the bizarre
notion that America's existence was not so much political as ontological. To
say this is not so much to repeat the truism that America has no sense of
history as to point out that history in America is contained within, and sub-
ordinated to, the drama of self-discovery. As Myra Jehlen (1986, 9) puts it:
"To be born an American is simultaneously to be born again. Americans
assume their national identity as the fulfillment of selfhood rather than its
point of origin, so that they travel their lives in a state of perpetual landing."
The organizing framework of this travel, Jehlen (12) argues, is the land itself;
hence, the ruling element in the narrative of America is not time, whose
movement is measured by the dialectics of difference and conflict, but space,
in whose expansiveness "opposites can cohabit indefinitely, unchanged and
independent." As the subject of the national narrative, the American self is
defined through possession of and by that expansive space.

The trajectory of the postnational narrative might thus be described as one
of dispossession. Specifically, the postnational narrative reveals the American subject's nonidentity with the subject of the national narrative; the shift
in focus is represented in the special issue's subtitle, *National Identities and
Postnational Narratives*. In the postnational narrative, Pease (1992, 6) explains,
national identity turns out to be "a permanent instability, an endless antagonism between figures integrated within ever changing social imaginaries and
singularities forever external to them." If the narrative of the nation is defined

by the unrepresentability of the antagonism it construes as the contamination of ontology by politics, the postnational narrative develops at the site
of that contamination, articulating through the struggles of disfranchised
people—African Americans, Chicanos, Native Americans, and gays and les-
bians—an American subjectivity whose integrity was always already frac-
tured, always already "political." In drawing attention to the constructed
"nature" of the subject of the American narrative, the postnational narrative outlined by Pease offers the possibility of transformation—and here one
is plagued by what, if one resists a more religious interpretation, can be described only as an odd sense of déjà vu.

   In answer to the implicit question of who will effect that transformation,
the figure of the American Adam, supposedly vanquished by the deconstructive forces of postnationalism, rises shakily to his feet, reborn in the heroic
stance of the New Americanist. In Pease's account, the latter figure quickly
betrays his provenance by obediently adhering to the Oedipal injunction,
expressed in James Russell Lowell's "Fable for Critics," to dispose of his critical forefather—in this case, Frederick Crews. Having demonstrated in the
introduction to the first volume of the *boundary 2* special issue the inadequacy
of Crews's critique of the New Americanists, Pease cannot resist smugly observing that at the end of his critique, Crews is forced to testify "to the New
Americanists' effectiveness in reorganizing the field of American Studies"
(1990, 29); this note of smugness is missing from the second introductory essay,
in which a slightly chastened Pease, acknowledging the criticism of other
members of the *boundary 2* collective, concedes that, in its exclusion of Crews,
the model of American studies he advanced in his first essay was as "monolithic, unidimensional and monocultural" as the model it purported to replace.
"I had," he admits "simply replaced one grand narrative of American Studies
with another" (1992, 2).

   The error is critical, and Pease's retraction is important, for as his second
essay makes clear, New Americanists are characterized by their refusal to be
interpellated by grand narratives. Like the American scholar who refuses to be
defined by the authoritative texts of the past, choosing instead to remain "free
even to the definition of freedom" (Emerson 1983, 65), the New Americanist
remains poised resolutely on the boundaries of his field, able, in Pease's words,
"to recognize as [his or her] disciplinary practice the sheer constructedness of
every one of the givens of the national narrative" (1992, 9). This recognition
stems not from privileged access to some abstract realm of unconstructed truth
but through a firm grasp on the connections between the abstract and the
concrete, the logical and the contingent, the universal and the political.

   In other words, the New Americanist, once again following his predeces-
sor, transcends the sphere of the merely academic, refusing, as Emerson's

American scholar refuses, to shrink from the realm of "politics or vexed questions" (Emerson 1983, 65) and grounding his scholarly authority in his vital connection to the community. But whereas the American scholar is connected organically to both the object and the audience of his scholarly work ("He is the world's eye. He is the world's heart" [Emerson 1983, 63]), the position of the New Americanist is somewhat more complicated, his advent on the scene of the postnational narrative appearing to be at once belated and fundamental. In a passage repeated in both introductory essays, Pease suggests that the New Americanists derive their authority from their status as *"liaisons between* cultural and public realms" (1990, 31; 1992, 3), a status he defines more explicitly in the second essay as "their different identifications with the disciplinary apparatuses in the new American Studies, as well as with social movements comprised of the 'disenfranchised groups' already cited [African Americanists, feminist Americanists, Chicano Americanists, Asian Americanists, or gay Americanists]" (1992, 3). Having established such scholars' places within these disfranchised groups, Pease goes on to prescribe for the New Americanists the responsibility of making these "absent subjects representable in [the field of American studies] past and present" (1990, 31), a seemingly insurmountable task unless the New Americanist also occupies a transcendent position above or at least beyond those unrepresentable subjects. The status of those subjects, and the relationship of the New Americanist to them, is made murkier by this narrative's political need to assert that those subjects have the capacity to represent themselves while denying them full subjectivity. He therefore asserts: "The agents for this [dismantling of the national narrative] were the national subject *peoples, figures* of race, class, and gender, who had been previously interpellated within the hegemonic category of disqualified social agency. As *motives* for changing existing social models, the *figures* of race, class, and gender moved from the status of *objects* of social regulation within the national narrative into performative *powers,* postnational *forces* able to change that narrative's assumptions" (1992, 4, emphasis added). It is difficult to figure out who did what in this account, where people, reduced to the sketchy status of figures, are then depersonified into motives that are somehow capable of changing from objects into forces and powers. Presumably, if these forces were identified as knowing subjects, the New Americanist would be out of a job. As it is, he retains his authority as his fathers did before him, by resolutely declaring his independence from the narrative that sanctions his speech and going on to fulfill that narrative's promise of transformation.

New Americanists 2: National Identities and Postnational Narratives concludes, appropriately, with an exemplum, recalling in style, if not in substance, the inspirational tradition of Puritan spiritual biography. Whereas writers

such as Cotton Mather trace the religious careers of the Pilgrim fathers as
models of Christian, protonational identity formation, Daniel O'Hara, in
Pease's approving terms,

> finds in Frank Lentriccia's literary career a way of living the postnational nar-
> rative as a rediscovery of what O'Hara calls "oneself." Because Lentricchia never
> identifies with any of the disciplinary practices . . . developing within the field
> of Literary Studies, he can discern the historicity of these developments as the
> basis for the discovery of his own imaginative agency. In "becoming himself,"
> instead of these academic personae, Lentricchia explains resistively the social
> imaginaries into which he otherwise would have been absorbed. (1992, 13)

Pease (1992, 13) explains that "because Lentricchia exemplifies the way an
identity always exceeds the social imaginaries in which it otherwise would
be interpellated," he concludes New Americanists 2 "with an account of his
exemplary postnational identity." "Go thou and do likewise," he might have
added, except it is not exactly clear for whom Lentricchia is meant to serve
as an exemplum, whether for identities hitherto excluded from the national
narrative by virtue of their interpellation as "other" or simply for those critics who would be identified as New Americanists.

   These questions are at once disingenuous and serious; in one sense it is
obvious (as Daniel O'Hara [1992, 232] claims in his essay) that Frank Lentricchia's career encapsulates nothing more than "the experience of his generation of oppositional literary critics." Nonetheless, in the context of a volume of essays that purports to initiate "an account of [New Americanists']
emergence from and continued interconnection with different emancipatory
social movements" (Pease 1992, 3), it seems reasonable to assume that the work
of the New Americanists somehow forwards the aims of these emancipatory
movements, that in "becoming oneself," as Frank Lentricchia does, the New
Americanist somehow extends the same privilege to those he represents. The
problem, of course, lies partly in determining exactly whom Lentricchia does
represent; while his "self" might be multiply determined by his affiliations
with Italian Americans (or African Americans or gay Americans), his capacity to articulate those components into a coherent account—to perform that
self—derives from his membership in a highly educated elite. The point is not
that his membership in that group should disqualify him from speech, or that
it proscribes his membership in other groups, but rather that it places special conditions—conditions that neither O'Hara nor Pease acknowledges—
on his capacity to identify with the socially disfranchised figures who have
been left out of the national narrative but who are promised key roles in the
postnational one.

   In tracing Pease's account of that narrative, I want to draw attention not
as much to the problem of academic hubris that prompts liberal critics to

claim that their work has broader social implications than it actually does (though I think that is a problem) as to the disturbing persistence, in the New Americanist narrative, of the Old Americanist trope of national redemption, whereby the emancipation of a people is figured as a process of individual self-discovery. The terrain of the New Americanist narrative begins to look suspiciously like the terrain of the New World, whereon European settlers, following the pattern set by such exemplary figures as John Winthrop, enacted their own dramas of self-discovery at the expense of those whose identities did not fit the pattern. It is at this narrative conjunction that the postnational critical project intersects with the more well-worn path of the postcolonial.

Numerous critics, Pease among them, have recently argued for the useful-ness of seeing the United States in postcolonial terms. Lawrence Buell (1992), for example, suggests that the emergence of a national literary tradition in the mid-nineteenth century represents not so much the transcendence of the lingering influence of British cultural norms as an anxious preoccupation with them. Borrowing Ashis Nandy's formulation of the intellectual climate of colonial India, Buell (1992, 415) suggests that the American tradition arose out of "a culture in which the ruled were constantly tempted to fight their rulers within the psychological limits set by the latter." Buell's argument is acknowledged in a footnote to Amy Kaplan's introduction to *Cultures of United States Imperialism* (Kaplan and Pease 1993), a collection of essays (ed-ited by Kaplan and Pease) that brings postcolonial literary theory to bear on the issue of imperialism in American culture. Although she cites Buell as an exception to postcolonial theory's prevailing tendency to omit discussion of the United States, Kaplan (1993, 21) suggests that his proposal to read early American writers as postcolonial not only ignores the nation's more recent imperial history[2] but "in a sense colonizes postcolonial theory by implicitly positioning the United States as the original postcolonial nation." Leaving aside the question of whether it makes logical sense to talk about colonizing a theory, Kaplan's move to defend the integrity of the postcolonial from con-tamination by an imperial force (Buell acting as an agent for the United States?) reveals something interesting about the role "the postcolonial" is invoked to play here, a role that is by no means peculiar to Kaplan's essay or to this collection.

To see the postcolonial as susceptible to colonization by the United States is to attribute to the postcolonial, at least implicitly, two important qualities. The first is its grounding in an emancipatory narrative framework, a frame-work whose moral authority is clearly sullied by association with a nation that, having loudly declared its independence, quickly acceded to the role of neocolonial bully. Second, and perhaps even more significant than its impli-cation in particular narrative structure, "the postcolonial," when seen as a potential victim of American bullying, invokes the nominally benign con-

cept of postcolonial identity: if it faces the risk of colonization, the postcolonial must already be identifiable as a coherent entity characterized by self-
possession—that is, it must already be sovereign. Thus Kaplan is invoking a
postcolonial framework that shares significant features with the postnational
framework invoked by Pease. Both imply a progressive, vaguely liberationist
movement; both are directed toward the affirmation of sovereignty. Both recall, as they renounce, the narrative of America's birth and ascendancy, as
figured in the development of the exemplary subject.[3]

Having examined narrative structure thus far in relatively abstract terms,
as a teleological framework that invisibly undergirds both traditional constructions of America and Americanism and contemporary critique of those constructions, I want now to turn to a more concrete example: Jamaica Kincaid's
Lucy, a text in which the process of narrative construction is self-consciously
foregrounded to highlight the path by which declarations of independence
become trapped in a framework of manifest destiny. The story of a West Indian immigrant's incomplete assimilation into the American cultural mainstream, *Lucy* follows the trajectory of the postnational narrative outlined by
Pease. Far from illustrating an "exemplary postnational identity," however,
Kincaid's text highlights the extent to which identity is structurally implicated
in narratives of nation. Although Lucy speaks to the necessity of resisting interpellation into the national mythology, the ethical (and aesthetic) reward
for such resistance—"becoming oneself"—is ultimately denied both to Lucy
and to the reader. The self that emerges from the novel is both partial and frac-
tured, offering neither the integrity of the sovereign subject nor the anchoring security of a grounding in community.

Lucy's eponymous narrator is a nineteen-year-old black West Indian
woman who goes to the United States as an au pair. At the outset of her journey, America represents for Lucy—as for many other West Indians—the
possibility of freedom not just from poverty and cultural isolation but also
from the constraints of colonial codes of propriety. Lucy's announcement
in a letter to her mother, written a year after her arrival in the United Sates,
that "life as a slut [is] quite enjoyable, thank you very much" (Kincaid 1991,
127–28), testifies to her anger at and, seemingly, her triumphant escape from
the bonds of maternal authority, bonds that are at once familial and cultural. Nevertheless, claiming the independent subjectivity that seems in a
parallel sense to be part of growing up and part of becoming an American
proves to be not as easy as Lucy anticipated.

She cannot, for example, accept the liberal feminist philosophy of her
employer, Mariah, which grounds her quest for liberation solely in her identity as a woman. "My life," Lucy explains, "was at once something more
simple and more complicated than that" (Kincaid 1991, 132). Lucy's life, like

the lives of the minority figures invoked in Pease's postnational narrative, contradicts the integrity of the universal subject "woman," which, like the universal subject "American," is predicated on the forgetting of the historical fracture that produced it. Mariah's doctrine of feminist liberation can never assuage Lucy's desire to be "free to take everything just as it [comes] and not see hundreds of years in every gesture, every word spoken, every face" (31)—can never, in other words, erase the legacy of colonial history that, in mapping the territory of the liberal subject, left her constitutionally out of bounds. Lucy's alien status is reflected in her observation, while on a train trip with Mariah, that "the other people sitting down to eat dinner all looked like Mariah's relatives; the people waiting on them all looked like mine" (32). The sign of her race does not permit Lucy to "pass" as a natural member of the universal/American family.

Her exclusion is figured concretely in the household in which she works, for Mariah and her husband, Lewis, frustrated by what they see as her stubborn refusal to become part of the family, teasingly nickname her "the Visitor." Their determination to consolidate her proper role in at least one family narrative is reflected in their response to a dream she recounts to them shortly after her arrival: she is naked, being chased by Lewis around the house on a yellow road that looks as if it were paved with cornmeal, and eventually falls into a pit of snakes. On hearing Lucy's dream, "Lewis made a chuckling noise, then said, Poor, poor Visitor. And Mariah said, Dr. Freud for Visitor, and I wondered why she said that, for I did not know who Freud was" (15). For Lewis and Mariah, Lucy's dream can be read as an index of her "normal" assimilation into the psychopathology of American family life and thus of her development as an individual. Once again, Lucy feels, they have completely misinterpreted her situation.

Read in the context of her own cultural background, the symbolic content of Lucy's dream confounds a psychoanalytical reading,[4] thus opening up the possibility of a different narrative of identity formation. More important, however, the *form* of the dream confounds translation into such a neat teleological framework. Rather, in departing from the text's realist surface to unearth buried historical symbols, the dream not only undermines the construction of the individual subject whose identity it putatively illustrates but it also interrupts the narrative convention of development on which such constructions are predicated. The dream is one of several devices that work in the text to inhibit the forward movement of the narrative, exploding into significations that are unassimilable to the progressive structure of the coming-of-age/immigrant success story. Metaphor has a similar function, as in Lucy's description of her bedroom in Lewis and Mariah's house. "The ceiling was very high," she notes, "and the walls went all the way up to the ceiling, enclosing the room

like a box—a box in which cargo travelling a long way should be shipped"
(7): a box, as Alison Donnell points out, that recalls the cargo holds in which
the African slaves were shipped to North America (Donnell 1992, 47). The
metaphor, whose aptness is conveyed in Lucy's attempt to dismiss it—"but I
was not cargo. I was only an unhappy young woman living in a maid's room,
and I was not even the maid" (Kincaid 1991, 8)—works to disrupt the liberal
myth of the global family (according to which slavery was a sordid episode
in the distant past), exposing its socioeconomic foundations and replacing it
in a deeper historical context. As Homi K. Bhabha has noted, "The space of
the modern nation-people [primarily diasporic people like Lucy] is never
simply horizontal. Their metaphoric movement requires a kind of 'doubleness' in writing; a temporality of representation that moves between cultural
formations and social processes without a 'centred' causal logic" (1990, 293).[5]
Breaking with the metonymic logic of realism, metaphor allows Kincaid to
figure the shifting ground of excluded meanings that lie beneath the "centered" causal logic of the narrative of individual/national identity formation.

Lucy further undermines the logical claims of that narrative by insistently
drawing attention to its status as narrative; each time Mariah makes a statement based on naturalistic assumptions about the world and her own place
in it, Lucy disingenuously asks, "How does a person get to be that way?" (17,
20, 41). To Mariah these questions can be seen only as an *un*natural display
of anger, anger that frequently thwarts communication between Lucy and
Mariah by challenging the terms of a liberal discourse that fetishizes difference without acknowledging inequality. Lucy's "irrational" bursts of anger
further obstruct the movement of a narrative whose progression depends on
the assurance that the "rational" use of language effectively forestalls the violent disruption of meaning. Accordingly, when Lucy does not restrain her
anger, she breaks not only an unspoken contract of "polite" conversation but
also the realist text's promise to deliver up a "meaningful" narrative.

Lucy's meaning may exceed the forms available to convey it, but she points
out that many of the forms by which Lewis and Mariah's worldview is sustained are devoid of meaning. Thus Lucy recognizes the emptiness of Lewis
and Mariah's marriage long before it ends in divorce, an unscripted turn in
the Oedipal drama that Lucy records by noting, "It was as if we had been
reading the last sentences of a very long paragraph and after that the page
turned blank" (128). The blank marks the end of Lucy's stay in the house, and
so, too, her achievement of a kind of independence. Having resisted interpellation into the colonial role of "a girl of whom certain things were expected" (133), she has also rejected the liberal humanist narrative—and its
feminist counterpart—that would suppress the markers of racial and cultural
difference that have signified her illegitimacy in the American family. For the
first time Lucy finds herself alone, without the support of those mythologies

that have both defined and erased her. "I understood," she explains, "that I was inventing myself, and that I was doing this more in the way of a painter than in the way of a scientist. I could not count on precision or calculation; I could only count on intuition. I did not have anything exactly in mind, but when the picture was complete I would know. I did not have position, I did not have money at my disposal. I had memory, I had anger, I had despair" (134). Against the disciplinary forces of conventional morality and science, Lucy embraces rebellion and art.

It is tempting to read this declaration as a climactic moment in the development of a postcolonial, if not a postnational, identity. "Lucy," suggests one critic, "has eluded numerous attempts to reimprison her, certain that she must discover herself alone"; thus, like the quintessential American scholar, who is "free even to the definition of freedom," "if Lucy is defined by anything now, it is her refusal to be defined" (Simmons 1994, 133). In a move perhaps more in keeping with the postcolonial than the (post)national narrative impulse, other critics extend the significance of Lucy's declaration of independence to an allegorical realm, arguing, for example, not only that Lucy "creates a new postcolonial cartography" but, more substantially, that "finally, at a symbolic level, [she] is also Antigua of 1967, a territory freeing itself from the colonizer" (Ferguson 1993, 256). The second reading makes explicit what the first only implies—that Lucy's independence somehow represents, if it does not actually portend, the liberation of an entire people.

The problem with both these readings is that they fail to take into account the lesson that Lucy has learned with difficulty, namely, that the search for freedom that her boyfriend, Paul, says is "part of the whole human situation" (129) is itself enabled and constrained by a culture of domination. Sitting in the car with Paul, listening to him talk about the "great explorers" who traveled the earth in search of freedom as well as riches, Lucy thinks, "Until that moment I had no idea that he had such a hobby—freedom. Along the side of the road were dead animals—deer, raccoons, badgers, squirrels—that had been trying to get from one side to another when fast-moving cars put a stop to them. I pointed out the dead animals to him. I tried to put a light note in my voice as I said, 'On their way to freedom, some people find riches, some people find death,' but I did not succeed" (129). The postcolonial dream of liberation, in other words—the dream that inspired the creation of the United States of America—is based on an irresolvable contradiction that is revealed in the violence that seeks to suppress it. Any attempt by Lucy to assume the role of the great explorer in order to "discover herself alone" must be qualified by her recognition of that contradiction.

Indeed, Lucy's final words, the ones she writes in the journal that will presumably initiate the process of her self-discovery, fall disappointingly short of the kind of declaration that might be expected of the postcolonial hero—

or even the American scholar: "'I wish,'" she writes, "'I could love someone so much that I would die from it.' And then as I looked at this sentence a great wave of shame came over me and I wept and wept so much that the tears fell on the page and caused all the words to become one great big blur" (163). The emotion of shame dampens the force of Lucy's redemptive anger by highlighting its entanglement with love. She has spent the last year trying to overcome two significant love affairs, not with the men who have been her lovers, but with the women who have been her principal oppressors—her mother and Mariah. Whether her shame comes from remorse at having abandoned both of them or—more likely—from disgust at herself for loving those who have tried to make her conform to their desires, Lucy's misery reflects the obduracy of the knots by which the rebel is entangled in the narratives that oppress her.

The ambiguity of her position reflects the symbolic legacy of her name, which her mother once told her is short for *Lucifer:* "I named you after Satan himself. . . . What a botheration from the moment you were conceived" (152). On learning this, Lucy embraces her name, recalling, "I was transformed from failure to triumph. It was the moment I knew who I was" (152). Thus Lucy assumes the role of the antihero in the story of Genesis, the figure who gets left out of the sanitized story of American Adam but who continues to haunt the margins of the American dream. To identify with Satan, however, is ultimately to remain trapped within the tautological frame of heaven and hell, condemned to play out the scriptural battle for sovereignty whose dramatic (and violent) conclusion only momentarily belies the hollowness of the victory. Lucy's final words in her journal can be read as an acceptance of Lucifer's fate—death—or they can be read as an acknowledgment of the unsustainability of the concept of the sovereign self, paradoxically underwritten by the pain of being alone.

In the end Lucy is still not completely independent, nor is her journey of self-discovery consecrated by her representative status within a particular community. Though she expresses a qualified identification with other women, she never does form an alliance with a group that might replace her family, to whom she remains connected only by the check she sends home each month. What she has lost in relationships she gains in a measure of economic independence: "I could do what suited me now," she observes, "as long as I could pay for it" (146). In the context of narratives about liberation and identity, the achievement of economic independence—and the structures of economic *inter*dependence by which such achievements are influenced, often invisibly— is at once mundane and critical. On the one hand, it is arguable that only from a situation of economic security is it possible to (mis)identify oneself with the ideal subject of the American narrative of independence; on the other hand, it is also her situation of (relative) economic comfort that enables Lucy to declare her resistance to that narrative.

The irony of writing oneself out of the dominant culture while earning a living within it is not lost on Kincaid, who, although insisting that she "loathe[s] the mainstream," and "would do everything . . . not to be a mainstream writer," goes on to concede, "If whatever I do ends up being mainstream, I can't deny it" (in Iyer 1993, 59). Kincaid's putatively reluctant acknowledgment of her success in "mainstream" literary circles highlights the contradictory status of the subversive identity in American culture, while her relative lack of defensiveness—"I can't deny it"—points, I think, to the futility of arguments about degrees of complicity and to the need to shift the terms of the debate away from identity and the mythological possibility of independence toward something perhaps less inspiring but ultimately more useful: the understanding of the difference that is constitutive of yet excluded by the assertion of identity. Lucy, while seeming to provide the attraction of the former, ends up speaking much more forcefully to the importance of the latter; as Lucy observes, "History is full of great events; when the great events are said and done, there will always be someone, a little person, unhappy, dissatisfied, discontented, not at home in her own skin, ready to stir up a whole set of great events again. I was not such a person, able to put in motion a set of great events, but I understood the phenomenon just the same" (Kincaid 1991, 147). Lucy's understanding finally grants her a measure of freedom from a narrative that has excluded her as it has held her captive. What it does not allow her to do is become the hero of the story she tells, overturning the American epic to create another anti-American epic. The blur of tears with which her story ends violates the progressive logic of a story in which growing up and becoming an American are inextricably woven. At the same time, by obscuring the words through which, according to narrative convention, the "truth" of the story is progressively revealed, Lucy's tears also dissolve the idealized image of identity on which the possibility of a countermythology—a "New America"—is predicated.

Although *Lucy*'s interrogation of identity highlights the hazards of identifying Lucy with her author (a temptation I have not entirely managed to resist), it would clearly make less sense to draw a line between Lucy and the New Americanist. Rather than hold up Lucy's story against the equally mythological story of Frank Lentricchia, I think it is useful to apply one of the interrogative strategies foregrounded in *Lucy* to the postnational narrative of America, asking, "How does a narrative get to be that way?"

When it is no longer hypostasized into the heroic figure of the New Americanist, the postnational narrative begins to look less like a subversion of than a reversion to the mythology of the national. The conjunction between the national and the postnational narratives of America is most visible at the point of their mutual intersection with the progressive rhetoric of the post-colonial, a rhetoric that ironically has until recently made only brief, reluctant forays into American territory. In that reluctance can be traced a critical desire to maintain the fictional integrity of a postcolonial moment that is belied by the postcolonial *history* of the United States. As Lawrence Buell (1992, 436) points out, the American situation reveals a worrying fracture in the progressivist logic of postcolonial theoretical discourse: "It begins to appear . . . that the old-world tropes whose ingestion by the new-world citizen marks his or her cultural subordination can in turn become reactivated, whether on the frontier within one's own borders or on the frontiers beyond, . . . to reproduce new versions of cultural subordination. This . . . is not the sole or inevitable consequence of postcolonialism, only the most disturbing, but it is by the same token the most dramatic reminder of the quixotism of positing a firm boundary between a postcolonial era and what follows it." To see the United States in postcolonial terms is disturbing not because postcolonial discourse does not work in an American context but because it *does* work—indeed, it has worked from the inception of the nation's culture—to naturalize a progression from dependence to sovereignty to global dominance. Thus, in a very significant sense, the narratives of the national and the postnational are both anticipated by and consummated in the narrative of the postcolonial.

In emphasizing the significance of this cultural conjunction, I am not suggesting that the postcolonial narrative should replace the postnational one as the most productive approach to traversing the field of the American studies; nor do I want to replace the old "posts" with new ones, thereby extending or reconfiguring the boundaries of that field. Instead, I am proposing that an analysis of the historical connections between those posts and the land claims they displace should precede—and perhaps forestall—the launching of any new ground-breaking ventures. To neglect such an analysis is at best to succumb to critical arrogance, following Lowell's mocking advice to "tear your own pasture for nought but to show what a nice pair of horns you're beginning to grow," and at worst to replicate blindly the sins of the fathers who abandoned the ravaged land of the old pastures to stake out the more promising territory of the New World.

Notes

1. The essays from the second volume are reprinted, with two additional essays, in Pease 1994.

2. In fact Buell (1992, 411) acknowledges this history as the reason most critics are reluctant to see the United States in postcolonial terms. Of course both post- or anticolonial and imperial energies can be identified as coexisting in American literary culture

dating back to the earliest debates on national independence. Laura Murray (1996) offers a cogent analysis of the way in which images of colonial disempowerment functioned in Euro-American writing to efface settlers' complicity in the colonizing venture. Similar strategies might be identified in the writing of postcolonial academicians today.

3. In this postcolonial narrative, as in the postnational one, the easy synecdochic relationship of nation and subject has been replaced by a more uneasy one that is still susceptible to the elevation of the scholar to a position of exemplary authority. David Carter (1992) describes the ethically satisfying operations that the postcolonial critic performs on particular literary texts as a kind of postcolonial self-fashioning. Whether the critic undertakes the deconstruction of a colonial text or the supportive reading of self-deconstructing contemporary postcolonial text, the reward is the empowerment of naming—and thus declaring one's critical distance from—the discourse of imperialism.

4. As Alison Donnell (1992) has argued, many of the elements of Lucy's dream—the image of cornmeal, which was the staple diet of slaves, and her sexual pursuit by her white employer—signify in the context not of Lucy's individual unconscious but of the collective memory of her slave ancestors.

5. The kind of "doubleness" to which Bhabha is referring informs and fatally undermines the principle of *e pluribus unum,* according to which the citizens of America are joined, by natural law and voluntary agreement, into a single body. Grounded simultaneously in an originary moment (the story of Genesis) and in the dynamic agency of its individuals, such a construction is by definition ambivalent, resulting in what Bhabha (1990, 297) describes as "a contested cultural territory where the people must be thought in a double time; the people are the historical 'objects' of a nationalist pedagogy, giving the discourse an authority that is based on the pre-given or constituted historical origin or event; the people are also the 'subjects' of a process of signification that must erase any prior or originary presence of the nation-people to demonstrate the prodigious, living principle of the people as that continual process by which the national life is redeemed and signified as a repeating and reproductive process." The nation, then, is the outcome of a narrative struggle in which nationalist pedagogy threatens to be undone by the performance through which it is continuously reproduced. As Bhabha (1990, 295) notes, "There is . . . always the distracting presence of another temporality that disturbs the contemporaneity of the national present." The space-time of the nation, conveyed in the realist narrative of the "everyday," is maintained, Bhabha argues, only through surmounting or repressing the disruptive conceptions of time that constitute what Freud described as the "cultural" unconscious. Through the "doubling" figures of dream and metaphor, these disruptive conceptions of time keep returning disturbingly to the surface.

Works Cited

Bercovitch, Sacvan. 1975. *The Puritan Origins of the American Self.* New Haven, Conn.: Yale University Press.

Bhabha, Homi K. 1990. "DisseminNation: Time, Narrative, and the Margins of the Modern Nation." In *Nation and Narration,* ed. Homi K. Bhabha, 291–322. New York: Routledge.

Buell, Lawrence. 1992. "American Literary Emergence as a Postcolonial Phenomenon." *American Literary History* 4:411–42.

Carter, David. 1992. "Tasteless Subjects: Postcolonial Literary Criticism, Realism, and the Subject of Taste." *Southern Review* 25:292–302.

Crews, Frederick. 1988. "Whose American Renaissance?" *New York Review of Books,* 27 Oct., 68–81.

Donnell, Alison. 1992. "Dreaming of Daffodils: Cultural Resistance in the Narratives of Theory." *Kunapipi* 14:45–52.

Emerson, Ralph Waldo. 1903a. *English Traits.* Vol. 5 of *The Complete Works of Ralph Waldo Emerson,* ed. Edward Waldo Emerson, 12 vols. Boston: Houghton-Mifflin.

———. 1903b. "The Future of the Republic." In *The Complete Works of Ralph Waldo Emerson,* ed. Edward Waldo Emerson, 12 vols, 11:511–44. Boston: Houghton-Mifflin.

———. 1983. "The American Scholar." In *Essays and Lectures,* ed. Joel Porte, 53–71. New York: Library of America.

Ferguson, Moira. 1993. "*Lucy* and the Mark of the Colonizer." *Modern Fiction Studies* 39:237–59.

Iyer, Pico. 1993. "The Empire Writes Back." *Time,* 8 Feb., 54–59.

Jehlen, Myra. 1986. *American Incarnation: The Individual, the Nation, and the Continent.* Cambridge, Mass.: Harvard University Press.

Kaplan, Amy. 1993. "Left Alone with America: The Absence of Empire in the Study of American Culture." In *Cultures of United States Imperialism,* ed. Amy Kaplan and Donald E. Pease, 3–21. Durham, N.C.: Duke University Press.

Kaplan, Amy, and Donald E. Pease, eds. 1993. *Cultures of United States Imperialism.* Durham, N.C.: Duke University Press.

Kincaid, Jamaica. 1991. *Lucy.* New York: Plume.

Lowell, James Russell. 1894. "A Fable for Critics." In *The Writings of James Russell Lowell,* 12 vols., 3:62–65. Boston: Houghton-Mifflin.

Murray, Laura J. 1996. "The Aesthetic of Dispossession: Washington Irving and Ideologies of (De)Colonization in the Early Republic." *American Literary History* 8:205–31.

O'Hara, Daniel T. 1992. "On Becoming Oneself in Frank Lentricchia." *boundary 2* 19:230–54.

Pease, Donald E. 1990. "New Americanists: Revisionist Interventions into the Canon." *boundary 2* 17:1–37.

———. 1992. "National Identities, Postmodern Artifacts, and Postnational Narratives." *boundary 2* 19:1–13.

———, ed. 1994. *National Identities and Post-Americanist Narratives.* Durham, N.C.: Duke University Press.

Simmons, Diane. 1994. *Jamaica Kincaid.* New York: Twayne.

Weinberg, Albert K. 1958. *Manifest Destiny: A Study of Nationalist Expansionism in American History.* Gloucester, Mass.: Smith.

3 Subject to Justice: The "Cultural Defense" and Legal Constructions of Race, Culture, and Nation

Donna Kay Maeda

> Due to the large influx of immigrants, particularly Asians, to the United States in recent years, the criminal justice system has encountered defendants who commit acts of violence that are illegal in the U.S. but which are condoned in the defendants' homelands. These crimes often involve domestic violence, highlighting the difference between American attitudes regarding women, children and family interactions and the attitudes of other cultures.
>
> — Alice J. Gallin (1994, 723)

> A fundamentally "pure" (unmediated) export of or import from the dominant countries, [feminism] indirectly serves the cause of tradition upholders and provides them with a pretext for muddling all issues of oppression raised by Third World women. Standardization continues its relentless course, while Tradition remains the sacred weapon oppressors repeatedly hold up whenever the need to maintain their privileges, hence to impose the form of the old on the content of the new, arises. One can say that fear and insecurity lie behind each attempt at opposing modernism with tradition and, likewise, at setting up ethnicity against womanhood.
>
> — Trinh T. Minh-ha (1989, 106)

To fulfill more fully the ideal of individualized justice in liberal society, contemporary legal theorists such as Alison Dundes Renteln, Deirdre Evans-Pritchard, Alice Gallin, and Taryn Goldstein consider the appropriateness of a formalized "cultural defense" in criminal law cases. Such a defense would allow the introduction of cultural information about actions that are illegal in the United States but may be considered acceptable in another country. Proponents suggest that the cultural defense would improve individualized justice by allowing the consideration of information that would explain individuals' behaviors and actions, while opponents argue for the same application of laws to all individuals, regardless of cultural background.

Rather than participate in such assessments of the strategy's contribution to individualized justice, this essay considers the defense in the context of continued legal productions of racial and cultural difference. Since legal writing on the cultural defense focuses on conflicts between cultural practices of Asian immigrants and U.S. law, this article considers perceptions of cultural otherness as a significant factor in continued productions of racial differentiation. Laws and policies that have the effect of categorizing "Asians" have long intersected with ideas about the inassimilability of persons from those cultures.

This essay thus attends to the legitimation of a nation and its subjects by legal discourse in postcolonial contexts. Postcolonial theory points to the law's role in policing subjects through the construction and maintenance of racial and cultural difference while maintaining boundaries of a nation and a people. Increasing cultural conflicts can be read as effects of global economic and political conditions that lead to the dislocations of transnational migrations. Current massive movements across national borders result not simply from matters of choice but from ongoing relations between formerly colonized and colonizer nations that create conditions for upheavals and dislocations. Global economic restructuring and changing labor force demands in global markets contribute to contexts about which Edward Said writes:

> Surely it is one of the unhappiest characteristics of the age to have produced more refugees, migrants, displaced persons, and exiles than ever before in history, most of them as an accompaniment to and, ironically enough, as afterthoughts of great post-colonial and imperial conflicts. As the struggle for independence produced new states and new boundaries, it also produced homeless wanderers, nomads, and vagrants, unassimilated to the emerging structures of institutional power, rejected by the established order for their intransigence and obdurate rebelliousness. And insofar as these people exist between the old and the new, between the old empire and the new state, their condition articulates the tensions, irresolutions, and contradictions in the overlapping territories shown on the cultural map of imperialism. (1994, 332)

Postcolonial theory calls to mind the United States as a global power shaping multiple economic and political factors that not only draw people to "us" but also contribute to conditions that push people away from "home." Remembering this context raises questions, then, about how law shapes who "we" in the United States are assumed to be as a nation and what constitutes "other" cultures. How is cultural difference named in case law and legal analysis? Where are boundaries set in understanding what other cultures are? Who is privileged in particular accounts of cultures? How does the focus on individuals as rights claimers serve to mask the production of cultural differentiation? What social positions are privileged by supposedly neutral laws, legal subjectivity, and presumptions about the "we" of the nation?

An examination of U.S. law through postcolonial theory also provides a location for linking cultural analysis to particular forms of resistance. Considering the rupture of difference in the United States as a postcolonial location makes clear that the ethical discourse linking the language of rights to the idea of justice serves the nation-forming function of law. Resisting those legitimizing, disciplining functions requires understanding the masked production of those whom the law and nation portray as "other" through the construction of race and cultural difference, as well as of appropriate subjectivity, understood to be the "I" of the West: the rational, rights-claiming, neutral individual who is to be protected by law. Further, the supposedly neutral language of rights discourse hides assumptions about the superiority of "American" culture in the global context. Conscious recognition of such productivity and a recontextualization of questions of law perform what Gayatri Spivak (1993, 283–84) calls a "persistent critique" that enables negotiations with structures of violence. Neither holding a utopian hope of escaping the productivity and disciplinarity of law and legal discourse nor simply accepting complicity in structures of dominance without resistance, such a persistent critique uses ruptures in the master narratives of rights, justice, and nation as locations of resistance.

A postcolonial reading of the cultural defense also acknowledges in these narratives (of rights, justice, and nation) the "other within," who resides in borderlands between us and them, "our" culture and "theirs." The cultural defense can be read here in a moment of rupture that uncovers the national subject's naming of difference that assumes homogeneity as well as the superiority of the dominant identity as constructed in the United States. In this reading, borders are blurred; American subjects are not clearly distinct from the Eastern otherness about which much legal discourse on the cultural defense is concerned. A postcolonial reading of the minority discourse through which the "other within" articulates alternative positionalities also denaturalizes assumed notions that support the disciplinarity of law and law's American individualist subject. Thus a postcolonial reading recontextualizes law, culture, race, and the formation of a nation and its people. This recontextualization of the cultural defense turns to articulations from in-between spaces in hybrid locations that resist enclosed notions of culture, race, and nation.

Silenced by Justice: Individual Rights and the Limits of Articulation

The question of cultural difference indicates the impossibility of reconciling individual rights with conditions of collectivities. Underlying the narrative of liberal justice are the epistemological and moral foundations of the individual. In liberal justice rights are to be applied "neutrally" and "objectively" to individual persons without regard to race, gender, culture, or other differences. Such differences, when acknowledged, are generally understood to be qualities of individuals. Given current hierarchical positionings along such differentials, however, treating persons the "same" (that is, applying the same rights) serves to maintain rather than transform inequalities of power and position. The language of equality, neutrality, and objectivity with regard to treatment of individuals masks the construction and maintenance of actual inequalities along group differential positionings. The "ethical" usage of this language serves to legitimize the masking.

The cultural defense resides in this liberal world in which rights are conceived first as attached to individuals. In the cultural defense, the collective idea of cultural difference indicates ruptures of liberal justice. By seeking to explain how culture shapes and affects an individual's behavior, the defense conceives of culture in the binary framework that splits individuals and groups. Individuals belong to groups that maintain or practice different cultures. Those different cultures can explain individualized behavior. Cultural difference is treated here as a matter of pluralism and limited tolerance for individuals' culturally different beliefs and practices. Nonetheless, the cultural defense also points to the boundary that is transgressed once attention to difference moves beyond merely placing the individual into the context of a collective. Cultural difference cannot be adequately addressed by identifying a group's practices and locating its impact on an individual's behavior.

The cultural defense can be understood as a mechanism for managing difference in a liberal world. Discussions about the defense consider not only whether particular behaviors ought to be tolerated under the notion of cultural difference but also whether an individual defendant is adequately "different" to qualify. A culture's otherness is measured by distance from a standard or cultureless norm of legally acceptable behavior. New analytical work in critical race theory interrogates assumptions behind this idea of the neutrality of law and investigates its role in the production of racial differentiation.

Critical Race Theory: Legal Productions of Racial Differentiations

Critical race theory (CRT) attends to the constructedness of liberal values. CRT considers positionalities, social locations, and group hierarchies as it challenges the association of fairness with the equal application of rules to individuals. Liberal neutrality, objectivity, and universal individualism actually protect and hide privileged group positionings. CRT thus recognizes not simply difference that is to be tolerated but hierarchies of power built into differentiations of gender and race.

Critical race theorists attend most specifically to race as a mode of differentiation that cannot be adequately confronted by attention to individual rights, neutrality, and objectivity. CRT looks to the production and maintenance of race by laws, legal structures, and legal norms. For example, in *White by Law: The Legal Construction of Race,* Ian Haney Lopez (1996) interrogates the legal construction of a "white" racial category. He examines cases challenging the racial prerequisite for citizenship in the United States from 1790 to 1952. He shows that in these cases, courts solidified the concept of whites as a race through the process of deciding on citizenship applications of persons who did not obviously fall within that category. Persons from Hawai'i, China, Japan, Burma, and the Philippines, as well as mixed-race persons, were deemed to be not white, whereas persons from Mexico and Armenia were found to be white. Courts gave varied decisions about persons from Syria, India, and Arabia (2). Lopez contextualizes such decisions by pointing to the prevalence of anti-Asian and nativist sentiments during the times in which most disputed cases were decided. He suggests that whiteness was constructed in such decisions not only as a race but as a superior one. Ambiguous cases were decided primarily on proximity to whiteness, both physically and culturally (33), based on notions of "common knowledge" or the understanding of the "common man."

Like other works in CRT, Lopez's analysis considers a primarily binary organization of race. Although he writes about various nonwhite races, Lopez attends to each in opposition to whiteness. He writes to uncover the taken-for-granted, naturalized status accorded to whiteness as the norm from which nonwhite deviates. Although it is clearly important to analyze the specificity of the construction of particular races by laws and legal structures, it is also necessary to consider how these foci constrain understandings of race as binary, oppositional categories. Attention to the category "Asian" challenges the binary understanding of racial constructions.

Although Lopez centers his work on the white/nonwhite oppositional understanding of race, *White by Law* begins to show ways that Asians and other "others" disrupt the black/white binary formation. Lopez notes that even after 1870, when Congress extended the right to naturalize to persons of African descent (1996, 44), no petitioners for citizenship attempted to be classified as "black," even though some non-African immigrant groups were considered to have "racial qualities" similar to blacks (51). Fear of further stigmatization caused applicants to attempt to be classified as white rather than black to gain citizenship.

Although the racial prerequisite required that petitioners be placed into a white or nonwhite category, applicants' rejection of another available route to citizenship indicates a more complicated classificatory scheme. The group of people who would later be legally classified as Asian did not simply provide a third term to a binary opposition. White/nonwhite and white/black were not simply parallel oppositions. The excess that escaped each opposition leaked into the other. *Nonwhite* did not mean *black*; neither did it include all who were not white. The absence of citizenship applicants attempting to be classified as black indicates the hierarchical ordering of the binary while disrupting its linear, oppositional organization.

Further, the racial prerequisite cases show that the eventual construction of an Asian racial category was built on perceptions of cultural difference that also served to break binary formations of race. Perceptions of cultural difference intersected with racial differentiation instead of merely fitting into firmly bounded categories of race. Asian immigrants were more closely associated with blacks than whites, but they were also marked as being even more different from the latter, culturally and religiously.

Lopez argues that in these cases, courts judged the nonwhiteness of Asian applicants based on perceptions not only of skin color but also of cultural, intellectual, and political unfitness for citizenship (1996, 56). He points out that court decisions increasingly turned to a rationale based on "common knowledge" of who fit the white racial category. Initially courts attempted to use scientific evidence in conjunction with common knowledge about race. Although the two rationales sometimes coincided because of proliferating social preconceptions that shaped both, the former became increasingly unstable and contested (65, 68). Common knowledge was called on in increasingly fixed ways. Even though scientific classifications of race were increasingly challenged by arguments about persons or groups who did not fit particular schemata, courts continued to base decisions on who was "generally known to be White" (77). Immigrants from Asia were "generally known" not to fit that category.

Lopez's analysis illustrates the complex intertwining of racial and cultural differentiation. Further examination of the cultural defense strategy points to intersecting differentials of gender, race, and culture in the context of nation formation.

The Cultural Defense and Race, Culture, and Nation

Culture, like gender and race, is not simply an attribute of individuals but instead marks intersecting collective social positionings. Racial categories have been produced in relation to perceptions of cultural difference. Attention to the ongoing historical construction of racial, cultural, and gendered differentiations shows that, in effect, the cultural defense continues the production of Eastern Others.

Legal discourse on the cultural defense raises important questions about the referent of the term *culture* as invoked by the use of such terms as *cultural traditions, values, customs, rituals, beliefs, background,* and *habits.* Such terminology is also mixed with more explicitly negative conceptions, where culture is conceived as ingrained impulses that dictate behavior (Gallin 1994, 736; Sheybani 1987, 775). Even more problematically, Alice Gallin (1994, 736) writes about "ritual traditions of violence against women," whereas Taryn Goldstein (1994, 146, 153–54) looks at negative "cultural experiences" intermingled with notions of "socio-economic culture" and "historical-sociological experience," which are both named as cultural difference.

Although legal scholars ostensibly point to a wide range of cultures that differ from that of the United States, Asian cultural difference is perceived as the source of most conflict. For example, Goldstein (1994, 141–42) points to a broad range of potential cultural defense cases, such as attempted *oyako shinju* (parent-child suicide) by a Japanese immigrant woman who walked into the ocean in Santa Monica with her two small children after learning of her husband's long-time mistress (the woman was rescued but the children died); *zij poj niam* ("marriage by capture") by a Hmong man who, after taking a bride-to-be from her home to consummate the marriage, was charged with rape; the murder during a fight of a man who had "culturally obligated" another Mexican man to drink; the murder of a Chinese woman by her husband after he learned of her extramarital affairs; the murder of a Caucasian man by three Native Americans who believed he was desecrating ancient burial grounds; and the murder of a white police officer by a Native American man who claimed that his cultural background influenced him to fear Caucasians. After compiling this wide range of cases, Goldstein focuses on Asian immigration as the source of most conflict between cultural values and American laws.

In the legal writings, strange and troubling slippages occur between the namings of cultural traditions, beliefs, rituals, practices, and values, and concepts such as Goldstein's "socio-economic culture." Legal terminology, concepts, and strategies matter for the ways that culture is named. What is named as culture actually concerns conceptualizations of difference. The naming of wife killing as a "Chinese ritual practice" (Gallin 1994, 736) indicates a slip from attempting to understand cultural factors that affect a defendant's mental state to a troublesome identification of cultural practice. Here, other cultures are conceived as compelling, impelling, and ingraining behaviors that limit rationality. These legal writings raise questions, then, about whose culture is perceived as different and different from what.

Attention to the naming of difference raises further questions about the interpretive strategies by which culture is investigated in legal discourse. Discussions about the cultural defense look at culture through liberal individualist and liberal pluralist frameworks that consider individual behavior and tolerance for differences. The two frameworks merge as pluralism is filtered into the understanding of individuals' actions. For example, Deirdre Evans-Pritchard and Alison Renteln (1994) argue that an anthropological approach offers insight into "true" understandings of culture that can explain individuals' behavior.

The cultural defense is also read from within feminist problematics that analyze gendered differentials, often using the trope of violence against women. For example, Gallin attends to an anti–domestic violence agenda as she considers the defense. According to Gallin (1994, 743), the cultural defense serves to condone culturally sanctioned violence against women and children: "Promoting cultural diversity by using a cultural defense also promotes domestic violence." She argues that U.S. law ought not to allow a backward move in justice for women and children in the name of tolerance for cultural difference. As she argues that immigrant women should not be forced to face the same "ritual traditions" of violence that they faced in their home countries (736), Gallin suggests that the United States is far more advanced in protecting the well-being of women than are other countries. She writes that "cultural defenses should not be used because the United States should not allow other cultures, which do not respect individual liberty and equality in the same manner as American culture does, to subvert the value we place on preventing domestic abuse" (725).

Similarly, Taryn Goldstein (1994, 162–63) writes that "a recognition of the cultural defense would demonstrate that the United States tacitly consents to the violence toward women that is practiced throughout the world. Other countries condone violence toward their women. . . . These women are sacrificed to a defense seemingly tailored toward the protection of wife-beaters and murderers." Although such feminist readings of the cultural defense attempt to consider individualized circumstances and the well-being of equal human beings, culture, expressed through values and traditions, is often conceived as harmful to women.

Even as these varied approaches attempt to address general problems of cultural difference and individualized justice by casting cultural defense cases broadly, legal scholarship turns to increasing Asian immigration as the source for excessive conflict with U.S. law. Particular attention is paid to cases of Asian cultural difference, such as *People v. Kimura,* the Santa Monica case of attempted oyako shinju; *People v. Moua,* a case of zij poj niam; *People v. Helen Wu* (in which a Chinese immigrant woman strangled her son and tried to kill herself after learning about the father's abusive behavior toward their son and also about his live-in girlfriend); and *People v. Dong Lu Chen* (in which Jian Wan Chen was beaten to death with a hammer by her husband after he became convinced that she was having an affair with another man). In this last case anthropologist Burton Pasternak was called as an expert witness. Pasternak testified to the "cultural appropriateness" of Dong Lu Chen's actions.

In assessing the use of the cultural defense in such cases, legal scholars consider what is Asian to be particularly different from what is American. Examples include the Alice Gallin quotation that opens this essay, as well as Taryn Goldstein's (1994, 145, emphasis added) comment that "today . . . , due to their large numbers and diverse cultural traditions, Asians are the group to whom the cultural defense seems most often to pertain. . . . Their Far Eastern culture is *drastically dissimilar than [sic] Western cultural and legal assumptions.*" This conception of Asian difference is remarkable in relation to Goldstein's assertion about cultures that "condone" wife beating and murder. In this moment of articulation, law continues to play a role in the production of Asians as racialized and culturally different Others. This view relies on essentialist notions of culture that hinge on binary understandings of insides/outsides of cultures and communities. As writers point to the dissimilarity of Asian culture, they fail to recognize their position in the ongoing historical context that produces East as other to the West.

In *Making and Remaking Asian America through Immigration Policy, 1850–1990,* Bill Ong Hing (1993) considers ways that immigration law has shaped the United States as a Western nation. Hing illustrates the impact of changing immigration laws on Asian presence and participation in the United States. He points out that historically immigration laws have reflected (1) perceptions of Asian immigrants as a source of cheap labor, (2) fears of economic competition and racial hostility, (3) changes in U.S. relations with Asian nations, and (4) the passage of other laws targeting Asians, such as alien land laws. Hing suggests that attention to Asians marked the first attempts to use immigration law as a tool for controlling particular populations:

Before 1965 the United States aimed to admit Asians only for specific purposes, exclude them altogether if necessary, and always to keep them in check. . . . The United States discovered that immigration might shape a self-serving relationship with those Asians it decided to admit. . . . It learned to selectively ignore,

rediscover, reinterpret, recombine, rewrite, and recycle laws, treaties, and agreements to respond to shifting and often conflicting views about Asians. . . . It
learned how to justify to itself—legally and morally—having to exclude first
some groups, then all Asians, as a necessary and perhaps vital aspect of the
reassertion of a control otherwise in doubt. (18)

Hing shows how the removal of legal limitations on immigration from Asia
in 1965 resulted in increased numbers of immigrants from that region. Hing's
analysis of the impact of changing immigration laws points to important
ways in which such laws shape the "we" of the United States. Along with
Lopez's analysis of racial prerequisite cases, Hing's work shows how law helps
to produce intertwining racial and cultural differentiations as it continues
to shape this "we-ness" of a Western nation. Legal approaches to the cultural
defense reproduce the East as most different, most inassimilable, and unchanging in its "drastic" and "violent" difference by ignoring transnational
migrations in a postcolonial context that lead to increasing permeations of
national and cultural borders.

The cultural defense continues the production of the East as Other as it
attempts to manage that otherness within the borders of the Western subject. In this moment of articulation, borders are illuminated; their construction becomes evident as notions of cultural difference are articulated through
the cultural defense. Just as immigration laws and decisions in racial prerequisite cases relied on notions of the cultural, religious, and political alienness
of the East, the cultural defense continues to read that difference as fixed and
essential. That is, readings of difference through the cultural defense participate not only in reifying classifications of cultural and racial differentiation
but also in maintaining an approach to such difference through a trope of
assimilability/inassimilability. The cultural defense continues to read anything Asian as especially different from all things American.

In-Between Differences: Asian American "Minority Discourse"

Looking at culture not as a matter of objectivity or anthropological truth
proceeding from a position of neutrality but rather from a location of complex positionings, Asian American "minority discourse" regarding the cultural defense indicates that the Other speaks back, rupturing binary formations of East/West and us/them. Legal scholars such as Leti Volpp (1994) and
Daina Chiu (1994) are positioned at the boundaries of these constructed
categories, thus making visible the enforcement of the divisions. Discursively
positioned as both Asian and American, yet not captured by either category,
these legal scholars indicate that Eastern is not necessarily so different from

American. In addition, Volpp and Chiu disrupt reified readings of culture defined through static notions of traditions, beliefs, and practices, as well as any presumed split between objective/subjective views, while attending to gendered positionings of such readings.

In a complex and problematic article entitled "The Cultural Defense: Beyond Exclusion, Assimilation, and Guilty Liberalism," Daina Chiu (1994) argues against essentialized versions of Asian culture. She notes that in essentialized versions, women are the ones who are silenced (1101). The cultural defense, Chiu argues,

> essentializes culture by defining it as the exclusive province of particular groups. Under the [cultural] defense proponents' conception of culture, some groups have culture, others do not. Where American society once essentialized Asian culture by stigmatizing and isolating the Chinese, the defense accomplishes the same result by demarcating whose cultural values are acceptable to excuse criminal conduct. By its very terms, the cultural defense is a strategy that is available only to those who have a culture different than white mainstream culture. The defense thus operates to reify the artificial metaphysical difference and distance between Asian Americans and white Americans. (1101)

Chiu places the cultural defense in the context of ongoing conceptualizations and managements of Asian difference (1055). Nevertheless, although Chiu contextualizes the cultural defense within histories of treatment of Asian difference, she also maintains separate Asian and American categories. She writes, "Asians are different from white Americans on many levels. Obvious differences include physical appearance, language, religion, food, and cultural traditions. The significant point, however, is that the social vision of dominant white society has magnified and manipulated these differences into social constructs that marginalize and isolate Asian people in American society" (1057–58). Further, Chiu seeks "to recognize legitimate cultural imperatives, while rejecting this metaphysical construction of Asian difference" (1056). Chiu maintains a firm boundary between Asian and American even while she recognizes the existence of Asian Americans.

Chiu notes that the anti–cultural defense position ignores the fact that U.S. law fails to embody values relevant to adjudicating culpability for Asian Americans who have committed certain crimes (1994, 1105). According to Chiu, the false assertion that Asian Americans should obey the law because it embodies their cultural norms obscures the dynamic of forced assimilation. In making this claim, she maintains the dangerous position that Asians and Asian Americans are truly different from Americans. Still, Chiu recognizes the continuing importance of the exclusion of Asians from widespread sociopolitical participation (1109). In the past the exclusion of Asian Americans from voting limited the contributions that Asian cultural values could make to American societal norms. As she considers patterns of coercive assimilation and continued exclusions, including criminal laws that prohibit certain Asian practices, Chiu notes the limitations of generalized societal norms that name customs as acceptable or unacceptable (1109). Still, Chiu's argument for the recognition of valid cultural differences is troubling in its essentializing implications.

Chiu argues for an approach that validates Asian American women's rebellion against both static notions of culture and misogynistic practices. She argues against confining Asian American identity to the acceptance of cultural traditions "created by men" that "privilege men" (1994, 1124). Arguing for an understanding of intersections of culture and gender, Chiu calls for an examination of gendered dynamics of power and subordination within Asian American communities (1124). She articulates a notion of "shifting, multiple selves, in which no aspect dominates. Identities in which contradictions and contradictory selves remain" (1125). This argument is limited, however, by her maintenance of other bounded categories (American and Asian) and her call for autonomous space in which ethnic communities can work out their values.

In "(Mis)Identifying Culture: Asian Women and the 'Cultural Defense,'" Leti Volpp (1994) offers a more careful analysis and articulation of the multiple, intersecting positionings of women of color. She considers the problem of the invisibility of women in approaches to understanding cultural communities that fail to attend to gender (62). Rather than argue for or against the cultural defense, Volpp sorts out what she considers to be appropriate uses of cultural information by analyzing *People v. Dong Lu Chen* and *People v. Helen Wu*. She considers multiple positionings in culture by attending to gendered differentials of power. Volpp argues for an antisubordination principle to mediate between a complete rejection of the cultural defense and an acceptance of a formalized version (59). For Volpp, a commitment to ending all forms of subordination ought to inform decisions about or interpretations of the use of cultural information in particular cases (59).

Volpp points to the invisibility of Jiang Wan Chen in the *People v. Dong Lu Chen* decision. Volpp examines the testimony of Burton Pasternak, the anthropologist who was set up as an expert witness on Chinese culture. Pasternak testified that Dong Lu Chen's behavior (killing his wife with a hammer after discovering her marital infidelity) was "normal" for a person from China. Volpp points out problems in Pasternak's testimony about Chinese attitudes toward adultery, as well as his view that "the Chinese" are much better able to control the community through social sanctions than are "Americans" (1994, 68). Volpp challenges Pasternak's notion that a Chinese individual carries "voices of the community" in his or her head as means of social control (68). She points out that the testimony about values and voices in Pasternak's description of Chinese society was in fact "his own American fantasy" (70). Volpp also criticizes Pasternak's division between "Chinese" and "American" for perpetuating the idea that Asians are always foreign. She argues that this testimony essentializes the categories while subordinating the latter through characterizations defined by the former (71). Volpp argues that in Pasternak's testimony, as well as in the court's decision, Jian Wan Chen was invisible as an Asian American woman. She writes, "This invisibility was manifest through the absence of Jian Wan Chen as a subject, a void that was filled only by stereotypes of the sexual relationships of 'Chinese women' and an image of her silent physicality. She appeared as an object, whose silence devalued her humanity to the extent that the taking of her life did not merit a prison sentence" (75). Volpp points out that this invisibility lies in the "intersection of race and gender that erases the existence of women of color" (75).

At the same time, Volpp criticizes white feminist approaches to cultural defense cases that also fail to recognize multiple subordinations in intersections of race and gender. In particular, Volpp criticizes the argument that culture ought not to be brought into court cases because of potential harms to "women" (1994, 81). She is particularly critical of the position of Western superiority such views assume (82). As she argues for the consideration of complex relations of subordination along multiple lines of difference, Volpp, like Chiu, points out that legal discourse on the cultural defense fails to recognize the cultural particularity of American law or to analyze what is presented as culture (61). Volpp points out that much feminist criticism repeats the notion that Asian Americans in particular are foreign, not American (61).

Volpp argues for the informal use of cultural information in assessing a defendant's state of mind. The defense ought not to be used to "fit an individual's behavior into perceptions about group behavior" (1994, 58). Volpp suggests that, rather than essentialize culture and render women invisible, this distinction allows for the consideration of cultural factors to explain a person's state of mind where actions "may stem from multiple oppressions" (91). Thus Volpp approves of the use of cultural information in *People v. Helen Wu*. Unlike Pasternak in *People v. Dong Lu Chen*, the expert witnesses solicited by Wu's attorney were trained in transcultural psychiatry and psychology (88). Volpp claims that these psychiatrists and psychologists were experts in the sense that they were immigrants to the United States and "were thus invested in representing the experience of immigrants from a subjective position" (89). Rather than set up oppositions of "Americans" and "Chinese," such testimony subverted the notion that U.S. law is cultureless (89). Volpp argues that as a result, neither Helen Wu nor Chinese culture was portrayed as alien or other (90). Still,

Volpp points out that with the use of cultural information, Wu was associated with a cultural group, resulting in a focus on "who she was rather than what she did" (90). For Volpp, the danger here is that Wu was an understandable or sympathetic character as long as she lived up to what a "traditional Chinese woman" should be. In this case, the court understood a "traditional Chinese woman" to be a "good mother" who was willing to sacrifice herself and who killed her son out of love (90). Volpp notes that this understanding perpetuates the stereotype of Asian women as self-sacrificing mothers. Volpp thus argues for the introduction of cultural factors as a means to explain state of mind, especially when actions may stem from multiple oppressions, rather than as a standardized approach to cultural difference (91).

As she argues for different positions on the use of cultural information in the Chen and Wu cases, Volpp turns to Gayatri Spivak's notion of strategic essentialism to distinguish ways in which culture ought to be associated with particular communities (1994, 95). Because she is concerned about reified notions of traditions that perpetuate the subordination of women, Volpp argues against cultural essentialism even while she notes the importance of considering culture to counter subordination. Strategic essentialism allows for the consideration of multiple positionings of gender, race, and culture: "Even when we attempt to use cultural information to explain an individual's oppressions or her state of mind, we are forced to label and define, in other words, to essentialize, certain behavior as 'cultural.' This can be done in the spirit of what might be called 'strategic essentialism'—consciously choosing to essentialize a particular community for the purpose of a specific political goal" (95). Volpp's turn to the notion of strategic essentialism suggests that intersectionality and multiple subordination need to be considered in the turn to notions of culture and community. Even as she writes toward an essentialism, she keeps in mind the multiplicity of positions within cultures. For Volpp, attention to political goals of undoing subordination provides a way to sort out uses of cultural information. Since she resists both the perpetuation of stereotypes and divisions between American and Asian, Volpp suggests that strategic essentialism allows for attention to culture in an antisubordination mode. This antisubordination mode of analysis allows for the consideration of multiple positions and the intersectionality of gender, race, and culture.

Both Chiu and Volpp participate in "minority discourse," for each marks her own positionality as Asian, as American, and as woman in writing about the cultural defense. Both write in the in-between space: neither solely Asian or American nor simply a combination of the two positions. Each disrupts simple or essential categories of culture, race, and gender by marking intersectionality and multiple positionalities. Nonetheless, Chiu and Volpp both turn to new kinds of stable positions. As was already noted, Chiu maintains notions of bounded categories (Asian and American), autonomous space for cultural communities, and valid cultural difference even as she calls for attention to multiple positionalities. Although Volpp pays closer attention to the constructedness of categories, she also stabilizes the category of Asian American women. In a sense, Volpp's use of strategic essentialism is still quite essential, even when she chooses political commitment to provide the category. Although her emphasis on being strategic provides an important approach to understanding the use of cultural information in court cases, she grounds the idea of antisubordination on fixed notions about which categories are most subordinate. For Volpp, intersectionality results in a new (strategically) essential category rather than a shifting positionality.

Postcolonial Readings of Culture, Difference, and Nation Formation

Postcolonial theories of Trinh T. Minh-ha, Gayatri Spivak, and Homi Bhabha provide ways to interrogate multiple differentials in the context of nation formation. The postcolonial theorists point to excess produced by any totalizing narrative, even that of antisubordination for those positioned at intersections of race, gender, and culture, if those intersections themselves become fixed locations. These theories challenge readings of culture that produce other, unremarked positionings of Western individualist subjects of knowledge and rights. Postcolonial theory provides alternative readings of culture and difference that rupture the narratives of justice.

In reading the cultural defense cases, Chiu and Volpp not only indicate the presence of a "minority discourse" within legal scholarship. They also raise the specter of Trinh Minh-ha's (1991) "Inappropriate Other," who challenges any attempt to look for an authentic representative of cultural difference. As she contests oppositions of inside and outside cultural difference, Trinh writes that the

> Inappropriate Other . . . affirm[s] "I am like you" while persisting in her difference and . . . remind[s] "I am different" while unsettling every definition of otherness arrived at. . . . Whether she turns the inside out or the outside in, she is . . . the same impure, both-in-one insider/outsider. There can hardly be such a thing as an essential inside that can be homogeneously represented by all insiders; an authentic insider in there, an absolute reality out there, or an incorrupted representative who can't be questioned by another incorrupted representative. (1991, 74–75)

Trinh pays special attention to attempts to understand cultural difference through anthropological expertise. Noting her own position as "na-

tive . . . among the anthropologists" (1989, 83), Trinh criticizes the claims
of Western knowing subjects who judge the authenticity of cultural representatives. She points out that the anthropological "conversation of 'us'
with 'us' about 'them' is a conversation in which 'them' is silenced" (1989,
67). The Western knowing subject relies on authentic natives to sustain a
position of knower. Trinh looks further to the "move from obnoxious ex-
teriority to obtrusive interiority" (1991, 66), in which the Western knower
attempts to "see into or to own the others' minds, whose knowledge these
others cannot, supposedly, have themselves" (1991, 66). Here Trinh's account echoes attempts in legal discourse to know the minds or mental states
of culturally different others.

Trinh also notes her problematic position between Asian and American
when these are seen as fixed enclosures (1991, 156). Considering the impossibility of that position, she articulates the multiplicity of boundaries that must
be crossed to resist "disfranchisement" (1991, 157). In Trinh the Inappropriate
Other speaks back, rupturing divisions of East/West, Asian/American, and
knower/known, thereby acknowledging the marginality imposed by firm enclosures of culture, gender, or ethnicity. For Trinh, who refuses these enclosures as well as any notion of authentic representativeness, the Inappropriate
Other exceeds, rather than rejects, knowledge that legitimates the position of
the sovereign knower (1991, 185). In doing so, she pushes Volpp's and Chiu's
positions in "minority discourse" to refuse the marginality imposed by any
attempts to offer representative claims to authentic culture.

Attention to Trinh's Inappropriate Other and her critique of anthropological claims brings new questions about the narrativization of culture. In the
attempt to translate culture into manageable terms, most legal scholars look
through the lens of assimilability. Culture is approached as beliefs, traditions,
and values that may affect individuals' mental states. Not only does this approach look for authentic versions of culture; it also frames such findings as
acceptable, tolerable, and excusable or unacceptable, intolerable, and inexcus-
able. In this framework, tales of authenticity attach to attempts at seeing the
inner mind of defendants to understand their "inability" to assimilate to "appropriate" behavioral norms.

These narrativizations of culture judge acceptability in relation to standards of Americanness. Cultures judged as other must translate into, approximate, and measure up to American norms. These narrativizations, however,
ignore histories and contexts that have already constructed Americanness
against cultural Others, especially Asians. Such narrativizations hold American standards to be objectively good or fair or neutral, whereas the others'
behaviors are seen as culturally bound. In doing so, these approaches ignore
ways that cultures judged as other are being measured by particular versions

of American cultural standards. For example, the Kimura case of attempted oyako shinju points to the power of tropes of motherhood, community, and family in interpretations of the case. Legal interpretations look to accounts of the closeness of mother-child bonds in Japanese culture as well as the emotional implications of adultery and its effects on family life. Each of these aspects is filtered back into proximity to American values of motherhood, family, and marriage. Kimura's actions are regarded as understandable in these terms in legal writings, even when disagreements arise about whether her behavior should have been excused. Malek-Mithra Sheybani (1987) suggests further that although zij poj niam must be punished so that Hmong men learn appropriate marital and sexual behaviors, America should learn to revalue the closeness found in Hmong communities. Sheybani suggests that we encourage those aspects of cultural difference that would be beneficial to America while discouraging, by punishment, aspects that would be harmful to the general good (782). In these cases interpretations of cultural difference are read into narrations of American culture without any attention to contestations over values or differential positionings in America.

These legal accounts of cultural difference ignore what Homi Bhabha (1994) calls the ambivalence at the origins of discourse. As he attends to regimes of truth and recognition, Bhabha points to the trace that remains in processes of cultural disavowal. For Bhabha, hybridity results not simply from the combination of separate or enclosed cultures but as an effect of colonial power (112). Hybridity marks a place of enunciation where the disavowed difference seeps by doubling and repetition; hybridity is "less than one and double" (118) and "neither the one nor the other" but something else (137). Through mimicry the hybridity of cultural difference does not simply reproduce the culture of coloniality but rather unsettles and displaces any enforced unitariness. "The display of hybridity—its peculiar 'replication'—terrorizes authority with the ruse of recognition, its mimicry, its mockery. . . . Such a reading of the hybridity of colonial authority profoundly unsettles the demand that figures at the centre of the originary myth of colonialist power. It is the demand that the space it occupies be unbounded, its reality coincident with the emergence of an imperialist narrative and history, its discourse non-dialogic, its enunciation unitary, unmarked by the trace of difference" (115).

Through the concepts of hybridity and mimicry, Bhabha suggests an effectiveness of cultural difference that both resists enclosures of culture and displaces the exclusive power of colonialist discourse. Hybridity escapes essentialized explanatory narrativizations of culture while marking a space of enunciation; in mimicry, cultural difference is a strategic process that does not rely on the intentionality of individual subjects. In hybrid locations,

cultural difference, as a form of intervention, participates in a logic of supplementary subversion similar to the strategies of minority discourse. . . . The
analytic of cultural difference intervenes to transform the scenario of articulation. . . . It changes the position of enunciation and the relations of address
within it; not only what is said but where it is said; not simply the logic of articulation but the topos of enunciation. The aim of cultural difference is to
rearticulate the sum of knowledge from the perspective of the signifying position of the minority that resists totalization—the repetition that will not return as the same, the minus-in-origin that results in political and discursive
strategies where adding to does not add up but serves to disturb the calculation of power and knowledge, producing other spaces of subaltern signification.
(Bhabha 1994, 162)

If the United States is considered as a location of hybridities rather than one
of competing American and other cultures, then questions about the cultural
defense point to the trace of difference that remains even under erasure.
Enclosed notions of culture ignore that America has been constructed in part
by that which it has sought to exclude. The trace of Asian difference remains
even in imagined origins of America as a source of positive construction. That
is, the United States has been shaped and consolidated in part by markings
of those outside its boundaries. As was previously noted, those markings have
been constructed in part through immigration and naturalization laws that
have participated in the construction of a Western nation. Such laws, as well
as current approaches to the cultural defense, participate in the management
of difference constructed in opposition to standards or norms that are considered to be both American and objective.

This contradiction indicates an ambivalence in originary and legitimating notions of the United States as a site of neutral justice. The modernist,
liberal approach to difference repeated in legal discourse on the cultural
defense attends to the value of tolerance while marking some cultural practices as simply wrong in the American context. Justice is to be both neutral
and American. This contradiction reveals the assumed but unnamed superiority of American culture that objectively measures higher than other cultures, especially Eastern ones.

This rupture between neutral and American justice unmasks the role of legal
justice in the formation of boundaries around the United States as a nation
and a people. American subjects are bounded not only by specific physical and
legal borders but also by the constitution of appropriate Western subjectivity. In this hybrid location, however, something else seeps—through the very
cultural difference against which the nation has been formed. The discourse
on the cultural defense indicates the seepage of unmanageable difference into
narratives of ostensibly neutral justice. Gayatri Spivak's attention to law, na-

tion formation, and strategic negotiations further illuminates this leakage of difference.

In "Scattered Speculations on the Question of Culture Studies," Spivak (1993) considers constitutional formations of "We the People" in the context of transnational postcoloniality. Speaking as "not-quite-not-citizen," Spivak notes the violent institution of origins of "the People" of the United States (262). Reading the Constitution as part of a nationalist agenda rather than as a text that simply illustrates American "neutral" justice, Spivak notes that "the making of an American must be defined by at least a desire to enter the 'We the People' of the Constitution" (279). She criticizes the conflation of internalized colonization in the United States (including the exploitation and domination of disfranchised groups) with colonization in the rest of the world (278–79). This conflation participates in centering the world in the United States and its dominant discourses of nation formation. At the same time Spivak acknowledges the impossibility of escaping structures of such nation formation. She writes, "Persistently to critique a structure that one cannot not (wish to) inhabit is the deconstructive stance" (284). Further, "the impossible 'no' to a structure which one critiques, yet inhabits intimately, is the deconstructive philosophical position, and the everyday here and now of 'postcoloniality' is a case of it" (281). For Spivak, persistent critique is intimately linked to "negotiating with enabling violence" (283). Although she notes the necessity of attending to what law makes possible and impossible, she also points to the necessity of seeing the provisional nature of gains there, not just in the United States, but also in relation to decolonized spaces on the global level.

Such a persistent critique points to an essentialism more provisional than the one to which Leti Volpp refers. Whereas Volpp uses a principle of anti-subordination to ground strategic essentialism, Spivak rejects any such grounding. Both attend to multiplicities of shifting differences, yet Spivak calls for constant recontextualization of the provisional essentialisms. She challenges U.S. structures of violence not only for those residing within its national borders but also in the global context. Thus her strategic negotiations attend to contexts in which the structures are both enabling and disabling. Provisional essentialisms for ethnic women in the United States, for example, may provide for negotiations with enabling violences—that is, with structures that are enabling in the national context—but hold violent consequences elsewhere. For Spivak, persons residing in the United States must confront differentials that its law produces. Attention to legal issues matters for negotiating structures of internal colonization and exploitation. Yet that system of law also serves to legitimize a nationalism that has deep transnational implications. To limit attention here participates in ideological, political, and economic structures that are violent in different ways in the global context. Negotiations with internal structures of violence (in this instance, legal productions of racial and cultural differentiations) participate in the legitimizing narrative of the United States even while rupturing the framework of justice. Recontextualization of questions of law suggests that cultural difference ought to be interrogated in postcolonial locations as transformative articulations of hybridity rather than as otherness that is to be disciplined and managed.

Works Cited

Bhabha, Homi. 1994. *The Location of Culture.* New York: Routledge.
Chiu, Daina C. 1994. "The Cultural Defense: Beyond Exclusion, Assimilation, and Guilty Liberalism." *California Law Review* 82:1053–1125.
Evans-Pritchard, Deirdre, and Alison Dundes Renteln. 1994. "The Interpretation and Distortion of Culture: A Hmong 'Marriage by Capture' Case in Fresno, California." *Southern California Interdisciplinary Law Journal* 4:1–48.
Gallin, Alice J. 1994. "The Cultural Defense: Undermining the Policies against Domestic Violence." *Boston College Law Review* 35:723–45.
Goldstein, Taryn F. 1994. "Cultural Conflicts in Court: Should the American Criminal Justice System Formally Recognize a 'Cultural Defense'?" *Dickinson Law Review* 99:141–68.
Hing, Bill Ong. 1993. *Making and Remaking Asian America through Immigration Policy, 1850–1990.* Stanford, Calif.: Stanford University Press, 1993.
Lopez, Ian Haney. 1996. *White by Law: The Legal Construction of Race.* New York: New York University Press.
People v. Dong Lu Chen. 1988. 87-7774 NY Sup. Ct.
People v. Kimura. 1985. A-091133 L.A. County Sup. Ct.
People v. Moua. 1985. 315972 Fresno Sup. Ct.
People v. Helen Wu. 1991. 286 Cal. Rptr. 868. Cal. Ct. App.
Said, Edward. 1994. *Culture and Imperialism.* New York: Vintage Books.
Sheybani, Malek-Mithra. 1987. "Cultural Defense: One Person's Culture Is Another's Crime." *Loyola L.A. International and Comparative Law Journal* 9:751–83.
Spivak, Gayatri. 1993. *Outside in the Teaching Machine.* New York: Routledge.
Trinh T. Minh-ha. 1989. *Woman, Native, Other: Writing Postcoloniality and Feminism.* Bloomington: Indiana University Press.
———. 1991. *When the Moon Waxes Red: Representation, Gender and Cultural Politics.* New York: Routledge.
Volpp, Leti. 1994. "(Mis)Identifying Culture: Asian Women and the 'Cultural Defense.'" *Harvard Women's Law Journal* 17:57–101.

PART 2

Unsettling the American Experience:
Immigration, Transnationalism,
and Globalization

4   Is the United States Postcolonial? Transnationalism, Immigration, and Race

Jenny Sharpe

When I completed my doctorate in 1987, postcolonial literature was not a clearly defined field. I and other diasporic Third World intellectuals with literary training applied for jobs in European literature, to which we introduced the critical frame of empire. Like them, I began to shift my research and teaching away from Europe and toward cultures of the former colonies. This shift occurred in response to the limitations of identifying colonial structures of power and knowledge without providing alternative frames of reference.[1] Even as I say that I turned toward Third World literatures in response to the demands of the classroom, however, I must admit that I cannot disentangle my *personal* decision from the *institutional* demand for diasporic Third World intellectuals to teach what has come to be known as "postcolonial literature."

A glance any English literature curriculum will reveal that courses on Anglophone writings of former British colonies are now essential offerings. This inclusion reflects the effort to reshape British literature in the same way that the canon of American literature has been transformed by the introduction of minority literatures and cultures. Recent hiring practices also suggest a resemblance between postcolonial and black/ethnic studies; affirmative action policies of U.S. minority programs have been extended to postcolonial studies, and diasporic Third World scholars are increasingly identified with their place of origin.[2] What began around 1978 as the analysis of colonial discourse and of institutions of power and domination is being reshaped as a minority discourse.

One indication of this reshaping is a turning of the critical gaze of post-colonial studies away from the ex-colonies and toward the United States. Given this nation's history of imported slave and contract labor, continental expansion, and overseas imperialism, an implication of American culture in the postcolonial study of empires is perhaps long overdue. When used to describe the United States, however, *postcolonial* does not name its past as a white settler colony or its emergence as a neocolonial power; rather, it designates the presence of racial minorities and Third World immigrants. For example, a recent reader on postcolonial theory includes writings by African Americans under the rubric of the "postcolonial," defined as a category that "includes diasporic communities [and] 'ethnic minority' communities within the overdeveloped world as well as formerly colonised national cultures" (Williams and Chrisman 1994, 373).

The designation of *postcolonial* as an umbrella term for diasporic and minority communities is derived in part from an understanding of decolonization as the beginning of an unprecedented migration from the former colonies to advanced industrial centers. In *The Location of Culture* Homi Bhabha describes the presence of diasporic peoples in Britain as the return of a repressed past that splits its national identity. By contrast, Member of Parliament Enoch Powell's perception of Black Britain as "detachments of communities in the West Indies, or India and Pakistan, encamped in certain areas of England" (1969, 236) understands Britain's postcolonial identity according to a nine-teenth-century logic of nation and empire. This logic underpins the regulations that in Britain, Germany, France, and (nonimperial) Switzerland have served to redefine the status of immigrants from outside the European Economic Community as guest workers. In Western Europe, the term *immigrant* expresses a racist policy that excludes Third World peoples from the "imagined community" of nation. The naming of Britain as *postcolonial*, then, recognizes the colonial history that precedes emigration from the empire and the racism that appears to have originated with the arrival of "immigrants."

The condition of the Third World migrant in Europe, however, has provided postcolonial studies a theoretical model for explaining *all* colonized cultures, past and present. When Bhabha offers Toni Morrison's *Beloved* as an instance of the "transnational histories of migrants, the colonized, or political refugees" (1994, 12), he brings the diasporic experience of African slaves into a narrative of postwar urban migration. Such a formulation fails to distinguish between the presence of racial minorities in Europe, which is a condition of its imperial past, and in the United States, where the history of race and empire is much more heterogeneous.

If the term *postcolonial* is to have any descriptive force at all, we need to account for the historical specificities of different national formations rather than treat "the West" as a single and homogeneous entity. The naming of the United States as a postcolonial society requires a different explanation than that applied to postwar migration in Western Europe.

Desiring to detach postcoloniality from its association with migrancy in the context of the United States, Gayatri Spivak argues that only the post–civil rights struggles of African Americans, Chicanos, and Native Americans can be called "postcolonial." She identifies the civil rights and Black Power struggles as a movement toward postcoloniality and the Latino-Chicano move of situating the United States (emphatically not recognized as America) in North-Central-South America as a refusal to be contained within the United States as its internal colonies (1992, 11). The idea of internal colonization also underpins Arnold Krupat's assertion that "Native American literature is among the postcolonial literatures of the World" (1994, 170), even though he considers Native Americans to remain colonized.

The historical antecedents to the use of *postcolonial* for U.S. racial minorities lie in the Third World movement of the late 1960s (Liu 1976). The Third World movement was a coalition of black, Native American, Asian American, Puerto Rican, and Chicana/o students who modeled their activities after Third World liberation struggles. Initiated at San Francisco State College, the movement spread to other campuses, where students articulated the disfranchisement of racial minorities as a form of colonization. Rejecting the preexisting national paradigm of immigration and assimilation, they declared the ghettos, barrios, internment camps, and reservations to be the "internal colonies" of the United States. Political activists belonging to Black Power organizations, La Raza, the Puerto Rican and Asian American movements, and the American Indian Movement (AIM), as well as sociologists wanting to align academic work with the militancy of radical politics, further developed the idea of U.S. racial minorities as internal colonized nations. They argued that these groups experienced the underdevelopment and dependency of Third World economies. As sociologist Robert Blauner declared in *Racial Oppression in America* (1972, 52): "The third world perspective returns us to the origins of the American experience, reminding us that this nation owes its very existence to colonialism, and that along with settlers and immigrants there have always been conquered Indians and black slaves, and later defeated Mexicans—that is, colonial subjects—on national soil."

As a descriptive term for U.S. racism, *internal colonization* is more relevant to a nineteenth-century experience of exclusion. Blauner's analogy between American racism and European colonization was a politically strategic move designed to harness the language of decolonization and has since been judged "politically, not analytically, grounded" (Omi and Winant 1994, 50). The internal colonial model too sharply distinguishes voluntary from involuntary movements of populations. In doing so, it equates immigration with assimilation and colonization with racism, thus neglecting racism in immigration. The limitations of this equation become evident in the historical example of Asians, for whom immigration was voluntary but who nonetheless experienced racism. Nor can the concept address class differences within minority groups. Describing the ghettos in which Chinese own businesses that exploit other Chinese, Blauner was forced to call America's Chinatowns "neocolonial enclaves" (1972, 88). Finally, the colonial analogy cannot address the indirect forms state racism assumes (such as the war on drugs and the control of crime and undocumented workers) during a post–civil rights era.

It is easy for those of us working within postcolonial studies to forget that *internal colonization* is only an analogy for describing the economic marginalization of racial minorities. Since people from Third World countries now inhabit the United States, the migrant can all too easily become the figure of racial exclusion. In this manner, a prior history of racism is written over (or worse yet, appropriated). This is why I agree with Ruth Frankenberg and Lata Mani that discussions of the United States require a periodization other than *postcolonial*. The term *postcolonial* does not fully capture the history of a white settler colony that appropriated land from Native Americans, incorporated parts of Mexico, and imported slaves and indentured labor from Africa and Asia and whose foreign policy in East Asia, the Philippines, Latin America, and the Caribbean accounts, in part, for its new immigrants. Frankenberg and Mani (1993, 293) suggest *post–civil rights* as a parallel to the anticolonial struggles that define the "after" to colonialism, but they admit that the term is inadequate for explaining the experience of recent immigrants and refugees.

If *postcoloniality* does not name the post–civil rights struggles of racial minorities or Third World immigrants in the United States, how should we understand the term? I want to propose that the postcolonial be theorized as the point at which internal social relations intersect with global capitalism and the international division of labor. In other words, I want us to define the "after" to colonialism as the neocolonial relations into which the United States entered with decolonized nations.

Critics of center-periphery models (such as neoimperialist, dependency, and world-system theories) point to the limitations of a state-centrist approach to defining global relations. In *Sociology of the Global System*, Leslie Sklair (1995) argues that these models are inadequate for explaining the uneven development on both sides of the East-West divide. The existence of Japan makes the equation of industrialization with the West obsolete. The peripheries that serve as sources of cheap labor for advanced industrial European nations, countries such as Ireland and Portugal, cannot be properly called "Third World." Perhaps Ireland may be said to have a neocolonized status vis-à-vis England, but Portugal was once a leading colonial power. Nor can center-periphery models explain the existence of Asian capital and what is known as "South-South" relations between adjacent Third World countries such as India and Sri Lanka or Vietnam and Cambodia. This is why Arjun Appadurai proposes a transnational model in which "the new global economy has to be seen as a complex, overlapping, disjunctive order" (1990, 6).

Yet those who favor an approach that is trans- or postnational rather than state centrist tend to downplay the continued existence of North-South, East-West relations. Sklair, for example, argues that transmissions by the Spanish International Network (SIN) to Latino audiences in the United States reverse the North-South flow of information suggested by theories of cultural imperialism (1995, 136). What he does not acknowledge is that the reversal is only partial: SIN is not made available to an English-speaking audience, while the American television shows that are broadcast internationally are translated into the languages of the receiving countries. It is important not to lose sight of the neocolonial relations sustained by institutions such as the International Monetary Fund, United States Aid for International Development, and the World Bank, as well as the emergence in the 1970s of free-trade zones that draw primarily on the cheaper Third World female labor force. At the same time, to account for diffused centers of power, we also need to address the emergence of Asian capital and increasingly transnational capitalist classes.

We need to define the "after" to colonialism in terms not only of neocolonial relations but also of indigenous elites who consolidate their wealth and power by cooperating with advanced industrialized nations. As Sklair points out, Third World elites do not form a comprador class in the sense of serving First World interests or assimilating into Western culture. Rather, they constitute a transnational capitalist class whose members act in the interest of the global system (1995, 117–19). Like transnational corporations (TNCs), their allegiance is not to the nation-state but to a global consumerism that thrives on cultural hybridities. What is the relationship between the diasporic identities we are calling "postcolonial" and the globalization of consumer culture? An equation of Third World diasporas with racial marginalization elides a question of this kind. Focusing critical attention on racism against diasporic communities forecloses a discussion of the workings of transnational capitalism.

In this essay I will be arguing that an understanding of the postcolonial condition as racial exclusion offers an explanation for the past history of internal colonies but not the present status of the United States as a neocolonial power. Although characterizing America as "postcolonial" is intended to displace the center/periphery binarism belonging to colonial systems of meaning, its effect has been to reconstitute the margins in the metropolitan center. The refashioning of postcolonial studies as a minority discourse has not only moved us far afield from the early objectives of colonial discourse analysis but also risks playing into a liberal multiculturalism that obfuscates the category of race.

Postcolonial Studies and the United States Multicultural Paradigm

The entry for postcolonial studies in *The Johns Hopkins Guide to Literary Theory and Criticism* includes the field as part of the educational reforms resulting from the post–civil rights and women's rights movements: "Postcolonial (cultural) studies (PCS) constitutes a major intervention in the widespread revisionist project that has impacted academia since the 1960s together with such other counter discourses that are gaining academic and disciplinary recognition as cultural studies, women's studies, Chicano studies, African-American studies, gender studies, and ethnic studies" (Gugelberger 1994, 581). Contrary to what this entry suggests, the institutional history of postcolonial studies is distinct from that of black and ethnic studies, even though the latter's borrowing from anticolonial writings suggests a shared origin. The concept of internal colonialism was important to the beginnings of black and ethnic studies, which were instituted some twenty-five years ago in response to student activism rooted in political movements. Inasmuch as traditionally white colleges excluded minority cultures from the curriculum and racial minorities from the student and faculty bodies, they were a microcosm of segregated America. Student demonstrations for minority representation brought the 1960s and 1970s civil protests against racial discrimination onto college campuses. The official response was to incorporate black and ethnic studies in the curriculum, to institute affirmative action hiring for faculty in these programs, and to recruit minority students.

Postcolonial studies, on the other hand, did not emerge in response to student demands for racial diversity or a political activism that spilled over onto college campuses. Rather, it constitutes an institutional reform "from within." Its beginnings are generally located in Edward Said's 1978 study of orientalism as a Western style of thought and institution of power for exercising control over Arabs and Islam (Williams and Chrisman 1994, 5). What distinguished Said's *Orientalism* (1978) from previous intellectual histories on West Asia is that it implicated academic learning in colonialism by establishing connections between images and institutions, the production of knowledge and the securing of power. His Foucauldian study cleared the space for a new kind of investigation that came to be known as "colonial discourse analysis."

Orientalism adhered to a colonial epistemology inasmuch as it failed to address native disruptions and restructurings of Eurocentric discourses. An inquiry into anticolonial resistance inevitably led critics from the literature of empires to that of decolonization and from colonial discourse analysis to postcolonial theory. In contrast to Said's description of "the Orient [as] the stage on which the whole East is confined" (1978, 63), anticolonial writings record how the drama of decolonization disturbed the exotic images fixed within the Western imagination. It is important that we acknowledge Frantz Fanon, C. L. R. James, Aimé Césaire, Amílcar Cabral, Ngugi wa Thiong'o, and Albert Memmi (among others) as the intellectual antecedents of postcolonial studies even as we remember that their writings were geographically and historically removed from the institutional beginnings of the field.

Whereas the literature of decolonization was intimately bound up with the national liberation movements of the 1960s and 1970s, postcolonial studies is primarily a First World academic discourse of the 1980s and 1990s. By calling attention to the temporal and geographical distance between anticolonial and academic writing, I do not mean to say that postcolonial studies should be narrowly defined in terms of what is produced in the university. Nor am I arguing that academic discourse has no political efficacy.[3] What I am contesting is a critical reading of the literature of decolonization according to the disciplinary demands of postcolonial studies. By suggesting that its institutional beginnings are rooted in political struggle, this reading fails to recognize the degree to which the shift from colonialism to postcolonialism was a response to the demands of U.S. multiculturalism.[4]

The rise of multiculturalism can be attributed to both the post–civil rights effort to desegregate education and the arrival of Third World immigrants who have transformed the racial and ethnic makeup of the United States. Following fast on the passage of the 1964 Civil Rights Act, the 1965 Immigration and Nationality Act signaled a dramatic change in U.S. policy. Prior to 1965, race was a determining factor for laws that prevented the unification of non-European families. The first of these restrictions was the Chinese Exclusion Act of 1882, which was passed in response to the perception of Chinese immigrants as degraded "coolie" labor and culturally unassimilable. It was followed by the 1907 "gentlemen's agreement" with Japan to limit emigration. The 1924 Immigration Act, which was upheld by the 1952 McCarran-Walter Act, established quotas for northern European nations alone and enforced a control of the United States–Mexican border. The Bracero Program, which ran between 1942 and 1964, coupled with Operation Wetback of the 1950s, is but one of the ways in which the United States ensured a continuous flow of cheap labor without relaxing its control of the border.

The 1965 Immigration Act, which became effective on 1 July 1968, eliminated prior restrictions against non-Nordic Europeans. It assigned a uniform quota for all countries (whether they were in the Eastern or Western hemisphere) and gave preferential treatment to technically skilled immigrants, regardless of their race. Policymakers did not then anticipate any dramatic change in the races of immigrants. Instead, they saw the reform as social redress for Catholics and Jews from southern and eastern Europe, against whom the 1924 Immigration Act had been equally directed (Glazer 1985, 7). They were unprepared for the demographic shift the new immigration law would introduce. During the last thirty years, Asians, Central Americans, Mexicans, and Caribbeans have constituted 80 percent of all immigrants to the United States. The 1980s, the economic boom years during which the demand for immigrant labor reached its peak, have been called "the decade of immigration" (Usdansky 1992).

With the global recession setting in by the 1990s, the United States responded to the arrival of mobile Third World populations by fortifying its borders and reentrenching itself as a nation. The term *immigrant* is now presumed to designate people of color even though those it denotes include Canadians, Soviet Jews, Germans, Italians, Irish, and English. Chicana and Chicano critics have responded to U.S. racism and xenophobia by claiming the "borderlands" as a culture that cuts across Mexico and the United States. In her bilingual book *Borderlands/La Frontera,* Gloria Anzaldúa (1987) reminds us that the border culture did not begin with the migration of Mexicans to North America. Rather, it was initiated with the migration of the border 100 miles south when the United States annexed northern Mexico. Anzaldúa shows the subsequent history of North American–Mexican relations to be one of border crossings—legal in the case of *maquiladoras* set up on the Mexican side and illegal in the case of Mexican workers on the United States side.

Appadurai (1993) also maintains that the idea of the United States as an autonomous and self-contained nation is untenable. Since travel and telecommunications permit immigrants to maintain close ties with their countries of origin, these communities exist as transnational diasporas that do not assimilate into the nation's dominant culture. To account for the postindustrial globalization of culture, he replaces a theory derived from the study of nations and empires with one that can address the current conditions of transnationalism and diasporas.[5] *Transnationalism* denotes the permeability of national borders in the electronic transmission of capital, labor, technology, and media images. *Diaspora* designates the political and economic refugees, immigrant and exile communities in advanced industrial and newly industrializing nations and city-states. The two terms, however, are inextricably linked. "Diasporas," explains Khachig Tölölyan (1991, 6), "are emblems of transnationalism because they embody the question of borders, which is at the heart of any adequate definition of the Others of the nation-state."

Alluding to the immigrant communities that cut across national borders, Appadurai (1993, 803) describes the United States as but "one node in a post-national network of diasporas." He calls on postcolonial critics to invoke the diasporic diversity of immigrant communities for entering debates on racism, affirmative action, and multiculturalism in the United States. His objective is to prevent postcolonial studies from becoming a means of containing the Third World as exotic cultures that exist "out there."

I agree with Appadurai that we should be concerned about nativism in the United States and the growing legitimacy of racial arguments such as the "bell curve" thesis. After all, I am employed by a state that recently passed a proposition denying health, educational, and welfare benefits to "illegal" (meaning Mexican) immigrants. A "civil rights initiative" whose objective is to roll back the advances of the civil rights (understood as affirmative action) and the women's movements is currently on the California ballot. In addition, however, I also want to warn that a lack of attention to the specific targets of such policy can be equally damaging to the groups who are being disfranchised. In the absence of addressing such specificities, our theories of ethnic diversity can just as easily contribute to a multiculturalism that elides the workings of "race."

The metaphors of "mosaic" or "quilt," which have replaced that of the nation as "melting pot," give ethnic pride a new (albeit problematical) legitimacy. The beginning of this new national paradigm can be traced to the late 1960s and early 1970s, when proponents of cultural pluralism challenged the melting pot hypothesis. They claimed that instead of melding into an undifferentiated nation, social groups maintained distinct ethnic identities to form a "nation of nations." Theories of cultural pluralism were paradoxically indebted to militant formations such as the Black Power movement, La Raza, and AIM, but they were primarily concerned with articulating the identities of white ethnics (Decker 1995). As a consequence, the nation of nations paradigm blurs the distinction between a racial identity formed in opposition to the idea of the United States as a nation of immigrants and an ethnic identity formed around the idea of the United States as a nation of unmeltable immigrants. The effect of this new national paradigm was to neutralize the radical racial identities informed by the race pride movements of the 1960s and 1970s. The appearance of an ancestry question on the U.S. census, which first occurred in 1980, is a sign that the nation of nations paradigm has become official.[6] Its legacy is the liberal multiculturalism that informs a popular understanding of race today.

Liberal multiculturalism effaces the different histories of native and immigrant populations and the specific histories of the different groups that constitute the nation. Thus formed around cultural difference rather than race (or racism) and the unequal distribution of power, it underpins the position that affirmative action policy is no longer necessary or, conversely, that affirmative action "must not be restricted to African-, Asian-, Mexican-, and Native-American writers; it must be extended to include the writers from European ethnic groups that have historically been ignored or marginalized by the Anglo-American literary-academic establishment" (Oliver 1991, 806). In view of such arguments, postcolonial critics should be particularly careful in articulating the social positioning of diasporic Third World communities in the United States.

Transnational Diasporas and the Politics of Race

Instead of treating transnational diasporas as homogeneous groups, we need to exercise vigilance about locating their members within specific racial formations. The tendency among critics, however, is to ignore the historical specificities governing migrations from the former colonies to different metropolitan centers. Feroza Jussawalla (1988), for example, treats Hanif Kureishi's representation of racism in Britain and Bharati Mukherjee's and Vikram Seth's descriptions of immigrant life in Canada and the United States as all expressing the same diasporic experience. Although she acknowledges that South Asians can assimilate in the United States but not in the United Kingdom, the singularity of the South Asian immigrant allows her to identify the conflict between a desire for assimilation and the drive to maintain "Indianness" as "the enigma of the South Asian immigrant in the new world—the enigma of success, of accomplishment, of having made an impact, and also of denigration, of discrimination" (584).

Because of the strategic role Indo-Pakistani intellectuals have played in consolidating the field of postcolonial studies (and because it is the diasporic group to which I belong), I want to examine in greater detail the immigration patterns of South Asians who move to Britain and the United States. My objective is to demonstrate that the postcolonial status of those in Britain cannot be extended to members of the diaspora living in the United States.

Indians have lived in Britain at least as long as the British have inhabited the Indian subcontinent. The first immigration of any significance, however, came during the postwar boom of the 1950s and 1960s, when Britain turned to its colonies and former colonies for cheap labor. Those "Asians" (the term used for people from the Indian subcontinent) who did journey to the imperial center found themselves restricted to unskilled factory jobs and segregated in areas surrounding their places of employment (Robinson 1986, 55–66). They were joined by "East African Indians" who were expelled from Kenya, Tanzania, and Uganda during the early 1970s. Whereas those from the Indian subcontinent tended to be economic migrants from poor rural backgrounds, those from East Africa were political refugees including white-collar workers and skilled laborers. Nevertheless, members of both groups found themselves to be second-class citizens employed in the low-paying, unskilled sector of Britain's work force.

The immigration that had been encouraged during the postwar era became a threat to the English national character once cheap labor was no longer needed. The state attempted to restrict immigration through a series of acts, beginning with the 1962 requirement of employment vouchers and ending with the 1971 act that effectively changed the status of nonpatrial immigrants into that of guest workers. These acts are rooted in the discourse of the British Empire inasmuch as they do not restrict immigration from the white dominions of Canada, Australia, and New Zealand. As late as 1978 the state was trying to discourage the unification of Asian families by subjecting women to an immigration test that included vaginal examinations for proof of virginity (Parmar 1982, 245). Colonial stereotyping was reanimated in media images of Asians as a backward and barbaric people invading Britain. They were called "natives," "niggers," and "wogs," racial slurs from a not-so-distant colonial past, and "Pakis," a newly invented term for expressing an internal form of racism, since Pakistan did not exist prior to 1947.

Asians, West Indians, and Africans constitute what Salman Rushdie calls "the new empire within Britain"—a phrase designating a domestic form of racism that reworks an old imperial paradigm (1991, 129–38). The Afro-Asian response was to organize around the concept of "Black Britain," a coupling of terms that both disrupted the nation's presumed whiteness and declared a solidarity between people of African and Asian descent. Afro-Asian unity was greatest from the late 1970s to the mid-1980s, when the radical appropriation of a racial category buckled under the weight of its colonial history. Some sectors of the Asian population, buying into the racial stereotyping of Africans and West Indians, objected to being called "black." An Asian middle class has recently emerged, and Indian names figure prominently in a list of the twenty most wealthy families in Britain (Jacob 1993, 169). Since there are no laws protecting the civil rights of minorities, however, Asians have no legal recourse for fighting Britain's increasing racial discrimination.

On the other side of the Atlantic, Indian immigration is usually traced to the several thousand Punjabi Sikhs who came to work on West Coast railway gangs between 1900 and 1910. The Sikhs, who eventually settled as farmers in California's Sacramento, San Joaquin, and Imperial Valleys, were subjected to the same discriminatory practices that Chinese and Japanese immigrants endured. They were not allowed to own land, and antimiscegenation laws prevented them from marrying white women. As a consequence, they married Spanish-speaking Mexican American and Mexican immigrant women. Their interracial descendants were known as "Mexican Hindus," or "Mexidus," even though the Sikh religion is distinct from Hinduism.[7]

Outside California educated Indians (which included Sikhs as well as upper-caste Hindus and Parsis) challenged the exclusionary practices of the U.S. naturalization policy, which restricted citizenship to "white" immigrants. They appealed to their Aryan origins as proof of belonging to the Caucasian rather than Asiatic race. Their success depended on where they lived and whether the judge decided to interpret "white" as a geographical or racial category (Jensen 1988, 246–69). Even if they were considered to be *racially* white, however, Indians were *culturally* defined as Asian. The compilers of the 1910 U.S. census, which classified the population as "White," "Black," "Mulatto," "Chinese," "Japanese," "Indian (American)," and "Other," explain that they had classified the 2,545 Indians as "Other" even though "pure-blood Hindus" were Caucasian because theirs was "a civilization distinctly different from that of Europe" (cited in Jensen 1988, 252). The designation of South Asians as "Other" indicates the absence of an identifiable group at this time.

The passage of the Immigration Restriction Act in 1924 effectively ended all Asian immigration, including that of Indians. The few Indians living in the United States were racially classified in the 1930 and 1940 censuses as "Hindus" (Lee 1993, 78). Since by 1940 there were slightly over 2,000 Indians, most of whom resided in California (Takaki 1989, 313–14), the category of "Hindu" was removed from subsequent reports. The 1980 census was the first to use the category "Asian Indians" (a term that includes Indians, Pakistanis, Sri Lankans, Bangladeshis, Nepalese, and East African Indians), placing their number at 361,531. In the 1990 census that figure had reached 815,447, indicating a population growth of 125.6 percent. The large number of undocumented workers who have also come to this country would make those figures even higher.

The sudden surge in South Asian immigration resulted from the 1965 act, particularly the clause stipulating preferential treatment for trained professionals. The shift in preferences from national origin to skill qualifications was made in response to the demand for scientists, engineers, physicians, and other highly skilled workers needed for an expanding U.S. economy. Members of the South Asian professional-managerial class were well suited for these jobs not only because of their high degree of education and specialized training (particularly in the sciences) but also because of their command of the English language. In this regard the British colonization of India was a precondition for the post-1965 migration of South Asians to the United States, just as the Sikh emigration from the Punjab region was the result of a colonial restructuring of the land tenure system. Unlike their Sikh predecessors, however, the post-1965 immigrants are skilled rather than unskilled workers who come from urban rather than rural areas.

Tracing the beginnings of the Asian Indian diaspora to the localized existence of the Californian Sikhs covers over discontinuities in immigration
patterns. The exclusionary practices that produced the hybrid culture of the
"Mexidus" are missing from a post-1965 immigrant experience. Instead, the
Sikhs who have recently settled in California's Yuba and Imperial Valleys are
imposing a new religious orthodoxy on the "Mexidus," whom they fault for
not being "of pure blood" (Jha 1992). Rather than treat race as a singular and
static category, then, it is more useful to think of racial formations as heterogeneous and historically produced.

South Asians who entered the United States under the protection of the
1965 Immigration Act did not arrive as economic or political refugees, as did
their British counterparts. Nor did they experience institutionalized racism
in the form of discrimination in housing and employment. Although they
have come up against the corporate glass ceiling that reserves the top-level
managerial positions for white males, the professional class of Indians was
able to adjust to the "Anglo-conformity" of the workplace (Saran 1985, xii;
Bhardwaj and Rao 1990, 209). Thus escaping the historical frame of racism
in the United States, South Asians are often paraded as examples of American success. There are anecdotes, such as that of the couple who suffered racial
discrimination in Britain but now own a $30-million-a-year computer com-
ponents company in California, and statistics showing that 16,280 South
Asians entered U.S. colleges in 1992, up from 5,491 in 1980 (Jacob 1993). In
this regard, they are the new model minority.

Critics of the model minority hypothesis point out that grouping people
from diverse historical and economic backgrounds permits the media to
present successful sectors of the Asian population as representative of the
larger community. The visibility of successful groups renders invisible (and
without access to social services) those members who are impoverished. In
1973, 83 percent of documented Asian Indian immigrants were skilled workers, whereas only 54 percent of all Asian immigrants were (Jones 1992, 270).
The latter figure demonstrates what Arthur Hu (1989) calls the "bipolar"
distribution of the Asian American community, which includes professional
and unskilled workers, fourth-generation Chinese and Japanese who have
assimilated and recent economic and political refugees from Vietnam, China,
and the Philippines. In 1982 the National Association of Americans of Asian
Indian Descent appealed for a minority-group designation so that they could
benefit from government affirmative action programs. The Indian League of
America opposed the move for fear of a backlash from "the truly disadvantaged minorities" (Varma 1980, 35; Takaki 1989, 446–47).

The recent racial attacks on Asian Indians are a sign of their increasingly
bipolar distribution. As the first generation of professionals sponsor their un-

educated and less affluent relatives for immigration, Indians increasingly move into lower-paying jobs in the service sector and operate small businesses such as grocery stores, motels, newspaper stands, movie theaters, and restaurants. In addition, the number of illegal immigrants working in the garment and restaurant industries is substantial. Indians' tendencies to live in tightly knit communities makes them more identifiable as "immigrants" during a time when nativist sentiment and racism is on the rise. In 1987 a racist gang known as the "Dotbusters" (in reference to the *bindi* Indian women wear on their foreheads) targeted the 15,000 Indian residents of Jersey City. A threatening letter was sent to a local newspaper, and several residents were beaten, one of them to death. In Middlesex County, thirty miles from New York City, a multiracial middle-class gang that called itself "The Lost Boys" terrorized a South Asian neighborhood. The gang's actions were fueled by older residents' resentment of the success Indian businesses were enjoying during uncertain economic times. In 1992 New York's South Asian taxi drivers formed the Lease Drivers Coalition to protest their racial harassment, particularly at the hands of the police.

Such racially motivated hate crimes and police harassment must be condemned, but we also have to contend with what this racism means in the face of the 1990 Immigration Reform Act, which has tripled quotas for skilled immigrants. Since the 1965 act extends to skilled non-Europeans a preference clause previously reserved for northern Europeans, models based on racial exclusion alone are inadequate for explaining the status of Third World diasporas in the United States. The priority given to skill over national origins shows that corporate America tolerates some degree of diversity. As Masao Miyoshi (1993, 741) observes, transnational identities are not necessarily the answer to the democratic failures of nation-states when TNCs "are at least officially and superficially trained to be color-blind and multicultural." Diasporic communities may threaten the integrity of the United States, but this does not mean that they threaten the interlinked economies of North America, Europe, and Japan (with Taiwan, Hong Kong, and Singapore as their junior partners).

Corporate investors rely not only on friendly Third World governments but also on those sectors of Third World diasporas that serve as mediators for the flow of capital, technology, and people. With the collapse of the Soviet Union, the United States has emerged as the largest foreign investor in India, an investment in which Indians living in the United States have played a crucial role. Meanwhile, Indian investors in California's computer industry run high-tech sweatshops, bringing trained programmers from India on short-term employment visas. The guest workers are often treated as virtual prisoners by their sponsors, who either hold their passports or make them liable for huge penalties should they quit before the termination of their contracts. These conditions cannot be understood as an aspect of postcoloniality unless they are tied into the complex workings of the global system.

Articulating the "Postcolonial" in Asian American Studies

For intellectuals working in Asian American studies, the global frame of race politics and ethnic identities is impossible to ignore. Twenty years ago Asian Americans were typically born in the United States; today the majority are born elsewhere. The term *Asian American* can no longer hold together a diverse group that includes not only American-born Chinese and Japanese but also Chinese and Filipino immigrants, whether skilled laborers, undocumented sweatshop workers or small-business owners, as well as Vietnamese, Hmong, and Mien refugees. Asian immigration to the United States also cannot be understood without explaining U.S. imperialism in Hawai'i, Vietnam, and the Philippines. As a result, critics have begun to shift their attention away from the presumed homogeneity of an Asian American community and toward the heterogeneity of the Asian diaspora. Nonetheless, homogeneity is often replaced with the singularity of, for example, a Korean or Filipino diaspora, thereby ignoring the cultural and economic transactions between Asia and the United States.

In her call for expanding the scope of Asian American studies to include a more global perspective, Shirley Hune enumerates the complex international relations that theories of transnational diasporas must address:

> There is a need to develop a theoretical explanation of the contemporary Asian diaspora in the post colonial period. Its political and economic context is qualitatively different from the previous era. It involves such forces as neo-colonialism, especially war, intervention and military regimes, national liberation movements, regional conflicts, revival of ethnic nationalism, underdevelopment and dependency, the Cold War, and recently an increasingly multipolar global power system that is coming to terms with the rise of Asian capitalism. The post World War II Asian emigration is also substantially different from earlier movements and in its global scope and scale will begin to dwarf that of the nineteenth century diaspora. (1989, xxii)

Hune's understanding of the Asian diaspora articulates an intersection between postcolonial and ethnic studies that I can endorse. At the same time, I want to insist that a common objective does not translate into a singularity of project.

Diasporic South Asian intellectuals who demand representation within Asian American studies abandon issues of postcoloniality in favor of multiculturalism. It may be argued that the impulse behind this demand is to form alliances with other minorities. My own position is not to undermine such alliances but to ask for a greater awareness of what I am calling the politics of race. Given the multicultural roles assigned them, diasporic Third World intellectuals occupy a place shot through with contradictions. Rather than legislate against South Asians working on issues of migrancy or forming alliances with racial minorities in the United States, I ask the following question: To what end is such an alliance being promoted? If it is to sanction a claim to marginality or racial minority status, I must interject the reminder that Third World immigrants do not constitute "the new empire within" the United States. Only by contending with the contradictions within diasporic communities can we transform postcolonialism into the study of transnationalism and differential power rather than marginality and oppression. It is at the very least with this in mind that we should approach the multicultural demand for teaching another kind of postcolonial culture.

Notes

I am grateful to Ali Behdad, King-Kok Cheung, Jinqi Ling, and Ellen Rooney, the reader for *Diaspora,* for their critical responses to an earlier draft of this essay.

1. The problem should be familiar to anyone who has attempted to teach Conrad's *Heart of Darkness* without the accompanying reversal of perspective offered by Chinua Achebe's *Things Fall Apart.* African culture and history, indeed, its humanity, have been so successfully effaced that American students have no conceptual framework with which to understand the colonial encounter other than the highly circumscribed one of Conrad's novel.

2. Although my discussion focuses on my own discipline, English literature, a similar hiring pattern exists in history and anthropology, the other primary sites of the field I am calling "postcolonial studies."

3. Said directed *Orientalism* at Middle East studies programs, which initiate U.S. policymakers into an orientalist mind-set. In his two subsequent books, *Tracking Islam* and *The Question of Palestine,* he shows how an orientalist epistemology underpins Western media images of Islam and the ideological formation of the Israeli nation-state. In this regard, Said's work has been particularly valuable to political organizations such as the Palestine Human Rights Campaign and the American Arab Anti-Discrimination Committee.

4. I am describing postcolonial studies as primarily a U.S. phenomenon; however, critics working in Commonwealth studies have contributed significantly to the field. Commonwealth studies was started in Britain during the mid-1960s to designate Anglophone cultures of its newly independent colonies. Although the literatures of the former colonies were formally recognized, they were treated as marginal (and, by implication, inferior) to English literature. In white settler colonies, such as Canada, Australia, and New Zealand, the idea of a "post" to colonialism is intended to dislodge the hegemony of English culture. As Bill Ashcroft, Gareth Griffiths, and Helen Tiffin (1989, 196), writing from Australia, declare: "The very idea of English Literature as a study which occludes its own specific

national, cultural, and political grounding and offers itself as a new system of development of 'universal' human values is exploded by the existence of the postcolonial literatures." Many of the epistemological problems with the use of the term *postcolonial* originated in Commonwealth studies. For example, by uniting the cultures of such diverse
regions as Kenya, Nigeria, Indian, Australia, Canada, and Jamaica on the basis of a past
relationship to Britain, Commonwealth literature effaces historical differences between
nations that emerged from decolonization and recenters their cultures around Europe.
For further criticism of the term *postcolonialism,* see McClintock 1992 and Shohat 1992.

5. Appadurai (1990, 16) explains that the globalization of culture is not the same as
cultural imperialism. Whereas cultural imperialism suggests uniformity in the spread of
Western consumer culture, the globalization of Western commodities involves their being transformed into indigenous, hybridized forms.

6. The impulse behind the ancestry question is to bring race under the hegemony of an
ethnic identity, but its instructions reveal the limits to the immigrant paradigm on which
the idea of ethnic identities is based. The traces of colonial conquest, which accounts for
the misnaming of the "First Nations," are visible in the census's demand for specificity: "If
ancestry is 'Indian' specify whether American Indian, Asian Indian, or West Indian" (fac-
simile of the 1980 census ancestry question in Waters 1990, 169). The examples of different
ancestries given—"Afro-Amer., English, French, German, Honduran, Hungarian, Irish, Italian, Jamaican, Korean, Lebanese, Mexican, Nigerian, Polish, Ukrainian, Venzuelan, etc."—
fail to provide a country of origin for African Americans but not for African Caribbeans.
Although the descendants of slaves on the mainland cannot be made to conform to an
immigration paradigm, those who have migrated from the islands split the racial identity
of black America. For a discussion of the racial *and* ethnic identity of African Caribbean
immigrants, see Kasinitz 1992.

7. For a discussion of this community of thinking, see Mankeker 1994 and Leonard 1992.

Works Cited

Anzaldúa, Gloria. 1987. *Borderlands/La Frontera: The New Mestiza.* San Francisco: Aunt
    Lute.
Appadurai, Arjun. 1990. "Disjuncture and Difference in the Global Cultural Economy."
    Public Culture 2, no. 2:1–24.
———. 1993. "The Heart of Whiteness." *Callaloo* 16:796–807.
Ashcroft, Bill, Gareth Griffiths, and Helen Tiffin. 1989. *The Empire Writes Back: Theory
    and Practice in Post-Colonial Literatures.* New York: Routledge.
Bhabha, Homi. 1994. *The Location of Culture.* New York: Routledge.
Bhardwaj, Surinder M., and N. Madhusundana Rao. 1990. "Asian Indians in the United
    States: A Geographical Appraisal." In *South Asians Overseas: Migration and Ethnicity,*
    ed. Colin Clarke, Ceri Peach, and Steven Vertovec, 197–217. Cambridge: Cambridge
    University Press.
Blauner, Robert. 1972. *Racial Oppression in America.* New York: Harper.
Decker, Jeffrey Louis. 1995. "Blood Lines: The 1970s Movement for White Ethnicity."
    Unpublished essay.
Frankenberg, Ruth, and Lata Mani. 1993. "Crosscurrents, Crosstalk: Race, 'Postcoloniality,'
    and the Politics of Location." *Cultural Studies* 7:292–310.
Glazer, Nathan, ed. 1985. *Clamor at the Gates: The New American Immigration.* San Fran-
    cisco: Institute for Contemporary Studies.

120 **JENNY SHARPE**

Gugelberger, Georg M. 1994. "Postcolonial Cultural Studies." In *The Johns Hopkins Guide to Literary Theory and Criticism,* ed. Michael Groden and Martin Kreishwirth, 581–85. Baltimore: Johns Hopkins University Press.

Hu, Arthur. 1989. "Asian Americans: Model Minority or Double Minority?" *Amerasia Journal* 15, no. 1:243–57.

Hune, Shirley. 1989. "Expanding the International Dimensions of Asian American Studies." *Amerasia Journal* 15, no. 2:xix–xxxiv.

Jacob, Rahul. 1993. "Overseas Indians Make It Big." *Fortune,* 15 Nov., 168–74.

Jensen, Joan M. 1988. *Passage from India: Asian Indian Immigrants in North America.* New Haven, Conn.: Yale University Press.

Jha, Ajit Kumar. 1992. "A Community of Discord." *India Today,* 15 Nov., 48b–48c.

Jones, Maldwyn Allen. 1992. *American Immigration.* 2d ed. Chicago: University of Chicago Press.

Jussawalla, Feroza. 1988. "Chiffon Saris: The Plight of South Asian Immigrants in the New World." *Massachusetts Review* 29:583–95.

Kasinitz, Philip. 1992. *Caribbean New York: Black Immigrants and the Politics of Race.* Ithaca, N.Y.: Cornell University Press.

Krupat, Arnold. 1994. "Postcoloniality and Native American Literature." *Yale Journal of Criticism* 7, no. 1:163–80.

Lee, Sharon M. 1993. "Racial Classification in the US Census: 1890–1990." *Ethnic and Racial Studies* 16, no. 1:75–94.

Leonard, Karen Isaksen. 1992. *Making Ethnic Choices: California's Punjabi Mexican Americans.* Philadelphia: Temple University Press.

Liu, John. 1976. "Towards an Understanding of the Internal Colonial Model." In *Counterpoint: Perspectives on Asian America,* ed. Emma Gee, 160–68. Los Angeles: Asian American Studies Center, University of California at Los Angeles.

Mankekar, Purnima. 1994. "Reflections on Diaporic Identities: A Prolegomenon to the Analysis of Political Bifocality." *Diaspora* 3:349–71.

McClintock, Anne. 1992. "The Angel of Progress: Pitfalls of the Term 'Post-colonialism.'" *Social Text* 31–32:84–98.

Miyoshi, Masao. 1993. "A Borderless World? From Colonialism to Transnationalism and the Decline of the Nation-State." *Critical Inquiry* 19:726–51.

Oliver, Lawrence J. 1991. "Deconstruction or Affirmative Action: The Literary-Political Debate over the 'Ethnic Question.'" *American Literary History* 3:792–808.

Omi, Michael, and Howard Winant. 1994. *Racial Formation in the United States: From the 1960s to the 1990s.* New York: Routledge.

Parmar, Pratibha. 1982. "Gender, Race, and Class: Asian Women in Resistance." In *The Empire Strikes Back,* Centre for Contemporary Cultural Studies, 236–75. London: Hutichson.

Powell, J. Enoch. 1969. *Freedom and Reality.* Ed. John Wood. London: Baksford.

Robinson, Vaughan. 1986. *Transients, Settlers, and Refugees: Asians in Britain.* Oxford: Clarendon.

Rushdie, Salman. 1991. *Imaginary Homelands: Essays and Criticism, 1981–1991.* London: Granta.

Said, Edward. 1978. *Orientalism.* New York: Vintage.

Saran, Parmatma. 1985. *The Asian Experience in the United States.* Cambridge, Mass.: Schenkman.

Shohat, Ella. 1992. "Notes on the 'Post-Colonial.'" *Social Text* 31–32:99–113.

Sklair, Leslie. 1995. *Sociology of the Global System.* Baltimore: Johns Hopkins University Press.

Spivak, Gayatri Chakravorty. 1992. "Teaching for the Times." *Journal of the Midwest Modern Language Association* 25, no. 1:3–22.

Takaki, Ronald. 1989. *Strangers from a Different Shore: A History of Asian Americans.* Boston: Little, Brown.

Tölölyan, Khachig. 1991. "The Nation-State and Its Others: In Lieu of a Preface." *Diaspora* 1:3–7.

Usdansky, Margaret. 1992. "'Diverse' Fits Nation Better than 'Normal.'" *USA Today,* 29–30 May, A1.

Varma, Baidya Nath. 1980. "Indians As New Ethnics: A Theoretical Note." In *The New Ethnics: Asian Indians in the United States,* ed. Parmatma Saran and Edwin Eames, 29–41. New York: Prager.

Waters, Mary C. 1990. *Ethnic Options: Choosing Identities in America.* Berkeley: University of California Press.

Williams, Patrick, and Laura Chrisman, eds. 1994. *Colonial Discourse and Post-Colonial Theory: A Reader.* New York: Columbia University Press.

5 Internal Frontiers, Transnational Politics, 1945–65: Im/Migration Policy as World Domination

Rachel Buff

> The phenomenon of migration thus stands at the crossroads between national and regional inequities and class exploitation. It is the way through which the exploited contribute to erect ever-expanding structures of economic domination and simultaneously the form in which they react to their power.
>
> — Alexandro Portes, "Migration and Underdevelopment"

Decolonization, Imperial Hat Tricks, and Postcolonial Im/Migration(s)

At the close of World War II, the United States consolidated its position as a world power. Like their European counterparts during the nineteenth-century "Age of Empire," American statesmen such as Henry Luce could now proclaim an "American century" where the sun would never set on the busy whir and hum of an internationalized economy. The spatial fix so crucial to capitalist development was available abroad as far as the imperial gaze could contemplate. Unlimited Third World markets clamored for glitzy American television and soda pop; workers throughout the world could labor in microelectronics and undergarments plants as well as coffee and banana fields. From the newly consolidated anticommunist alliance of the North Atlantic Treaty Organization (NATO) to the U.S.-backed Southeast Asia Treaty Organization, and from hemispheric domination perpetrated by single companies and backed by the U.S. Central Intelligence Agency in Latin America to a developing mission to stop the spread of communism in Africa, the

United States would dominate resources, diplomacy, and internal politics throughout much of the so-called Free World.

At the same time that the United States consolidated its international hegemony, nations all over the world were engaged in decolonization struggles. National liberation movements begun before World War II won political victories after 1945 in Asia, the Caribbean, and Africa. Weakened by centuries of colonial rule, these nations would nonetheless define themselves as politically independent. These new nations, as demonstrated at the 1955 Bandung Afro-Asian Conference, struggled to resist neocolonialism and to assert economic and political sovereignty.[1] Although they met with limited success in combating a world-system based on maintaining the economic benefits of colonialism, these decolonized nations did limit the ability of the United States and other First World nations to intervene directly in their affairs of state.

The rhetoric of decolonization abroad had substantial echoes within the borders of the United States. Popular African American politicians such as Adam Clayton Powell identified the parallels between full civil rights here and the emergence of strong, independent states in Africa and Asia after decolonization. A strong voice for the emerging civil rights agenda after World War II, Powell also pressured Congress for a less racist immigration policy and urged the State Department to send an official U.S. representative to Bandung (Plummer 1996, 249). Many African American activists came out of the war years recognizing the international as well as national dimension of Du Bois's famous color line. In the postwar period they struggled to assert a political agenda that both connected them to international struggles for colonial independence and attempted to realize the equal opportunities at home promised by U.S. victory in the war to defend democracy. They were met, however, with great opposition. As Gayle Plummer points out, "The Cold War reaffirmed the dominance of states over world organizations and blocked entry to the open hearing on race relations that black activists sought" (194).

For Native Americans, the immediate postwar period was also a time of changing consciousness. Native veterans such as Ira Hayes and the 382d Platoon of Navajo codetalkers returned from distinguishing themselves in defense of democracy to impoverished reservations and to a mainstream national community that recognized them as citizens only in theory. In the immediate postwar period, organizations such as the National Congress of the American Indian (NCAI, founded in 1944) contested the status of Indian people as an internal, stateless minority. Just as Powell and other civil rights leaders recognized the parallels between their situation and those of newly decolonized nations throughout the world, organizations such as the NCAI increasingly connected their struggles for land claims and sovereignty to the rhetoric of decolonization. Through such agencies, Indian people would come together to claim their rights, first as U.S. citizens and later as Fourth World peoples, members of colonized nations that had been militarily defeated but had maintained strong affective and political allegiances among their denizens.

At the same time that the NCAI pressed claims to citizenship and sovereignty, a conservative Congress moved to permit development in native lands in the western United States. Resisting the sway of internationalist arguments, cold warriors such as Patrick McCarran (R-Nev.) and Arthur Watkins (D-Utah) eyed American Indian land claims, arguing that the United States could become self-sufficient if it were to fully develop the resources within its borders. For white politicians backing the termination of the federal trust relationship with Indian nations, a discourse of citizenship rights served to absorb a potentially troublesome minority population into the mainstream of national life. Although the Snyder Act of 1924 had made Indians citizens under law, supporters of the "Termination policy" would rediscover them as candidates for assimilation, arguing for their recruitment into the American family in language oddly redolent of the late nineteenth century.[2] Ironically the vocabulary of civil rights would be used against the claims of native organizations attempting to advocate a democratic agenda for their constituencies.

American hegemony in the postwar period was a matter of both controlling the flow of international labor and extending the development of national resources to include lands guaranteed to Indian peoples. The extractive power of First World capital increasingly involved transforming Third World workers into domestic laborers, either through plants built by multinational corporations in the home countries, through austerity or "import substitution" programs implemented by the World Bank or other international development agencies under the aegis of world anticommunism, or through the migration of large sections of the labor force away from the Third World and into the United States. At the same time federal Indian policy attempted to resolve the long-standing messy business of relations with Indian nations, "domestic, dependent" peoples defeated in the nineteenth century. The Bureau of Indian Affairs established the Indian Claims Commission in 1946 to resolve unsettled land titles, clearing the way for unrestricted exploitation of western lands. The hat trick of neocolonialism, then, was to control labor power with or without the consent of newly independent nations and to cast a "veneer of legality" over the continued violation of the treaty relationship with sovereign Indian nations within U.S. borders (Churchill 1992, 147). At the same time that postwar economic development relied on the transformation of an international work force into cheap labor for U.S. multinationals as well as the marginalization of minority workers, conservative nationalists in the West claimed the semisovereign lands of Indian nations.

Along with a gradualist approach to civil rights policy, immigration and Indian policy became crucial components of U.S. hegemony during the postwar period. The novelties of domestic prosperity and global leadership were premised on an older contradiction in the practice and distribution of the democratic goods. Internal war on organizations such as labor unions or Indian nations that might threaten the national good by asserting and maintaining loyalties beyond that of citizenship paralleled the surveillance of internationalist sentiments both within the United States and in the decolonizing world. For Americans of color, of course, the cold war represented an assault on their rights, which have always been granted only in response to political opposition and struggle. Race, then, was a crucial component of a supposedly colorblind corporate liberalism. David Theo Goldberg (1993, 6) calls this contradiction the "liberal paradox": "As modernity commits itself progressively to idealized principles of liberty, equality, and fraternity, as it increasingly insists upon the moral irrelevance of race, there is a multiplication of racial identities and the sets of exclusions they prompt and rationalize, enable and sustain."

My essay traces the transition between the comparatively isolationist immigration restriction imposed by a conservative Congress in 1954 to a liberalized policy that allowed for a dramatic increase in the legal arrival of Third World workers. Implemented by a nationalist bloc in congress, the McCarran-Walter Act was concerned with maintaining strong borders and developing the American West. At the same time, of course, the West that this legislation was intended to protect from foreign hordes was being amply stocked with cheap labor by the Bracero Program, which ran between 1946 and 1964. The McCarran-Walter Act, then, constituted a rhetoric of isolationism operative in a time of increasing U.S. dependence on Third World labor. Although this legislation was eventually reformed by the Immigration and Nationality Act of 1965, it put into place crucial categories applicable to immigrants effective through the present time. Based on cold war as well as colonialist distinctions, these categories sort immigrants into "political" and "economic" groups consonant with the United States' political and economic alliances in the postwar international arena.

Promoting "America first" also meant further abrogation of the federal trust relationship in the West, so that Indian lands could become available for the newly reconsolidated American empire. Thus my essay also looks at the assemblage of a rhetoric to support the Termination policy of ending Indians' special status within the nation—a twentieth-century equivalent to Colonel Henry Pratt's folkloric notion of "killing the Indian to civilize the man." Ann Laura Stoler (1996, 90) comments perceptively about the way racial discourse "invariably draws on a cultural density of prior representa-

tions that are recast in new forms." She argues that such racial discourse is
invariably correlated with national consolidation. In its concern to cast the
United States as a free nation in a world threatened by communist totalitarianism and its use of nineteenth-century racial categories to explain the necessity of termination, federal Indian policy in the 1950s and early 1960s very
much paralleled contemporary immigration policy. Both immigration and
Indian policies not only generated resistance from the communities that were
subject to them but also implemented a regime of postcolonialism within the
borders of the United States.

The National Romance, 1945–65

In the postwar period transmigrants from all over the world, as well as from
Native American reservations within the nation, arrived in U.S. urban centers in record numbers. Pushed by federal policy as well as underdeveloped
reservation economies, American Indians came to cities in search of the
democratic opportunities that the war was fought to defend. Refugees from
war-torn Europe waited in the war camps and devastated cities of their homelands for permission to immigrate to the United States. As newly consolidated
U.S. power reshaped the world political economy, Third World people were
pulled to seek opportunities away from the ravaged economies of their home
nations. These transmigrants joined communities that had existed in the
United States for as long as the intrahemispheric, intercultural economies of
colonialism had been bringing North American and Caribbean Indians into
contact with Euro-American settlers and African slaves—that is, for as long
as immigrants had gone back and forth across the oceans in search of economic opportunity and political liberties, leaving their homes for temporary
work in the Americas, from which many of them never returned.

Both recent arrivals and existing communities were affected by ongoing
national debates over immigration and Indian policies. Centering on the ideal
of assimilation, policies of termination and relocation during the 1950s and
early 1960s sought to move Indians off the reservations, desolve the trust
relationship under which the federal government held land for Indian nations, and move Indians into cities, where they could "become Americans."
In a similar quest for good Americans, immigration policy during this period attempted to screen potential immigrants for their likelihood of becoming trustworthy and loyal citizens. The debates over these policies, ideologically focused on questions of citizenship and national health, framed larger
issues of racial formation and cultural acceptability in the immediate postwar period. In turn the debates shaped policies that brought transmigrants
into U.S. cities.

This essay also analyzes the ways that cold war ideologists attempted to write Indians and immigrants into the dominant imaginings of national life during the postwar period at the same time that domestic politics delimited the efforts of these groups to assert their claims to the economic and political goods of corporate liberalism. These trends are contiguous with attitudes toward internal and external minorities throughout U.S. history, but it is for the postwar period that a reexamination of national borders, as they are created both internally and externally through imaginings of race and citizenship, becomes most crucial. The emergence of the United States as an international power after World War II made possible capital's current tremendous mobility. Historians and cultural critics must respond to this mobility by considering the fiction of the nation and what is done in the name of this powerful story.

The historical experiences of Indian and Third World peoples in this hemisphere brought these transmigrants to identify home with multiple political geographies, some of which were not illustrated on the maps available in cold war America. At the same time, organizations representing these groups within the United States struggled for their members' broader access to citizenship. During the 1950s and 1960s, however, state institutions such as the Bureau of Indian Affairs and the Immigration and Naturalization Service attempted to construct transmigrant peoples as citizens possessing singular loyalties and affinities. Even though a great disparity existed between imaginative alliances and official constructions of citizenship, cold war policy screened loyalties and racial fitness for eligibility into the American democracy.

Finally, this essay explains the ideas of citizenship central to these policies as a product of a more general, "foundational fiction" of national formation in the postwar period. The nation relies on discursive formations—metaphors and other stories—to shore up its legitimacy and to make claims on its citizen-subjects. Nationalism stakes its claims to the souls of citizen-subjects through its ability to write a singular story that defines and describes the life of the people.[3] "Foundational fictions," according to Doris Sommer, attempt to reconcile social inequalities by writing romantic fantasies of collective national destiny. Inevitably these fictions betray their origins; they are specifically gendered, highly racialized imaginings of national unity that rely on a familiar cast of characters for their heroes, villains, and walk-ons. The importance of Sommer's work is that it teaches us about "the inextricability of politics from fiction in the history of nation building" (1990, 75).

Nationalist ideology must somehow reconcile the struggle among very different visions of community and sovereignty, presenting the illusion of a harmonious and organic national family. But all fiction is culturally produced.

The master narratives of nation, the ideologies that rationalize domination and hierarchy, are thus just as arbitrary as the counternarratives generated by colonized people that are often dismissed as magical realism or fantastic folklore. The difference between foundational fictions and counternarratives turns on the power available to produce from a specific fiction a disciplined set of practices that we come to recognize as truth.

My research on immigration and Indian policy focuses on the period between 1947, when U.S. policy toward European refugees and American Indian GIs was first instituted, and 1965, when some of the more hard-line aspects of cold war policies were reformed. Taking a cue from Sommer's imaginative scholarship, I read the rhetoric of policy debate as foundational fictions that sought to rationalize and disseminate national identity. My research draws on readings of the *Congressional Record,* state and federal reports on policy, and the debates found in media organs such as the *New York Times.*[4] Government agencies such as the Immigration and Naturalization Service (INS) and the Bureau of Indian Affairs (BIA) are semiautonomous political entities, as much ensnared in the contradictions of state structures as they are responsive to public opinion or debate (Calavita 1992). My effort here has been not as much to uncover the machinations of policy implementation, however, as to understand its ideological underpinnings. Although the specific policies discussed in the 1950s were eventually reformed, the public debate that accompanied them set the stage for enduring conceptions of citizenship, race, and culture.

Both the BIA and the INS were charged with writing populations marginal to national social and economic orders into the foundational fictions of postwar consolidation. Accordingly these agencies attempted to implement policies that reflected well on newly established U.S. international hegemony and that appeared best to distribute the ideological goods of democratic capitalism to new immigrants and reservation-dwelling Indians.

Nationalist narratives such as that of cold war democracy invoke and sustain an identity on the grounds of common homeland and biological descent, language, and civil religion: all those private arenas of identity that are held to be beyond the rationalization and control of the public, political sphere. Nationalism as a narrative project claims an organic motion from past to present, an unassailable and totalizing sovereignty in the name of intimate practices of language and culture. Nationalist narratives are epics; they represent the present in terms of a determinate, glorious national past.[5] This remove from the practices of everyday life, in which territory, race, language, and belief are all arenas for contestation, keeps nationalist ideology outside the social. At the same time, foundational fictions construct an ideal organic body that is supposed to maintain the spirit and the highest aims of a unified people. In the 1950s this move toward ideological consolidation was concurrent with a profound reshaping of the U.S. political economy. While the state functioned ideologically to bolster the postwar foundational fiction of cold war democracy, it increasingly represented the consolidation of an alliance among industrial, military, and national interests.

At the same time that World War II brought Indians into the public consciousness, allowing the discourse of national policy to scrutinize them as both "first Americans" and potential citizens, the war had also turned national economic attention to the West. Federal expenditures on economic development in the West increased, in the instance of California, by as much as ten times. By no coincidence, many of the most strongly proterminationist members of congress belonged to a coalition of political and corporate interests that saw the postwar West as the site of a new America. For a senator such as Nevada's Patrick McCarran, the development of the West promised American economic autonomy and the certain replication of a familiar foundational fiction. He wrote: "The West today is the land of empire, of opportunity, of destiny. Today, more than ever, the West is plain every day American for 'opportunity'" (in Nash 1990, 187). If this glorious and familiar future was to be realized, of course, the rich "opportunities" that existed on Indian land would have to be made available to the national project. "Emancipation" of Indians through termination of their federal trust relationship would allow for the exploitation of Indian lands.

In the years following World War II, the United States was positioned to consolidate an empire, both abroad and at home. Geopolitically the nation had ascended to the leadership of the "Free World," while domestically the military-industrial complex had expanded and consolidated, using war production as the machine to pull the national economy out of the depression. The percentage of goods produced by the hundred largest corporations zoomed in the first two years of the war, from 30 percent in 1941 to 70 percent in 1943 (Nash 1990, 8); this war machine, along with the propaganda apparatus generated to support the war effort, readily translated into the production and marketing of consumer goods after the war. Geopolitical and economic consolidation presented an ideological challenge: how could the foundational fictions that would support U.S. imperialism and expansion, both at home and abroad, also appear to foster egalitarian democracy and individualism?

Just as federal Indian policy had to legitimize local claims to land guaranteed to Indian nations, immigration policy in the postwar period attempted to maintain the foundational fiction of the cold war whereby the United States was a "beacon of freedom" to oppressed and appropriate people. At the same time immigration policy was charged with screening out "unde-

sirable immigrants" who would not make good citizens. "Undesirable immigrants" were those whose loyalties were questionable on grounds of their
ties to other nations or political systems or those who sought refuge in the
United States not because of access to democracy but because of economic
opportunities.

As the paradigmatic new Americans, immigrants, particularly those fleeing
communism, were expected to assimilate into the "American way" much less
problematically than were Native Americans. Determining competence for
citizenship, then, was not a matter of individual preparation, as it was with
Indians. Instead, the assimilability of these new immigrants pertained to their
loyalties. The pressure to receive immigrants democratically and to be the
traditional "golden door" for the poor and oppressed of the world was miti-
gated by an overarching cold war concern for national security. McCarran
argued that immigration policy should err on the side of the latter: "Our
entire immigration system has been so weakened as to make it often impossible for our country to protect its security in this black era of fifth column
infiltration and cold warfare with the ruthless masters of the Kremlin. The
time has long since passed when we can afford to open our borders indis-
criminately to give unstinting hospitality to any person whose purpose, whose
ideological aim is to overthrow our institutions and replace them with the
evil oppression of totalitarianism" (*CR* 25 April 1946, 4993).

Cold war ideology translated the mythologized democracy of the western
frontier into Third World skirmishes as actively as possible, but the reinven-
tion of America as a land of opportunity was contradictory. Many of the
opportunities for new immigrants were maintained by agribusiness and industry at the minimal wage scales made possible by cheap labor provided by
the Bracero Program.[6] The logic of assimilation here was contradictory: for
many new immigrants, particularly those of color, it would be difficult or
impossible to participate in what writers such as Daniel Bell touted as a "class-
less society."

The national romance narrated in postwar discourse about immigration
and Indian policy is one of assimilation, of equal access to the democracy and
affluence promised by postwar capitalist development. As Sommer argues
about the nineteenth-century novels she studied, the national romance of
policy debate in the postwar United States produced, through marriage, a
homogeneous national body out of the diverse bodies of the lovers who were
to come into citizenship, the official body of the nation. In contrast to the
optimistic and expansive tone of the Latin American novels, however, these
foundational fictions worried about maintaining national homeostasis in the
face of cultural differences—both those within the nation and those among
the refugees and migrants clamoring at its borders to be "let in."

Taking place in a cold war context charged with fears of subversion and anti-Americanism, debates on immigration and Indian policy in the immediate postwar period emphasized the importance of citizenship as qualifying these individuals for entry into the national family. These policies sought to manufacture good citizens out of potentially subversive denizens and refugees. How these citizens were produced, however, was a key component of the romance of national unity and marriage.

The national romance of assimilation and homogenization through citizenship authored formative discourses of race and ethnicity in this period. In producing the nation, this foundational fiction sponsored state policy toward what Vine Deloria (Deloria and Lytle 1984) has called "the nations within"—historically and culturally sovereign Indian nations—as well as toward denizens from other countries. Such stories constructed and implemented racialized ideas of citizenship. The idea that there is equal access to citizenship and that it is equally desirable to all individuals and collectivities dwelling within the nation proposes a limited national subjectivity at the same time that it supports the liberal claim of equal access to both social and economic democracy. Nonetheless, just as different denizens of the state would be required to take different routes to full citizenship—whether genealogical or legislative—the liberal idea of citizenship for all is always undercut by the racialization of public policy and of the very Enlightenment model of equality.

As the close of World War II inaugurated the cold war—a military standoff internationally and an ideological war of attrition domestically—classical bulwarks of the liberal state, such as the notions of progress through assimilation and social harmony through democratic emancipation, became increasingly important to the coherence of nationalist fictions. Egalitarian ideologies such as that of cold war democracy rely on the centrality of individual identity as well as the ability of these individual identities to compose an organic social body (Kapferer 1988, 14–16). The ideal qualities of the nation are reproduced in the individual bodies of its citizens; state policies that enforce the construction of such an organic unity are seen to stand outside the charged and sacred sphere of national and individual identity. Cold war ideology had to produce a sense of national purpose that extended to all American citizens; at the same time, the repressive policies deemed necessary for national security brought more regulation of sites, such as universities and the arts, that were traditionally considered to be arbiters of democratic freedom. Contestation over the definition of citizenship in this period, then, was central to the discursive field that defined and protected national identity.

Cold war immigration and Indian policy sought to assimilate citizens se-

lectively into the national family. Ostensibly designed to strengthen and protect this national family, these policies implemented racialized practices that
governed the ways individuals would be recognized as citizens: how they were
to qualify and become citizens, and what, implicitly, they would give up to
join the national family. Whereas Indian people had become citizens by national law in 1924, federal Termination policy attempted to "integrate" them
"into the social, political, and economic life of the nation" (*NYT* 24 July 1952,
17), "emancipating" them from the federal trust relationship that protected
their treaty rights to the land.[7] Emphasizing on *Meet the Press* that Indians'
current nonassimilated status made them inferior Americans, Secretary of
the Interior Douglas McKay stated: "Any time anybody lives as a ward of the
Government, they are of no value" (*NYT* 6 April 1953, 24). Fear of Indian
dependence readily slid into the rhetoric of anticommunism: in 1946, Con-
gressman George Schwabe stated that it would be a good idea "to get rid of
the Indian Bureau as soon as possible[;] it is a drain upon the taxpayers
and . . . a poor guardian for the Indians. I think it tends to encourage pater-
nalism and socialistic and communistic thinking" (in Fixico 1986, 17).

Calls for immigration restriction during this period were also couched in
the rhetoric of civic responsibility and anticommunism. Demanding restriction of immigration and naturalization in 1951, Senator Patrick McCarran
"indicated that the bill would call for a careful 'screening' of persons seeking to come to the United States to see if they were 'adapted to our way of
life.' . . . [under the current system] proof of good moral character, adapt-
ability to our way of life, and general conduct have been most laxly dealt with"
(*NYT* 1 Jan. 1951, 20).

The foundational fictions of postwar immigration and Indian policy racialized ideas of citizenship and subjectivity. The struggle over citizenship in the
postwar period posed crucial questions about the identities of those who
would be included in the nation's social body. In turn, this struggle confronted
the highly racialized concepts of assimilation and emancipation. Although
these ideals purport to be universal, they are always charged with a sense of
who is, and who is not, eligible for these rights. These policies represent a
racialized paradigm of modernization that developed in the immediate postwar period and remains potent today. Premised on the notions of assimilation and social amelioration, this paradigm draws on liberal constructions
of citizenship and equal rights, offering progress as a resolution for previous
inequities. These racialized ideas defined the terrain of struggle over these
policies. Because assimilation and racial hierarchy are ideologically coterminous in liberal political theory, the idea of modernization will always generate inequality, even as it seeks to ameliorate it (Goldberg 1993; Escobar 1988).
Although the policies on which this essay focuses were eventually reformed,

what is important to the ongoing narrative of U.S. national foundations in the postwar period is the way that they were able to affect discourses of citizenship and subjectivity.

In emphasizing individual citizenship over group self-determination, Termination policy continued a history of federal and state Indian policy unable to acknowledge the centrality of the relationship between Indian people and the land. Fictions of citizenship and emancipation wrote over existing Indian narratives of nation and identity. Similarly, policies that came to emphasize the assimilability of new immigrants screened legal immigrants on the basis of cultural traits deemed acceptable to mainstream national values. Even after Native Americans had successfully resisted termination and a coalition of ethnic and progressive groups overturned the racist preference system of the McCarran-Walter Act, the more subtle aspects of this racialization remained, maintaining division and inequity within the national family that was meant, in the story of the postwar period, to coalesce around corporate liberalism and economic affluence. Stoler (1996, 90) writes: "Racial discourse is not opposed to emancipatory claims; on the contrary, it effectively appropriates them."

Producing Citizens

The foundational fictions informing immigration and Indian policies in the postwar period can be divided into different chapters according to how they created citizens. Sometimes citizenship was written as a narrative of descent, where citizens are produced through the bodies of other citizens, through biological reproduction and the socializing institution of the family. In the case of naturalization, however, citizenship becomes a narrative of ascent, where the legitimating body of the nation stands in for the actual bodies and genealogies of subjects. In the case of naturalization, the state is the parent bringing already existing individuals into the national fold (Sollors 1986, 4–6). These various origins of citizenship point to different constructions of race and ethnicity in the postwar period.

Immediately after the war, between 1945 and 1952, policy debates focused on bloodlines, reproduction, and the ways that new citizens were related to the actual bodies and immediate families of those already inhabiting the national family. Policies concerning nonnational "war brides" and the families of returning Indian veterans in this period emphasized lineage and reproduction. After 1952 social scientists and policymakers shifted their attention away from the military heroics and physical depredations of war. Social fictions in this period did not correspond so directly to bodily incarnations of citizenship. As they considered the domestic ramifications of "the American century," the authors of immigration and Indian policy turned to the legal production and naturalization of new citizens, and cultural conceptions of race and citizenship came to supplant biological distinctions. Finally, as the coalitions that opposed both Termination and immigration policies during the 1950s, in concert with the ascendant civil rights movement, challenged these restrictive assimilatory practices, a more liberalized approach to assimilation emerged. After 1965 reformed Indian and immigration policies would emphasize ethnicity over race, liberalizing the terms of inclusion into the national body. Whereas Termination and immigration policies had adopted racialized definitions of culture, reform efforts responded to the influence of the civil rights movement in implementing an ethnicity-based model of access to economic and political rights. These different models of citizenship and assimilation overlap to a great degree: although the reforms changed the immediate racial hierarchies of policy, they maintained continuity with racialized social thought and continued to limit access to full citizenship.

This periodization is in some ways artificial, given the ideological slippage among different policies and the overall continuity of what I have called "the modernization paradigm." As Goldberg (1993, 74) writes, a concept such as race or citizenship is "a fluid, transforming, historically specific concept parasitic on theoretical and social discourses for the meaning it assumes at any historical moment." This having been said, however, these different chapters of the postwar romance do point to specific ideological tensions and romantic resolutions possible within national fictions of assimilation and citizenship.

We Are Family: Citizenship Embodied

In 1945, as Congress was beginning to debate issues of national origin, immigration, and ancestry, the War Brides Act passed both houses and was signed into law by President Truman. Under this law the spouses and minor children of U.S. citizens serving in the military were allowed to enter the country as nonquota immigrants. McCarran-Walter legislation, passed seven years later, upheld this special right for families of GIs (Reimers 1985, 17–22). Women married to American servicemen and the children of these marriages were beyond the suspicion and racialized scrutiny applicable to other refugees and immigrants.[8]

The War Brides Act rested on two assumptions about the family and citizenship. First, American GIs, the defenders of democracy, would be unlikely to select wives who would make bad citizens. Second, these foreign women, because of their gender and their status as wives, were unlikely to be the same immigrants that Congress worried would "not leave behind them their loyalties to foreign governments and foreign ideologies" (CR 25 April 1949,

4993).[9] Both these assumptions suggest, as did later immigration reform strategies, that the family was to function as a crucible for assimilation and for the screening of loyalties to the nation.

At the same time that "war brides" were unproblematically admitted as potential U.S. citizens, Congress debated the status of American Indian veterans. Because of the federal trust relationship, Indian veterans were not eligible for Veteran's Administration mortgages (*NCAI* vol. 1, no. 4 [1946]). House Resolution 1113 addressed this problem in 1947: "The Secretary of the Interior is authorized and directed, upon application of any Indian who shall have served honorably in the armed forces of the United States in time of war, to remove all restrictions upon the lands, interest in lands, funds, or other properties of such Indian, and, if such lands or interests in lands are held in trust for such Indian, to issue an unrestricted patent in fee therefore" (*CR* 21 July 1947, 9562).

Although veterans had shown themselves to be worthy of inclusion in a country for which they had fought and died, Congress saw fit to amend the initial bill providing for the removal of restrictions on land owned by Indian veterans by requiring them to take a competence test. Veterans over the age of twenty-one could "apply to any naturalization court for the area in which he resides for a 'writ of competency'" (*CR* 21 July 1947, 9562). A second amendment, debated at length during the same congressional session, restricted the rights of citizenship to the individual Indian veteran who successfully applied, granting the offspring of Indians who had achieved competence the right only to apply for citizenship on becoming twenty-one. In other words, Indians were capable of becoming citizens, but not of engendering them; being an Indian born in the United States did not necessarily grant an individual the right to claim citizenship in the national body. Indian veterans, ideologically, would have to enter the nation in a more profound and less threatening way than as warriors.[10]

The "emancipation" of Indian veterans through competence tests set a precedent that would lie at the center of Termination policy: Indians had to be transformed to enter the national family. This affected Indian families as well as Indian nations. Representative Francis Case, of South Dakota, argued that when individual Indians became citizens, they should be allowed to become the legal guardians for their minor children (*CR* 21 July 1947, 9562). Entrance into the national family here entitled prospective citizens to responsibility for their biological family. In an ideologically parallel gesture, Senator Barry Goldwater used the debate over Indian citizenship and competence as a platform to argue for transforming the racial definition of Indian status. Goldwater charged that, just as Indians needed to prove their competence to become U.S. citizens, individuals should be required to be of full-blood

status to claim any Indian identity at all (*CR* 16 Jan. 1954, 625). This assertion contradicted the laws and practices of both Indian nations and the federal government. What it attests to, however, is the importance of bloodlines
and reproduction in this debate over membership in the national body. Stoler
(1992, 52) calls these racialized boundaries "internal frontiers," which she uses
to track the emergence of legal discourse about citizenship in colonial culture. The internal frontiers delimited by postwar discourse about the bodies
and families of Indians and immigrants also construct racialized fictions of
citizenship and nation.

The national romance, as it was written into the War Brides Act and House
resolutions for competence testing of Indian veterans, centered on a national
family constructed on biological descent, shored up by the offices of federally adjudicated competence. In a minor but illuminating subplot of this
postwar romance, House Resolution 2108 in 1949 allowed refugee physicians
to practice medicine in Indian hospitals, even though the complexities of
passing national certification tests ordinarily prevented them from doing so
elsewhere in this country (*NCAI* 1, no. 2 [July 1947]). On the one hand, citizen-subjects deemed incompetent to operate on the bodies of full citizens
were allowed to practice on Indian bodies. On the other, Indian bodies needed
legal operations to enter the national family.[11]

Indian people took note of the discussion of their status in Congress. The
NCAI dubbed House Resolution 1113 the "phony emancipation bill." Jose
Carpio, the governor of Isleta Pueblo, pointed out the injustice of such policies: "In our recent struggle for freedom from European aggression, many
Indian boys donned the uniforms of Uncle Sam to fight the threats of the
aggressors. But it seems that it resulted in vain, because by the so-called
'emancipation bill' many are going to be affected to the end of our natural
lives. It seems like our white brother is shaking us with his left hand and stab-
bing us with his right" (*NCAI* 2, no. 2 [July 1948]).

In 1949 the NCAI's sixth annual convention resolution on "emancipation"
pointed out the bill's problematic construction of Indians as "foreigners" and
its inherent unconstitutionality: "This bill operates under a false premise:
namely, that Indians are foreigners who must apply and prove their competency; no other native citizen is required to humiliate himself to prove his
competency; this again, is in conflict with the rights of native-born citizens
as prescribed within the framework of the United States Constitution; the
whole tone of the bill stresses the approach that the Indian is inferior and
not really a citizen; for example, he is put on the same level as aliens" (*NCAI*
3, no. 2 [June 1949]).

Here the NCAI points to the central contradiction in the policy of naturalizing Indians. The BIA attempted to resolve this contradiction through a

civil rights rhetoric of the "emancipation" and "desegregation" of American Indians during the 1950s. At the same time, immigration policy implemented a biologically based discourse of race, screening immigrants for their potential assimilability by the restrictive policies of national-origins quotas and loyalty tests.

The Recombinance of Race: Natural Selection of Citizens

The national romance's reliance on the physical family and on explicitly biological constructions of race and citizenship gave way after 1952 to a functionalist model of the nation as a homogenizing social body. The actual bodies and families of American GIs could not be the only incubators of good American citizens. Increasingly the national romance relied on discourses of assimilation and selection for the integration of new bodies into the national family. Cultural and biological racism entwine here in defining the good citizen; it is important to recognize how interdependent these discourses have been in the shaping of national identities. The political technology of biopower shapes the citizen-subjects of the nation-state; race and sexuality are key discourses that determine membership and exclusion in this entity. In addition, more elusive cultural definitions of appropriate citizenship rely on these markers of difference as well. "Nationalist discourse drew on and gave force to a wider politics of exclusion. This version was not concerned solely with the visual markers of difference, but with the relationship between visible characteristics and invisible properties, outer form and inner essence. Assessment of these untraceable identity markers could seal economic, political, and social fates" (Stoler 1996, 8).

The McCarran-Walter Act was the culmination of debates on immigration that took place between 1947 and the act's passage into law under Eisenhower in 1952. Like the Termination policy pursued during the same time period, immigration policy under McCarran-Walter legislation gestured toward American egalitarianism while at the same time mandating a racialized selection process for the assimilation of new citizens. Harry N. Rosenfeld, commissioner of the unpopular Displaced Persons Bureau, pointed out that the law "would remove racial barriers from our current laws but would tighten the provisions for admissions and deportation on security grounds" (*NYT* 4 Mar. 1952, 19). Although the law did eliminate restrictions against the naturalization of Asians as citizens, it implemented national-origins quotas that applied the 1920s "Nordic race theory" of immigration restriction. In accordance with Nordic race theory, this law gave preference to immigrants of northern European backgrounds. Quotas diminished in size moving from southern Europe to Latin America and then to Asia and Africa: newly decolonized nations such as Mali were granted a yearly quota of one hundred. Nordic race theory also distinguished the national origins of people under foreign sovereignty.

In concert with the Internal Security Act of 1950, McCarran-Walter legislation set up strict and subjective loyalty tests for potential immigrants.[12] Finally, and most important in terms of writing fictions of citizenship, assimilation, and national inclusion, the law distinguished between political and economic immigrants.

The enduring ideological success of the McCarran-Walter Act, even after its abrogation by the Hart-Cellar Immigration Reform Bill of 1965, lay in its ability to conflate biological racism with the discourse of political loyalties. From the 1950s through contemporary debates, immigration and refugee policy take as a given the distinction between economic and political refugees that McCarran-Walter legislation recognized. Under this policy individuals fleeing "communist-totalitarian" regimes are given preference and considered "political" refugees. This ironic cold war vote of confidence in the economies of the Eastern Bloc meant that non-Eastern-Bloc refugees fleeing "friendly" governments such as Salazar's Portugal, Reza Shah Pahlavi's Iran, or Anastasio Somoza's Nicaragua were designated "economic" refugees. This distinction between political and economic migrants is what Goldberg (1993, 99) calls a "racialized exclusion," which he defines as follows: "If it is reasonably clear that some institutional practice gives rise to racially patterned exclusionary or discriminatory outcomes, no matter the institutional aims, and the institution does little or nothing to avoid, diminish, or alleviate these outcomes, the reasonable presumption must be that the institution is racist or effectively promotes racism of a sort."

Conceiving of political migrants as rational subjects able to assess their situation and opt for the democratic freedom offered by the United States, immigration policy posits economic migrants—almost without exception from developing countries—as part of "push-pull" cycles of hemispheric and international migrations, not as viable democratic citizen-subjects. In this cold war romance, political migrants assess their situations in an analytical manner, whereas economic migrants seem to wash up on our national shores, out of control of their lives, family economies, and destinies. Ironically, the political "freedom" touted in cold war discourse is largely economic: the freedom of the free market, the abundance of economic opportunities for hardworking and deserving families. Predictably the immigrants deemed political subjects by this distinction tend to be Europeans fleeing state socialism, whereas the economic immigrants so often referred to as faceless hordes or tidal waves tend to be nonwhite people attempting to escape the grim austerity imposed on friends of democracy around the globe.[13]

Controversy over the McCarran-Walter Act preceded its congressional approval and accompanied the law's thirteen-year dominance of national immigration policy. Support for the bill came from the same western senators who backed Termination policy, from hard-line cold warriors such as Mississippi Democrat James O. Eastland,[14] and from eastern conservatives such as Francis Walter (R-Penn.). These policymakers saw the postwar epic arising from western lands and domestic ingenuity. In addition, segregationists such as Eastland utilized fears of domestic subversion to legitimate the maintenance of the long-standing internal frontiers monitored by the regime of Jim Crow (Plummer 1996, 168).

This romance of national development through isolationism and selection contradicted the logic of postwar capitalist development. By 1956 even John Foster Dulles had concluded that national health and biologistic selection were incompatible. The national-origins system, he argued, "which draws a distinction between the blood of one person and the blood of another, cannot be reconciled with the fundamental concepts of our Declaration of Independence" (*NYT* 26 Apr. 1956, 13). National homeostasis needed to be maintained, but the discourse of blood and competence was to be transformed into a discourse of social assimilation.

As the nation economy boomed during the 1950s, riding the "peacetime conversion" of military-industrial development into consumer goods, the family assumed ongoing importance as a social and economic unit. Cold war economics as well as political rhetoric depended on a story about "the American way of life" that in turn took family life as its moral and cultural justification (see May 1988). The continuity with earlier narratives of reproduction, biology, and competence is important here as what Goldberg (1993, 68) calls a "hybrid of significations" between older conceptions of natural law grounded in the individual bodies of citizens and emerging ideas of social development that allowed entrance into the national family through the romance of assimilation.

Notions of assimilation and emancipation came to replace the biologistic thinking prevalent during the immediate postwar period. During the 1950s cold war concern for the loyalties of citizen-subjects coincided with racially laden ideas about the assimilation of minorities into "mainstream" American society. For example, Secretary of the Interior Douglas McKay argued that Indian nations should not have a right of "consent" to Termination policies beyond their rights, as American citizens, to vote for elective office. In a 1955 letter McKay conflates his distaste for Indian self-determination with a cold war aversion to nongovernmental political organizations: "The issue of consent has most serious Constitutional implications . . . for Indians would thus be given over and above the normal rights of citizenship, a special veto power

over legislation which might affect them. . . . No other element in our population (aside from the President himself) now has such a power, and none
has ever had in the history of our country. . . . it would be extremely dangerous to pick out any segment of the population and arm its members with
the ability to frustrate the will of the Congress which the whole people have
elected" (*Amerindian* 4, no. 3 [Jan.–Feb. 1956]).[15]

Termination, then, was presented as the "emancipation" of Indians from
their "segregated" status as owners of reservation land and participants in self-
determining politics. The national romance here offered Indians the chance
to marry into the family, to emerge from their more primitive relationship
to the federal government into full rights as citizen-spouses. Proterminationist
figures such as Senator Butler compared Indian "emancipation" to civil rights
for African Americans: "Let me say frankly that I do not believe Negroes
should be segregated, and I do not believe Indians should be segregated. Any
institution or any public policy which strengthens and enforces segregation
for these two minority racial groups in my judgment is wrong" (*CR* 7 Oct.
1949, 14118). Particularly instructive were the ways that these dominant national romances dealt with opposition from within during the mid-1950s.
Congress devoted time and energy into debating with an absent Eleanor
Roosevelt, who had written a letter to the *Washington Times* opposing Termination policies. John Collier, the former BIA director and architect of the
Indian Reorganization Act whose vocal criticism of Termination and Relocation policies appeared in newspapers as well as government debates, was
largely branded as too left-leaning to be taken seriously.

Like many colonial marriages, however, Indian "emancipation" required
an education in economics and social life for the weaker partner. A racialized
and sexualized social body grants inclusion to such partners only after they
have demonstrated their cultural propensities for assimilation. The paternal-
ism of Termination policy, as well as its disciplinary intentions, were well
expressed by Assistant Secretary of the Interior Bill Warne, who said at a
meeting with the Association of Indian Americans in 1949, "What we need
most is the knowledge which will enable us to awake in our Indian fellow
citizens a desire to move away from the past of their fathers into the future
we have arranged for every youngster" (in Fixico 1986, 49).

Although some Indian people followed the assimilation narrative suggested
by the story of Ira Hayes, proclaiming that Indians "no longer feel attached
to tribal custom (and) are leaving the reservation to make their own independent way in the world" (*NYT* 16 Sept. 1956, 21), many commentators and
policymakers worried about how Indian citizens would fare in the mainstream economy. Their questions primarily concerned how members of the
Klamath and Menominee nations, the first to be targeted for termination,

would spend their allotment money and what kinds of households they would establish off the reservations. In 1961 each Klamath willing to accept termination was eligible to receive $43,000 (Fixico 1986, 185). Reverend Harvey Zeller, who worked in a Methodist mission on the Klamath reservation from 1945 to 1963, reassured *New York Times* reporters: "The Klamaths are behaving just like white men. Some blew their cash, others put it to work. Some bought new cars, lots are buying new houses" (*NYT* 7 Feb. 1963, 17).

Nevertheless, the transition from partial self-determination to Termination and Relocation policies required the ministering of a coalition of university social science, state, county, and federal agencies: this marriage required a rigorous regime of prenuptial education. The termination coalition wrote the attachment of American Indians to their land and culture as typical "laboring class psychological problems (that) often come from the lack of requisite practical social skills, or from lack of opportunity to fulfill white middle class goals—not from a reluctance to adopt them or inability to fully assimilate them" (Ames and Fisher 1954).[16] The coalition's psychologization of Menominee resistance to termination is worth quoting at length here, because it exemplifies how the romance of assimilation dealt with different conceptions of citizenship and subjectivity.

> Most Menominees would prefer to maintain the present federal guardianship status rather than accept termination. The widespread belief that they were bribed or coerced into accepting termination is a poor psychological foundation for a program which demands the utmost cooperation and efforts of the tribal membership. . . . Underlying this feeling is the strong attachment that the Menominees have for their "homeland," a birthright that they feel is worthy of and entitled to protection. This feeling is reinforced by: The exceptional beauty of the Reservation forest, streams and lakes, the passion of the Menominees for hunting and fishing, and its symbolic significance for them as Indians; and on the human side, the fact that the Reservation psychologically represents an island in the white man's world, where one is relatively certain to be treated in a friendly and permissive way. (103)

Not surprisingly, the Termination policy coalition attempted to override these sentimental objections, implementing assimilation by drawing on the related discourses of citizenship and family. The BIA offered Menominee adults classes on citizenship and government and hired a home agent to help Menominee women prepare their households for termination and relocation. *The Menominee News,* a proterminationist paper, carried regular tips on sanitation, canning, and gardening, as well as advice on buying appropriate clothing for children attending integrated county or city schools (*Menominee News,* Aug. 1956, Sept.–Oct. 1957). In his monthly column, Relocation Officer George McKay offered fatherly advice on home economics: "We all desire to have something better for our home, to improve our living conditions, but we must work and save in order to obtain this type of living" (29 Oct. 1958).

Under pressure from the terminationist coalition, Wisconsin Public Law 399 changed the legality of Indian heirship in 1956. Unlike Goldwater's earlier suggestion that only full-bloods be considered Indian, this law made it possible for all legal heirs, not just those eligible for tribal enrollment, to receive a "certificate of beneficial interest." A share of tribal property, then, would be passed on to all legal heirs (*Menominee News* 27 Feb. 1956, 23 Mar. 1956). This law undermined the limited legal sovereignty of the trust relationship and allowed for the eventual dissolution of Menominee land claims along with the tribe members' inevitable—to the coalition—intermarriage into white society. The terminationist coalition here made war on the internal frontiers of Indian self-determination, opening sovereign nations to literal and figurative marriage and the social and economic exploitation accompanying both.

Under Termination policy the national romance replaced its emphasis on bloodlines and kinship with the legally administered conversion of citizens. During the 1950s the state took on a therapeutic attitude toward Indian people: they would be converted to citizens through social psychology and political education. The "internal frontiers" here are no less racialized that those drawn on biological conceptions of race. Instead of operating through the exclusions of biology and reproduction, however, they emphasize culture and social standing. As Fixico (1986, 91) points out, "The real circumstances of terminating trust relations set the stage for scrutinizing the Indian ability to exchange traditional life for that of dominant middle class values." The coalition of state, federal, county, and university forces in this period authored a narrative of transformation. Under their scrutiny, Indians were to give up their national identity and, through the ministrations of the therapeutic state, become singular American citizens.

In their work on East Indian colonial history, Kumkum Sangari and Sudesh Vaid (1989, 6) describe policies closely parallel to those of termination and relocation in the United States: "Such ostensibly gender-neutral land settlements . . . , in fact, began a process of social restructuring which was simultaneously and necessarily a process of reconstituting patriarchies in every social strata [*sic*]." Termination and Relocation policies wrote Indians as the child brides of the state, emerging from the infancy of the trust relationship into citizenship and wifely maturity. These policies, ultimately designed to abolish the separate national and cultural status of Indian people, offered a citizenship that was specifically gendered and racialized.

The McCarran-Walter Act, by far the most important immigration legislation of the immediate postwar period, combined an anachronistic focus on "national origins" with a cold war discourse of national loyalty and potential subversion. I have already discussed the biologistic aspects of Nordic race theory, and their continuing influence through the cold war discourse of political and economic motivations for migration. These same biological discourses of race also provided the grounds for the coalition that challenged the basis of nationality quotas and immigration restriction throughout the 1950s and succeeding in overturning these policies with the Hart-Cellar Immigration Reform Act in 1965. Just as Termination policy moved away from a concern with bloodlines and physical reproduction toward a discourse of therapeutic social amelioration, immigration policy in this period also replaced the controversial idea of national origins with an emphasis on family reunification and the productive health of the nation.

A diverse coalition opposed the McCarran-Walter Act. African American organizations such as the National Association for the Advancement of Colored People (NAACP) contested its racialized basis. Civil rights groups were well aware that U.S. citizenship constituted a terrain of struggle, as Reverend William J. Harvey noted at the NAACP's forty-third convention in 1952: "We want you, our guests, to know that nearly every privilege of citizenship which we now enjoy has been fought for." The NAACP's yearly resolutions between 1952 and 1964 called for immigration reform and "the fair and equal treatment for all immigrants and prospective immigrants." In addition, because of the presence of Caribbean Americans in civil rights organizations as well as the influence of pan-African and anticolonial discourses in the black community, African American groups generally recognized the interdependence of Northern and Southern Hemispheres. In 1961, while Congress debated immigration reform, Representative Adam Clayton Powell Jr. presented a bill in the House calling for unlimited immigration from the British West Indies and the nascent West Indian federation (*NYT* 6 Jan. 1961, 10).

Ethnic organizations such as the Sons of Italy and the Anti-Defamation League of B'nai B'rith, as well as Christian organizations like the Church World Service, sought a more liberalized policy of admission for southern and eastern Europeans hardest hit by the aftermath of the war.[17] Because of the lobbying efforts of Italian organizations, for example, Columbus Day in East Coast cities was likely to occasion political rhetoric in support of immigration reform. In 1958 Governor Averil Harriman of New York used his Columbus Day address to support changing the racialized basis of the law, calling for a "new age of discovery" and progress in the United States based on "continuous infusion of new vigor and new ideas from other countries. . . . Italians and peoples from other countries of southern and eastern Europe have added enormously to our culture, our progress, our strength" (*NYT* 12 Oct. 1958, 44). Columbus Day speeches like this one wrote a narrative of ethnic assimilation onto the story of heroic national origins.

For ethnic associations, the romance of assimilation was key to their claims to citizenship for themselves and their friends and relatives in Europe. To write themselves into this narrative of assimilation, Jews and Italians emphasized their good citizenship and downplayed any potential rivalries for their loyalties to the nation. In a heated exchange with Representative Emmanuel Cellar at the 1956 Democratic Convention, Clarence L. Coleman, president of the American Council for Judaism, insisted that being Jewish was a religious rather than a national matter and that Jews had no extranational loyalties. He argued: "We regret the Zionist thesis that all of the Jewish faith by virtue of being Jews hold a common Jewish nationality" (*NYT* 8 Aug. 1956, 12).

Similarly, organizations such as the Sons of Italy argued for enlarging the quotas for their ethnic group rather than against the idea of national origins itself.[18] Claiming citizenship for themselves and potential citizenship for other immigrants, "ethnic" groups such as Jews and Italians in the immediate postwar period emphasized their assimilability; although they were temporarily allied with African American groups in achieving reform, their identifications were for the most part as "white ethnics" who wanted to allow their friends and relatives into the country.[19]

Finally, a coalition of eastern and midwestern members of Congress supported immigration reform. This coalition sought greater immigration, in the words of Senator Jacob Javitz (R-N.Y.), "not only in the name of humanity but in our own enlightened self-interest" (*NYT Magazine*, 8 July 1951, 8).[20] In contrast to the coalition that supported termination and immigration restriction in Congress, supporters of immigration reform saw postwar prosperity founded on increasing internationalization of both capital and labor. Javitz stressed the increased productivity that new laborers would bring to the country, as did John F. Kennedy's popular, posthumously released book *A Nation of Immigrants.*

Proterminationist members of Congress, who generally also favored immigration restriction, saw the sovereignty of the nation within its geographic borders as all-important. They sought to extend state hegemony over separately governed Indian land, creating a return to a heroic national economy. Immigration reformers such as John F. Kennedy and Herbert Lehman were more likely to see national progress wedded to the international expansion of markets and the ingenuity and hard work of immigrants. "Who can say how far ahead in science we would be today," asked Lehman in 1959, "if Congress had not created so many immigration barriers and kept out of our country so many individuals of ability and promise. The loss is not only in the scientific field but in the whole fabric of American life" (*NYT* 17 Mar. 1959, 37).

In the vision of immigration restrictionists, national interest lay in strictly policing both internal and external frontiers. A 1956 *New York Times* editorial worried that the days of the "golden door" for immigrants were over: "There are no new lands on which they might settle; no unpopulated prairies, no shores where orchards have never been planted" (10 Feb. 1956, 20). In 1959 a proposal was made in Congress that control over immigration be moved to the House Un-American Activities Committee (HUAC), so that potential threats to the national order might be nipped in the bud. Richard Arens, the director of HUAC, commented, "If the liberal groups succeed in the destruction of the immigration system, it will be the destruction of the first line of defense of this country" (*NYT* 19 Apr. 1957, 8).

The contradictions between the nation's ideological needs to maintain sovereignty by screening new immigrants and the internationalization of labor and capital in the postwar period were resolved domestically through discourses of social assimilation. Just as competence tests and immediate families proved to provide criteria too limited for judging individual Indians' readiness for "civilized" life, national-origins quotas were controversial as well as unrealistic in the light of the increasingly hemispheric economy of the Americas and the Caribbean in the postwar period. Cornelius and Montoya argue that traditional immigration restriction had been part of the pact between capital and organized labor since 1924. After World War II and the reorganization of capital and labor, unauthorized immigrant labor became particularly important, particularly in the Southwest (see Davis 1986).

Debates on immigration policy during the late 1950s and early 1960s focused on discourses of family and productivity to ensure national stability and allow new immigrants to provide the inexpensive labor needed for economic expansion. Immigration reform efforts consolidated around family reunification and domestic labor market needs, as well as continuing the cold war aim of providing refuge for persons fleeing persecution or disaster abroad. This new set of immigration restrictions was implemented in the Immigration and Nationality Amendments of 1965. The law specified these restrictions to apply to Eastern Hemisphere immigrants, whereas a general ceiling and a nation-by-nation quota remained in effect for Western Hemisphere immigrants until 1976, when they were included in general policy. The reforms of 1965 set a 120,000-person limit on Western Hemisphere immigration and a 170,000-person limit on immigration from the Eastern Hemisphere. For Western nations, a national quota of 20,000 each was established. This amplified by 100 percent the numbers of Caribbean people eligible to immigrate and, along with Great Britain's restrictions on immigration from former colonies in 1962, accounts for the drastic increase of immigration from the Caribbean during the late 1960s and 1970s.

In 1959 Senator John F. Kennedy proposed amending immigration policy by allowing unrestricted immigration to relatives of citizens and resident aliens. Family reunification as a central component of immigration policy would "make it easier for future immigrants to assimilate into the United States and eliminate much of the bitterness engendered by the present system" (*NYT* 3 Jan. 1956, 7). The discourse of family reunification attempted to counter fears that immigration could spiral out of control by naturalizing new arrivals through the auspices of extant family ties. As Jasso and Rosenzweig (1990, 425) point out, the assumption of family reunification policy is consonant with cold war policies that sought to screen out unsuitable immigrants: "If the characteristics of family members are similar, then given that priority in sponsorship is provided to naturalized immigrants, who presumably have had some success in the United States, the family preference system will select new immigrants who are also likely to succeed."

Like the War Brides Act, family reunification, a central component of immigration reforms from 1965 through the present, presumes that the family is a competent crucible for selecting likely citizens. Unlike the War Brides Act, however, family reunification is administered by the Immigration and Naturalization Service, drawing on a complicated set of laws governing relationships and their relative priorities for admission. As in Termination policy, the discourse of family value and home economics here stands in for a therapeutic state. Potential citizen-subjects are operated on under the auspices of this state.

The problem with family reunification as a reform of national-origins law is twofold. First, if preference is to be given to the family members of citizens or legal immigrants, family reunification will maintain an algebraic relationship to an immigrant population maintained by racialized national-origins laws. Jasso and Rosenzweig estimate that family reunification has been the central factor in legal immigration since 1965: fewer than 4 percent of immigrants since that date have entered under labor market categories, whereas 95 percent of people who qualify for admission for legal, permanent residence do so through the law favoring family reunification (1990, 425, 185). Second, family reunification as a policy necessarily favors a culturally specific notion of family relationships. Immigrants attempting to utilize family reunification policy to gain entrance into the United States must draw on a culturally acceptable model of kin relations (see Garrison and Weiss 1987). By 1988, for example, more than one-third of all adult immigrants who did not come under refugee/asylum status got visas through marriage (Jasso and Rosenzweig 1990, 185).[21]

The second component of the immigration reform that supplanted national origins was the discourse of "special skills" and "domestic labor market needs." This component of the law allowed preference to professionals and skilled workers who could find employers to vouch for their importance on the job. As Whitney Young observed in an *Amsterdam News* editorial, this idea of special skills "is likely again to discriminate in favor of the industrialized nations of Europe, while excluding those from Africa and Asia, which are not as highly developed" (3 Oct. 1964, 18).

Even though the particular provisions of immigration reform maintained a national romance of assimilation through the discourses of family and work, the 1965 amendments largely satisfied the coalition backing reform. Kennedy's *Nation of Immigrants,* itself a foundational fiction of the diverse nationalities that had come together to form the United States, was widely acclaimed as endorsing a more tolerant immigration policy. Praising the talents and hard work of America's immigrant stock, Kennedy celebrated the marriage of new blood into the family of the nation: "Somehow the difficult adjustments are made and people get down to earning a living, raising a family, and building a nation" (Kennedy 1964, 17).

Fictions of Empire: Toward Re-Vision

In the 1950s and 1960s Congress and the Bureau of Indian Affairs, in concert with social scientists and western business interests, installed policies that undermined Indian sovereignty and cultural self-determination in the name of epic narratives of democracy and progress. Immigration policy implemented a racially based national-origins quota system and used political loyalty tests to determine the eligibility of potential immigrants for the American way of life. State policy draws on and imposes the foundational fictions of national life: the termination and relocation policies of the 1950s used the epic of the national struggle for freedom to claim to "emancipate" Indians from "primitive" reservation conditions. Correspondingly, immigration policy invoked narratives of upward mobility and American love of freedom, screening immigrants on the basis of their ability to "assimilate" into the national community. At the same time, of course, "emancipating" Indians meant that their land would be open for development; "assimilating" new immigrants meant accepting those who were presumed to become a loyal citizens and a docile labor force.

Viewing state policy as a discourse allows for elaboration of the practices and politics of specific regimes. On the one hand, state policies construct disciplined populations. Both Indian and immigration policy in the post–World War II period extended an institutional gaze to marginalized populations, studying their preparedness for emancipation and assimilation. Indians and immigrants were carefully studied in this period so that their social lives, their very existence as subjects of the state and citizens of the nation, might be remapped. In this context social policy provides "a technique of power/knowledge that enabled administrators to manage their institutional populations by creating and exploiting a new kind of visibility" (Fraser 1989, 22).

Understanding state policy as a discursive field lets us use this field to articulate oppositional claims. If the state writes foundational fictions of the nation, it also provides an arena where these fictions may be edited, revised, or altogether rewritten by social movements and groups that do not have access to hegemonic power. Whereas Termination policies articulated a discourse of emancipation, Indian groups such as the National Congress of American Indians were able to use the contradictions in social policy to argue that true emancipation should mean not the end of the federal trust relationship and the Indians' relocation from their land to cities but rather broader access to their constitutional rights. Similarly, groups opposed to restrictive immigration policies drew on discourses generated by the civil rights movement that attempted to claim equal status under the Constitution for people of all races.

Although resistance to Termination and restrictive immigration policies were crucial to their subsequent reform, it is important to see that the kinds of reform available, authored through the racialized discourses of national citizenship, maintained continuities with the discriminatory policies of the immediate postwar period. Where the nation claims a subject in the form of a citizen, alternative imaginings of citizen status are crucial in undermining the totalizing claims of nationalist ideology. Instead of identifying with the national narrative of assimilation, new immigrants often think of themselves as citizens of more than one homeland; similarly, Indians in the 1950s and 1960s systematically refused to be "emancipated" into the mainstream of national life. Whenever the nation creates a foundational fiction, the result gives life to the discursive struggle to write alternative narratives.

Almost by definition, then, the narrative of the nation cannot recognize the dual identities maintained by groups of people whose historical experiences place them in positions where the claims of dominant foundational fictions are less convincing than those of alternative discourses of nation and community. The existence of citizens with cultural and political loyalties to more than one homeland challenges liberal ideas of what the state is, as well as its relationship to the nation. Assimilation, as Howard Winant (1990) points out, is part of a modernist framework for understanding social relations; equality and social harmony are presumed to come about as various classes, races, and ethnicities grow to be alike under the generalizing rubric of the nation. Emancipation is part of the enlightenment project that sought to discipline various ethnic, class, and regional factors into national harmony through education and the gradual absorption of difference (Boyarin 1992).

Citizenship became a crucial site of political struggle in the 1950s and 1960s.

African Americans drew on the discourse of national consolidation to claim the equality promised to them as citizens under the Thirteenth Amendment and reaffirmed by Truman's desegregation of American troops with Executive Order 8801 in 1948. The civil rights movement's achievement in asserting African American claims to citizenship and equality rearranged the field in which foundational fictions of the nation could be written. Similarly, the celebration of Indian veterans as American heroes changed the ability of Indian political organizations such as the NCAI to make claims in nationalist discourse. At the same time, decolonizing African and Caribbean countries created newly conscious citizens who had struggled for their identities; immigrants from these countries were unlikely to easily accept melting pot paradigms of assimilation and national unity. The civil rights movement, and the struggles of Indians and immigrants in this period, accepted the ideological claims of cold war egalitarianism at the same time that it used these claims to pressure the state for additional rights. This refusal to let the state manage the terms of national ideology set up a challenge to primary U.S. foundational fictions in this period.

Immigration and federal Indian policy were and are part of a complex system of both global and hemispheric domination. Of necessity, the struggle to reform repressive policies takes place in a national arena. The contradiction here is that the factors that make immigration such a crucial source of cheap labor, as well as the reasons that Indian lands are perennially sought by western land and mineral developers, are part of much larger, more global processes. The national results of these processes are still underway, as many states consider legislation like California's Proposition 187, the Save Our State Initiative in Florida, or the House "Responsibility" Bill (2202); the U.S. Senate passed a restrictive immigration bill, which was signed into law in 1996. Because there is no protection for immigrants based on their human rights, rather than their specific rights under foundational fictions of national life, both legal and illegal immigrants continue to be at risk from increasing attacks. Similarly, the national movement toward antifederalism and block grants to the states threatens to undermine the limited sovereignty that native peoples have achieved within the confines of the United States. Until we have a new story, one that recognizes that multiple experiences of citizenship and denizenship are part of international capitalist hegemony, we will be repeatedly confronted by the dazzling solidity of colonialist fictions.

Notes

This essay has benefited from the intelligent readings and generous comments of Joe Austin, C. Richard King, George Lipsitz, and Steve Ziliak. My thanks to them. A version of it will appear in *CALLING HOME: Im/Migration, Race, and Popular Memory in Car-*

ibbean Brooklyn and Native American Minneapolis, 1945–1992 (University of California Press, forthcoming).

1. For a discussion of the importance of Bandung in both international and U.S. domestic context, see Plummer 1996, 247–54.

2. Jean O'Brien-Kehoe noticed the parallel between termination- and allotment-era rhetoric; I am indebted to her insight on this matter.

3. I am using *soul* here in the sense used by Michel Foucault (1979, 5): "A real subjection is born mechanically from a fictitious relation. So it is not necessary to use force to constrain the convict to good behaviour, the madman to calm, the worker to work, the schoolboy to application, the patient to the observation of the regulations."

4. These sources will be cited parenthetically in the text as follows: *Congressional Record* (*CR*), the *New York Times* (*NYT*), and the *National Congress of American Indians Bulletin* (*NCAI*).

5. Mikhail Bakhtin writes about this past: "The epic past, walled off from all subsequent times by an impenetrable boundary, is preserved and revealed only in the form of national tradition. . . . By its very nature the epic world of the absolute past is inaccessible to personal experience, and does not permit an individual, personal point of view or evaluation" (1981, 17). The idea here is that those who do not participate in authoring the "foundational fictions" of national life cannot revise them to fit their experiences; there are no footnotes to this official account.

6. Public Law 40 was passed in April 1947 to provide emergency labor through December of the same year. With pressure from western agricultural interests, as well as State Department intervention, an accord was arranged with the Mexican government to continue the importation of labor into the United States; the Bracero Program continued until 1964.

7. Rich Kees suggests that the concern over "citizenship" during the 1950s focused on the issue of state citizenship rather than that of national citizenship (personal communication, Apr. 1993). It is true that Indians were not considered to be citizens of the states in which they lived because of the federal trust relationship. In New Mexico and Arizona this was used to make it difficult for Indians to vote. As the debate about Termination policy was disseminated through Congress and the press, however, references to state and national citizenship were dropped. Most Americans, including policymakers, considered the idea of "Indian emancipation" to represent access to citizenship in the nation.

8. See Ann Stoler 1992 for a discussion of marriage as it functions in a multiracial colonial context to create a boundary for national inclusion and exclusion. In addition, the excellent work of the Women, Immigration, and Nationality Group (WINGS) has pointed to the connections between race, gender, and immigration policy; see Bhaba, Klug, and Shutter 1985.

9. Husbands were barred from unrestricted immigration until 1952; parents, until 1965 (Jasso and Rosenzweig 1990, 412).

10. Cultural anxiety over the role of Indian men as warriors has been played out in popular narratives such as the Western since the inception of the film industry in the 1910s, the anxiety being portrayed with increased vigour during the Termination policy period. Anthropological studies echoed this anxiety, observing that reservation Indians were "warriors without battles."

11. The operating metaphor, with its particularly Foucauldian and vampiric overtones, is lifted from Zipes 1991.

12. The components of the McCarran-Walter Act that remain on the books have been used against American citizens such as the poet Margaret Randall, as well as against gay

and lesbian activists. In addition, such controversial nonnational artists as the South African performers Mahlathini and the Mahotella Queens, the Haitian band Boukman Eksperyans, and the Scottish pop band Big Country have encountered difficulty entering the country under these regulations.

13. The salient exception here, of course, is Cuba. Cuban refugees range from appearing "white" to "black" to people in the United States and have generally been given more and less warm receptions on our shores accordingly.

14. "Senator James O. Eastland contended today that the relaxation of refugee immigration requirements would flood the United States with 'criminals and communist agents'" (*NYT* 17 Sept. 1955, 10).

15. A *New York Times* editorial, indicative of the lack of support for Termination policies among eastern Democrats, criticized McKay's interpretation of the constitution in January 1956: "The circumstance in which our tribal Indian populations find themselves are obviously different from those of any other American citizen, and we therefore think that the Interior Department is straining a point in stating that the principle of Indian consent 'has most serious constitutional implications'" (26).

16. Ames and Fisher, the authors of the quoted article, were both University of Wisconsin faculty members (in sociology and anthropology, respectively) who worked on the University Committee and Wisconsin Legislative Council for Menominee Indian Study and the Governance Committee on Human Rights. This coalition attempted first to study the conditions for termination and then to implement it. The article is included in the folders of *The Menominee News,* a reservation-based BIA paper, collected in the State Historical Society of Wisconsin in Madison.

17. Among the Jewish components of this alliance were the American Jewish Committee, the Anti-Defamation League, the Jewish War Veterans of the USA, the National Commission on Religion Advisory Council, the National Council of Jewish Women, the Synagogue Council of America, the Union of American Hebrew Congregations, and the United Service for New Americans. In addition, leaders of local Jewish communities often took part in political work as it concerned local elections.

The American Committee for Special Migration was a coalition of thirty-five groups, including the Church World Service and the National Lutheran Council. Other groups included the Catholic Resettlement Commission, the International Longshoremen's and Warehousemen's Union, the American Committee to Aid Homeless Armenians, and the American Committee on Italian Immigrants.

18. Immigration History Research Center, Minneapolis, Minn., OSIA News Office, Box 2, Folder 9. This research is the work of Lee Bernstein, who generously brought it to my attention.

19. Because the timing of the immigration reform coalition coincides with that of other civil rights alliances between African American and "white ethnic" groups—Jewish-Americans in particular—this is a point that calls for further research. To what extent were Jewish efforts against national-origins quotas in line with the broader antiracist agendas of the NAACP? I suspect that this was a cause for division and debate within the Jewish community. A progressive interpretation would see the national-origins quotas as posing a racialized threat to both Jewish and African American communities. This further research project was suggested to me in a conversation with George Lipsitz.

20. Other congressmen who supported immigration reform included Philip Hart (D-Mich.), Kenneth Keating (R-N.Y.), Jacob Javits (R-N.Y.), Frank Clark (D-Pa.), Richard Neuberger (D-Ore.), Hubert Humphrey (D-Minn.), Patrick McNamara (D-Mich.), Herbert Lehman (D-N.Y.), and Emmanuel Cellar (D-N.Y.).

21. Current family sponsored preferences are ranked as follows: unmarried sons and daughters of U.S. citizens and their children; spouses and children of alien residents and unmarried sons and daughters of alien residents, twenty-one years of age or older; married sons and daughters of U.S. citizens; their spouses and children (*An Immigrant Nation: United States Regulation of Immigration, 1798–1991* [Washington, D.C.: U.S. Department of Justice, Immigration and Naturalization Service, 1991], appendix A). At the time of this writing (March 1997), these categories were being challenged by a bill proposing to restrict family preferences to a much greater degree.

Works Cited

Ames, David, and Burton R. Fisher. 1954. "The Menominee Termination Crisis: Barriers in the Way of a Rapid Cultural Transition." *Human Organization* 18, no. 3:105.

Bakhtin, Mikhail. 1981. *The Dialogic Imagination: Four Essays.* Trans. Michael Holquist. Austin: University of Texas Press.

Bhaba, Jacqueline, Francesca Klug, and Sue Shutter, eds. 1985. *Worlds Apart: Women under Immigration and Nationality Law.* London: Pluto.

Boyarin, Jonathan. 1992. *Storm from Paradise: The Politics of Jewish Memory.* Minneapolis: University of Minnesota Press.

Calavita, Kitty. 1992. *Inside the State: The Bracero Program, Immigration, and the INS.* New York: Routledge.

Churchill, Ward. 1992. *Fantasies of the Master Race: Literature, Cinema, and the Colonization of American Indians.* Ed. Annette Jaimes. Monroe, Me.: Common Courage.

Davis, Mike. 1986. *Prisoners of the American Dream.* London: Verso.

Deloria, Vine, and Clifford Lytle. 1984. *The Nations Within: The Past and Future of Indian Sovereignty.* New York: Pantheon.

Escobar, Arturo. 1988. "Power and Visibility: Development and the Invention and Management of the Third World." *Cultural Anthropology* 3, no. 4: 428–43.

Fixico, Donald. 1986. *Termination and Relocation: Federal Indian Policy, 1945–1960.* Albuquerque: University of New Mexico Press.

Foucault, Michel. 1979. *Discipline and Punish: The Birth of the Prison.* Trans. Alan Sheridan. New York: Vintage Books.

Fraser, Nancy. 1989. *Unruly Practices: Power, Discourse, and Gender in Contemporary Social Theory.* Minneapolis: University of Minnesota Press.

Garrison, Vivian, and Carol Weiss. 1987. "Dominican Family Networks and United States Immigration Policy: A Case Study." In *Caribbean Life in New York City,* ed. Constance Sutton and Elsa Chaney, 235–55. New York: Center for Migration Studies.

Goldberg, David Theo. 1993. *Racist Culture: Philosophy and the Politics of Meaning.* Cambridge, Mass.: Blackwell.

Jasso, Guillermina, and Mark R. Rosenzweig. 1990. *The New Chosen People: Immigrants in the United States.* New York: Sage.

Kapferer, Bruce. 1988. *Legends of People, Myths of State: Violence, Intolerance, and Political Culture in Sri Lanka and Australia.* Washington, D.C.: Smithsonian Institution Press.

Kennedy, John F. 1964. *A Nation of Immigrants.* New York: Harper and Row.

May, Elaine Tyler. 1988. *Homeward Bound: American Families in the Cold War Era.* New York: Basic Books.

Nash, Gerald. 1990. *World War II and the West: Reshaping the Economy.* Lincoln: University of Nebraska Press.

Plummer, Brenda Gayle. 1996. *Rising Wind: Black Americans and U.S. Foreign Affairs, 1935–1960*. Chapel Hill: University of North Carolina Press.

Portes, Alexandro. 1978. "Migration and Underdevelopment." *Latin American Immigration Project Occasional Papers,* February.

Reimers, David. 1985. *Still the Golden Door: The Third World Comes to America.* New York: Columbia University Press.

Sangari, Kumkum, and Sudesh Vaid, eds. 1989. "Introduction." *Recasting Women: Essays in Colonial History.* New Delhi: Kali for Women.

Sollors, Werner. 1986. *Beyond Ethnicity: Consent and Descent in American Culture.* New York: Oxford University Press.

Sommer, Doris. 1990. "Irresistible Romance: The Foundational Fictions of Latin America." In *Nation and Narration,* ed. Homi Bhaba, 71–98. London: Routledge.

Stoler, Ann. 1992. "Sexual Affronts and Racial Frontiers: National Identities, 'Mixed Bloods,' and the Cultural Genealogies of Europeans in Colonial Southeast Asia." *Working Papers of the History and Society Program, University of Minnesota* 34, no. 3.

———. 1996. *Race and the Education of Desire.* Durham, N.C.: Duke University Press.

Winant, Howard. 1990. "Postmodern Racial Politics in the United States: Difference and Inequality." *Socialist Review* 20, no. 1:121–47.

Zipes, Jack. 1991. *The Operated Jew: Two Tales of Anti-Semitism.* New York: Routledge.

6 On the Road with Chrysler: From Nation to Virtual Empire

Elena Glasberg

In a well-known 1950s television ad, Dinah Shore invited American TV viewers to "see the USA in your Chevrolet," thereby linking the post–World War II interstate highway system, Fordist automobile production, and nationalist discourses to a specifically American landscape. Aligning individual, nation, and land as integral features of a naturalized national consumer order, this Chevrolet ad demonstrated what advertising historian Roland Marchand (1985) calls the marketing of the American Dream in the postwar era. Such a strategy continued to dominate automobile advertising throughout the 1970s and 1980s, even as U.S. automakers began moving their production sites overseas to take advantage of lower labor costs and to avoid expensive negotiations with powerful unions. Not until the 1990s did the automobile industry's advertising campaigns hail its audience from sites completely divorced from U.S.-based images. In a widely circulated 1994 ad, for instance, Chrysler Corporation views Antarctica through the "lens" of the ozone hole, which opens down onto a South Pole inhabited solely by plaintive and anthropomorphic penguins. The captions reads: "The ozone layer has protected us for 1.5 billion years. It's time we returned the favor." The company further promises to "solve a problem that's been hanging over all our heads." Fixing its attention on the South Pole, the ad markets a global postnational consciousness, for Antarctica is not only home to the hole in the ozone layer but also the only continent still undivided into nations.

Chrysler's use of Antarctica is a telling instance of the way nationalist imaginaries are being refigured by and through the rise of transnational corporations (TNCs), whose modes of operation are not settled once and for all in particular nations or locations but rather, like weather and climate conditions, constellate and move across borders. Neither permanent nor ephemeral, neither wholly unattached to national formations nor entirely subject to nations, transnational corporate modes of production both respond to and shape economic and cultural resources "in situ," so to speak, not in fixed places. No longer does "buy American" strike consumers as a necessary and radical act for claiming U.S. world power by consolidating U.S. workers and consumption; in fact, the slogan has been rendered materially incoherent by automobile production practices such as subcontracting for parts and by foreign factories that obscure the relation between national labor and national brand. As both a factor and a consequence of such practices, the auto industry in particular and the business and consumer worlds in general have become more comfortable with the cachet of globalism. Only labor, intellectuals, and environmentalists seem particularly alarmed by the transformations of economy and culture inherent in transnational ties, mobility, and profit potential.

Much of the newfound comfort with the transnational can be attributed to its everyday presence in information circuits and recent advertising campaigns that link televisual, print, and electronic modes of representation. As the "information highway" metaphorically and materially merges the old U.S. interstate of the postwar era with the global cybersphere, U.S. TNCs, such as Chrysler, boldly market the international nature of production. Such marketing strategies seek to resolve tensions between the nation and the TNC within the larger context of the globalization of commodity culture. In its focus on the nonnational and exotic Antarctic, the Chrysler ad stages its investment in a postnational imaginary by highlighting the positive environmentalism of postindustrial production. By reading the Chrysler ad as evidence of the representational shift toward global consciousness as a marketable strategy, this essay works through the currently problematic terms *global, postcolonial,* and *transnational* as they converge in "American studies." In particular, I use Chrysler to explore how the unprecedented global arrangements, both material and symbolic, of the TNC have produced a "virtual empire" of value and meaning unavailable and perhaps unthinkable under the rule of nation. It is this virtual empire that replaces the colony as the material location for imperial accumulation, posting the nation and ensuring the ultimate survival of the TNC to rescue the globe, as the ad promises, "from a problem hanging over all our heads."

Postings of American Studies

At the same time that Dinah Shore was enjoining a U.S. consumer public to "see" the nation as a coproduction of industrialization and national identification, academicians were putting the finishing touches on a field appropriate to the new postwar power of that United States: American studies. In its disciplinary and institutional emergence in the American Studies Association, American studies heralded the nationalist ideologies of the postwar years, approaching the nation as an object of study seemingly natural in its exceptionalism. The doctrine of the "separate creation" of American culture, its individuality, and isolation—evident in such founding documents of American studies criticism as R. W. B. Lewis's *American Adam* (1955) and Perry Miller's *Errand into the Wilderness* (1956) and *Nature's Nation* (1963)— emerged paradoxically in the context of a United States increasingly unable to disengage from the rest of the globe. Ignoring or otherwise mitigating the evidence of immigration flows from Europe, the urbanizing of African American migrations, and the presence of native inhabitants, scholars of the master narrative of American identity codified a continental national cultural origin that defied the histories of specific populations, the acquisition of national territories, and the ongoing processes of nation formation. Undoing this legacy of exceptionalism and relinking the United States to global history has been the disciplinary imperative of American studies for the past decade.

In questioning the foundational narratives of U.S. nationality, American studies scholars have simultaneously reexamined U.S. imperial history and exposed the assumptions and motives of the field or interdiscipline itself. "New Americanists," named after the title of the Duke University Press series edited by Donald Pease, work to take apart and reassemble the naturalized spatial, historical, and material aspects of the Americanist national imaginary. Pease cites the globalization of democracy as one of the impulses fueling the New Americanist project. As he explains, the globalization of democracy has created new alliances and higher levels of expectations for international control of overly aggressive national interest. The new peacetime alliances and relative security of the post–cold war era developed parallel to a multicultural analysis of power that, in Pease's words, would "no longer authorize belief in an Americanness that somehow contained a plurality it also transcended" (1994, vii). Thus New Americanist critiques refuse the grand narratives of assimilation, of universal citizenship and equality, and of individual or collective American identity.

Accordingly, "postnational studies," another Pease project related to that of the New Americanists, concerns itself with unearthing a specifically imperial U.S. history. Much of the work collected in the highly influential anthology *Cultures of United States Imperialism* (1993), coedited by Pease and Amy Kaplan, contributes to the debate over the applicability to the United States of critical concepts that developed within European studies, especially postcolonialism. As Kaplan writes, "The history of American imperialism strains the definition of the postcolonial, which implies a temporal development (from 'colonial' to 'post') that relies heavily on the spatial coordinates of European empires, in their formal acquisition of territories and the subsequent history of decolonization and national independence" (1993, 17). To be critically useful, the U.S. postcolonial must take on a history and a mapped shape different from those of the European model. But what would that shape be? One refinement of the postcolonial model, "internal colonization," was developed within a Chicano/a studies paradigm to reference the internal incoherence of any monolithic account of the United States. This model has come under critique by scholars who argue that the notion of internal colonization reinstates the legitimacy of the U.S. national borders it seeks to explode by affirming a stable inside/outside binary opposition. As Kaplan puts it, to link America "as a colony and an empire to the imperial enterprises of other nations in a global system . . . without either collapsing them into European models or propagating a new model of American exceptionalism" (1993, 18), it is important to think of the global as a shift in material economic and cultural conditions of production that cannot be properly understood in terms of any U.S.-centered analysis. Even the promising concept of the postimperial cannot be extended to the United States or to the contemporary period, since the concept of nation has been superseded not simply by the global but by a more precisely defined aspect of the global: the transnationalization of capital.

One of the foremost recent critics to discuss the influence of the transnationalization of capital on U.S. global cultural and political formations is Masao Miyoshi. Although not set in the context of American studies, Miyoshi's analysis begins and ends with a critique of the academic "preoccupation" with the postcolonial, which he says "looks suspiciously like another alibi to conceal the actuality of global politics" in which "colonialism is even more active now in the form of transnational corporatism" (1993, 728). For Miyoshi, the proliferation of transnational corporate operations does not necessarily indicate a break from the postcolonial condition of cultural and economic production. Rather, the postcolonial and the transnational are phases of a historical development of capital differentiated only in the mode of their capital and social association. Whereas the colony is tied to the nation-state, the locations (factories, zones, and material and symbolic spaces) produced by TNCs "no longer wholly depend on the nation-state of their origin for protection and facilitation" (1993, 732). Transnational production practices move factories to sites in various parts of the globe based on factors such as the availability of natural resources, the attractiveness of taxation policies and infrastructures, and the cost and skill level of labor. In doing so, TNCs associate with but do not incorporate territories, governments, or populations, and in this they demonstrate Miyoshi's claim that the transnational is a neocolonial, not postcolonial, form extending to various locations the process of extracting value for the benefit of sites disassociated from and often ultimately unaccountable to these new colonies. The transnationalization of capital can thus be understood as a necessary reformulation of bourgeois culture itself, which to follow the postcolonialist critic Ranajit Guha (1989, 277), has "hit" its limit in empire. That is, colonialist expansion, while seeming to reproduce the bourgeois center to its peripheries, destabilizes the very foundations of its reproductive practice. Transnationalism thus rescues the imperial project in the face of its internal contradictions.

Miyoshi's demonstration of the postcolonial model's inapplicability to transnational formations offers a way to read the reframing of the global picture in the image of Antarctica presented by Chrysler. If the image is read as depicting Antarctica as a territory to be colonized in some way by imperial powers, specifically national ones, or as a territory newly brought into view under the aegis of an established imperial power, we have not understood the contradictions and complicities between transnational virtual empires and national-colonialist formations. In other words, the image cannot be read as postcolonial precisely because it destabilizes the temporal-spatial underpinnings of the postcolonial by offering us not a colony but a virtual empire of mobile locations. Virtual Antarctica is a non- or extra-place that invokes the icy limits of the reproduction of capital as colonial accumulation while bringing into crisis the epistemological frame of the national imaginary itself.

This form of virtual Antarctica has been made available, if not activated, by the discourse of terrestrial mapping since the invention of the globe. It is, however, Chrysler's version of Antarctica as virtual empire—that representational place of industry and profit neither national nor material—that demands attention. Chrysler's claim on the virtual territory is not exactly that of a colonizer or nation; its globalization strategy is not precisely American in logic, for it waves no flag and makes no other overt national references.

But it is post-American; it is postnational; and in the fantasy of agentless vision from a location detached from the globe itself, it is postindustrial. Given the ad's universalizing and corporatizing strategies, how can American studies methodologies operate to read the ad as not Americanizing, or as resisting the very corporatization of "America" in which American studies is itself implicated? How can American studies methodologies distinguish their own corporatizing logic from that of the TNCs?

One way, it seems to me, is to follow Miyoshi's lead. He suggests that TNCs need to be investigated as key operators in the fundamental realignment of capital flows and cultural and geographical boundaries in which nation-states seem to recede from power even while retaining a nostalgic appeal on the level of representation to their populations. The TNCs operate as the mobile nodes of a new style of colonialism no longer formed on a center-periphery model. Not only are TNCs the agents of capitalization, international association, and political and economic formations unimaginable under nationalist enterprise, but their activities create new kinds of spatial relations for capitalization and new images for both production and consumption. They are crucial points of investigation for a postnational American studies or a transnational U.S. studies. To investigate further the TNC's new postnational horizon, however, we must cruise in a vehicle quite different from the one Dinah had in mind. This car has no doors, no seats, and no windshield, but it is definitely going to take us places—eventually to Antarctica, a place that has historically not registered as a place and thus occupies, so to speak, a problematic position under the rubric of nationality.

On the Road with Chrysler

This new vehicle is the PC, or home computer, and the new road is the much-touted "information highway," the "Web," or "cyberspace," all designations for the electronic transnational sphere of communication and capital operation, which is our nonterritorial "antidestination." Situated on the worldwide electronic web, Web sites are not immediately accessed through national localities nor are they locatable as national sites. The user of Chrysler's Web page "clicks" on icons representing an array of products, services, and places associated with Chrysler to arrive at destinations organized through Chrysler. Through the now familiar transnational operations of the Internet, Chrysler represents itself as both national in origin (you can read that the company has headquarters in Auburn, Mich.) and as originless, just one location, one connection point, on the Web. This indicates the power of transnational capitalization as it shifts from global to local or national significations to create new markets by unmooring consumers from their own national constraints. The creation within this "transnational web" of a transnational or postnational consumer is simply good business, with Chrysler exploiting the instabilities between nation and transnational association by involuting globe and nation.

The Web site's home page presents the viewer with a quaint automobile front grille, an association of the most national-historical-local kind for Chrysler as automaker. In its virtual reproduction, however, the Fordist auto-body (like the nation it represents) is fragmented and reassembled within a network of related icons: the rugged stick shift, the U.S. flag, a set of car keys, a dashboard radio dial, a rudimentary mechanical engine, and a miniaturized globe. These assembled fragments—the identifiably American retro style and the computerized, modern, and global images—are smoothly linked within the associational net created by Chrysler's cybermechanical "reassembly line." In this way the Web page becomes a kind of post-post-Fordist interactive factory in which users produce their own associations for Chrysler in and among its many locations. The user is instructed that this site is "about Great Cars . . . and how we build them. It's about people and passion. Resources and resourcefulness. It's about us, and about you. Now go discover." What the unspecified "you" might discover is the transnational mobility offered by buying and selling, even as the "you" of the consumer and the "us" of the corporation remain unclear in terms of material or local specification. The formerly U.S.-specific image of Chrysler Corporation has exploded or morphed into a commodity service hub ready to connect any consumer to dealers and sites all over the world.

The user accesses Chrysler's international links by clicking on the small globe icon arrayed among exploded engine parts. Placed among the network of accessories associated within the national/autobody, the icon functions to internalize or colonize the external territoriality of the globe. In other words, Chrysler's Web page inverts the traditional inside/outside relations of the local/global, making the "global" icon an aspect of the "local" Web page. When users click on the globe icon, they are presented with another screen whose heading reads: "Who sells CHEROKEES in Australia?" This iconic display also redirects the relation between nation and globe, but this time in an opposite fashion. Below the caption is a flag-shaped rectangular grid formed by the assembled individual flags of a variety of nations, except for the United States. The Web site thus takes an internally colonized symbolic and exports it to a new territorial site; in the process, the expropriated trademark, Cherokee, exemplifies both the contradictory arrangements available through the transnational and the political stakes of recognizing such global mobilities. Chrysler thus simultaneously draws on its value as a historically recognizable U.S. corporation associated with specifically U.S. products, peoples (however disfranchised), and practices while offering consumers links and access to its operations over the globe, beyond the conceptual and material limits of the United States. Out of sight of transnationalism's impact on trade deficits and job loss, Chrysler promotes a consumer-driven benevolent virtual empire of power that leaves unquestioned (though entirely fictional) the protean priority of the United States in the global network.

Chrysler represents its interests as operating simultaneously on three levels: as separate from, central to, and coterminous with the interests of nation, individual, environment, and globe. This transnational net of associations in which nation, corporation, consumer, citizen, and natural environment (globe) have been assembled, disassembled, and reassembled through the representations of the Web sites and the activity of clicking on icons indicates the powerful realignments of affiliations of feeling, identity, and capital that transnational capital offers. Under the cybernetic unification offered by the TNC, the globe is no longer broken up into nations, colonies, or even geographically distinct continents. Nevertheless, the reconstitution offered by the TNC is not a mere reassembly of already identifiable, unitary, and unchanging parts. The globe as factory of the future has gone beyond interchangeable parts. The parts themselves—populations, nations, places, products, the globe—are subject to change; they themselves hold little integrity. Rather, their meaning is constituted in the forms of their relations. The TNC, therefore, is not so much an always identifiable controlling entity but rather a node and mode of connection that in its own mobility and mutability provides the grammar of a "new world order," one in which the TNC promises a cure for the failures of industrialization. In this, Chrysler demonstrates the creation of a new transnational consumer who will not be afraid of the foreign but instead will see him- or herself as implicated in and excited by the consumer possibilities of the Cherokee in an Australian utopia, however it might serve to continue exploitive arrangements. Chrysler is working to create a transnational representational economy where nation has not wholly given way but is differently positioned to take advantage of new possibilities of profit, new markets, and new places hitherto unattainable through national or international modes of production.

Rescuing the End of the Earth

One of the most useful strategies of the TNCs in their efforts to find new markets and to integrate and reorient existing ones is to marshal consumers under a sufficiently global purpose. To this end the problem of global environmental degradation serves well: a global problem demands a global actor, and the TNC is well invested in taking up the global position vacated by the fall of national superpowers. But how can the TNC dare be so cheerful and optimistic about what looks like the end of the earth? In part, it does so because that ending enables a revamped consumer protectionism that shifts the power of oversight and perpetuity from the state to the TNC itself. It is thus no surprise that Chrysler has been especially drawn to the environmental trope. In fact, the Antarctic ad is part of a larger environmentally focused Chrysler campaign that ran nationally in 1994–95 in magazines such as *National Geographic, Time,* and *Newsweek.* All the ads share a similar format, with a large color image of a natural phenomenon or animals and accompanying public-service-style text touting one of Chrysler's environmentally friendly policies; none depicts humans, buildings, or machines. In one ad, armlike extremities (flippers, tails, trunks) of exotic animals from across the ecosystems join in a circle as if in preparation for a team cheer. In the good fight for the preservation of the natural world, Chrysler acts here as the inaccessible agency offering a helping "hand" to endangered species. Chrysler's projection of its internationalizing prowess is imaged through the seemingly universal aegis of the natural world, whose anthropomorphized concerns most clearly cross national borders by inviting global claims.

For my purposes, of course, the ad that focuses on the globe seen from space offers the most striking enactment of Chrysler's transnational pursuit. As I suggested at the outset, there is something deeply significant about Chrysler's appeal to global consciousness via an image of the environmental degradation of Antarctica. When I say that Antarctica has been unrepresentable, I am indexing a brief but distinct history of visual illegibility that is best epitomized by the images that accompany the so-called discovery of the South Pole in 1912. Roald Amundsen of Norway and Sir Robert Scott of Britain each raced in nationalistic frenzy to become the first to claim the South Pole for his nation, and Amundsen won. Scott came in second, and then he and his team froze to death on their way back to base. Both parties, however, took photos to commemorate their achievements. What the rest of the world had to trust as proof that men had reached the South Pole were images that looked as if they could have been taken in a clever photographer's studio. Against an undistinguished dirty white background stand a few men, their solemn, smudged faces nearly unrecognizable beneath heavy gear. No sense of foreground, background, season, or time can be adduced from the "realistic" photographic representation. Antarctica resists realist representation even as its terrain has become, with the introduction of airplane overflights in the 1920s and satellite and robotic technologies in later decades, the locus for the development of visual knowledge based on replications and enhancements of the human eye. In this regard, much of the current critical attention to the human body's "posting" in representational practices—the rise, that is, of the "virtual" as an arena of commerce and production—might be traced to certain technological changes wrought by the twentieth-century development of private, military, and scientific exploration of Antarctica, among other places, such undertakings being precursors to the contemporary aerospace conglomerates such as Chrysler. The disembodied, antirealistic view from outer space—or beyond the limits of the globe—is technologically, historically, and symbolically central to the development of the TNC's representational practices.

Both imaginative and scientific discourses have linked Antarctica and outer space. With no indigenous population or habitable landmass, Antarctica defies the reigning logic of nation: its territory is not yet divisible into nations, and it has no human culture to register it as a place. Even the cute penguins of the Chrysler image in reality live on the peninsula, well off the center of the continent. Contrary to the ad's jaunty picture, the bulk of the continent is a frozen desert lacking free-flowing water. Adventurers and sports people have trekked, skied, and sledded across the continent, always to return to their point of origin. Although carefully monitored scientific settlements have more recently enabled people to live in Antarctica, no individual or group can consider it home. To borrow the language of early postcolonial discourse, the Antarctic is radically "other" in relation not just to Western civilization but to the entire human-centered earth. Since 1959 an international organization of states called the Antarctic Treaty System (ATS), composed originally of twelve imperial and industrial nations including the United States, has legislated access and use of the region. This law regime was reratified in 1993 and specifies that for the next fifty years the now twenty-one consulting nations agree that Antarctica will remain a designated international science zone, free of nuclear or mining development and exempt from all military use (Beck 1986; Joyner and Theis 1997; Klotz 1990; Peterson 1988; Sahurie 1992).

Despite the utopianism of the concept of a "frozen laboratory" for science, the associations conjured by the Antarctic congeal more often in dystopia. As a symbolic and material image of the "end of the earth," Antarctica certainly works as a focus of environmental drama. Each week, it seems, the *New York Times* reports the latest oil spill, mass bio death, and of course, widening of the ozone hole. Nothing degrades in the Antarctic. Every footprint marring the permafrost—from those left by dinosaurs roaming a once-tropical southern landmass to explorers and now the latest tourists—testifies to the incompatibility of human and Antarctic time and place. Chrysler's advertisement for the continent plays off this incompatibility by, on one hand, inserting Antarctica into public consciousness as potential resource and, on the other hand, promoting the power of TNC capital to incorporate the marginal, to recuperate the wasted, and to heal the damage begun by formerly national-based industrialism. Chrysler's map of the south recenters the globe around Antarctica, populates (with animals) the uninhabitable, and projects conventional life onto the radically other. In short, the ad successfully absorbs Antarctica into the global economy as preserve and as territory—and of course as material place in need of the kind of capital and reform that only the TNC can provide.

In troping the posthuman exploration image of the globe seen from the comforting distance of space, the ad gives readers a historyless globalism: "The Ozone layer has protected us for 1.5 billion years. It's time we returned the favor." Just as Benedict Anderson (1982) writes that nations must justify themselves as ancient, Chrysler too imagines this newest continental territory as ancient—1.5 billion years ancient. In the same way that the narrative of the discovery of America by Amerigo Vespucci, Christopher Columbus, or even Pacific Islanders reinforces the naturalness of America as a place and a nation, we find that Antarctica has always been there, waiting for Chrysler to represent it. By narrativizing the history of place that has led to this moment of mediated representation, Chrysler creates Antarctica as the newest global entity with a recognizable history that, though suppressed, seems to require for its fulfillment only the simple reciprocity of a business deal.

Nonetheless, this transnational representational regime, smooth as its appeal may be, does not entirely avoid contradiction. A TNC symbolic is just as fictional as a national symbolic. Even within the TNC network of the ad, nation intervenes: Chrysler, the ozone-destroying avatar of Fordist production, comes to the rescue of its own creation of Antarctica as an otherworldly, nonnationalized, and nonindustrialized place through its zealous compliance with "government guidelines" on the atmospheric pollutants known as CFCs (chlorofluorocarbons). In the first place, however, nonaligned scientists consider the government guidelines insufficient. Not only is the logic of Chrysler's appeal faulty, but the rescue is a sham, for the TNC rescues us from a problem it has produced, thereby securing the inevitability and necessity of its interventions. In addition, the simple business deal proposed by the ad, a deal that enlists the reader's help in the rescue of the continent, has an even more contradictory reference: the 1982 Chrysler "bailout." At one point in its transition from national industry to transnational and diversified entity, Chrysler, a sick corporation, needed the nation's help in the form of government-guaranteed loans; presumably, through the promise of association with Chrysler's powerful transnationality—which paradoxically figures as a national reinvigoration—the nation has been repaid.

Chrysler thus produces both problem and cure, along with the place on which it stages its rescue drama. Chrysler's vision of Antarctica as the last place on earth is also the first place for the technological development of new representational practices and new ways of tying the unusable (or wasted) earth to the engines of capital accumulation that have propelled the world's economies into transnational exchange. It is only the TNC's combined virtual and material operations that have delivered Antarctica from margin to center and into profitability. Chrysler has thus pulled off the capitalist's impossible dream by creating value from a wasteland in a global economy marked by increasing stricture and scarcity. Moreover, it circumvents the problem of ecological degradation that it congratulates itself for solving by extracting value from Antarctica without leaving a single footprint on the continent itself.

Competing Ends

Whereas Antarctica poses a problem for postcolonial theory as it encounters a nonexceptionalist American studies, our recent arrival at a discourse of the "virtual" seems to take us into the theoretical territory of Jean Baudrillard's simulacrum, for which there can never have been an original Antarctica to be sullied. There is only the "generation by models of the real without origin or reality," a situation in which the "territory no longer precedes the map," for "it is the map that engenders the territory" (1983, 2). From this perspective, the Antarctic is the perfect simulacrum, a place defined by its inaccessibility (its value in its remoteness from circuits of value) and a territory whose very map, with its crosshatches of latitude and longitude and its artificially designated sectors, most resembles the pure metaphysics of mapmaking. Nevertheless, the simulacrum fails as a model for Antarctica because Baudrillard's hyperreal requires a temporal mode of succession impossible for the complex makings of the last continent. Rather, in a simultaneity model nothing precedes anything as original or center or as the new virtual or a nonoriginal natural referent—all are evacuated from the representational scheme. Antarctica is there but not yet there, mapped but wholly unimagined, excessive to the circuits of knowability. As you might expect, such a situation results in a surfeit of regimes of simulacra. In proportion to the limitations of both the representational theory of simulacra and postcolonial theories of the shape of imperialism, as well as limitations of the nation as organizing principle, we find competing simulacra of Antarctica. What are these and what are the stakes of their proliferation?

The first competing simulacrum regime is the law regime of the ATS. By constellating unequal national stewardship and especially by authorizing a mapped sectoring of the continent into the contesting national territorial claims that it protects for futurity, it functions as a simulacrum, which as Baudrillard argues "deters" the real. As in the Chrysler ad as simulacrum, however it is this notion of the simulacrum's deterrence of the real that creates problems. The concept of the simulacrum's "precession" implies a spacialized temporality that is even more hierarchically operative in the center-periphery relation of postcolonial theory. Neither the postcolonial nor the simulacrum, strictly understood, can offer a model of simultaneity or of a relation between the real and the hyperreal that, given Antarctica's history as simultaneously mapped and inaccessible as well as its escalating environmental degradation, is desperately necessary to ensure the region even a provisional future .

The inability of the ATS to control the borders of its simulacrum map is made evident in the resistance of nonindustrial nations to its reratification, a resistance that not surprisingly took the form of a competing simulacrum. In 1982, during negotiations in the United Nations preceding the reratification of the ATS, the delegate from Malaysia, a nation not among the treaty's twelve original signatories, protested the control of the ATS, and thus the potential wealth of the continent, by powerful industrial and primarily European nations. To replace this First World stewardship over Antarctica, Malaysia offered the "Common Heritage" concept, calling for First World nations to share technology, modes of production, and profits with formerly dependent nations. Although it generated much debate, the Common Heritage concept failed on a practical level simply because powerful nations refused to be directed in their neoimperial fantasies by a small subtropical state. The concept fails on a theoretical level as well, however, because its goal of reapportioning global wealth among nations reinstates the primacy of nationality just as postcolonial independence movements reproduced nation, extending rather than refiguring competing national claims to Antarctica (see Klotz 1990; Suter 1991).

Another dubious principle of modernity reinscribed by the Common Heritage concept was the inevitability and even desirability of industrial activity on the fragile continent, an eventuality that many groups would fervently like to defer eternally. The prospect of mining and other development, though still unrealizable, invokes the environmental doom that even Chrysler takes up cynically but that is central to the activities of several powerful nongovernmental agencies (NGOs) concerned with the environment. Because these NGOs are not attached to the limits of nation, they are better positioned to engage a multinodal, postnational regime over the Antarctic. Greenpeace, an environmental NGO active in monitoring the use of the Antarctic, has promulgated the "World Park," or "Public Heritage," concept. Designating the Antarctic a world park entails the continuation of the antidevelopment regime now in place with the ATS. Unlike the ATS, however, such a program would preclude national or private ownership and industrial development in perpetuity. Nevertheless, this concept too suffers a unimodal relation to Antarctica as simulacrum, for "Yosemite Antarctica" reverts to a fantasy of the pristine. The world park concept's reliance on a reconstitution of precontact conditions recalls one of the more limiting and discredited aspects of the postcolonial: the return to the precolonial. As many scholars and politicians have pointed out, that relation is no longer available and should not underwrite any political or theoretical horizons. The environmentalist rescue of the Antarctic begins to sound, if less sinister than Chrysler's, then at least as limited.

Nevertheless, in its own Web site for Antarctica, Greenpeace provides a competing alternative to the cartoon provided by the TNC (see also May 1988). Because it can move from one environmental hot spot to another and because it amasses and connects environmental workers into a professional class, Greenpeace often looks like a mobile transnational concern. Its activities are not motivated by profit, however, and the organization targets for criticism rather than congratulation the effects that TNC activity has on the environment. Not surprisingly, Greenpeace's publicity strategies vie in sophistication with those of the TNC. Greenpeace has an elaborate Web page that includes a link to Antarctica. By clicking on icons, the environmental consumer can see images of Greenpeace operatives presently in the Antarctic and read their diaries and descriptions of their activities. Other icons let you watch a clip of an iceberg calving, see images of those infamous penguins, or read about the latest scientific research as well as environmental reforms, efforts, and challenges. The Web page may not be as conceptually rich (i.e., contradictory) as Chrysler's, but it is a well-planned virtual Antarctic produced to attract publicity and to disseminate knowledge to individuals (as opposed to nations) that might grow to resemble a force that can counter that of the TNC.

Will Antarctica become a wilderness park or an industrial park? Imagine the environmentalists taking a lesson from the TNCs and marketing images of Antarctica, the Last Wilderness. Already a company called Terraquest has a Web site that will take you on a virtual exploration of Antarctica (free for now). Although there are many virtual exploration possibilities available on the Web for places that do exist, have existed, or might never exist, the difference in the concept of virtual Antarctica lies in the particular history of the place. Having long represented the projected classical end of the earth— an end that materialized as men stood at the South Pole in 1912—Antarctica as the end of the world in the new transnational regime must somehow project beyond that end. Antarctica indeed signals twin paradoxes at the heart of modernity in its impossible promise of the end of nation-states and post-Fordist production and the beginning of another world order, a both/and scenario that invites fantasies of both the apocalypse of industrial ruin and the utopia of pure production.

The example of Antarctica shows that resistance to transnational capital cannot come from the "local," since Antarctica does not register in the circuits of the world. How can one address a place that by definition has no population and so is not a place as that term has been critically developed? What world and what locality would the Antarctic inhabit in the global/local conceptual model? The Fifth World? If Antarctica is the Fifth World, the contestations over its present and future meaning and value reside not only in economic and representational transformations but in the critical analytics that might hope to control our destinations.

Transnational U.S. Studies

It is worthwhile to reiterate the cultural illegibility of Antarctica, the colony at the end of the world, in the terms of intellectual projects such as national studies, postcolonial studies, or even postnational studies as they have developed to describe the organizations of the world. The actors involved—the resistant territory, the TNCs, the ATS, the NGOs, and the representations circulated without and beyond the site or object of study—all defy traditional definitions and relations of power. The conceptual tools to describe the state of nonstates or transstates such as Antarctica need to go beyond the existing rubrics of the national, the colonial, or the global/local. To what extent can one consider the actions and effects of Chrysler Corporation as a U.S. entity, and to what extent must its operation be considered in the context of global economics, as a TNC? What is American about Chrysler's approach to, say, the Antarctic or to any other territory or market on earth? To ask such questions, American studies too must be unmoored from both nation and from global/local rubrics to produce an American transnational studies.

The transnational must distinguish itself from the postcolonial, a model that because it has been primarily tied to a center-periphery model of national imaginary cannot approach places such as Antarctica or cyberspace locations, malls, and other built economic environments, all of which are calling for a restructuring of national feeling from citizen-subjects on the one hand and a new understanding of the relation between place and publics on the other. In addition, a transnational focus on study of the nation-state might highlight the dynamics produced by the inequality among nation-states and the ways that TNCs interrupt the center-periphery model, often rendering those inequalities less powerful or putting them in novel arrangements.

Transnational studies would thus release American studies and other national or area studies from fictions of place and nation by tracking new relations among markets, places, populations, governments, and supra- or nongovernmental organizations or the interstitial sites that have yet to be incorporated into the regimes of the known and knowable; it would con-sciously question the formation of nation, its historical legacies of thought and discipline, and the connections among nation, diaspora (and its theo-rized decline), and deterritorialized nation-states. Reading Antarctica—and other postnational spaces—becomes possible under this program; move-ments of people within and through borders, their complex economic loops and migrations, become more ready to analysis, and new national belong-ings and unbelongings can be compared apart from presuppositions about nation and citizenship or culture. As Miyoshi (1992, 1993) suggests, trans-national studies would not be wedded to the academy as a national struc-turing or to the academy's corporatization. It might be better positioned to resist these powerful structurings of the academy. Perhaps the most pro-vocative promise of this conception of transnational studies is in its abil-ity to trace the tentacle ends of empire, even when those ends are in inter-nalized or virtualized spaces.

Works Cited

Anderson, Benedict. 1983. *Imagined Communities: Reflections on the Origin and Spread of Nationalism*. London: Verso.

Baudrillard, Jean. 1983. *Simulations*. Trans. Paul Foss, Paul Patton, and Philip Beitchman. New York: Semiotext(e).

Beck, Peter J. 1986. *The International Politics of Antarctica*. London: Croom Helm.

Chrysler Corporation. 1997a. "Welcome to the Uncommon Approach of Chrysler." <http://www.chryslercorp.com/default2.html>. 4 March.

———. 1997b. "A Global Perspective." World Wide Web page linked to Chrysler Corpo-ration 1997a at "International." 4 March.

Greenpeace. 1997a. "Greenpeace Antarctica Tour 1997." <http://www.greenpeace.org/meltdown/tstindex.html>. 15 March.

———. 1997b. "Greenpeace National Offices." <http://www.greenpeace.org/swor.html>. 15 March.

Guha, Ranajit. 1989. "Dominance without Hegemony and Its Historiography." *Subaltern Studies* 6:277–99.

Joyner, C., and E. Theis. 1997. *Eagle over the Ice: The U.S. in the Antarctic*. Hanover, N.H.: University Press of New England.

Kaplan, Amy. 1993. "'Left Alone with America': The Absence of Empire in the Study of American Culture." In *Cultures of United States Imperialism*, ed. Amy Kaplan and Donald E. Pease, 3–21. Durham, N.C.: Duke University Press.

Kaplan, Amy, and Donald E. Pease, eds. 1993. *Cultures of United States Imperialism*. Durham, N.C.: Duke University Press.

Klotz, Frank. 1990. *America on the Ice: Antarctic Policy Issues*. Washington, D.C.: National Defense University Press.

Lewis, R. W. B. 1955. *The American Adam: Innocence and Tradition in the Nineteenth Cen-tury*. Chicago: University of Chicago Press.

Marchand, Roland. 1985. *Advertising the American Dream: Making Way for Modernity, 1920–1940*. Berkeley: University of California Press.

May, J. 1988. *The Greenpeace Book of Antarctica: A New View of the Seventh Continent.* London: Dorling Kindersley.

Miller, Perry. 1956. *Errand into the Wilderness.* Cambridge, Mass.: Belknap.

———. 1963. *Nature's Nation.* Cambridge, Mass.: Belknap.

Miyoshi, Masao. 1992. "Sites of Resistance in the Global Economy." *boundary 2* 19:61–84.

———. 1993. "A Borderless World? From Colonialism to Transnationalism and the De-cline of the Nation-State." *Critical Inquiry* 19:726–51.

Pease, Donald E., ed. 1994. *National Identities and Post-Americanist Narratives.* Durham, N.C.: Duke University Press.

Peterson, M. J. 1988. *Managing the Frozen South: The Creation and Evolution of the Antarctic Treaty System.* Berkeley: University of California Press.

Sahurie, E. 1992. *The International Law of Antarctica.* New Haven, Conn.: Yale University Press.

Suter, K. 1991. *Antarctica: Private Property or Public Heritage?* Brisbane, Australia: Pluto.

Terraquest. 1997. "Virtual Antarctica Expedition." <http://www.terraquest.com/va/expedition/maps/cont.map.html>. 16 March.

7 Establishment Postcolonialism and Its Alter/Native Others: Deciding to Be Accountable in a World of Permanent Emergency

E. San Juan Jr.

In her introduction to a recent issue of *Publications of the Modern Language Association* devoted to colonialism and the postcolonial condition, Linda Hutcheon placed her imprimatur on the institutionalization of postcolonial theory and discourse, ascribing to the field "complexities" that scholars privilege as the mark of legitimacy. "Heterogeneity" is the salient code word that characterizes this "broad anti-imperialist emancipatory project," a "counter-discourse" of dissensus that is also "performative, provisional, and situated" (1995, 12). Indeed, the prefix *post-*, for Hutcheon and like-minded colleagues, becomes emblematic of "the dynamics of cultural resistance and retention" (10): *post-* implies not only "after" but also "inclusive," being even more explicitly anticolonial in its task of valorizing the "multiplication of identities." Adding to the *PMLA*'s official blessing, the entry "Postcolonial Cultural Studies" in *The Johns Hopkins Guide to Literary Theory and Criticism* surveys the genre's variety from a historical perspective. Postcolonial cultural studies (PCS), according to Georg Gugelberger, "is the study of the totality of 'texts' (in the largest sense of 'text') that participate in hegemonizing other cultures and the study of texts that write back to correct or undo Western hegemony," but he also observes that the term *postcolonial* has a "jargonizing quality and lacks precision" (1994, 582, 583). Although asserting that PCS inadequately problematizes Western hegemonic discourse paradigms, Gugelberger claims that it is "essentially radical in the sense of demanding change" (584). One is left to wonder, change from what to what?[1]

Despite PCS's prima facie radicalism, I contend in this essay that post-colonial discourse mystifies the political and ideological effects of Western postmodernist hegemony and prevents change. It does so by espousing a metaphysics of textualism, as in Gayatri Spivak's (1985) fetishism of "the archives of imperialist governance" or in Bhabha's (1990) analogous cult of linguistic/psychological ambivalence. Such idealist frameworks of cognition void the history of people's resistance to imperialism, liquidate popular memory, and renounce responsibility for any ethical consequence of thought. Decentering a unitary discourse of Enlightenment modernity or, conversely, repudiating Eurocentric models to advance a unique postcolonial mode of decolonization (e.g., Katrak 1989) does not liberate oppressed people of color such as the Guatemalan Indians or overturn in any way the World Bank or International Monetary Fund conditionalities imposed on superexploited nations such as the Philippines, Jamaica, and Tanzania. I endorse Kumkum Sangari's timely intervention here: "To believe that a critique of the centered subject and of representation is equal to a critique of colonialism and its accoutrements is in fact to disregard the different historical formation of subjects and ways of seeing that have actually obtained from colonization" (1987, 146; see also Callinicos 1989; Appiah 1995).

Postcolonial theory entrenched in Western institutions denounces historical specificity and with it projects of national-popular liberation and socialist transformation. By ignoring or discounting "Third World" communities' efforts to survive the havoc of global imperialism, postcolonial critics and their subtle stratagems only serve the interests of the global status quo, in particular the asymmetry between North and South (Magdoff 1992). One suspects complicity with transnational and "transcultural" interests. If the postcolonial desire is "the desire of decolonized communities for an identity" (During 1987), this desire is negotiated not through the imagination enabled by print capitalism or an uncontaminated indigenous language equivalent to a precolonial culture. It is negotiated through diverse counterhegemonic struggles (in wars of both position and maneuver, to use Gramsci's [1971] terms) that dismantle the intricate play of sameness and difference in the constitution of otherness in material practices and institutions. Such struggles (three examples of which are discussed later) are historically specific, with their own infinitely variegated strands of residual, dominant, and emergent formations that need to be inventoried and configured within the world-system of global capitalism. To label these struggles "totalizing" and "totalitarian" only confirms the presence of the enemy's not-so-invisible hand.

Scenarios of the "Postcolonial" Stigmata

One site for this struggle may be found in the semantic historicity of the term *postcolonial* and its politically determinate inflections. Using the genealogy of sedimentations, I would like first to record the term's semantic shift by registering its initial use within the 1970s debate on the "postcolonial state." Hamza Alavi, among others, argued then for the relatively autonomous nature of the postcolonial state: "The role of the bureaucratic-military oligarchy is relatively autonomous because, once the controlling hand of the metropolitan bourgeoisie is lifted at the moment of independence, no single class has exclusive control over it" (1973, 147). The petit bourgeois class in newly independent countries is credited with playing a progressive role in such institutions as the civil service bureaucracy and the military; hence the Arusha Declaration in Tanzania is interpreted as an initial victory for the progressive wing of the petite bourgeoisie. Following the failures of the radical experiments of Nkrumah in Ghana, Lumumba in the Congo, and Sukarno in Indonesia, the idea that the postcolonial state is independent of foreign interests (the former colonizer, among others) and can be harnessed for nationalist goals has been definitively refuted. From a historical-materialist perspective, the postcolonial state can only reproduce the general conditions needed to perpetuate unequal property and power relations and their effects. In most of the Third World the weakness of the native elite's capitalist fraction forces it to depend on the military or a despot to administer the state apparatus, which explains why these states often take the form of a ruling junta characterized by Bonapartism. The structural legacy of colonialism thus includes the postcolonial state, a mechanism to replace direct by indirect ideological or economic domination.

After the demise of the classic imperial system in 1945, the United States, as the successor to the debilitated European states, opted for a strategy of neocolonialism (Woddis 1972) or neoimperialism (Parenti 1995). In this framework the postcolonial state may appear independent or sovereign, but in reality its economic and political policies are dictated by the former colonizer and other foreign interests through the indigenous elite, the civil service, and the military, with its network of ties with Western governments during the cold war and after. Aside from its economic control, the West's ideological and cultural stranglehold reduces political independence to mere formality: "Through its control of the institutions of education, the media and communication systems, the West is in a position to subvert whole spheres of Third World social life" (Hadjor 1993, 216). Neocolonialism thus designates the persistence of economic ascendancy and cultural hegemony underneath the mask of political independence, demarcating the real democratic right of the people to exercise self-determination (which is effectively undermined by built-in mechanisms) from the formal or nominally procedural rights of citizens in a market-driven polity.

Instead of the rubric *neocolonial* to describe the discrepancy between, and paradoxical imbrication of, formal independence and real subservience, the specter of the "postcolonial state" now revives to fabricate the illusion that we have gone beyond the neocolonial stage. In fact, some argue that we have entered the postimperialist era, one in which transnational corporations are integrating national economies into one supranational world market. Dependency theory in the 1960s failed to account for the growth of the power of the transnational corporations. Today world-systems theory (Wallerstein 1983; Amin 1995) seeks to comprehend the new globalizing trend of capital by a systemic cosmological trope of center and periphery. Consequently, postcolonialism is offered, according to Vijay Mishra and Bob Hodge, because "it foregrounds a politics of opposition and struggle, and problematizes the key relationship between centre and periphery" (1994, 276). They qualify this, however, by postulating a complicit postcolonialism underpinning *The Empire Writes Back* (*EWB*), one that confuses self-misrecognizing mastery of difference with empowerment of citizens. Because postcolonial critics are heavily invested in the complicitous critique offered by postmodernism via irony, allegory, and self-reflexive tropes of doubleness, they reduce everything to metanarratives of contingency and indeterminacy. By reifying terms such as *nation* and *people*, they commit the same fallacies they ascribe to everyone else except their disciples. In defense, the Australian authors of *EWB* argue that their position cannot be conflated with a postmodernist consensus. Disavowing the link between the deconstruction of Eurocentric master narratives (concepts of progress, logocentric subjectivity, essentialism, teleology) and the project of "dismantling the Center/Margin binarism of imperial discourse," they assert that postcolonial critics confirm the "political agency of the colonized subject" (Ashcroft, Griffiths, and Tiffin 1989, 195). Such agency, however, is posited but not really theorized or concretized as an immanent historical process that subverts worldwide commodification.

Fundamentalist Disseminations

Postcolonial theory acquires its most doctrinaire instigator in Homi Bhabha. For Bhabha, the poststructuralist paradigm of linguistic or textual difference legitimizes a new master narrative of indeterminism and contingency. The triumphalist note in the celebrations of postcolonial theory's "coming of age" (exemplified by Hutcheon 1995 and Gugelberger 1994) is epitomized by

Bhabha's chapter "Postcolonial Criticism" in an academic guidebook entitled *Redrawing the Boundaries: The Transformation of English and American Literary Studies*. We find here a distillation of Bhabha's axioms concerning cultural translation, deferred or postponed meanings, and the "incommensurability of cultural values and priorities that the postcolonial critic represents" (1992, 439). The fundamental premise is that the colonial experience of marginality and displacement can be figured as analogous to the arbitrary position of the signifier in a system of differences; following Lacan, Bhabha asserts that the signifier is constantly suspended in a chain that never connects with the signified, forever caught in perpetual slippage, because of differential temporalities and spaces that resist comprehensive, systematic explanations. The postcolonial discourse of cultural difference is essentially ambivalent, liminal, hybrid, disjunctive, and chockful of ironies and aporias; unpresentable by definition, it refuses the logic of representation and all principles of intelligibility (Bhabha 1990).

It is indeed somewhat of a surprise that Bhabha or I can speak of postcolonial themes and rhetoric in this manner. But let us proceed anyway in a hypothetical mode, since plenitude of meaning or communicative "good faith" is unwarranted here.

Because of the experiences of oppression, diaspora, migration, exile, and so on, the postcolonial subject—the most controversial prototype is Salman Rushdie—occupies the locus of enunciation (distinguished from the enunciated) and inhabits it indefinitely. For Bhabha, postcolonial culture as enunciation or enunciative practice is an uninterrupted process of performance, never achieving the closure of the enounced or the sentence. Because it refuses to be bound to fixed referents or significations, postcolonial discourse undermines the logic of representation that accompanies "consensual and collusive" liberal society, the "holistic and organic notions of cultural value" (Bhabha 1992, 441). Postcolonial culture and identity privilege "the enunciatory present as a liberatory discursive strategy. . . . The contingent and the liminal become the times and the spaces for the historical representation of the subjects of cultural difference in a postcolonial criticism where the dialectic of culture and identification is neither binary nor sublatory" (1992, 444–45). With structuralism and dialectics refused, Bhabha elevates the "language" metaphor to transcendental aprioristic status. In this context Barthes's playful and agonistic semiotics is invoked as a model. Its performative textuality, the libertinism of the signifier, the "hybrid moment outside the sentence," finally leads to Derrida, whose example "opens up disjunctive, incommensurable relations of spacing and temporality within the sign," ushering us into a borderland filled with time lags, alterity, mimicry, and "sly civility." Authorities proliferate. Bhabha invokes

Guha, then Bakhtin and Arendt (revised accordingly to fit Bhabha's purpose), and then Rorty and Foucault, finally stopping in an anticlimactic orgy of archival legerdemain.

What is symptomatic in this version of postcolonial ratiocination (if it can be called that) is its claim to plausibility. Except for Guha and Fanon, none of the authorities mentioned really belongs to any conceivable geopolitical milieu—unless the imperial metropoles already are included in the slippage of the signifier *postcolonial*. What is more telling in this exercise in eclectic citatology and paraphrase is the way Bakhtin's idea of dialogism is appropriated in complete opposition to Bakhtin's politico-ethical commitment (see Bakhtin 1981). Bhabha, for instance, attempts to impute a deconstructive motive to Bakhtin: "Bakhtin's use of the metaphor of the chain of communication picks up the sense of contingency as contiguity, while the question of the 'link' immediately raises the issue of contingency as the indeterminate" (1992, 454). On the contrary, Bakhtin precisely rejects the contingency of *parole,* or utterance, because the speech act is triangulated by the constitutive roles of speaker, theme, and addressee. In other words, utterance addressed to a specific listener in a specific situation is concretely determinate, not contingent; moreover, utterance considered as "a link in the chain of communication" (quoted by Bhabha himself) is rooted in an intersubjective, stratified totality of social assemblages locked in ideological-political antagonisms, hence the "multiaccentuality of the sign" (Voloshinov [Bakhtin] 1986, 23). Utterance (acts of communication) is thus a crucial arena of class warfare. Whereas Bhabha repudiates the categories of history and class subjects, Bakhtin situates language and speakers in an "uninterrupted process of historical becoming" (1981, 271) where official and oppositional discourses fight for supremacy.

Demobilizing Fanon

Although Bhabha's fallacies and inadequacies have already been examined by Parry (1994), Callinicos (1995), and others, I would like to show how Bhabha's subordination of everything to the language metaphor and its exorbitant implications compels him to distort and thus render useless the praxis-oriented voice of Frantz Fanon.

One example of Bhabha's relentless insistence on the grammatological syndrome can be demonstrated by analyzing his essay "Remembering Fanon: Self, Psyche, and the Colonial Condition." In a typical move, Bhabha situates Fanon in the topos of ambivalence, in the "uncertain interstices of historical change." Challenging Enlightenment historicism (Hegel and Marx) and the "representative structure of a General Will," Fanon's *Black Skin,*

White Masks (according to Bhabha) "rarely historicizes the colonial experience. There is no master narrative or realist perspective that provides a background of social and historical facts against which emerge the problem of the individual or collective psyche" (Bhabha 1994, 115). This incredible claim that Fanon's primordial question ("What does the black man want?") is posed in a vacuum—in spite of the numerous references to "colonial racism" in Africa, Algeria, the United States, and elsewhere—blunts the text's political edge and mystifies Fanon's argument. It also undercuts Bhabha's thesis that "the emergence of the human subject as socially and psychically authenticated depends upon the negation of an originary narrative of fulfillment or an imaginary coincidence between individual interest or instinct and the General Will" (1994, 118). Lacking that "originary narrative," any negation seems pointless. Bhabha insists that the answer to Fanon's question is the psychoanalytic—more precisely, Lacanian—doctrine of "the splitting moment of desire" that defines the Other. The black man wants "the objectifying confrontation with otherness." Bhabha posits the following injunction: this "Other must be seen as the necessary negation of a primordial identity—cultural or psychic—that introduces the system of differentiation which enables the 'cultural' to be signified as a linguistic, symbolic, historical reality" (1994, 119). In plain language, the psyche can be understood as a sociohistorical construction inserted into a web of cultural artifices and artificial boundaries.[2] From this semiotic anatomy of Fanon's desire, Bhabha makes Fanon reject the Hegelian "dream for a human reality in itself–for itself" for a nondialectical Manichaeanism. Bhabha thus reifies the colonial Manichaean world that Fanon poignantly delineated in *The Wretched of the Earth* for the sake of freezing Fanon in that twilight zone of difference, the in-between of displacement, dispossession, and dislocation that Bhabha hypostatizes as the ineluctable essence of postcoloniality. Reductive closure of Fanon is complete.

This hermeneutic sabotage would not be a serious matter if we took Bhabha's version of Fanon as one possible reading or interpretation, albeit a highly fanciful one. To claim that this version captures the substantive, integral, and most subversive quality of Fanon's thought is, however, to expose the pathos if not reactionary function of postcolonial theorizing. Fanon analyzed the case of a real patient, relied on empirical research, and interrogated the conclusions of O. Mannoni and Jean-Paul Sartre. His observations of everyday life and the general conditions of blacks in Africa, the Caribbean, the United States, and Europe led him to an existentialist affirmation of creative freedom enabled by a Hegelian problematic that Bhabha nevertheless claims Fanon abandons. In the concluding chapter of *Black Skin, White Masks*, Fanon writes:

[The] former slave wants to make himself recognized. At the foundation of
Hegelian dialectic there is an absolute reciprocity which must be emphasized.
. . . The only means of breaking this vicious circle [of colonial, racist domina-
tion] that throws me back on myself is to restore to the other, through mediation and recognition, his human reality, which is different from natural reality. The other has to perform the same operation. "Action from one side only
would be useless because what is to happen can only be brought about by
means of both . . . they recognize themselves as mutually recognizing each
other." (1967, 217)

Because he distrusted Western philosophy as complicit with the ruses of
racism, Fanon relied on his own experiences and his diagnosis of others to liberate blacks from the "epidermalization" of the inferiority complex produced
by historical structures and economic circumstances. His book ends with a
humanistic shibboleth reminiscent of Rousseau, Voltaire, and the philosophes
and anathema to postcolonial bricolage: "I am my own foundations. . . . It is
through the effort to recapture the self and to scrutinize the self, it is through
the lasting tension of their freedom that men will be able to create the ideal
conditions of existence for a human world" (231). His ultimate "prayer" already
signals a departure from the positions enunciated in the book: "O my body,
make of me always a man who questions!" Three years later Fanon criticized
his formulaic psychoanalysis of racism thus: "Here we have proof that questions of race are but a superstructure, a mantle, an obscure ideological ema-
nation concealing an economic reality" (in Zahar 1974, 34). Even then, however, as he immersed himself in the unequivocal exigencies of anticolonial
revolution, Fanon never succumbed to a purely dualistic (Manichaean) metaphysics or to a formalist valorization of anarchistic decentering and dispersal.[3]
Like Rigoberta Menchú, C. L. R. James, and Maria Lorena Barros, my other
exemplars here, Fanon sought solidarity with Europe's "Others" and commu-
nicated this desire to all who shared his anti-imperialist principles and their
potential for generating communities of activists. Feeling responsible to the
mass of "Calibans" constructed by the West's "civilizing" hubris, he decided
to serve the cause of the victims and their project of collective transformation.

The victims in fact multiply at the hands of postcolonialists. The premium
assigned to hybridity, pastiche, parodic performance, and so on as constitutive of the postcolonial weltanschauung is rendered suspect when we encounter the dissidence of aboriginal peoples. Diana Brydon argues that the
claim to authenticity of Canada's native peoples "condemns them to a continued marginality and an eventual death" (1995, 141). To transcend the
impasse of liberal pluralism manifest in the postmodernist cult of difference, to move beyond "myths of cultural purity or authenticity" that isolate natives from "contemporary life and full citizenhood," Brydon urges a

strategy of "contamination" that will not homogenize or co-opt. She envisions a "new globalism that is neither the old universalism nor the Disney simulacrum" in a postcolonial recuperation of deconstructive energies (141). As a "white Inuit," this white middle-class intellectual intends to bring "differences together into creative contact" (136). From these notions of the "multiple, shifting, and often self-contradictory identity" of the postcolonial subject, can we properly appreciate the political sagacity embedded in North American native vernacular speech—say, in works by Pauline Johnson (a Tekahionwake) or Alootook Ipellie (Caws and Prendergast 1994, 2517–19, 2704–7)?

The claim of postcolonial theory (as exemplified by assorted Australian, Indian, and Canadian ventriloquists of "speechless" subalterns) to be more radical than avant-garde modernism is problematic especially for people of color seeking to affirm their autochthonous traditions of resistance. What is at stake is their survival, their authentic and incommensurable dignities. Also cast in the wager are their counterhegemonic projects to recover and reaffirm the integrity of their cultures, which are often anchored to the land or habitat, to events of dwelling and communion with their environment. What we have discerned so far is that a transcendental politics of aporia and equivocation is substituted for a critique of hegemonic authority. The ironic or minimal self of the theorist intervenes to mediate between Western epistemes and the self-empowering expression of multitudes, thus recuperating in "bad faith" the fraud of representation originally denounced.

Critics ranging from Arif Dirlik (1994) and Aijaz Ahmad (1995) to indigenous partisans at the front lines have contended that the postcolonial repudiation of "foundations" undermines any move to generate new forms of resistance against globalized capitalism and its centrifugal hierarchies (Magdoff 1992). Hybrid contrivances, discrepant local epistemes, cyborgs, border crossings, creole or metissage texts—such performative slogans tend to obfuscate the realities of what Leslie Sklair (1994) calls the transnational ideology of capitalist consumerism. Postcolonial theory generated in "First World" academies turns out to be one product of flexible, post-Fordist capitalism, not its antithesis. I suggest a dialectical counterpoint to this orthodoxy (satirized by Jacoby 1995) in the practices of Guatemalan activist Rigoberta Menchú and of the socialist revolutionary thinker C. L. R. James, from Trinidad. To provide a contrast to the postcolonial posture of recalcitrance, I offer the life work of a guerrilla combatant in the New People's Army in the Philippines, Maria Lorena Barros, whose martyrdom speaks more eloquently about the human condition under imperialism than does any hyperreal, labyrinthine discourse from the metropole. These are three possible embodiments of the Fanonian figure who questions; their identities cannot be

"postalized" or romanticized because their illocutionary force rests in the
border between trauma and utopia.

Menchú: Speak Truth to Power

Counterpointing the postcolonial devaluation of the Cartesian unitary subject, Menchú's narrative *Me llamo Rigoberta Menchú y asi me nacio la conciencia*
strives to synthesize the fragmented lives and the disintegrated families of
Guatamelan Indians, the Quiche people, as well as ladinos and other indigenous
groups. Menchú asserts that her story is not just a private or purely personal
account; it speaks for "all poor Guatemalans" exploited and manipulated by
the local elite and their foreign patrons. Pursuing this avowal of intent, John
Beverley considers Menchú's *testimonio* (testimonial narrative) an example of
"an emergent popular-democratic culture" transcending bourgeois humanism, Eurocentric decorum of proper style, and all existing ideological apparatuses of alienation and domination (1989, 20). Menchú's narrative may be said
to approximate a plot of education, the personal yet collective learning of the
operations of a brutal racist system based on combined tributary-capitalist
property relations (for U.S. intervention in Guatemala, see Greene 1970; Chomsky 1992; Hawkins 1994). It is also a reciprocal interrogation of the self and
others, of accounting for one's responsibility to beleaguered communities tra-
versed by one's labor and suffering.

For Menchú, the impulse to communicate is integral to the liberatory and
nurturing *conatus* of her life. Her speech act is also a "form of survival" (Rice-
Sayre 1986, 52). In chapters 1 to 15 of her *testimonio,* we are given an ethnographic account of the life cycle of the Quiche Indians, their traditional beliefs and rituals, as experienced by a young woman whose maturation coincides
with our exposure to the degradation suffered by the Indians.[4] This montage
of scenes, conveyed in the style of expressive realism, culminates in the torture and burning of her brother in chapter 24, followed first by the killing of
her father in a revolutionary engagement and then by the torture and murder
of her mother. Despite the destruction of her family and her subsequent exile, Menchú is reunited with her sister; her "family" becomes all the *compañeros*
in the Peasant Unity Committee and the Quiche people. She reaffirms her
commitment:

> My life does not belong to me. I've decided to offer it to a cause. . . . The world
> I live in is so evil, so bloodthirsty, that it can take my life away from one move-
> ment to the next. So the only road open to me is our struggle, the just war. . . . we
> can build the people's church . . . a real change inside people. I chose this as my
> contribution to the people's war. I am convinced that the people, the masses, are
> the only ones capable of transforming society. That is my cause. . . . it wasn't born

out of something good, it was born out of wretchedness and bitterness. It has been radicalized by the poverty in which my people live. It has been radicalized by the malnutrition which I, as an Indian, have seen and experienced. And by the exploitation and discrimination which I've felt in the flesh. And by the oppression which prevents us performing our ceremonies, and shows no respect for our way of life, the way we are. (1983, 246–47)

One cannot deny a unifying telos immanent in the unfolding of Menchú's lived experiences. The autobiographical redaction unites in a precarious but heuristic tension the political and scientific concerns of both the anthropologist Elizabeth Burgos-Debray and the protagonist Menchú. Ethnography mutates into a unique practice of dissent combining both alternative and oppositional stances (Sommer 1993; Portillo 1995).

In her study of this anticanonical genre, Barbara Harlow underscores the dynamics of resistance in the narrative blending of "the social transformation of traditional family structure into a political organization and the personal transformation of the daughter into a political organizer" (1987, 191). Although Menchú, the signified subject position, may be conceived as an effect interpellated by a rhetoric of exposure and indictment, such discourse is itself inscribed in the overdetermined specificity of the Guatemalan sociopolitical formation judged in the context of geopolitical conflicts of the 1960s and 1970s: U.S. support for the Guatemalan military to contain the threat of the Nicaraguan Sandinistas, the Cuban revolution, and so on. Formulated another way, one can characterize Menchú's discourse as both referential and self-reflexive: it speaks truth to power. Its illocutionary force lies in its programmatic resonance—more exactly, in the provocation of agencies or instrumentalities committed to destroying the system of injustice in Guatemala and the entire hemisphere.

Contamination by a received agenda of popular-democratic socialism as well as a Latin American theology of liberation may be apprehended in the narrative's "silences." Nevertheless, this does not result in an infinitely polysemous and finally unintelligible, playful text. On the contrary, Menchú's project is diametrically opposed to the postcolonial one of undecidable mixture: an integration of the personal and the communal, the forging of a new universality (to use a term C. L. R. James frequently deploys) that will connect the Quiche people with all humans fighting for equality, justice, and respect for all peoples' integrity and right to self-determination. This quest for a radical universality is sustained by an impulse to preserve something unique, something distinctive, whose substance can be only precariously named by the term *ethnic*—the aboriginal signature, which resists codification, hermeneutic gloss, or co-optative translation. Menchú's act of witnessing is rooted in the call for solidarity sanctioned by the community's distinctive, inviolate ethos: "Therefore, my commitment to our struggle knows no boundaries or limits. This is why I've travelled to many places where I've had the opportunity to talk about my people. . . . Nevertheless, I'm still keeping my Indian identity a secret. I'm still keeping secret what I think no one should know. Not even anthropologists or intellectuals, no matter how many books they have, can find out all our secrets" (1983, 247). Menchú's "secrets"—not just her Indian nom de guerre—will continue to resist the appropriation and abrogation strategy of postcolonial theory as long as imperialism and the client "postcolonial" state seek to destroy the habitat and spiritual ecology of the Indian peoples in Guatemala (Beverley and Zimmerman 1990). I am confident that, as the *testimonios* of the silenced multiply, this genre is bound to neutralize any postcolonial ludic machinery geared to destabilizing representation and obstructing communication.[5]

C. L. R. James: Deterritorializing Individualism

Let us examine another transcription of *la vida reál*. In *The Empire Writes Back,* Bill Ashcroft, Gareth Griffiths, and Helen Tiffin uphold the Caribbean as "the crucible of the most extensive and challenging post-colonial literary theory" on account of the works of Edward Braithwaite, Wilson Harris, and others. What I find revealing, however, is that the book never mentions C. L. R. James, the great West Indian Marxist innovator. Throughout his entire oeuvre, spanning the interwar years and the cold war, from *The Black Jacobins* (1963) to *Mariners, Renegades, and Castaways* (1985), *American Civilization* (1993a), and *Beyond a Boundary* (1993b) James showed how to incorporate Western thought and art dialectically in a peculiar Third World sensibility that is neither hybrid, syncretic, nor pastiche but singular in its commitment to the popular overthrow of the imperial world-system. James's thesis of a "permanent revolution" in the domain of cultural practice may be illustrated by his insightful commentaries on popular culture (cinema, detective novels) and especially by his chronicle of cricket as performed in the colony, *Beyond a Boundary.*

James's text is less an autobiography than a discourse on the Caribbeanization of British and, more largely, European culture. On the surface, it may be read as an endeavor to syncopate the chronological sequence of his life with his exploration of the aesthetic pleasure and ethical value of cricket in the national life of Trinidad and the West Indies. James serves both as witness and experiencer of contradictory forces, the lines of power and difference generated in a typical colonial milieu. Cricket happens to be a terrain of hegemonic compromise where the natives are given access to an imported "form of life." James's interest centers in the pedagogical and symbolic function of cricket. Although cricket is appraised as an educational and moral force in shaping Anglophone West Indian identity and social mores, it also serves as "a privileged site for the playing out and imaginary resolution of social antagonisms" (Lazarus 1992, 78). In other words, cricket functions as an ideological apparatus that can interpellate subjects as colonized natives or independent agents. In chapter 16 James conceives of cricket as an art form that resembles classic Greek drama, "so organized that at all times it is compelled to reproduce the central action," where the characters are engaged in a conflict that is both personal and representative of social groups. James expounds on the allegorical character of the players and movements of the game, especially the "significant form" of stylized bodily motion:

> This fundamental relation of the One and the Many, Individual and Social, Individual and Universal, leader and followers, representative and ranks, the part and the whole, is structurally imposed on the players of cricket. . . . Thus the game is founded upon a dramatic, a human, relation which is universally recognized as the most objectively pervasive and psychologically stimulating in life and therefore in that artificial representation of it which is drama. [Hence] the greatness of the great batsman is not so much in his own skill as that he sets in motion all the immense possibilities that are contained in the game as structurally organized. (1993b, 197, 198)

Aside from noting this aesthetic "heightening of vitality," however, James focuses on the game's political resonance by analogy with Greek drama and the Olympic games, both of which are associated with the birth of democracy and individualism. The striving for a "more complete human existence" (1993b, 211) is expressed not just by individual players but by the mass audience that, for James, participated in the rendering of its socially "significant form."

Beyond a Boundary is James's genealogy of his intellectual and ethical formation. It is a memoir relating how questions of race, class, and nationality (no matter how elided or peripheral) could not be repressed from the texture of everyday life in the colony. Loyalty, restraint, moral discipline, a critical attitude, adherence to a code of conduct or a structure of feeling—these are what for James constitute the positive legacy of colonial sports. His life history coincides with the political struggle to define the emergence of West Indian integrity and initiative within this imperial scaffolding in a way that transforms this material, together with the indigenous elements, into something new and original, not a mimicry or counterfeit image. Although James acknowledges his debt to colonial schooling, to British literature (from Bunyan to Thackeray and Arnold), in the end he affirms his rootedness in place: "We are of the West Indies West Indian" (1993b, 255). The "Puritan sense of discipline" he discerns in his own extended family is not something foreign but already indigenized, not a mimicry of Western "Othering" but a creative response to imposed circumstances.

In the public arena James always acknowledged himself as a product of European learning. In the lecture "Discovering Literature in Trinidad: The 1930s," James located himself in a world-system and took his bearings from this extraterritorial vantage point: "We live in one world, and we have to find out what is taking place in the world. And I, a man of the Caribbean, have found that it is in the study of Western literature, Western philosophy and Western history that I have found out the things I have found out, even about the underveloped countries" (1993b, 238). If he was a "hybrid" from a postcolonial optic, he can also claim to have made himself an "original" in his own terms.

Following the Marxian vision that capitalism begets its own gravediggers, James suggested that artists such as Wilson Harris, St. John Perse, Aimé Césaire, and others who broke away from the Eurocentric tradition disavowed the premises but operated within the same parameters. It is an instance not of syncretic adaptation but of dialectical sublation, a simultaneous canceling and preserving of selected cultural materials. The process, however, occurs within the new horizon of an emancipatory agenda. The center/periphery dualistic paradigm is thereby problematized. Given that English literature is largely a creation of "foreigners" such as Joseph Conrad, Henry James, Ezra Pound, T. S. Eliot and an assemblage of Irish writers from Shaw to Yeats, Joyce, and O'Casey, James contends that the Caribbean artist can also participate in modifying or de-Westernizing "civilization" as both insider and outsider: "And it is when you are outside, but can take part as a member, that you see differently from the ways they see, and you are able to write independently" (1980, 244). This standpoint, which problematizes outside/inside boundaries, fosters a symptomatic reading that lets us appreciate James's idea of British colonialism in the West Indies as a mode of begetting its gravediggers. His association with the celebrated cricket player Learie Constantine witnessed the manner of its begetting via James's pioneering advocacy for West Indian self-government. I should qualify this, however, by interpolating here the subsequent catalyzing role of the militant socialist tradition: it was the influence of Marxism, particularly American Trotskyism, along with radical French historiography, Herman Melville's fiction, and U.S. popular culture filtered through the mass media, that served as midwife to the anti-imperialist rebirth of cricket as an allegory of the West Indian quest for national recognition and self-determination. In this framework the process of mediation or transition becomes thematized. The Jamesian text becomes the site for calculating the precise determinants of native agency, what postcolonial

critics would call the self-referential "happening" of translation and intrac-
table displacement.

The profoundly instructive value of James's trajectory—from historian of
the Haitian slave revolt as part of the European bourgeois revolution to the
cultural activist of *American Civilization* and *Beyond a Boundary*—cannot
be captured by the postcolonial epistemology of hybridity and ambivalence.
Nor can it account for the difference between influence and reception. Within
the framework of permanent world revolution challenging state capitalism
in East and West, James discovers new life in the system's "weak links." This
is shown by his wide-ranging inventory of struggles foregrounded in "From
Toussaint L'Ouverture to Fidel Castro," "The People of the Gold Coast," and
"The Revolutionary Answer to the Negro Problem in the USA" (James 1992).
More than thirty years after his departure from Trinidad, he discovers the
moment of autonomy, his Caribbean voice and persona, in the search for the
universality first claimed by the European Enlightenment but already for-
feited by cold war capitalism in a stage of protracted crisis. There is a lesson
for postcolonials in recalling that James was languishing as a prisoner in an
Ellis Island facility when he completed his magisterial cultural study *Mariners, Renegades, and Castaways.*

Barros: Hope and the Will for Transformation

In an insightful critique of postcolonial dogma, Aijaz Ahmad argues that
within the orbit of transmigrant, multinational capitalism and its consumerist ethos, the nation-state remains as an effective horizon of politics. Popular democratic struggle for national liberation, not identity politics based on
ethnic particularisms, is a legitimate and historically timely response to the
structural offensive of transnational corporations and their instrumentalities (such as the World Bank and International Monetary Fund): "It is in this
framework that the nation-state remains, globally, the horizon for any form
of politics that adopts the life-processes of the working classes as its point of
departure, and which seeks to address the issue of the exploitation of poorer
women, the destruction of the natural environment by national as well as
transnational capitals, or the rightward drift of ideological superstructures,
all of which are deeply connected with labour regimes, gender-related legis-
lations and ideologies, and investment and extraction plans guaranteed by
the nation-state" (Ahmad 1995, 12–13). It is in this context that I call attention to the cultural politics of the National Democratic Front in the Philippines (which includes the partisans of the New People's Army [NPA] led by
the Communist Party of the Philippines) spearheading the struggle against
the neocolonial U.S.-supported regimes from the time of the Marcos dicta-

torship (1972–86) to Corazon Aquino (1986–92) and the present Ramos administration.

Anticolonial insurrections against centuries of Spanish tyranny in the Philippines climaxed in the 1896 revolution, but complete and genuine independence was aborted by U.S. military forces. The Filipino-American War (1899–1902) marked the beginning of U.S. political, ideological, and economic domination over the Filipino people. This conquest was punctuated by numerous peasant revolts for half a century, culminating in the Huk uprising of 1949–51 at the height of the cold war. Set amid world-epochal upheavals, notably the Cultural Revolution in China, popular uprisings in Africa and Latin America, and the protest against intensified U.S. aggression in Indochina, the founding of the NPA in 1969 initiated a new epoch of popular-democratic resistance throughout the archipelago.

The vicissitudes of the armed struggle against the postcolonial state (the United States granted the Philippines formal independence in 1946) can be emblematized by the life of Maria Lorena Barros, founder of the pioneering women's organization Makibaka (Malayang Kilusan ng Bagong Kababaihan, or Liberation Movement of New Women). This appraisal is not intended to romanticize a single individual but to deploy a life history as a condensation of the rich, durable tradition of women's resistance to colonialism and patriarchy beginning with figures such as Gabriela Silang, Teresa Magbanua, and Melchora Aquino to twentieth-century heroines such as Salud Algabre, Consolacion Chiva, Liza Balando, and many others now enshrined in the pantheon of Filipina feminism.

Born on 18 March 1948, Barros matured during the 1968 student rebellions and mass demonstrations against the Marcos government's complicity in the Vietnam War. Deeply influenced by her mother's views about social injustice and inequality, Barros graduated in 1970 with a degree in anthropology from the University of the Philippines, where she taught for some time. She led in organizing Makibaka with a program of action linking women's emancipation from male domination to class exploitation and national oppression. On the "woman question" her stance was profoundly oppositional: "In our system of values, a woman who uses her brains is regarded as an anomaly. The women in our society are encouraged to be passive creatures good only for bearing and rearing children" (in San Juan 1986, 156). In this she concurs with the finding of the 1980 Permanent People's Tribunal that Filipina women suffer "double oppression and exploitation" by the dominant classes and by "male authority" (Komite ng Sambayanang Pilipino 1981).

Given the uneven, tortuous development of the Filipino struggle for genuine independence amid persistent U.S. domination of civil society and state, the issue of gender equality and the potential of women as an autonomous force for radical transformation remain contentious for all sides (Aguilar 1988). Nevertheless, it is difficult even during Barros's lifetime to ignore the specificity of women's oppression that defies the peremptory foreclosure of postcolonial eclecticism and ambivalence.

I review the most relevant background facts here (Evasco et al. 1990; Eviota 1992). Composing more than one-half of the population, Filipino women most often live in the countryside, performing two-thirds of the work but receiving only one-tenth of the usual income of male peasants and rural workers. In the urban regions women are subjected to substandard wages, limited benefits, sexual abuse, and degrading, substandard conditions. In the 1970s the unemployment rate for women was 75 percent; for men, 10 percent. Sexist segregation of the labor force confined women to traditionally female jobs with lower wages, longer hours, and accelerated pace: domestic work, nursing, sales, clerical work, and unskilled labor. Over 300,000 women in the cities worked as prostitutes, with at least 60,000 (many of them teenagers) earning subsistence wages around the U.S. military bases. With martial law under the Marcos dictatorship, the lives of women considerably worsened, driving many of them to engage in the "hospitality" trade, their bodies converted into exchangeable commodities or fetishized as "mail-order brides" or "warm-body export." That was the sociopolitical context of Barros's decision to join the national democratic struggle against U.S. neocolonialism and its client regime.

In line with Barros's agenda of transgressing patriarchal and neocolonial borders, Makibaka urged women's total participation in politics. It targeted traditional sexist practices that quarantined women in the domestic sphere of civil society. It sought to unleash "the vigor, intelligence and creativity of Filipino women," to mobilize them (particularly students in the Catholic colleges) in programs combating sexual discrimination and exploitation. After studying the roots of women's oppression in the history of the Filipino family, Barros observed: "You have to convince them [women in the middle stratum of society] that there really is exploitation in the Philippines. . . . The principal problem is our culture, a culture that subordinates women to men. Makibaka aims to project this problem in the context of the national democratic struggle. Its purpose is to present more dramatically the need for emancipation and involvement" (in Davis 1989, 139).

After experiments in consciousness raising (influenced by Paulo Freire's conscientization pedagogy) of petit bourgeois women, Makibaka decided to widen its range of action by trying to organize peasant women in the rural villages as well as women in the factories. Barros realized that the right to abortion was not a priority for peasant women in the countryside, where the basic needs for food, clothing, and medicine (including reproductive health care) were urgent concerns. The major demands of tenant farmers and workers concerned land reform, elimination of usury, reduction of land rent, and improvement of the quality of life in general. Various chapters of Makibaka were established throughout the islands: a workers' bureau for peasants and urban poor and the Mother's Corps for housewives who were more pressured by the rising prices of basic staples, high tuition fees, and so on. Barros set up nursery classes for preschool children in cooperation with her mother's coactivists. In the course of her work, Barros discovered how the majority of women workers were not aware of their individual human rights, simply accepting subhuman working conditions. In actualizing participatory democracy, Barros was forced to go underground when the writ of habeas corpus was suspended in August 1971; the government had already announced a reward of 500 pesos for her capture.

At this juncture I want to interject some background information for those not familiar with political events in the Philippines in the last three decades. Since the reestablishment of the Communist Party of the Philippines in 1968, tremendous efforts have been made to involve women in both the legal and the clandestine sectors of the national democratic struggle (Chapman 1987). Of immense significance is the direct participation of women in guerrilla actions, with the formation of a Red Detachment of Women in the New People's Army, part of the coalition called the National Democratic Front. Women partisans of the NPA have distinguished themselves in ambushes, raids, organizing work, and so on. They have assisted in consolidating the liberated base areas and supervising the creation of the Barrio Revolutionary Committees (the chief administrative bodies for initiating revolutionary land reform), building up the people's army, and strengthening the united front of all progressive forces (for an update, see the interview with Makibaka by Prairie Fire Organizing Committee [1989]; Justiniani 1987; Aguilar 1993). The opportunities for reclaiming territory (physical and spiritual) from patriarchal capitalist control had considerably expanded by the time Barros fled the city in 1971 for the battlefield in the northern province of Isabela.

After Marcos imposed martial law in 1972, Barros married a fellow activist and subsequently gave birth to her first child in a private clinic in Manila. She had to return to the hills, however, leaving her son in the care of relatives. In October 1973, four months pregnant, Barros was arrested while organizing the rural masses; she was supposedly armed with a .32 caliber pistol and bound for Sorsogon City, Sorsogon Province, several hundred miles south of Manila, to establish a revolutionary base. She was first detained at Camp Vicente Lim for interrogation. She refused to cooperate and so was placed in *bartolina* (isolation), where she remained for several months. When she was allowed to mix

with other prisoners, Barros began to organize them and counter the demor-
alization they suffered, prompting the military to transfer her to the seclu-
sion of the Ipil Rehabilitation Center in Fort Bonifacio, at the outskirts of
Manila.

In January 1974 Barros was interviewed by a correspondent from the
Manchester Guardian. She had refused to disclose the whereabouts of other
guerrilla partisans in exchange for milder prison treatment. She recalled a
mercenary government officer's attempt to elicit cooperation: "He told me,
'You'll be inside for thirty years and then you'll be an old woman and you
won't be able to get married.' I was shocked that he thought that such a
threat would frighten me. I told him, all right, I said, 'I've been married once
already, and that was enough to last until I die'" (in San Juan 1986, 159).
Her husband, an NPA combatant, was killed five months later in an encounter with government troops. In her work organizing village committees of
peasants, Barros immersed herself in the lives of the over 75 percent of Filipinos who live in the impoverished countryside. In the rigor of integrating with the people, she grasped what Raymond Williams (1977) calls the
peculiar "structure of feeling" immanent in communities desiring and
wanting revolutionary change. She found that "the people in the villages
wanted to know all about communism. We tell them that under communism there will be no landlords, that the land will really be theirs and their
families; we teach them the problem of bringing about communism in a
feudal society like the Philippines; that the first stage of the struggle would
be to industrialize the Philippines, but that this cannot be done as long as
we are a semi-colony of U.S. imperialism" (in San Juan 1986, 159).

Barros's artistic sensibility envisioned breaks, transitions, rituals of passage. It was during her confinement in July 1974 that she wrote about her
distress, her grief at being separated from her loved ones, which she compares to "a tear shed for a leaf, / pain unassuaged / by the promise of a new
bud / at the tip" (Barros 1975–76). She invokes the "rich soil of people's war"
that will fructify and sustain the cycle of natural life. In another poem entitled "Sampaguita" (written a year earlier), she engages in "cross-address-
ing," emphasizing commonalities instead of singularities and inscribing directions on what would otherwise be a site of undecidability or postcolonial
ambiguity (Barros 1975–76):

> This morning Little Comrade
> gave me a flower's bud.
> I look at it now
> remembering you, Felix,
> dear friend and comrade

and all the brave sons and daughters
of our suffering land
whose death
makes our blades sharper
gives our bullets
surer aim. . . .

How like this pure white bud
are our martyrs
fiercely fragrant with love
for our country and people!
With what radiance they should still have unfolded!

But sadness should not be
their monument.
Whipped and lashed desperately
by bomb-raised storms,
has not our Asian land
continued to bloom?

Look how bravely our ranks
bloom into each gap.
With the same intense purity and fragrance
we are learning to overcome.

In another poem Barros shifts to a relaxed mood reminiscent of the "exteriorism" of the Nicaraguan poet Ernesto Cardenal and the Cuban writer Roberto Fernandez Retamar. She abandons the sentimental exuberance of images derived from organic nature and recounts her talk with an old man who spoke "of patience, / in his voice a whole season / of cool, summed-up sorrows." The dialogic evocation of differences engenders the occasion for learning the wages of responsibility: "Comrade, dear friend, / teach me how not to flinch" through adversities (Barros 1975–76). In such verses, the architectonic of exchange mediates both realism and utopian longing. I call this genre of interlocution "emergency writing" after Walter Benjamin's reminder that the state of emergency is not the exception but the rule for the oppressed (San Juan 1995, 103).[6]

Barros's writings are dispersed in many underground publications and private archives, still uncollected. We can infer that because of their insistence on recovering agency and rational critique, on transcending multiplicity and striving for wholeness via solidarity and cooperation with others, her art goes against the grain of orthodox postcolonial theory. It is an art of decision and risk taking, an imagination sworn to determining accountability and articulating responsibility for what is going on in her part of the world. On the whole, Barros's militant melancholy foresees personal defeat but inscribes this in the public sphere created by the national liberation struggle, in the immortal life of the community of workers and peasants.

On 1 November 1974 Barros and four companions escaped with the help of other political prisoners who distracted the guards. She rejoined the NPA and became the leader of a squad operating in the Bicol provinces. Even while engaged in military operations, Barros reserved time to listen to people's problems, especially women combatants. Surrounded by literally endangered lives, Barros had to sacrifice the luxury of claiming an oxymoronic, shifting, and plural identity expressed in tropes of positional or border identities. In such situations of unmitigated and unrelenting emergency, the strategy of self-positioning requires drawing up priorities during the interval of defense and attack, a nuanced maneuver that affords a sense of wholeness from which one is enabled to defamiliarize the status quo:

> Considering the quality of the young people today, the country has a good future. . . . The interest of the ruling class and of the exploited masses are dia-metrically opposed; the former will never allow the latter to wrest power with-out a struggle. . . . The revolution is inevitable, it is dictated by necessity. The Philippines might become another Vietnam. If we don't endure and do some-thing about it now, the succeeding generations will suffer even more. . . . If an armed conflict does arise, we will fight alongside the men. We should take up arms, if necessary. We are working for a better society for men and women alike, so why should the men always bear the brunt of the struggle?" (in San Juan 1986, 156)

Such retrieval and inventory of trends in the geopolitical terrain may serve as Barros's autograph in unifying the particular and the universal. In the early morning of 24 March 1976, in the town of Mauban, Quezon Province, Barros was killed in an encounter with ruthless government troops. She was twenty-eight years old. Her mother commented on her daughter's funeral: "When-ever there is a struggle there is a sacrifice, and death is a common occurrence" (in Davis 1989, 142).

Postcolonial indeterminacy breaks down here in the site of the destroyed female body. Refusing the strangeness of the Other, of death as ultimate uncrossable boundary, Barros's mother and all her comrades sought to read the young woman's life as a performance of a feminist identity beyond the category of "national allegory" (Jameson 1986). From the perspective of the embattled subalterns, Barros's life may be construed as a project (in the Sartrean sense) of achieving subject-hood and enfranchisement beyond Bhabha's "interstices" or "Third Space," beyond Rushdie's "imaginary homelands." Among engaged feminists in the Philippines today, Barros functions as a model of a learning process, a resource for discovering the nexus between personal experience and history. She serves as a legible sign, an intelligible configuration, of life's value as deeply imbricated in communal desires, concerns, and aspirations. I might add here that for thousands of underground revolutionaries in the Philippines, the homeland is not imagined or fantasized but actually lived, suffered, and endured; their collective experiences signify the questioning body that Fanon celebrated as an icon of permanent resistance (San Juan 1994).

Signs of Indifference

Whether those of the Quiche Indians, Filipina women, or Caribbean intellectuals, the practices of national popular struggle (in Gramsci's sense) are richer than any categorical description. Nonetheless, I will venture some theoretical reflections on the inadequacy of orthodox postcolonialism. My three examples of alternative antipostal practice in the domain of expression are all attempts to counter the universal deracination, loss of foundations, and totalized marginality posited by postcolonial theory. They are concerned with undertaking initiatives, discovering roots and sources, laying the groundwork for partisanship that would bind "we" and "they," "you" and "I"—all shifters that acquire determinate concreteness in actual, feasible projects. Alterity is inscribed in a situation of permanent emergency—Menchú's beleaguered people, James's diasporic quest, Barros's theme of metamorphosis—that temporalizes space. Time becomes fundamental for emergence of the new, the Novus.

In this alternative cultural milieu, we become enmeshed in a web of significance constituted by a literature of reconnaissance and transition—all three activists perform inventories of their lives in the act of surpassing the past, of valorizing the transitional moments of decision and existential becoming. Consequently, we have not the in-between but transition and the interregnum as privileged sites of self-recognition via the community; we have not ambivalence but resolve, commitment, and determination to face specific problems and crisis. We have not the local but a striving for coalitions and counterhegemonic blocs to prefigure a universal public space. We have not the syncretic and hybrid but creative demarcations and the crafting of the architectonic of the new, the emergent, the Novus. We have not the polyvocal but the beginning of articulation from the silenced grassroots, the loci of invention and resourceful innovation. Here the trope of difference is displaced by the trope of possibilities; the binary impasse of reified hegemonic culture is deconstructed by the imagination of materialist critique and extrapolation. Utterance is not private or solipsistic but collective, not heteroglossic but triangulated, not contingent but charted by cognitive mapping and provisional orientations.

What is at stake in thus counterpointing standpoints is the future—justice for the oppressed, equality for the deprived, and liberation for all. Given necessities and limited possibilities, oppressed people of color endeavor to shape a future freed from the nightmare of colonial history. Such endeavors are central, not marginal, to any attempt to renew humane learning everywhere. What Edward Said (1994) calls "the centrality of imperial culture" insinuates itself into the postcolonial claim to speak for all "the Rest," thus negating its self-proclaimed commitment to difference and radical alterity.

As though repudiating the ventriloquism of postcolonial experts, James and Menchú in their disparate ways provide a strategy of popular anticolonialism premised on historical retrospection and narratives of "belonging" and solidarity (Eagleton 1990). In analogous fashion Barros's laconic verses also present a synthesis of the personal and the collective in the process of trying to dismantle neocolonial repression and its floating signifiers of "free enterprise," "individual freedom," and mass consumerism (Featherstone 1991). After this complex encounter with the unequal division of intellectual labor, we return to history, the repressed corpus, via popular memory (in Menchú's *testimonio*), by tracing the variable genealogy of cricket (in James's memoir), and by documentary witnessing (in my appraisal of Barros's trajectory as feminist underground combatant). All three revolutionaries reject the academic historicist renunciation of conflicts and apotheosis of museumized fragments. They welcome "thick description" of events, of accountabilities—the conflicted texture of experience of change, discontinuity, transmutations, and breakthroughs. What happened? Who is responsible? After all, we are complicit in the fate of humanity anywhere on this planet.

All three figures I have surveyed here represent modalities of cultural production different from the mainly British Commonwealth "subaltern" archetype that today dominates postcolonial doctrine. Overall, I opt for replacing "postcolonial" foundationalism with a hypothesis of situated "national popular" cultures that in their concrete dynamics of engagement with global capitalism in specific sites express the varied forms of responses by people of color (including aborigines, women, peasants and workers, ethnic communities, and the dissident petite bourgeoisie) to commodification. (One example that quickly comes to mind is the work of Basil Davidson [1982] on African history.) Such responses also illustrate their modes of inventing autochthonous traditions that defy postmodernist skepticism or irony and offer materials for articulating hopes and dreams not found in the classic European Enlightenment and its mirror opposite, postcolonial relativism and pragmatic nominalism.

Notes

1. I endorse the qualified review of postcolonial theory vis-à-vis Establishment disciplinary canon by Apter (1995).

2. For a comparison and contrast to Bhabha's approach to racism, see Kovel 1984. For the communicative rationality of Fanon's antipsychoanalytic stance, see Gendzier 1973.

3. But Fanon's "ethical universal" is not the same as Appiah's notion of postcolonial humanism, which embraces a mystical transnational in-between, what remains after rejecting the modernist binarism of Self and Other, "a unitary Africa over against a monolithic West" (Appiah 1995, 124).

4. For an excellent analysis of ethnography as critique of assimilation, see Portillo 1995; for Menchú's rhetoric of resistance, see Sommer 1993.

5. For examples of *testimonios* by Filipina women, see Wynne 1979. For an example of collective feminist expression, see Arriola 1989.

6. Compare the heuristic notion of "emergent writing" suggested by Godzich (1988).

Works Cited

Aguilar, Delia. 1988. *The Feminist Challenge.* Manila: Asian Social Institute.

———. 1993. "Engendering the Philippine Revolution: An Interview with Vicvic." *Monthly Review,* Sept., 25–37.

Ahmad, Aijaz. 1995. "The Politics of Literary Postcoloniality." *Race and Class* 36, no. 3:1–20.

Alavi, Hamza. 1973. "The State in Post-Colonial Societies: Pakistan and Bangladesh." In *Imperialism and Revolution in South Asia,* ed. Kathleen Gough and Hari Sharma, 145–73. New York: Monthly Review Press.

Amin, Samir. 1995. *Re-Reading the Postwar Period.* New York: Monthly Review Press.

Appiah, Kwame Anthony. 1995. "The Postcolonial and the Postmodern." In *The Postcolonial Studies Reader,* ed. Bill Ashcroft, Gareth Griffiths, and Helen Tiffin, 119–24. New York: Routledge.

Apter, Emily. 1995. "Comparative Exile: Competing Margins in the History of Comparative Literature." In *Comparative Literature in the Age of Multiculturalism,* ed. Charles Bernheimer, 86–96. New York: Modern Language Association.

Arriola, Fe Capellan. 1989. *Si Maria, Nena, Gabriela atbp.* Manila: Gabriela and Institute of Women's Studies, St. Scholastica.

Ashcroft, Bill, Gareth Griffiths, and Helen Tiffin. 1989. *The Empire Writes Back: Theory and Practice in Post-Colonial Literatures.* New York: Routledge.

Bakhtin, Mikhail. 1981. *The Dialogic Imagination: Four Essays.* Trans. Michael Holquist. Austin: University of Texas Press.

Barros, Maria Lorena. 1975–76. "Three Poems: Sampaguita, Ipil, Yesterday I Had a Talk." *Collegian Folio* 12.

Beverley, John. 1989. "The Margin at the Center: On Testimonio (Testimonial Narrative)." *Modern Fiction Studies* 35, no. 1:11–28.

Beverley, John, and Marc Zimmerman. 1990. *Literature and Politics in the Central American Revolution.* Austin: University of Texas Press.

Bhabha, Homi. 1992. "Postcolonial Criticism." In *Redrawing the Boundaries: The Transformation of English and American Literary Studies,* ed. Stephen Greenblatt and Giles Gunn, 437–65. New York: Modern Language Association.

————. 1994. "Remembering Fanon: Self, Psyche, and the Colonial Condition." In *Colonial Discourse and Post-Colonial Theory: A Reader,* ed. Patrick Williams and Laura Chrisman, 112–23. New York: Columbia University Press.

————, ed. 1990. *Nation and Narration.* London: Routledge.

Brydon, Diana. 1995. "The White Unit Speaks." In *The Postcolonial Studies Reader,* ed. Bill Ashcroft, Gareth Griffiths, and Helen Tiffin, 136–42. New York: Routledge.

Callinicos, Alex. 1989. *Against Postmodernism: A Marxist Critique.* New York: St. Martin's.

————. 1995. "Wonders Taken for Signs: Homi Bhabha's Postcolonialism." In *Postality: Marxism and Postmodernism,* ed. Masud Zavarzadeh, 98–112. Washington, D.C.: Maisonneuve.

Caws, Mary Ann, and Christopher Prendergast, eds. 1994. *The HarperCollins World Reader.* New York: HarperCollins.

Chapman, William. 1987. *Inside the Philippine Revolution.* New York: Norton.

Chomsky, Noam. 1992. *What Uncle Sam Really Wants.* Berkeley: Odonian.

Davidson, Basil. 1982. "Ideology and Identity: An Approach from History." In *Introduction to the Sociology of "Developing Societies,"* ed. Hamza Alavi and Theodor Shanin, 435–58. New York: Monthly Review Press.

Davis, Leonard. 1989. *Revolutionary Struggle in the Philippines.* London: Macmillan.

Dirlik, Arif. 1994. "The Postcolonial Aura: Third World Criticism in the Age of Global Capitalism." *Critical Inquiry* 20:328–56.

During, Simon. 1987. "Postmodernism or Postcolonialism Today." *Landfall* 39, no. 3:366–80.

Eagleton, Terry. 1990. "Nationalism: Irony and Commitment." In *Nationalism, Colonialism, and Literature,* ed. Seamus Deane, 23–42. Minneapolis: University of Minnesota Press.

Evasco, Marjorie, et al., eds. 1990. *Women's Springbook.* Quezon City, Philippines: Women's Resource and Research Center.

Eviota, Elizabeth. 1992. *The Political Economy of Gender.* London: Zed Books.

Fanon, Frantz. 1967. *Black Skin, White Masks.* Trans. Charles Lam Markmann. New York: Grove.

Featherstone, Mike. 1991. *Consumer Culture and Postmodernism.* London: Sage.

Gendzier, Irene. 1973. *Frantz Fanon.* New York: Grove.

Godzich, Wlad. 1988. "Emergent Literature and the Field of Comparative Literature." In *The Comparative Perspective on Literature,* ed. Clayton Koelb and Susan Noakes, 18–36. Ithaca, N.Y.: Cornell University Press.

Gramsci, Antonio. 1971. *Selections from the Prison Notebooks.* New York: International.

Greene, Felix. 1970. *The Enemy: What Every American Should Know about Imperialism.* New York: Random House.

Gugelberger, Georg. 1994. "Postcolonial Cultural Studies." In *The Johns Hopkins Guide to Literary Theory and Criticism,* ed. Michael Groden and Martin Kreiswirth, 581–85. Baltimore: Johns Hopkins University Press.

Hadjor, Kofi. 1993. *Dictionary of Third World Terms.* New York: Penguin Books.

Harlow, Barbara. 1987. *Resistance Literature.* New York: Methuen.

Hawkins, Janet. 1994. "Confronting a 'Culture of Lies.'" *Harvard Magazine* 97, no. 1:49–57.

Hutcheon, Linda. 1995. "Colonialism and the Postcolonial Condition: Complexities Abounding." *Publications of the Modern Language Association* 110, no. 1:7–16.

Jacoby, Russell. 1995. "Marginal Returns: The Trouble with Post-Colonial Theory." *Lingua Franca* 5 (Sept.-Oct.): 30–37.

James, C. L. R. 1963. *The Black Jacobins.* New York: Vintage Books.

196 **E. SAN JUAN JR.**

————. 1980. *Spheres of Existence*. Westport, Conn.: Lawrence Hill.

————. 1985. *Mariners, Renegades, and Castaways*. London: Allison and Busby.

————. 1992. *The C. L. R. James Reader*. Oxford: Blackwell.

————. 1993a. *American Civilization*. Oxford: Blackwell.

————. 1993b. *Beyond a Boundary*. Durham, N.C.: Duke University Press.

Jameson, Fredric. 1986. "Third-World Literature in the Era of Multinational Capitalism." *Social Text* 15:65–88.

Justiniani, Victoria. 1987. "*Makibaka* Statement." *The Manila Chronicle*, 22 Feb., 10.

Katrak, Ketu. 1995. "Decolonizing Culture: Toward a Theory for Post-colonial Women's Texts." In *The Post-Colonial Studies Reader*, ed. Bill Ashcroft, Gareth Griffiths, and Helen Tiffin, 255–58. New York: Routledge.

Komite ng Sambayanang Pilipino. 1981. *Philippines: Repression and Resistance*. Utrecht, the Netherlands: KSP and Permanent People's Tribunal.

Kovel, Joel. 1984. *White Racism: A Psychohistory*. New York: Columbia University Press.

Lazarus, Neil. 1992. "Cricket and National Culture in the Writings of C. L. R. James." In *C. L.R. James's Caribbean*, ed. Henry Paget and Paul Buhle, 92–110. Durham, N.C.: Duke University Press.

Magdoff, Harry. 1992. *Globalization: To What End?* New York: Monthly Review Press.

Menchú, Rigoberta. 1983. *I, Rigoberta Menchú*. New York: Verso.

Mishra, Vijay, and Bob Hodge. 1994. "What is Post(-)colonialism?" In *Colonial Discourse and Post-Colonial Theory: A Reader*, ed. Patrick Williams and Laura Chrisman, 276–90. New York: Columbia University Press.

Parenti, Michael. 1995. *Against Empire*. San Francisco: City Lights Books.

Parry, Benita. 1994. "Signs of Our Times: Discussion of Homi Bhabha's *The Location of Culture*." *Third Text* 28/29 (Autumn/Winter): 5–24.

Portillo, Ma. Josefina Saldana. 1995. "Re-Guarding Myself." *Socialist Review* 24, nos. 1–2:85–114.

Prairie Fire Organizing Committee. 1989. "Interview with Makibaka." *Breakthrough* 13, no. 1 (Spring): 22–31.

Rice-Sayre, Laura. 1986. "Witnessing History: Diplomacy versus Testimony." In *Testimonio y Literatura*, ed. Rene Jara and Hernan Vidal. Minneapolis: Institute for the Study of Ideologies and Literature.

Said, Edward. 1994. *Culture and Imperialism*. New York: Alfred Knopf.

Sangari, Kumkum. 1987. "The Politics of the Possible." *Cultural Critique* 7:157–86.

San Juan, E. 1986. *Crisis in the Philippines: The Making of a Revolution*. South Hadley, Mass.: Bergin and Garvey.

————. 1994. *From the Masses to the Masses: Third World Literature and Revolution*. Minneapolis: Marxist Educational Press.

————. 1995. "On the Limits of Postcolonial Theory: Trespassing Letters from the Third World." *Ariel* 26, no. 3:89–116.

Sklair, Leslie. 1994. *Sociology of the Global System*. Baltimore: Johns Hopkins University Press.

Sommer, Doris. 1993. "Resisting the Heat: Menchú, Morrison, and Incompetent Readers." In *Cultures of United States Imperialism*, ed. Amy Kaplan and Donald E. Pease, 407–32. Durham, N.C.: Duke University Press.

Spivak, Gayatri Chakravorty. 1985. "Three Women's Texts and a Critique of Imperialism." *Critical Inquiry* 12, no. 1:43–61.

Voloshinov, V. [Mikhail Bakhtin]. 1986. *Marxism and the Philosophy of Language*. Cambridge, Mass.: Harvard University Press.

Wallerstein, Immanuel. 1983. *Historical Capitalism*. New York: Monthly Review Press.

Williams, Raymond. 1977. *Marxism and Literature*. New York: Oxford University Press.

Woddis, Jack. 1972. *Introduction to Neo-Colonialism*. New York: International.

Wynne, Alison. 1979. *No Time for Crying*. Hong Kong: Resource Center for Philippine Concerns.

Zahar, Renate. 1974. *Frantz Fanon: Colonialism and Alienation*. New York: Monthly Review Press.

PART 3

Postcolonial Formations:
Complicity, Opposition, and Possibility

8 Son of the Forest, Child of God: William Apess and the Scene of Postcolonial Nativity

Laura E. Donaldson

The rise of postcolonial studies during the past decade has been nothing short of spectacular. However, because critics such as Gayatri Spivak, Anthony Appiah, Homi Bhabha, and Edward Said have dominated the discussions, the axis of its interdisciplinary field has tilted primarily from East to West and has consistently neglected the relevance of American Indian cultures—or any cultures of the so-called Fourth World—to current postcolonial debates. This state of affairs arose partly because institutionally situated academicians know little about indigenous peoples, but equally important is a conflicted attitude toward the postcolonial paradigm among Native intellectuals themselves. For example, although Louis Owens (Choctaw) chastises Bill Ashcroft, Gareth Griffiths, and Helen Tiffin (1989) for ignoring the contribution of American Indians in their widely cited text *The Empire Writes Back: Theory and Practice in Post-Colonial Literatures,* Thomas King (Cherokee) emphatically rejects the postcolonial as an adequate concept for describing Native literatures. In his essay "Godzilla vs. Post-Colonial," King (1990) denounces not only the book's assumption of European contact as the starting point for American Indian literary production but also the way it "organizes the literature progressively suggesting that there is both progress and improvement" (11–12). Yet this objection begs the question of how one defines the postcolonial and how exactly it pertains to the lives of American Indian peoples.

Most critics repudiate a simplistic chronological articulation of postcolonialism, although the prefix *post-* always implies some sort of movement through time. Some also contest the assumption that this movement is always anticolonial and progressive. As Bob Hodge and Vijay Mishra note, "'postcolonialism' as the period that follows a stage of colonisation is not necessarily subversive, and in most cases it incorporates much from its colonial past" (Hodge and Mishra 1990, xi). In order to restore some definitional coherence to its usage, Hodge and Mishra differentiate between "complicit" and "oppositional" modes of the post-colonial: the former designates eras of political decolonization that repeat many colonial tendencies; the latter, the potentially insurgent underside of any colonial context. Such a distinction is valuable because it "corrects the misleading impression that subversion reigns equally everywhere in all 'postcolonial' societies" (xii) and transforms the postcolonial into a less absolute and totalizing construct.

Although I agree that colonialism—both pre- and post—traces only certain parameters of American Indian cultures (and strongly resist the myth that Native life begins with white contact and ends with the latest Euro-American exploitation), I also do not underestimate its influence, since everything from the disintegration of family and clan structures to the depletion of natural resources and the storage of nuclear waste on reservations can be construed as legacies not only of colonialism but also of "complicit" postcolonialism. Indeed, one could argue that the novels so dazzlingly written by King himself facilitate this complicity because they strengthen capitalism's penetration into the tribal realm (i.e., they appear in the form of print commodities) and circulate elements of Native cultures that have become available through the processes previously described. The point here is not to criticize King, whose work I admire and have enthusiastically discussed elsewhere (see Donaldson 1995); it is instead to highlight the dangers of constructing the postcolonial as a critical monolith rather than recognizing it as an important, but necessarily partial, explanatory frame.

My essay will examine these political and theoretical conundrums through the figure of William Apess,[1] a nineteenth-century Pequot whose vocations as a writer, Methodist circuit preacher, and architect of the 1833 Mashpee Revolt persuasively mark him as one of the first "oppositional" postcolonial intellectuals in the emerging United States. I use the term *oppositional* because Apess appropriated the skills of biblical literacy—reading and writing the signs of God—to attack a racist and imperialist Christianity as well as to construct one of the earliest appeals for solidarity among peoples of color. As someone who articulated the terrible ironies of those who continued to be colonized within the newly "decolonized" America (and one could hardly find a better example of complicit postcolonialism than the nation's treatment of nonwhite peoples), Apess raises profoundly important questions about the relation of theory to praxis, the politics of representation, and the role of Christianity in the Euro-American imperial project. Before we can explore these more protracted matters, however, we need to investigate a troubling episode in the life of a young Indian child.

Colonial Conflagrations

> Voted, that the earth is the Lord's and the fulness thereof; voted,
> that the earth is given to the Saints; voted, we are the Saints.
>
> — A 1640 resolution of the Milford, Connecticut, town council in
>   celebration of Connecticut colony's defeat of the Pequot

In 1806 an eight-year-old mixed-blood Pequot boy named William Apess fell ill with "a very curious" illness that neither the attending doctor nor the patient himself could explain: "The physician could not account for it, and how should I be able to do it? Neither had those who were about me ever witnessed any disorder of the kind. I felt continually as if I was about being suffocated and was consequently a great deal of trouble to the family, as someone had to be with me" (Apess 1992, 13). The family for whom he caused such a great deal of trouble was not related to the boy biologically; rather, it constituted the household of a Mr. Furman, to whom Apess had been "bound out" at the tender age of five.[2] Apess recalls this harrowing incident in his 1829 autobiography, *A Son of the Forest: The Experiences of William Apess, a Native of the Forest (Written by Himself)*, a story that borrows heavily from the assurance, decline, and reassurance pattern of the Christian conversion narratives common at the time. Because of this, and because readers soon discover that immediately prior to his mysterious ailment, an encounter with a transient evangelical group had left Apess "intent upon learning the lesson of righteousness," one might be tempted to diagnose his illness as the psychosomatic manifestations of an exaggerated theory of sin and damnation— or as editor Barry O'Connell (1992, lviii) suggests, "a frightening spiritual crisis."

Although Apess's religious angst certainly played a role in his illness, it is also an embodiment of what I would call "colonial hysteria." To paraphrase Sigmund Freud (1961, 5), Apess's illness represents an enigmatic interaction of mind and body that produces the capacity to simulate a number of serious ailments. More specifically, the interaction of Pequot mind and body in the context of Euro-American imperialism and nineteenth-century Indian-white relations induced within Apess the inability to breathe properly and a fear of suffocation. The other likely medical candidate for these symptoms, a collapsed lung, was commonly known to physicians during this era and would almost certainly have been properly diagnosed. If understanding the hysteric crisis depends on exposing the entire chain of pathogens in reverse chronological sequence, "the last ones first and the earliest ones last" (Freud 1961, 10), then we must return to its earliest roots in Apess's life story—the colonial scene of indentureship and the Euro-American patriarchal family.

According to historian James Axtell, children of England and its colonies traditionally prepared for their life's work by becoming apprenticed to a master of some trade or skill for a specified number of years. In exchange, apprentices were supposed to receive social discipline, religious nurture, some formal education, and on-the-job training (Axtell 1985, 159). For the New England Puritans, this time-honored practice of "binding out" seemed an effective panacea for the lack of industry they perceived in aboriginal peoples, since it allegedly inculcated within them an Anglo-Protestant work ethic (159). When this practice (not surprisingly) failed to achieve its goal, binding out eventually functioned "less as an educational institution than as an instrument of social control" (160). The Indians who became subject to indentureship were the children of paupers and debtors or those, like Apess, who were victims of familial abuse.

In Apess's case, the presumed exchange of labor for education was patently fraudulent. No evidence exists that Mr. Furman ever seriously considered teaching Apess the secrets of his trade as a working-class cooper, or repairer of casks and barrels; on the contrary, the little we know overwhelmingly suggests that the boy was nothing more than a virtual slave.[3] Despite these grim realities, however, Apess desperately longed to become a full-fledged member of the Furman family: he called their dwelling "home" (Apess 1992, 15), addressed Mr. Furman's mother-in-law as "mother," and developed a strong attachment to Mrs. Furman. Unfortunately, a cavernous gap separated desire and fulfillment, and what he received was not an invitation to join the family but rather intimate lessons in differential consciousness.

Frantz Fanon—a psychoanalyst of colonialism as well as a mixed-blood Martinician—clarifies the nature of this consciousness when, in *Black Skin, White Masks,* he observes that a normal black (or Indian) child who has grown up within the embrace of a normal family will become abnormal on contact with the white world. Why? Because, according to Fanon (1967, 146), the individual is confronted with the whole weight of a difference from whites that is cast in demonic terms: "The Wolf, the Devil, the Evil Spirit, the Bad Man, the Savage are always symbolized by Negroes or Indians." He further argues that this projection of negative value becomes an important cathartic vehicle in the psychology of imperialism, since "blackness" (or Indianness) functions much like a hysterical symptom in channeling the dominant culture's collective aggression. In the context of Apess's New England, this process of channeling occurred through what Herman Melville so aptly named "the metaphysics of Indian-hating," or the conversion of white fantasies about Indians' lying, theft, double-dealing, want of conscience, and bloodthirstiness (to name but a few in *The Confidence-Man*'s litany of ills) into incontrovertible natural laws (Melville 1984, 146; see also Takaki 1994). All too often, however, individuals in targeted groups internalize these projections instead of recognizing their virulent social pathology, and, I would argue, Apess's colonial hysteria originates in this misrecognition.

Immediately prior to his illness, for example, Apess was deeply troubled by Mr. Furman's attitudes toward the "poor Indian" child whom he forbade from attending Methodist meeting. As Apess explains, "He supposed that I only went for the purpose of seeing the boys and playing with them" (1992, 13). Mr. Furman's denigration of Apess's spiritual aspirations—as a child and an Indian, he was considered incapable of serious intentions—perpetuated a pattern of racist stereotyping common in the nineteenth century (and continues in transposed forms even now). Indeed, a scant year before his bout with suffocation, Apess experienced an incident that functioned as a microcosm of the terrible conflicts engendered by the metaphysics of Indian hating. In this incident, a girl "belonging to the house" sought revenge on Apess by telling Furman that he "had not only threatened to kill her but had actually pursued her with a knife" (12). Furman unquestioningly accepted her version of the story as truthful and whipped the boy severely (12)—a response motivated, even if unconsciously, by the negative fantasy of the Indian as a hypersexualized threat to nonnatives.

Although Furman subsequently conducted an investigation confirming young William's innocence and "regretted being so hasty," he showed no remorse for his prejudgment and continued to mobilize similar views as epistemic weapons against the child. One should not wonder, then, that Furman reacted to Apess's illness much like the traditional medical practitioner, whose training, according to Freud (1961, 7), fails in the face of hysterical phenomena: "He regards them [hysterical patients] as people who are . . . like heretics in the eyes of the orthodox. He attributes every kind of wickedness to them, accuses them of exaggeration, of deliberate deceit, of malingering." Indeed, Furman associated Apess's disorder with possession by the devil and "supposed that the birch was the best mode of ejecting him" (Apess 1992, 13). Once again, however, the "poor man's" exorcism proved futile: the "dreadful whipping" failed to cure his charge, and Furman discovered "his mistake, like many others who act without discretion" (14).

That an eight year old should survive such psychological and physical abuse is remarkable; that he not only survived but also became a nationally known Native leader is nothing short of miraculous (Apess himself would likely have attributed this to God's intervention on his behalf). Clearly he possessed a strength of mind and will that eludes many adults. Nevertheless, Apess paid an extremely high price for his lessons in differential consciousness, since the combination of its negative projections and Apess's destructive family relationships (both biological and surrogate) facilitated a symptomatic bout with the illness I have named "colonial hysteria." Apess's affliction implies an even greater suffering than just individual pain, however; it also conjures the genocidal history underlying the successful colonization of New England.

Freud provides an especially important clue for understanding this relationship between Apess's individual illness and the collective suffering of American Indians in his observation that hysteric patients *suffer from reminiscences* whose bodily symptoms exist as displaced "residues and mnemic symbols of particular (traumatic) experiences" (1961, 12). In other words, hysterics literally inscribe the wounds of memory on their bodies and, through a specific constellation of symptoms, publicly commemorate them. Freud illustrates this process by comparing the "mnemic" quality of hysteria to such memorials as Charing Cross, which marks a resting place of Eleanor of Aquitaine's coffin, or the monument to those who died in the 1666 London Fire. He asks: "What should we think of a Londoner who shed tears before the Monument that commemorates the reduction of his beloved Metropolis to ashes although it has long since risen again in far greater brilliance? Yet every single hysteric . . . behaves like these unpractical Londoners. Not only do they remember painful experiences of the remote past, but they still cling to them emotionally" (13). The monument's evocation of a catastrophic fire is especially apt in this context, since Apess's illness bears an intrinsic relationship to the First Puritan Conquest (also known as the 1637 Pequot War) and the burning of Mystic Fort by the Connecticut militia.

A complete account of the first major war involving New England's colonizers and its indigenous peoples lies outside the scope of this essay, and other scholars have provided superb discussions of this topic (see Jennings 1976; Axtell 1985). There are two aspects of the First Puritan Conquest, however, that have a direct bearing on the "mnemic," or commemorative, quality of Apess's hysteric disorder: the incendiary destruction of the Indian village of Mystic (mistakenly termed a "fort" because of its hastily erected stockade) and the postwar consequences of this massacre for the Pequot. Before the First Puritan Conquest, the Pequot—whose name translates loosely as "the destroyers" or "manslayers"—were among the Northeast's most powerful and influential tribes. After the war a population of 13,000 was reduced to 1,000, and they became the first Native culture subjected to coercive termination—literally dispersed from the homeland "where reposed the ashes of their sires" (Apess 1992, 7).[4] For Apess, these last words are not metaphorical but literal, since he refers to the 26 May 1637 massacre of 700 men, women, and children—the warriors were largely absent—from the village on the Mystic River. In less than an hour, Pequot hegemony in the region was broken (Hauptman and Wherry 1990, xiv) and their souls put to the test. John Underhill, the soldier who trained the Connecticut militia, was a participant in this action, and his eyewitness account stunningly catalogs the horrors of that day:

> But seeing the fort was too hot for us, we devised a way how we might save ourselves and prejudice them. Captain [John] Mason entering into a wigwam, brought out a firebrand, after he had wounded many in the house. Then he set fire on the west side, where he entered; myself set fire on the south end with a train of powder. The fires of both meeting in the center of the fort blazed most terribly, and burnt all in the space of half an hour . . . Many were burnt in the fort, both men, women, and children. Others were forced out, and came in troops to the Indians, twenty and thirty at a time, which our soldiers received and entertained with the point of the sword. Down fell men, women, and children . . . It is reported by themselves [the Pequot] that there were about four hundred souls in this fort, and not above five of them escaped out of our hands. (in Segal and Stineback 1977, 136–37)

Richard Hayward, a contemporary leader of the Mashantucket (Connecticut) Pequot, affirms that the terrible events of 1637 haunt tribal memory even to the present (Hauptman 1990, 70). Its similarly traumatic effect on Apess cannot be doubted since his allusion to both the conflagration and its consequences frame his colonial dis-ease.

Under the terms specified by the 1638 Hartford Treaty, the Pequot were officially suppressed and forbidden to speak the name of their tribe. Since, like all societies dependent on oral tradition, they stood only one generation away from silence, the intent of the treaty remains clear: in the words of Captain John Mason, architect of the Mystic slaughter, it was "to cut off the Remembrance of them from the Earth." Is it any surprise, then, that a feeling of suffocation—commemorating not only the struggle of his fellow Pequot to breathe on that fiery day in May but also the Puritans' legislative attempt to suck the life out of them—should appear as Apess's primary symptom? As Homi Bhabha remarks, however, every state of emergency is also always a state of *emergence* (1994, 41), and one could also interpret Apess's incipient asphyxiation as a re-membering of the Pequot nation, a daring to speak its name by publicly memorializing it in and through his own body.

Fortunately, William Apess survived his sickness and in fact experienced something akin to a spontaneous recovery: "One morning after this [Furman's flogging] I went out in the yard to assist Mrs. Furman milk the cows. We had not been out long before I felt very singular and began to make a strange noise. I believed that I was going to die and ran up to the house; she followed me immediately, expecting me to breathe my last. Every effort to breathe was accompanied by this strange noise, which was so loud as to be heard a considerable distance. However, contrary to all expectation I began to revive, and from that very day my disorder began to abate, and I gradually regained my former health" (Apess 1992, 14). The expectation of mortality becomes the harbinger of life, and a presumed death rattle, the boisterous expression of . . . what? Although Apess himself makes no attempt to answer this question, a close analysis of the episode provides some salient hints about Apess's healing and his subsequent career as a preacher, pan-Indian activist, and politically engaged writer. If Freud's first hysteric patient was "brought back to normal mental life" by putting "into words her freshly constructed phantasies" (Freud 1961, 8), then perhaps Apess's "strange noise" produced a similar catharsis through its long overdue verbalization of his own rage and pain. Nothing less than expelling his internalized psychology of "Indian hating" could effect such a dramatic restoration to health.

This enunciative cure emphatically contests Arnold Krupat's assertion in *The Voice in The Margin* that "in Apes's case . . . there is the implication that when the Native lost his land, he lost his voice as well" (1989, 147). According to Krupat, the loss of American Indian utterance clears the way for the inculcation of a dominant Christian "voice of salvationism" that assimilates "the heteroglossia of craftsmen and merchants, Natives and whites, common soldiers and officers, pious and profane into the single strict monologue" (151). For Krupat, Apess is nothing more than a "mimic man" who parrots the colonizer's discourse and whose voice is completely subsumed under its rubric. On the contrary, I would argue that Apess's "strange noise" articulates what he might say to Krupat and all others who succumb to the myth of the "Vanishing and Silent Indian": "I would speak, and I could wish it might be like the voice of thunder, that it might be heard afar off, even to the ends of the earth" (Apess 1992, 301). Interestingly, soon after regaining his health Apess continued his "cure" by trading the lifeless brand of Christianity endorsed by his owner-employers for the much less respectable (but much more lively) meetings of the evangelical Methodists: "I therefore went to hear the *noisy Methodists*" (18, emphasis added).

These individual and religious vocalizations mark the beginning of Apess's postcolonial nativity because they signify his self-identified birth as both a revolutionary Christian and a sovereigntist "native." Rather than positioning him as "the licensed speaker of a dominant voice" (Krupat 1989, 148), Apess's recovery from colonial hysteria and his decision to join the Methodists granted him a license to *make* noise, that is, to insert "the poor Indian's" dissident voice into the imperialist social text. But first he had to translate this voice into the ciphers of English literacy. The talking cure had to metamorphose into a writing cure.

Like many other New England Indians (Axtell 1985, 188), Apess appropriated the skills of reading and writing English as a powerful tool of survival in an increasingly Anglicized world. The rhetoric of appropriation I use is intended to suggest a geocritical territory whose "ragged and vague" boundaries conform much more closely to the ambiguous "frontier zones" described by ethnohistorian Francis Jennings (1993, 52) than to any conception of the frontier as a stark line dividing savagery from civilization and degeneracy from assimilation. In the context of Apess, it suggests a postcolonial reality somewhere between relentless victimization and outright confiscation—or between resistance and complicity—since his appropriation of English writing implies not only mimicking the language of the colonizer; the power of the pen also grants him access to an extraordinarily useful means of resistance. Indeed, as Apess observes (quoting Elias Boudinot's 1816 history *Star in the West*): "Had the Indians [in the First and Second Puritan Conquest] . . . been able to answer in writing, they might have formed a contrast between themselves and their mortal enemies, the civilized subjects of Great Britain. They might have recapitulated their conduct in the persecution of *Indians, witches, and Quakers* in New England—*Indians* and *Negroes* in New York, and the cruelty with which the aborigines were treated in Virginia" (1992, 58). They might, in other words, have turned English literacy against its previous owners and waged a defensive struggle over the politics of representation as well as their ancestral homelands. This recognition of English literacy as a vehicle for resistance enabled Apess to parlay his anticolonial critique of Christianity into the more constructive evocation of an imagined postcolonial community. It is to this vexed question that I now direct my attention.

Signs of Spectacular Resistance

> To the extent to which discourse is a form of defensive warfare, mimicry marks those moments of civil disobedience within the discipline of civility: signs of spectacular resistance.
>
> — Homi K. Bhabha (1994)

There is an alternative to conceiving the frontier as a kind of Maginot line, one that depends on a much more ambivalent enactment of "camouflage, mimicry, black skins/white masks" (Bhabha 1994, 120). As one of the most effective yet elusive strategies of colonial power, mimicry is an identity imposed on the colonized, who must then reflect back the image of the colonizer—but always in imperfect form (McClintock 1995, 62). It is precisely this deviation, characterized by Bhabha as "almost the same, but not white," that Krupat ignores in his insistence on Apess's Christian ventriloquism. The fact that Apess—like other "mimic men" and women—can never exactly mirror the image of the colonizer allows his imitation to emerge "as a *question* of colonial authority, an agonistic space" that also becomes the site of an irregular hybridity (Bhabha 1994, 121). And this, according to Bhabha, gives birth to "the warlike, subaltern sign of the native" that may not only read between the lines but also change the often coercive reality it contains (ibid.). Almost 150 years before Bhabha's provocative analysis, however, William Apess demonstrated a sophisticated understanding of this same dynamic in his 1833 polemic *An Indian's Looking-Glass for the White Man.*

This essay was originally paired with a collection of short conversion tales in a book entitled *The Experiences of Five Christian Indians; or, An Indian's Looking-Glass for the White Man* (in the 1992 collected works, it is again published as part of *Five Christian Indians*). The joining of these two works is important because it implicitly recognizes the contradictory dynamic of colonial mirroring that Bhabha calls "mimicry." As critic David Murray (1991, 61) notes, the ambiguity of the text's initial title suggests either an Indian looking at himself for the benefit of whites or an Indian holding up a mirror so that whites can see themselves. At first glance the personal narratives anthologized by Apess appear to signify Indians looking at themselves for the benefit of whites, since they resoundingly endorse each person's conversion to Christianity—even seventy-one-year-old Anne Wampy, who had successfully resisted Christian proselytizing for most of her adult life.

Like many Pequot women, Anne Wampy wove and sold baskets, "some made of very fine splints, some of coarse, and many skillfully ornamented in various colors" (in Apess 1992, 153n15). In his local history of Ledyard, Connecticut, the Reverend John Avery recalled that a large portion of what Anne Wampy received from the sale of her baskets was usually spent on "strong drink." Avery's anecdote eerily echoes a story from Apess's own autobiography in which his grandmother, having "been out among the whites, with her baskets and brooms . . . had fomented herself with the fiery waters of the earth" (1992, 120) and beaten him so violently that he almost died. Although we have no record of Apess's grandmother after this incident, we do know of Anne Wampy's ultimate conversion to Christianity, after which she shunned any more episodes of rum drinking: "Me love everybody, me want to drink no more *rum*. I want this good religion all the time" (in Apess 1992, 152). Although one might interpret this statement as an apologia for the religion of the colonizers, when it is read in tandem with *An Indian's Looking-Glass,* a very different perspective emerges.

In each published edition of *Five Christian Indians, An Indian's Looking-Glass* comes after the conversion stories and consequently acts as a kind of theological and political gloss on them. It is significant, then, that Apess begins this text with the status of reservation Indians in the different areas of New England: "With but few exceptions, we shall find them as follows: the most mean, abject, miserable race of beings in the world" (1992, 155). Nothing illustrates this abjection more poignantly than the basket selling of Anne Wampy and Apess's grandmother, since the practice that once transmitted important skills and spiritual values now signified a desperate means of survival within a capitalist economy (Moon n.d., 47–48). How, Apess asks with great rhetorical power, have these "ingenious" Native people become so degraded? His own answer to this question lies neither in blaming the victim nor in promoting conversion to Christianity but rather in constructing a complex metaphor of mirroring. For Apess, the Indian's looking glass does not reflect the dehumanized image of the colonized but instead exposes the reason for this dehumanization: "The unbecoming black principle" of racism, "which is ten times blacker than any skin that you will find in the universe" (1992, 157). Like the surface of a mirror, a racist society looks no deeper than skin color in determining a person's value. The Indian's looking glass thus stands as an epistemological and moral rebuke and turns the power of representation—the same power that marked all Indians as "savages"—back onto the alleged "civilizers." In so doing, however, the mirror mutates from a vehicle of mimicry into a much more active political instrument.

Like Cheryl Walker in *Indian Nation: Native American Literature and Nineteenth-Century Nationalisms*, I perceive Apess's thought in *An Indian's Looking-Glass* to be evolving from mimicry, or imagining how each entity (person, group, or political unit) might occupy the space of its opposite (Walker 1997, 16), to a more actively resistant discourse focusing on differential power relations and the theme of oppression. As Walker notes, a transpositional rhetoric such as mimicry does not suffice for Apess because he realizes that Indians *cannot* change places with whites: "Difference (including differences of power and interest) obstructs this" (53). And thus resistance is born. The nativity of resistance also raises questions of agency, and it is here where Apess makes a distinctive contribution to contemporary debates. It is also here that my analysis departs most significantly from Walker's, since she locates the beginnings of Apess's imagining the nation in later treatises such as *Indian Nullification* and, as I will show, imbues it with much more limited goals.

Anne McClintock (1995, 63) questions the politics of agency implicit within Homi Bhabha's concept of mimicry; although she recognizes "the vital importance of the concept of ambivalence," the question becomes "whether it is sufficient to locate agency in the internal fissures of discourse." That is, because Bhabha contends that colonialism is subverted more by the formal ambivalence of representation than by changing social contradictions or the militant strategies of the colonized, his analysis risks what McClintock calls "a formalist fetishism that effectively elides the messier questions of historical change and social activism" (64). It is only when mimicry indicates less a self-defeating colonial strategy and more an anticolonial refusal (64) that it comes closest to Apess's articulation of mirroring in *An Indian's Looking-Glass.*

There is probably no clearer example of an anticolonial refusal than Apess's recollection of his youthful distress at being called "Indian"—that misnomer imposed on the Arawak by a geographically challenged Columbus: "I know of nothing so trying to a child as to be repeatedly called by an improper name. I thought it disgraceful to be called an Indian; it was considered as a slur upon an oppressed and scattered nation, and I have often been led to inquire where the whites received this word, which they so often threw as an opprobrious epithet at the sons of the forest" (1992, 10). With all its pejorative overtones of racial and cultural difference, the term *Indian* attempted to force the people of Turtle Island to perceive themselves through the mirror of others. Apess defies such deformation by surpassing the Christians in exegesis and pronouncing the term "unbiblical" (although he himself used it in his later career as a preacher and writer): "I could not find it in the bible [*sic*] and therefore concluded that it was a word imported for the special purpose of degrading us" (10). Even this stronger sense of mirroring as anticolonial refusal has limits, however, because one is always chained to that which one repudiates. It is for this reason that Apess, unlike Bhabha, ventures into the enterprise of solidarity building, or what I call the creation of an imagined postcolonial community.

An Indian's Looking-Glass anticipates not only how to produce such a community but also what its function might be. In a remarkable moment Apess asks his readers to engage in an act of what we would now call creative visualization: "Assemble all nations together in your imagination, and then let the whites be seated among them, and then let us look for the whites, and I doubt not it would be hard finding them; for to the rest of the nations, they are still but a handful. Now suppose these skins were put together, and each skin had its national crimes written upon it—which skin do you think would have the greatest? . . . I know that when I cast my eye upon that white skin, and if I saw those crimes written upon it, I should enter my protest against it immediately and cleave to that which is more honorable" (1992, 157). The parallel of this image to an international court investigating the crimes of imperialism and racism takes Apess's rhetorical and political vision further along the road to anticolonial activism. For example, the statement's construction of white skin as a text whose ciphers reveal its social transgressions and of Apess as its skilled, accusing reader adds even more metaphorical power to his appropriation of Christian literacy. Particularly interesting is his use of the pronoun *us* to elicit rhetorically a particular community of readers: "And then let *us* look for the whites, and I doubt not it would be hard finding them; for to the rest of the nations, they are still but a handful." The collective constituted by "us" includes all those who are not white and who, like Apess, share a passion for justice. Although this counterhegemonic "us" appears in *An Indian's Looking-Glass* only briefly, Apess's appeal to it sets the stage for a more comprehensive evocation of this imagined community in his later works.

I borrow the term "imagined community" from Benedict Anderson (1991), who first defined this concept in his widely cited book *Imagined Communities: Reflections on the Origin and Spread of Nationalism*. Although Anderson's specific hypotheses about the origins of modern European and Asian nationalism have been extensively debated and subsequently revised, his larger discussion of "nationness" as a function of social imagination remains relevant not only to the work of William Apess but also to the larger context of postcolonial criticism. As Anderson explains, he uses the term "*imagined* because the members of even the smallest nation will never know most of their fellow-members, meet them, or even hear of them, yet in the minds of each lives the image of their communion"; he uses the term *community* because, despite actual discrimination and exploitation, the nation "is always conceived as a deep horizontal comradeship" (1991, 6, 7). He further contends that we should distinguish communities by the style through which they are imagined—as "indefinitely stretchable nets of kinship and clientship" or an *ancien régime*, for example (6)—rather than through appeals to their alleged truth or falsity. According to this rubric, one might describe the style through which Apess's community is imagined as the mode of a citizen's jury that convicts rather than acquits the iniquities of white racism and Euro-American imperialism.

This production of an alternative nationness surely existed as one of the most powerful critical weapons available in an era that also witnessed the explosive growth of a new American nationalism. Apess realized that if Indians, or indeed any people of color, were to secure a future in the emerging United States, he must challenge any promotion of a public identity based on the divine right of Euro-Americans to seize lands of indigenous peoples or to drive out the "red Canaanites," as the Reverend Nahum Gold so descriptively termed Indians in 1835. For the Reverend Gold and many others who shared his views, ridding America of its first peoples was the only way to prevent them from "trampling down" the vineyard God had so graciously planted in America. Perhaps the most influential architect of this nascent nationalism was Daniel Webster, the famed lawyer and orator, whom Apess characterized as "distinguished" and praised for his advocacy of American Indian interests (in Webster 1894, 160).

Although Webster did oppose the 1830 Indian Removal Bill, Apess's suggestion that whites bury "the [Plymouth] rock that [their] fathers first put their foot upon" nevertheless entailed burying the very mythology that Webster created and successfully promoted. Many scholars have noted how Webster constructed his own version of America's early past to serve the political necessities of his antebellum present. To quote Webster himself: "The wintry forests become fields and gardens; cities and temples rise with civilization's victory over wilderness; and the Constitution and Union stem from the Mayflower Compact" (in Erickson 1984, 49). One cannot comprehend Webster's narrative of the American socius, however, without also understanding his assumptions about the European colonial project and its difference from the "settling" of America by the English.

For Webster, there were two kinds of colonialism: Spanish and English, "bad" and "good." Spain's colonization of the Americas was "bad" because it operated through motives of greed, that is, the love of gold and the aggrandizement of royal power. In contrast to Spain, which "descended on the New World in the armed and terrible image of her monarchy and her soldiery . . . , England approached it in the winning and popular garb of personal rights, public protection, and civil freedom" (Webster 1894, 145). Spain brought to the Americas only an avaricious brutality and the institution of the *encomienda*,[5] whereas England transplanted liberty, most especially religious liberty, and the traditions of common law. In the 1843 address he delivered for the completion of the Bunker Hill monument, Webster rhapsodically summarized this pronounced (and highly questionable) historical contrast: "The Mayflower sought our shores under no highwrought spirit of commercial adventure, no love of gold, no mixture of purpose warlike or hostile to any human being. Like the dove from the ark, she had put forth only to find rest. . . . The stars which guided her were the unobscured constellations of civil and religious liberty. Her deck was the altar of the living God" (143). In this passage the disinterested and altruistic light of English colonialism shines forth serenely and purely, and no scenario illustrates its essence more dramatically than the arrival of God's Book on the shores of Turtle Island. Besides touting all the virtues just enumerated, Webster also emphasizes that the Mayflower's passengers carried the Bible, whose "free and universal reading" enabled them to bequeath future Americans a legacy of civil liberty, individual responsibility, human dignity and equality (148).

Just two years after Webster's Bunker Hill speech, John O'Sullivan condensed its revisionist history into the popular concept of "Manifest Destiny" and, in words reminiscent of the golden-throated rhetor himself, argued that democracy is nothing other than "Christianity in its earthly aspect—Christianity made effective among the political relations of men" by eliminating "the obstacles reared by artificial life" (in Stephanson 1995, 40). As the Cherokee, Choctaw, Muscogee, Chickasaw, and Seminole had already discovered, however, they were the "artificial life" standing in the way of progress. O'Sullivan's euphemistic allusion to the need for eliminating obstacles actually connoted the concrete tragedy of Indian removal and attempted to erase the thousands who died on the *Nuna-da-ut-sun'y,* or "the place where they cried" (the Trail of Tears).

In his extensive introduction to Apess's collected works, Barry O'Connell notes that Apess's 1836 *Eulogy on King Philip* recontextualizes Webster's tale of the Pilgrims to expose its "ideologically seductive elisions" and to disable white Americans' presumptions of a "seamlessly glorious and singular American story" (1992, xxi). One of the ways it accomplishes this is by juxtaposing the figure of "King Philip"—Metacomet, *sachem*[6] of the Wampanoags and leader against the whites in the Second Puritan Conquest (also known as "King Philip's War")—to the mythologized character of George Washington: "As the immortal Washington lives endeared and engraven on the hearts of every white in America, never to be forgotten in time—even such is the immortal Philip honored . . . by the degraded but yet grateful descendants who appreciate his character. . . . Where, then, shall we place the hero of the wilderness?" (Apess 1992, 277). According to O'Connell, Apess's pairing of Metacomet and Washington induces a kind of "historical vertigo" that eventually reorients the American Dream even as it questions the credentials of America's most revered patriot. Walker summarizes this strategy as the use of a transpositional discourse in which an Indian and a white man mirror one another, causing the reader to acknowledge the Indian rather than the white man as the true American hero (1997, 176).

Other examples of such transpositions abound, performed on figures such as Miles Standish, military commander of the Mayflower expedition and later of the Plymouth Colony, whom Webster recalls in terms of his "decisive and soldier-like air and manner" (1894, 27) but whom Apess characterizes as a "midnight robber and assassin" (1992, 285).[7] Alternatively, one might consider the way Apess revalues the Pilgrims' introduction of Christianity as a "hypocritical proceeding" dependent on duplicity and flattery: "Flattered by informing the Indians that their God was going to speak to them, and then place them before the cannon's mouth in a line, and then putting the match to it and kill thousands of them" (1992, 285). Nonetheless, however strongly such reversals contest Webster's history, they cannot eclipse its most influential strategy: the casting of America in the mold of a tightly knit family directly descended from the Pilgrims and bound together by common heroes and common goals. Indeed, Webster so effectively envisioned America in these terms that it has haunted political and civil discourse ever since.

As Anders Stephanson (1995, 28) has noted, such amber waves of nationalism were constituted more by a shared structure of feeling than by any explicit ideology. Each participant in this evolving entity known as the "United States" subscribed to the view that it was a country uniquely marked not only by social, economic, and spatial openness but also by a "mission of world-historical importance in a designated continental setting of no determinate limits" (Stephanson 1995, 28). In Webster's speech on the settlement of New England—an address honoring the bicentennial of the Pilgrims' landing that became one of the most widely known cultural expressions of Apess's era (O'Connell 1992, 286n15)—the orator vividly thematizes the theory and practice of this imagined patriotic community: "By ascending to an association with our ancestors; by contemplating their example and studying their character; by partaking their sentiments, and imbibing their spirit; by accompanying them in their toils, by sympathizing in their sufferings, and rejoicing in their successes and their triumphs; we seem to belong to their age, and to mingle our own existence with theirs. . . . We become their contemporaries, live the lives which they lived, endure what they endured, and partake in the rewards which they enjoyed" (Webster 1894, 26). The simultaneous connection between Pilgrim past and postrevolutionary present and the almost mystical mingling of the two provided the primary sentiment of American nationalism's emotional structure and wove together the disparate threads of its social text.

If Apess were to counter this social, psychological, and ideological nexus, he would have to mobilize an equally powerful countercommunity consisting of all those excluded or rendered invisible by the Mayflower Compact. We glimpsed the beginnings of this collective in *An Indian's Looking-Glass;* in the *Eulogy for King Philip* it is embodied much more comprehensively through a complex interplay of rhetorical text and political context. To the America that Webster so poetically imagined as formed of scions of the first Pilgrims, Apess opposes a nation descended from Massasoit, the Pokanoket *sachem* who repaid the intrusions of the English with "peace and universal benevolence toward all men" (1992, 278), and his son Philip, "an independent chief of a powerful nation." In fact, Philip's response to the English might provide a model for Apess's invocation of another United States of (Native) America: "For during some time he had been cementing his countrymen together, as it appears that he had sent to all the disaffected tribes, who also had watched the movements of the comers from the New World and were as dissatisfied as Philip himself was with their proceedings" (294). The members of this nation are free from subjection and, like Philip, are "as active as the wind, as dexterous as a giant, firm as the pillows of heaven, and fierce as a lion, a powerful foe to contend with indeed, and as swift as an eagle, gathering together his forces to prepare them for battle" (296). Its borders lie beyond the boundaries of New England, since it includes all those whose cultures have been threatened by the colonizer's "spirit of avarice and usurpation of power."

This counternation far surpasses Walker's contention that Apess's main task in the *Eulogy* "was to assert 'I—I also—AM AN AMERICAN' and to elevate his (Indian) people so that they could take their appropriate place among Americans of all description, protected by the laws and exercising the rights of full citizens" (1997, 180). His goal was to obtain parity for American Indians in the life of the nation and to argue that America could not be an egalitarian society until major changes were made in economic, social, and spiritual realms (Walker 1997, 53). Thus, Walker sees Apess's "imagined community" in the much more confined sense of influencing the dominant, hegemonic nation rather than constructing a potent and resistant counternation. Whether or not Apess intended to produce such a community, it nevertheless comes to life in the *Eulogy* through narrative strategies that echo Webster's musings on the Pilgrim's first settlement. By "ascending to an association with our ancestors"— *with Massasoit and King Philip rather than the Pilgrims;* by "contemplating their example and studying their character"—*both the greatness of Philip as well as the hypocrisy of many Christians;* by "partaking their sentiments, and imbibing their spirit"—*that is, learning who Philip was and why he fought to preserve his traditions;* by "accompanying them in their toils, by sympathizing in their sufferings, and rejoicing in their successes and their triumphs; we seem to belong to their age, and to mingle our own existence with theirs"—*but in this case, the* Eulogy's *readers mingle their existence with the first victims of the Mayflower Compact and rejoice in the fact that, although they were militarily defeated, they never surrendered their humanity or their sovereignty.*

The story of how Philip literally and metaphorically fed his people with the coat off his back nicely illustrates this community-building process. During the throes of the Second Puritan Conquest, some of Philip's men experienced severe shortages of food and lacked the materials to make weapons for battle. Apess recounts that, on hearing this, Philip ordered that his *sachem*'s coat, "neatly wrought with mampampeag (i.e., Indian money) ... be cut into pieces and distributed ... among all his chiefs and warriors" (1992, 297). This magnanimous act possessed both religious and economic significance since *mampampeag*—the Pequot word badly transliterated into English as "wampum"—traditionally consisted of purple and white clam shell beads that were then threaded into strings and belts. Although the original function of *mampampeag* was to record sacred texts and certify the validity of treaties, "wampum" eventually became the transnational exchange currency of seventeenth-century New England.[8] Metacomet's act consequently involved carving his *mampampeag*—those markers of wealth and tribal authority—into individual portions that could be exchanged as "wampum." This so cheered the hearts of the Wampanoag that they were motivated "still to persevere to maintain their rights and expel their enemies" (Apess 1992, 297). How could one fail to identify with such a generous and heroic—although admittedly apocryphal—figure? Apess's characterization is designed to elicit such identification and to make readers want to become a part of Philip's historical and the *Eulogy*'s textual confederacy, each of which worked to defend and maintain the rights of the oppressed.

This imagined postcolonial community expanded beyond pan-Indian concerns to encompass all those brought to the New World against their will and, indeed, all peoples of color. Interestingly, O'Connell notes that Apess's attitude toward African Americans underwent a change after 1831. Whereas in his earlier writings he took pains to distance himself from them, in *An Indian's Looking-Glass* he joins the experience of Native North Americans to that of African Americans, both of whom possessed the dubious distinction of having their oppression rationalized in the name of Christianity (O'Connell 1992, lxx). Both groups also experienced the humiliating subjugation of having dark skin in a white-skinned world. Because of these similarities, the anniversaries of the Pilgrims' landing on Plymouth Rock and American independence evoked only the harshest sentiments from Apess: "We say, therefore, let every man of color wrap himself in mourning for the 22nd of December and the 4th of July are days of mourning and not of joy" (1992, 286). This textually assembled, multiracial collective aspires to nothing less than all-out assault on those degrading principles that rob a person "of all rights, merely because he is ignorant and of a little different color" (307). Instead, according to Apess, his countercommunity will give the Indian—and presumably the slave as well—his or her "due" according to the principles of true Christian equality. Of course, the dismal histories of removal, Sand Creek, the Dawes Act, and Wounded Knee confront us with the ultimate failure of Apess's visionary nation. Imperialist banality and viciousness triumphed—but only temporarily, to which the contemporary revitalization of Indian populations and cultures attests.

In his essay "William Apess and Writing White," Randall Moon (n.d., 52) identifies a kind of "political unease" over Apess "because he writes too much like a white person" and is too Christianized to be recognized as an "authentic" representative of "Native America." This discomfort stems, I believe, from a misunderstanding of Apess's complicated cultural positioning as well as a failure to recognize that he inhabits a "frontier zone" somewhere between complicit and oppositional postcolonialism. Although in his published life Apess never eschewed the religion of the colonizers (we will never know what happened after he stopped writing in 1838), his version of Christianity tapped the potentially insurgent underside of the Euro-American context, and his creation of an alternative nationness tried to reconstruct America from the standpoint of the colonized.

Perhaps instead of writing too Christian and too white, William Apess actually wrote too far ahead of his time. Perhaps we are only now discovering how much he illuminates the strategies that our ancestors used to divert, displace, and transcend the onerous burdens of colonialism. Indeed, long before theorists distilled postcolonial criticism into its current configurations, Apess articulated his own understanding of the politics of representation and such strategic concepts as mimicry and imagined communities. Perhaps this "son of the forest" inscribes a scene of postcolonial nativity whose creative negotiations might instruct those who have heretofore ignored the contributions of American Indians to the ongoing debates within critical and cultural studies. Perhaps, when all is said and done, it is the limitations of his readers and not of Apess himself that have prevented this complex and important figure from gaining the attention he so richly deserves.

Notes

1. The name William Apess has usually been spelled with one *s*. Throughout this essay, however, I will use the two-*s* spelling, which necessitates that the name be pronounced in two syllables and which Apess himself preferred. O'Connell (1992, xiv*n*2) presents an informative discussion of the one-*s* versus two-*s* spelling and their respective histories.

2. Apess's mother and father left him with his paternal grandparents when it became impossible for them to support their children. There is also some suggestion of marital discord. Apess was removed from his grandparents' custody, however, after his grandmother beat him so severely at age four that it took him a year to recover. With characteristic critical insight and generosity of spirit, he refused to place all the blame on his grandparents for their violent treatment of him: "I attribute it in a great measure to the whites, inasmuch as they introduced among my countrymen that bane of comfort and happiness, ardent spirits . . . I do not make this statement in order to justify those who had treated me so unkindly, but simply to show that, inasmuch as I was thus treated only when they were under the influence of spirituous liquor, that the whites were justly chargeable with at least some portion of my sufferings" (1992, 7).

3. Indeed, barely three years after his recovery, the Furmans sold Apess's indentures to Judge William Hillhouse, chief judge of the county court in New London, Connecticut, for twenty dollars. This began a rapid series of transfers to which Apess (1992, 16) responds: "If my consent had been solicited as a matter of form, I should not have felt so bad. But

to be sold to and treated unkindly by those who had got our fathers' lands for nothing was too much to bear."

4. I invoke the concept of diaspora advisedly here, since for American Indian cultures, ancestral lands are not replaceable: it is *this* land and *these* woods that in Apess's poignant words contain "the ashes" of one's ancestors, that is, the core of what makes the Pequot Pequot and bequeaths them a unique identity.

5. Although Webster does not name it explicitly, what he describes is surely the *encomienda*. This institution granted the services of a certain number of Indians to each *encomendero*, most likely a former conquistador, in recognition of their services to the Crown. While theoretically these Indians were free, the *encomienda* signified a brutal system of exploitive labor that killed just as surely as slavery or disease. For example, thousands of Quechua and Aymara died—one out of four in their first year of labor—in the Cerro Rico silver mines of Potosí, Bolivia, the first mines worked under the system of *encomienda*.

6. The word *sachem*, like many other American Indian terms for leaders, is not translatable by the much more hierarchical "chief." Among American Indian cultures in New England, it was primarily a high-status position and, although both men and women could be *sachems*, it followed the male line. *Sachems* were civil officials providing leadership for communities on a day-to-day basis, and like most traditional tribal leaders, they maintained influence largely through their persuasive abilities (Starna 1990, 41–42).

7. Accounts from the time have vindicated Apess's view. For example, to suppress trouble brewing in nearby Wessagusset, one of Plymouth's competitors for Indian corn, Standish pretended to the Massachusett—the tribe expected to supply Wessagusset with rations—that he had come to trade. After inviting the Massachusett *sachem* Witumawet and several followers to a feast honoring their supposed partnership, he and his men killed them with their own knives and then repeated this scenario with other Massachusett throughout the day. Standish then took Witumawet's decapitated head back to Plymouth, where he put it on display as a warning to any other Indians who thought they could defy the colony. For a detailed discussion of this episode, see Salisbury 1982, 125–40.

8. In 1622 a Dutch trader named Jacques Elekens seized the Pequot *sachem* named Tatobem and threatened to behead him if he did not pay a hefty ransom. Tatobem swiftly paid the equivalent of an enormous sum in *mampampeag*, and as a result of this incident, the West India Company discovered the value of these strings of small beads. Wampum became the currency of choice in payments for furs and mercantile goods. Ironically, it was Philip's refusal to pay England's demand for tributary wampum that, among other factors, precipitated King Philip's War. For a discussion of the origins of wampum, see Salisbury 1982, 148–49; and Ceci 1990.

Works Cited

Anderson, Benedict. 1991. *Imagined Communities: Reflections on the Origin and Spread of Nationalism.* Rev. ed. New York: Verso.

Apess, William. 1992. *On Our Own Ground: The Complete Writings of William Apess, a Pequot.* Ed. Barry O'Connell. Amherst: University of Massachusetts Press.

Ashcroft, Bill, Gareth Griffiths, and Helen Tiffin. 1989. *The Empire Writes Back: Theory and Practice in Post-Colonial Literatures.* New York: Routledge.

Axtell, James. 1985. *The Invasion Within: The Contest of Cultures in Colonial North America.* Oxford: Oxford University Press.

Bhabha, Homi K. 1994. *The Location of Culture*. New York: Routledge.

Ceci, Lynn. 1990. "Native Wampum as a Peripheral Resource in the Seventeenth-Century World-System." In *The Pequots in Southern New England: The Fall and Rise of an American Indian Nation*, ed. Laurence M. Hauptman and James D. Wherry, 48–63. Norman: University of Oklahoma Press.

Donaldson, Laura E. 1995. "Noah Meets Old Coyote, or Singing in the Rain: Intertextuality in Thomas King's *Green Grass, Running Water*." *Studies in American Indian Literature* 7, no. 2:35–51.

Erickson, Paul D. 1984. "Daniel Webster's Myth of the Pilgrims." *The New England Quarterly* 57:44–64.

Fanon, Frantz. 1967. *Black Skin, White Masks*. Trans. Charles Lam Markmann. New York: Grove.

Freud, Sigmund. 1961. *Five Lectures On Psycho-analysis*. Trans. James Strachey. New York: Norton.

Hauptman, Laurence M. 1990. "The Pequot War and Its Legacies." In *The Pequots in Southern New England: The Fall and Rise of an American Indian Nation*, ed. Laurence M. Hauptman and James D. Wherry, 69–80. Norman: University of Oklahoma Press.

Hauptman, Laurence M., and James D. Wherry. 1990. "Preface." In *The Pequots in Southern New England: The Fall and Rise of an American Indian Nation*, ed. Laurence M. Hauptman and James D. Wherry, xiii–xix. Norman: University of Oklahoma Press.

Hodge, Bob, and Vijay Mishra. 1990. *Dark Side of the Dream: Australian Literature and the Postcolonial Mind*. Sydney: Allen and Unwin.

Jennings, Francis. 1976. *The Invasion of America: Indians, Colonialism, and the Cant of Conquest*. New York: Norton.

———. 1993. *The Founders of America: How Indians Discovered the Land, Pioneered in It, and Created Great Classical Civilizations; How They Were Plunged into a Dark Age by Invasion and Conquest; and How They Are Reviving*. New York: Norton.

King, Thomas. 1990. "Godzilla vs. Post-Colonial." *World Literature Written in English* 30, no. 2:10–16.

Krupat, Arnold. 1989. *The Voice in the Margin: Native American Literature and the Canon*. Berkeley: University of California Press.

McClintock, Anne. 1995. *Imperial Leather: Race, Gender, and Sexuality in the Colonial Contest*. New York: Routledge.

Melville, Herman. 1984. *The Confidence-Man: His Masquerade*. Evanston, Ill.: Northwestern University Press and the Newberry Library.

Moon, Randall. n.d. "William Apess and Writing White." *Studies in American Indian Literatures* 5, no. 4:45–54.

Murray, David. 1991. *Forked Tongues: Speech, Writing, and Representation in North American Indian Texts*. Bloomington: Indiana University Press.

O'Connell, Barry. 1992. "Introduction." In *On Our Own Ground: The Complete Writings of William Apess, a Pequot*, ed. Barry O'Connell, xiii–lxxxi. Amherst: University of Massachusetts Press.

Salisbury, Neal. 1982. *Manitou and Providence: Indians, Europeans, and the Making of New England, 1500–1643*. Oxford: Oxford University Press.

Segal, Charles M., and David C. Stineback. 1977. *Puritans, Indians, and Manifest Destiny*. New York: Putnam's.

Starna, William A. 1990. "The Pequots in the Early Seventeenth Century." In *The Pequots in Southern New England: The Fall and Rise of an American Indian Nation*, ed. Laurence M. Hauptman and James D. Wherry, 33–47. Norman: University of Oklahoma Press.

Stephanson, Anders. 1995. *Manifest Destiny: American Expansionism and the Empire of Right.* New York: Hill and Wang.

Takaki, Ronald. 1994. "The Metaphysics of Civilization: Indians and the Age of Jackson." In *From Different Shores: Perspectives on Race and Ethnicity in America,* 2d ed., ed. Ronald Takaki, 52–66. Oxford: Oxford University Press.

Walker, Cheryl. 1997. *Indian Nation: Native American Literature and Nineteenth-Century Nationalisms.* Durham, N.C.: Duke University Press.

Webster, Daniel. 1894. *The Great Speeches and Orations of Daniel Webster.* Ed. Edwin P. Whipple. Boston: Little, Brown.

9 Modern Colonization and the Will to Alterity: Public Culture and Migrant Lifecraft in a New Mexico Town

Arthur Martin

alternative *adjective* 2.a. Existing outside traditional or established institutions or systems. b. Espousing or reflecting values that are different from those of the establishment.

— *American Heritage Dictionary,* 3d ed.

In some places and in some senses, the United States may be postcolonial. In the high desert mesas and mountains of northern New Mexico, however, there is nothing "post" about colonization. Although the form of modernity in the Taos, New Mexico, area is rooted in romantic, expressivist sentiments associated with a desire to be alternative, a "will to alterity," the production and reproduction of that form, modern life as lived in this place, remains a colonizing process, a taking over by and making over into a site of capitalist modernity. If we think of postcoloniality as the project of analyzing coloni- zations as historically located discourses, practices, and relations, a project animated by the idea that such analyses can help us move beyond coloniza- tion, then ethnographic studies of U.S. sites such as Taos, where modern colonization is ongoing, seem particularly relevant. In this essay I build on the insights of postcolonial theorists (e.g., Fanon 1963; Said 1978, 1993; Willis 1991) into the interconstitutive relations between colonizing "center" and colonized "periphery," arguing that modernity and colonization are inher- ently linked, that colonization (expansion into new territories, taking and remaking places, populations, and persons) is a key way that modernity pro- duces and reproduces itself. From this perspective, the will to alterity (the desire to be alternative to, beyond, or postmodern) appears to be a cultural form or practice that is constituted and captured by the logic of modernity, a resource in its expansive reproduction. This essay explores how the modern colonization of Taos works through the will to alterity and suggests that the desire to transcend "coloniality" found among culturally elite U.S. citizens (including many Taos migrants, some academicians, and myself) aims at a complicated and problematic goal.

For one hundred years modern middle-class migrants and tourists have been going to Taos to experience the dramatic otherness they find and create there in the natural environment, the Pueblo Indian and Hispano settler cultures, and the rustic bohemian artist lifestyles of many migrants. During the twentieth century the experiences of otherness modern people have enjoyed there have been seized on as Taos has been constructed as an aesthetic periphery of the modern United States, an internal colony of exotic, alternative, and even utopian experiences. Today Taos is one of the Rocky Mountain West's hypermodern boomtowns. Places such as these (other well-known examples include Santa Fe; Sedona, Arizona; and Moab, Utah) undergo social, cultural, and economic restructuring as they become sites of romantic-alternative colonization, attracting modern tourists and migrants in search of unique experiences. Two key aspects of a "hypermodern" colonization are the construction of a public culture of commodified experiences and the in-migration of modern individuals and families seeking better lives or different lifestyles. The first aspect is based on constructing or controlling certain kinds of extraordinary leisure experiences, commodifying those experiences so that they can generate income, and promoting them to outsiders. Through promotion hypermodern places become associated with the particular cluster of experiences available there. This commodified place identity is a site's "public culture." The second aspect of hypermodern colonization is the transformation of a place into an aesthetic suburb, a place to which people migrate to craft alternative lifestyles. In rural places such as Taos, these lifestyles are marked by their distance from the "hurly-burly of modern life." As people migrate to and make modern lives and selves in new places, they make modernity in those places. Such migrants are generally socioeconomic elites relative to local people, arriving with more money and education than is available in peripheral areas, and they generally remake places in terms of their own meanings and practices. Local peoples and their ways of life are incrementally supplanted as places are remade into more glamorous and expensive sites of lifestyle alterity. In Taos the process of modern colonization through a will to alterity is one hundred years old and ongoing.

The Culture of Capitalist Modernity

Modernity in Taos is a particular manifestation of the culture of capitalist modernity, itself a latest manifestation of the historical dialectic of Euro-American Enlightenment—the systems of meanings and practices emerging from postfeudal Europe. This whole period since the hegemony of feudalism began to be challenged can be characterized as the modern era, a period when certain ideas and practices were crafted and transformed through time. Capitalist modernity is a particular articulation of modern trends that, beginning in the late nineteenth century, structured a new cultural world, a new culture-power framework of identity in environment.

Early Enlightenment thinkers such as René Descartes and Francis Bacon understood themselves to be at a threshold. Whereas medieval persons would have looked around their world and seen everywhere the hand of God, leading-edge moderns looked around theirs and saw worldly phenomena to explain, problems to solve, and situations to manage and control using the rational capacities of thought. For these newly enlightened people (as they thought of themselves), the world became significantly more secular, a place in the here and now of natural history, to be explained and understood first and foremost in terms of its worldly self, without hasty recourse to supernatural or spiritual explanations. Among the bourgeois elites who were imagining this new modern world, there were two prominent intellectual responses. First, a rationalist utilitarian mode of thought was invoked, an instrumentalist search for patterns that could be managed to produce efficient results. Second, reacting to the first trend as an alternative interpretation of a secularized world, there was a romantic, expressivist sensibility centrally concerned with individual experience, aesthetics, and creative expression; romantics sought "totality" or some new form of meaningfulness in a newly disenchanted world. Although divergent on the surface, both these trends of modern thought, utilitarian and romantic, share the basic modern conception of a secularized reality: on the one hand a reality to be explained, accounted for, managed, and controlled and on the other a reality in which human activity and experience are constitutive—primary components of reality, and able to affect it in creative ways. A helpful fact to consider is that David Ricardo and Samuel Taylor Coleridge were contemporary members of the same English bourgeoisie.

An important aspect of the modern secular worldview is the particular form of temporality built into it. This temporality, this cultural mode of being in time, has the modern world constantly sliding toward a progressive future susceptible to human agency. Like any temporality, this modern form is tied to a particular cultural logic of meaningful action. Modernity's progressive temporality structures a dynamic of newness into modern life, a logic of meaningful activity that builds into an open future. Modern values such as accumulation and individualist expression, or utilitarian quests for profit and romantic quests for meaning, imply a cultural space-time of newness into which movement is possible. In fact, enacting this expansive logic and producing this newness seem to be a basic part of the production and reproduction of modernity as a cultural reality.

Pursuing this progressive-expansive logic, the modern Enlightenment world reached a critical point in the late nineteenth century. Bourgeois advances in science, industry, government, and imperialism had radically altered the lifeworld of the elite middle classes in a short span of time. The expanding commodification of everyday life created feelings of being "unreal" and "overcivilized." A sense of self-identity and the general meaningfulness of life were becoming problematic, something less ascribed (assigned by their group) and more achieved—people were becoming more individually responsible for crafting themselves, for their own "self-realization" in a significant phrase from the time (Lears 1994). As Anthony Giddens (1991) has described, a modern self came to be crafted in projects or quests that take the form of reflexively organized, continuously revisable autobiographical narratives. This new sense of self and the advance of the modern capitalist economy combined to form the dual imperatives of modern life: individuals are required to create both meaningful identities and money-based livelihoods from fields of differentially accessible possibilities—to do so is to engage in modern lifecraft, practice modern life, be a modern individual.

The emergence of the modern form of self-identity occurred more or less simultaneously with the development of the modern capitalist corporation and the professionalization of the advertising industry. The result, as described by historians such as Jackson Lears (1983) and Stuart Ewen (1976), was the creation of the modern consumer culture, where individuals were encouraged to craft their lives by acquiring ensembles of commodities appropriate to their economic level. For the mainstream of middle-class people, the goal of acquiring such commodities was to create a "modern," "respectable" self. Others— for example, the "antimoderns" described by Lears (1994)—drew on the modern tradition of romantic expressivism and sought to create more distinct lifecraft projects, often characterized by meanings and practices evoking otherness, differentness, alterity. For these moderns, life and self became a work of art, and they accordingly sought dramatic, aesthetic experiences and people to incorporate into their aestheticized modern lifecraft. Lears (1994) shows how these pursuits (including the arts and crafts movement, turns to medieval and "oriental" styles, and therapy) often contradicted their intent and ended up creatively extending bourgeois hegemony, facilitating rather than resisting the growth of a modern consumer culture. My analysis of lifestyle migrants in Taos builds on Lears's idea, suggesting that the yearnings (and the resolutions of those yearnings) of various antimodern movements—manifestations of the romantic-expressivist, "leftist" segment of the middle class—have played and continue to play a crucial role in the development and hegemonic spread of capitalist modernity.

The history of the twentieth-century United States can be read in part as the spread of the modern identity form and the commodified environmental framework throughout society and the economy. Sociocultural analysts of this history have identified an important trend since around 1970 (see, e.g., Harvey 1989; Jameson 1991). To greatly simplify, the social disorder in the middle classes during the late 1960s was partly due to a growing sense, particularly among young people, that they were stifled by the restrictions of the respectable middle-class lives they were expected to lead. Capitalist modernity's dialectical response was to draw on the tradition of aesthetic alterity seekers and expand the possibilities for diverse lifestyles, proliferating the kinds of styles, experiences, and entertainments available to individuals for creating personal meaning.

The creation of a hyperconsumption public culture of multiple possibilities for multiple tastes was enhanced by "postindustrial" shifts in capitalist investment. As the increasingly transnational corporate sector moved industrial production to overseas areas with cheaper labor and resources, investment in the formerly industrial areas turned to service industries, focusing more on the consumption side of commerce than on production (Harvey 1989; Sassen 1988). Postindustrial investment strategies have come to structure a hypermodern commodity environment of omnipresent corporate media, shopping malls, stylized imagery, and aesthetic experiences. Individuals are expected to experience the public culture as a giant supermarket of goods and experiences from which to craft an identity, either one based on images provided in the mass media or a more personal one (Kellner 1992). Characterizing this condition as "hyper" (very) modern seems more accurate than the more common "post" (after).

Contemporary hypermodern culture is visible in physical places from gentrified urban areas (Mills 1993; Zukin 1989, 1991) to aesthetic suburbs such as Chadds Ford, Pennsylvania, as described by John Dorst (1989), where an "ideological discourse" comes to frame the construction and experience of public and personal space. By transforming or intensifying the built environment for aesthetic experience, such places can be themed in a variety of ways (e.g., as "history," "country," or ethno-other), evoking different kinds of sentiments, construing different kinds of experiences, and attracting residents, shoppers, and experience seekers who find those themes intriguing. The proliferation of aesthetic styles and gentrified sites is part of an increasingly differentiated sphere of consumption in which diverse meanings, experiences, and tactics are available for identity making (as well as money-making). The hypermodern cultural environment includes diverse commodified possibilities available to different people with different tastes or desires, encompassing mainstreams of respectability as well as various kinds of alterities. These alterities become increasingly significant as more people seek to create or participate in distinct, stylized identities evoking difference of various sorts.

The Modern Colonization of Taos: Constructing a Periphery of Alternative Experience

The modern colonization of Taos has not always been in a postindustrial mode. In the years before 1900, the major commercial attempts to capitalize the Taos region (to make money there) focused on industrial-scale stock production and prospecting for gold and other minerals. Ultimately, these enterprises served only to degrade the area's tenuous range lands and create a string of abandoned mining towns in remote mountain valleys (Barrera 1979, 24; Pearson 1986; Rodríguez 1987, 339). Although these early attempts at large-scale accumulation were not successful, the region's incorporation into the Anglo-American legal-economic-administrative framework moved ahead.

When New Mexico came under U.S. control during the Mexican-American War a few decades earlier (1846), hundreds of thousands of acres in the northern part of the territory were communally controlled by villages under the community land-grant system of the Spanish colonial and Mexican governments. The Treaty of Guadalupe Hidalgo, which ended the war, guaranteed the property rights of Mexicans in the areas taken over by the United States. The U.S. judicial system, however, through the specially created Court of Private Land Claims, was unable or unwilling to comprehend the community-based system of land ownership in northern New Mexico, eventually breaking up most of the grants and turning huge tracts into federally controlled fee-for-use national forests. Much of the private land that remained in Hispano control fell into the hands of Anglos and Hispano elites in various ways: families were swindled by lawyers and government officials, could not pay taxes or debts, or succumbed to attractive cash offers (Ebright 1994; Hall 1989; Rodríguez 1987). In this way the foreign system of law imposed on New Mexico after the U.S. takeover was largely responsible for the deterioration of traditional Hispano landholdings that had formed the resource base for their agricultural and pastoral way of life (Barrera 1979). Perhaps the key symbol of the conflict in basic orientations to and definitions of the land is the image of the Hispano land-grant basins, marked off by natural landmarks and designed for subsistence, being overlaid by the rationalized U.S. township grid system in which every parcel was uniform and legally equivalent. Increasingly cut off from their subsistence base, and increasingly in need of cash to acquire commodities, many northern New Mexico Hispanos adapted by taking seasonal wage employment away from home (with the railroad, in the beet harvest, or at commercial ranches). This adaptation helped to preserve home villages by bringing in cash while allowing a continuing degree of local autonomy (Deutsch 1987, 36–38).

Modernity in New Mexico entered a new phase beginning in 1900, when the Fred Harvey chain of hotels, restaurants, and shops extended further west on the Atchison, Topeka, and Santa Fe Railway Company's line into New Mexico and Arizona, and the railroad began promoting the region as a place of natural wonder and cultural exotica (Weigle 1989). Much of this promotion consisted of purchasing and commissioning representational paintings of western landscapes and Native Americans that were used for posters, calendars, and other promotional materials (D'Emilio and Campbell 1991). The images selected for purchase and promotion by the Santa Fe Railway's general advertising agent, W. H. Simpson, were created by "talented artists who, inspired by their quest for the romantic southwestern subject, were painting the region in a manner that greatly appealed to Simpson . . . , [who] looked for brilliant colors and a romantic realism in the pictures" (D'Emilio and Campbell 1991, 17). As Sylvia Rodríguez (1989, 83) writes of the work of early Taos artists, however, "It is important to emphasize that the Indian paintings were not realistic portraits of individuals as they actually appeared in everyday life, but rather romantic compositions for which the subjects dressed in prototypical costume [often the Plains-style dress most familiar to Anglo-Americans of the time]. Indians tended to be portrayed as ideal types in harmony with Nature, caught at some pristine, eternal moment."

This imagined moment of romantic timelessness, so easily evoked in the minds of middle-class European Americans, is a key part of the systematic production of an "Other" that defines the modern Southwest. Discussing popular culture images of Pueblo women and the potteries they make, Barbara Babcock notes that such representations—construing the women and their crafts as "outside history, outside industrial capitalism"—are part a colonial discourse akin to the orientalism described by Edward Said (Babcock 1994, 187). The colonial discourse of "the Southwest" in the twentieth century is largely a promotional discourse, ultimately designed to attract modern middle-class consumers. Interestingly, just as European orientalism created an object—the Orient—that did not exist prior to its articulation in colonial discourse and practice (Said 1978), the "Southwest" to which the Santa Fe railroad and Fred Harvey Company attracted modern Americans consisted significantly of their own creations. Primary among these were the hotels and gift shops built at train stations in the region. The station in Albuquerque featured the sprawling Alvarado Hotel (built in the Spanish Mission revival style developed by Anglos in California) and the Indian Building, which "provided the model for developing middle-class tastes for Indian arts and peoples" (Weigle 1989, 125). The Indian Building, designed by Harvey Company architect Mary Colter, was a combination museum and store intended to introduce train travelers to the Southwest and give them the opportunity to buy some of it. Marta Weigle describes the scene: "Visitors alighted from the train, passed between Indians displaying wares on the platform, entered a museum room of fine Native American and Hispanic arts to educate their tastes for these exotic new forms, went through a demonstration area where 'real' Indian craftspeople were at work, and finally came to the salesrooms, ready to purchase articles resembling those just seen before exiting to train or Alvarado accommodations" (1989, 125). Employees and promoters of the fledgling tourism industry not only created Southwest-style "shopping experience architecture" such as the Indian Building but also, by designing displays and selecting inventories for these sites, helped to construct a general "Southwest style," a system of modern meanings using images of local peoples and scenes and elements of local material culture (architecture, domestic wares, religious objects, jewelry) to evoke a simpler, more authentic "premodern" way of life (Babcock 1990, 1994; Weigle 1989, 1992, 1994a, 1994b; Wilson 1990).

The construction of a modern Southwest, accessible through modern transportation, attracted to northern New Mexico not only tourists but also increasing numbers of middle-class lifestyle migrants, or "art colonists," who sought to escape the modern industrial world and imagined New Mexico to be "the quintessential frontier experience—vast desert-mountain spaces, wild but noble savages, and unlimited personal freedom" (Rodríguez 1989, 80). Chris Wilson writes that the "internal expatriates" of the Santa Fe and Taos art colonies "formed the romantic wing of the New York intelligentsia. . . . many had lived in New York before relocating to New Mexico, and they were joined by a steady stream of summer visitors from New York . . . and like artists and intellectuals the world over, they sought to broaden their understanding of human experience through the study of primitive cultures" (Wilson 1990, 184–85). Migrants seeking to craft aesthetic lives of alterity or differentness could master the code of Southwest-style meanings in their homes and personal fashions, bringing the otherness of Taos and New Mexico into their lives and identities. As "members of an alien, superordinate and colonizing society," however, these romantic art colonists "appropriated indigenous symbols as their own in a manner that relied on and yet belied a social system of stringent ethnic-racial stratification and segregation" (Rodríguez 1987, 344).

Enchanted by the natural environment, the rustic Hispano villages, and especially the Pueblo Indians living in a multistoried mud village, migrants experienced Taos as a premodern wonderland, evoking and articulating with romantic and bohemian/utopian sentiments (Rodríguez 1989, 1994). Through individual migrant lives, commercial development, and the establishment of institutions, Taos was incorporated into the modern United States as an exotic internal colony, an outpost for "a peculiar breed of artists, intellectuals, scholars, and dropouts . . . , culturally disaffected refugees from urban industrial America" (Rodríguez 1987, 344).

Since the land of the Pueblo people was deemed communal and shielded from market forces through their official designation as a "tribe" in 1913, most of the Taos-area land available for new migration and development belonged to the Hispano population. Although bohemian Indianist migrants such as Mabel Dodge Luhan revered the local Indian culture, they seem to have seen Hispanos as picturesque peasants and servants, sources of cheap land and labor. Through the development of a modern, outsider-oriented "economy of enchantment" in which the Pueblo culture was the star celebrity, the Hispano population was caught in what John Bodine (1968) calls a "tri-ethnic trap." Anglos' valorization of the Pueblo culture and their dominance in the local capitalist economy largely relegate Hispanos to low-paying service jobs, increasingly cut off from their traditional land-based system of identity and community. (Of course, there is a well-educated Hispano middle class as well, but it is often not clear whether their interests lie more with the majority of Hispanos or with the Anglo-run system.) The various Hispano responses to this situation include grass-roots and personal attempts to preserve the traditional agricultural and pastoral way of life (see Rodríguez 1987, 1990). These efforts necessarily run up against the legal power and profit momentum of the capitalist development system and its legal ontology. The money-profit logic of modern capitalist development is continuing to erode the Taos Hispanos' agricultural and pastoral way of life—since it is not the fastest way to make the most money, this pattern of land use is by definition "inefficient" and "irrational," and the modern Anglo-American legal-economic system is set up to eliminate such things. As migration-oriented development continues to accelerate (the price of undeveloped land in Taos Valley appreciated as much as 69 percent annually in the early 1990s), more intense pressures will continue to mount against the local Hispano way of life, the main casualty in the modern colonization of Taos.

Taos's Modern Place Identity: A Hypermodern Public Culture

Over the last twenty years, with the ascendance of postindustrial capital accumulation and the hypermodern consumer culture that goes with it, Taos
has boomed. Taos was already established as a site of lifestyle alterity, and as
these kinds of places have become a more important part of the cultural landscape, the area has attracted more investment, lifestyle migration, and development. An important part of this rising tide of modern activity has been
an increasingly professionalized and commodified place identity, a "public
culture" of images, narratives, sites, and experiences that attracts outsiders,
the primary source of profit making.

Three main experience-activity domains constitute Taos's public culture.
The first is the historical and ethno-other complex. This domain takes up and
builds on the historical and continuing cultural otherness that characterizes
Taos. Modern people have in particular been enchanted by the Taos Pueblo
village, composed primarily of two multistoried mud structures facing each
other across a mountain stream. The feeling of romantic timelessness evoked
by the pueblo is enhanced by the centuries-long presence of rustic Hispano
villages and the more recent frontier/mountain-man history of mid-nineteenth-century Anglos in the area. The presence of these cultures and histories gives modern outsiders a sense of stepping back in time, an experience
of an "other" place in an "other" time.

The second domain of the local public culture is nature, the natural environment as both scenery and site of activity experiences. With forested green
mountains and rolling high-desert mesas broken by the valleys and gorges
of mountain streams coursing to the Rio Grande and its dramatic gorge, the
scenery of Taos's natural environment has always played a role in enchant-
ing modern visitors. The sky is an important part of the aesthetic experience
of nature: broad views across plains to isolated peaks and distant ranges, the
much-remarked "crystal-clear" character of the light, and the dramatic cu-
mulus clouds and thunderstorms that can be seen forming near or far. At
certain times of year incredible sunsets light up the mountains in deep pink
tones for less than a minute. Certain view spots around the valley, notable
for the angles of vision and the ranges of geography and sky visible, typify
the modern "scenic" experience of nature in Taos and become the subject
of recurrent artistic rendering. Nature recreation (hiking, skiing, rafting,
horseback riding, and hunting) is also a significant part of Taos as a topography of experiences.

The third major place identity component is the bourgeois arts domain
set up by early migrants. Modern migrants and tourists have found Taos to

be particularly potent in inspiring creative activity and have set up institutions and businesses that promote a general environment of aesthetic activity and experience. Eventually the original academic realist painters, who focused on romantic and nostalgic scenes, were joined by artists of the emerging modernist sensibility. These too were inspired to creativity, but in a more "expressive" mode. These two trends, representational and expressivist, continue generally to characterize modern cultural production in Taos.

A final domain of public culture, one that integrates the others, is the human built environment. An adobe village atmosphere pervades the area, particularly around the downtown central business district, where zoning ensures the adobe appearance is maintained. As with nature, the built environment has a visual rhetoric and typical views and scenes that are endlessly reproduced. The most famous specific site is the San Francisco de Asis church in Ranchos de Taos (whose bulging buttressed rear was made famous by Georgia O'Keeffe). More general elements of the visual rhetoric of adobe enchantment include adobe walls with windows and doors painted "Taos blue" (light blue), adobe walls with *ristras* of red chile hanging along them from protruding vigas (log rafters), and hollyhocks flowering red against adobe walls. For modern outsiders (tourists and migrants), views such as these tend to produce a yearning, either a nostalgic one for the simpler life of an imagined past or a utopic one for a simpler life in an imagined future. In either case, the sense is one of alterity, of something different, which is the dominant symbol of Taos as a modern place, the theme of this hypermodern theme park.

A key component of a hypermodern place identity is a promotional master narrative that defines officially recognized aspects or domains (sites of experience within a place) and ties them together in some unifying image or identity through which consumer-citizens are expected to understand, anticipate, and experience that place. Taos's master narrative is found in visitor guides and maps, travel magazine articles, and advertising for Taos businesses aimed at people in other places. The genre is exemplified by the annual *Taos Vacation Guide,* published and distributed by local business promotion organizations (the Taos County Chamber of Commerce and the Taos County Lodgers Association), partially using money from local governments and American Express, which has small ads for their charge card throughout the guide. The guide is a slickly produced thirty-six-page collection of activity- and domain-specific texts and accompanying montages of color photos, as well as a special events calendar and the names and addresses of appropriate domain-specific businesses and institutions. It is distributed locally at the Chamber of Commerce Visitor Center and on brochure racks throughout the region and is mailed to travel agencies and thousands of potential visitors who inquire by phone or mail.

Blurring the distinction between information and promotion, the guide provides an official account of Taos as a topography of experience, directing visitors into commodified activities within the different domains that, taken as a whole in this totalizing discourse, make Taos the "Soul of the Southwest," as the guide declares. Most of the guide consists of two-page spreads of texts and bright color photos, with key site experiences in bold and significant institutions and businesses listed in the differently colored sidebars. The guide's opening text sets the overarching theme for the textual and visual descriptions that follow: "Prepare to enter the theatre-in-the-round that is Taos, where our diverse landscape and our multi-cultural community enact a drama of rich contrasts." It then continues, after sentences about the natural setting and people coming "millenniums ago": "You are the latest in the history of people journeying to Taos. We invite you to enter our theatre and participate in the drama that is Taos." This is the unifying theme of the experiences that are to be described, the general themed experience that renders hypermodern Taos whole as a public culture: be a part of the historic, aesthetic production that is Taos; insert yourself in the dramatic historical trajectory and aesthetic present by "exploring," "experiencing," and "participating"—"adventure awaits you in every direction," the guide notes toward the end (22).

The first section, "History Alive Today," consists of photos and textual descriptions of historical buildings, museumized as sites of "olden times" experiences for modern consumers. Nevertheless, the guide emphasizes these objects of experience as present: "The Taos drama is not merely a period piece. Our legacy is not a thing of the past." One can "step back in time" at the area's two Pueblo Indian villages, yet two historic Hispano plazas "now have many fascinating shops and galleries." As prefigured by the guide's opening text, these paragraphs present Taos's history and cultural groups as aesthetic productions that visitors can experience and in which they can participate: "We invite you to join our daily celebration of Taos past and present, respecting our customs and our home." Significantly, the ghostly "we" that speaks throughout the guide remains unidentified. The guide's producers assume the right to speak for the community as a whole. The subject who can refer to "our Native American and Spanish cultures" clearly speaks from a colonialist position, assuming the right to define history and cultures to the "outside" in order to attract outsiders and their money. Since the guide's key producers are migrants and would be considered outsiders by many locals (and some migrants),[1] this "we" narrating the guide is, in some ways, the outside defining Taos to the outside from a position understood as being inside. Although the narrator voice does ask for respect for "our customs," it still constructs the local peoples and their traditions as aesthetic experiences. These experiences are mostly "preserved," museumized homes, maintained and equipped in ways deemed historically appropriate. Local churches are promoted and attract tourists as well.

The guide's two sections on art and culture draw attention to more museumized homes and note annual performing arts events, arts festivals, crafts fairs, schools, and workshops, emphasizing that "art is an active experience in Taos. You can participate." The text invites "you" on a "journey into Taos art." Art is "a constant theme. . . . It's everywhere. . . . If you notice a certain spirited atmosphere, it's the wonderful synergy of cultures, generations and personalities creating and interacting. . . . The artists of Taos encourage you to be on the look-out for that one piece of art that speaks to your soul. Ask questions and enjoy your journey into the spirit of southwestern art." Through texts and photos of paintings, galleries, and artists at work, the vacation guide construes Taos as a site of hyperaesthetic experience—art is "everywhere," creating "a certain spirited atmosphere," speaking "to your soul," and, it is hoped, inducing you to buy. A certain kind of active experience is emphasized: "stroll," "be on the look-out," "ask questions," and spend money.

The *Taos Vacation Guide* is a slick promotional magazine, written and designed by publicity specialists under the direction of the main local business promotion organization. It is intended to open up, shape, and construe the experience of Taos for outsiders, doing so through carefully constructed images and texts that provide information and promote particular site experiences. Other texts contributing to a public culture master narrative for Taos include the several freely distributed foldout maps. One of these is published by the local Kiwanis Club; the rest are commercial enterprises. These items are street maps, graphic representations, or in one case an aerial photo of downtown Taos that indicate notable sights and institutions, along with businesses that pay to appear on the maps. Some maps are encircled by ads for these businesses and include business directories listing the advertisers under subject headings. Maps may define territories, but existence in a hypermodern setting is dependent on one's ability to buy a place on a promotional map. Like the vacation guide, these maps conflate information with promotion, a key strategy in the construction of this hypermodern public culture.

Nature recreation is another key component of Taos's public culture. The natural environment becomes part of a topography of activity experiences through the practices of recreation entrepreneurs and land management agencies. Acting under federal and state government mandates, the latter play crucial roles in the mapping, management, and construction of nature experiences. Two federal agencies, the Bureau of Land Management (Interior Department) and the National Forest Service (Agriculture Department), control slightly over 50 percent of the land in Taos County, and their mandates center on managing land and resources to produce value. For most of their histories, these agencies have interpreted value in the modern industrial production sense and sought to create it through extractive industries (mining and logging) and large-scale ranching. More recently, though, as hypermodern postindustrial trends have become more significant, so has a definition of value that emphasizes making nature recreation available to consumers.[2] Thus, the Bureau of Land Management (BLM) and Forest Service construct picnic and camping areas and trails for hiking, biking, and cross-country skiing and then produce and distribute maps and guides for these sites, registering and promoting them as parts of the local topography of experience.

A notable example of such a nature experience site is the Wild Rivers Recreation Area, twenty miles north of Taos. The BLM controls most of the Rio Grande Gorge corridor in Taos County under the federal Wild and Scenic Rivers Act of 1968. In accordance with this legislation, the agency creates recreation sites and manages river rafting traffic, supposedly in such a way as to provide recreation opportunities while protecting the environment. At the Wild Rivers site, where the gorge of the Red River joins the Rio Grande Gorge in one of the many incredibly beautiful sites of erosion throughout the West, the BLM has constructed and manages long trails running down from the mesa tops along the sides of the gorges to the rivers below. The most dramatic trail, La Junta, partially consists of a metal staircase set in concrete down the sheerest drop. Up on the mesa, along with picnic tables and shelters, camping and RV sites, and portable outhouses, a visitors' center ("staffed during summer months") offers maps of trails, nature books, and postcards for sale; "interpretive displays [serving] as an introduction to the area"; and a six-foot-by-three-foot three-dimensional topographic representation of the Taos Valley. This BLM visitor's center also boasts a small amphitheater, used during the summer for fireside lectures, slide shows, and storytelling by BLM rangers. A BLM brochure for the Wild Rivers area includes a map of the area and sections entitled "Access," "Recreation Opportunities," and "What You Will See." In these ways and others, land managers, acting under government mandates, serve to construct, contain, and manage the experience of nature in the Taos area. Although these are not-for-profit enterprises, their stated purpose is to use the land's resources to create value. In a hypermodern setting, this value is increasingly tied to recreational consumption and making the land over into a commodified topography of experience.

Government agencies also work with entrepreneurs, making land available for ski trails and authorizing and facilitating river rafting, hunting, horseback riding, and trekking businesses (including a growing "llama trek" industry—overnight or day hikes with llamas carrying the luggage, including gourmet organic meals). These are mostly small-scale nature-experience commodification enterprises, which in turn articulate with other small businesses, such as outfitters and outdoor equipment shops. The major for-profit force in the outdoor recreation realm is the Taos Ski Valley and other smaller ski basins. The Ski Valley consists of a family-owned base/mall and lift operation, with trails cut on mountains controlled by the Forest Service, plus an area of privately owned lodges, condominiums, and homes. Taos Ski Valley is a major presence in hypermodern Taos, particularly during the winter, when skiing becomes the primary attractor of outsiders. Not surprisingly, the Ski Valley is financially involved in every major promotional effort (such as the vacation guide) and assumes a central place in such promotions.

The human built environment—the rustic, adobe look of downtown, village, and rural areas—is an important part of the experience of alterity in Taos and thus an important part of its modern place identity. Certain parts of downtown and outlying village areas still retain the aesthetic romantic look and "feel" of a premodern adobe village—low clusters of tightly packed mud buildings. Walking around such places, where people often have planted hollyhocks and hung *ristras* of red chile and painted doors and sills sky blue, with flowing ridges of the Sangre de Cristo mountains overhead, is like stepping into a three-dimensional Southwest-style painting, an aesthetic "theatre-in-the-round" (as the vacation guide says), a Santa Fe–style theme park. This image captures the "adobe-nature complex" that Etsuko Kuroda (1981, 39) identifies as the "dominant symbol of Taos," the joining of "the beauty of the mountains" with "a human factor in the adobe construction" that "symbolizes a sense of happiness."

Although some structures in the Taos area are old and have been "preserved," many others were built or rebuilt in the twentieth century in the pueblo revival architectural style designed by modern architects and made popular in homes, hotels, and government buildings throughout New Mexico.[3] Pueblo revival style emphasizes an explicitly adobe look, "organic" with big rounded brown walls, viga ceilings, *portales,* and carved corbels—a look that produces exciting feelings and experiences of "olden times" for modern people. The process of constructing a "preserved" downtown is legally inscribed in Taos's Land Use Development Code, which defines downtown as a "Historic Preservation Overlay Zone," mandating architectural uniformity through preservation of old buildings and strict aesthetic standards for new ones. As Sylvia Rodríguez (1994) has described it, the twentieth-century transformation of the downtown plaza area of Taos is an ongoing rural version of gentrification, including both the remaking of the physical appearance of the built environment and changes in the uses of public spaces. Since the arrival of modern migrants, the downtown area has been rebuilt in pueblo revival style. Some of the architectural transformations of Taos plaza can be seen in historical photographs contained in the book *Taos: A Pictorial History* (Sherman 1990). A photo from the early 1880s shows the west side of the plaza as it had probably been for decades: a single one-story, flat-roofed structure and portal (the traditional covered walkway) running the length of the square, with a plain door and window about every twenty feet. Sherman's discussion of the photo notes that the *portales* "were removed to make the plaza more 'modern' in 1887" (1990, 31). Photos from around 1900 reveal this project was successful. The single structure of the west side is broken into distinct storefronts, several with their front walls converted into paneled picture windows; some sections have a new second story, and the portal is gone, replaced in some places with individual storefront awnings. Although there is no visible signage in the 1880s view, by 1900 signs proliferate, with most businesses displaying more than one. There is no doubt the new eclecticism of the plaza would have appeared "modern" compared to earlier incarnations, but not long into the twentieth century local businesspeople began to realize that the growing tourist industry was better served by a more regionally distinct style. By 1940 three sides of the plaza had been rebuilt or remodeled into pueblo revival style buildings that remain today (see photo, Sherman 1990, 110). Gentrification claimed the plaza's east side in the 1970s with the construction of Plaza Real, a two-story minimall with seven shops and an inside courtyard on the first floor and a restaurant with a balcony on the second. Finally, in the early 1990s an old building and parking lot on the southeast corner of the plaza were replaced with a small version of the plaza itself, modeled on the previously gentrified and now "historic" sections.

The changing of the public space into one designed for modern experience has affected the use of the space as well as its appearance (Rodríguez 1994, 114). The plaza was once the center of community life—photos show general merchandise stores, drug stores, restaurants, coffee shops, a movie theater, pool parlors, saloons, banks, and an electric supply store. Today Taos plaza is almost wholly given over to the trinket, souvenir, and T-shirt shops, art galleries, and boutiques that define a hypermodern public space, transformed into an aestheticized place to shop for tokens of experience and lifestyle accoutrements (clothing, jewelry, home stuff) in stores with names such as Coyote Club, Six Directions, Images, Buffalo Dancer, and Artwares. A recent example of the hypermodern remake or colonization of Taos's public culture occurred in 1994 when a J.C. Penney store that had been located just off the plaza for over fifty years was told to vacate its building so the owner could convert it into a minimall of five art galleries and craft shops called Galeria de Taos. As uses change, so do the users. Except for small groups of teenagers, a few shop owners, and some shop workers (usually young or older women), Hispanos largely avoid the plaza area.

Gentrification of the downtown area into a shopping experience theme park has companion transformations in other parts of the valley. The kind of modernization that goes along with a developing place such as Taos produces the growing, corporate urbanized strip south of town, with its Wal-Mart, Holiday Inn, Mail Boxes Etc., and pueblo-style Long John Silver's. Many previously open areas—farmland, pastures, hillsides, and the mesas outside of town—are being developed and sold as residential subdivisions as hundreds of new migrants arrive every year. These subdivisions take a variety of forms, from regularized suburban-style neighborhoods within the Taos town limits to remote parcels of land sold to individuals. Many new developments are notably upscale and have the kinds of restrictive covenants on density and minimum lot size that tend to keep out people with subaffluent incomes. Until recently, most Anglos, even wealthy ones, lived near local, relatively poor people; current forms of development tend to put more space between relative haves and have-nots. These transformations of public space, the gentrification of previously occupied areas and the development of new ones, constitute the human geography of hypermodern colonization in the Taos area.

Through gentrification and development, commodification of nature experiences, saturation of the public space with artwork and adobe, and the construction of local history and cultural groups as aesthetic experiences, Taos is colonized for modern people, made over into a hypermodern place, a site of alternative experience.

Migrant Lifecraft

Another way hypermodern places such as Taos are colonized is through the in-migration of relatively elite outsider Anglos. "Anglos," or non-Hispanic whites, have grown from only 8 percent of the Taos County population in 1970 to 28 percent in 1990, with more arriving all the time. Conservative estimates based on census data suggest at least 85 percent of the Anglos were born outside Taos County. Compared to the overall U.S. Anglo population, the 5,000 Anglos eighteen years or older in Taos in 1990 included a slightly higher percentage of females and singles and were more educated and poorer (although there have always been affluent migrants, and their percentage seems to be growing). The largest age group for both men and women was thirty-five to forty-four, with the remaining people skewed slightly toward the older side. The unusually high level of "educational attainment" by Anglos in Taos indicates the migrant community is overwhelmingly elite middle class. Following Pierre Bourdieu (1984), I understand modern classes to be based in particular half-conscious cultural practices and orientations, and I assume that a good (but never foolproof) measure of membership in the middle class is the educational history of a person and her or his parents.

Comparisons of the three ethnic groups' census figures for income, educational attainment, and money spent on buying or renting a place to live show that in these terms Anglos are clearly elites relative to Hispano and Native American people, just as one would expect in a situation of colonization.

Being a modern person entails taking up the dual imperatives of modern lifecraft: the creation of a meaningful self-identity and the money-based maintenance of livelihood. As Giddens (1991) has observed, a key way modern people make meaningful lives and self-identities is by telling themselves and others stories about themselves, stories that explain what has happened before and how it has led to where, what, and who they are in an ever-shifting now. Besides creating such a self-narrative, modern people must also find or make places in structured flows of capital, "make money," to purchase necessary and desired goods. As migrants craft modern lives in Taos, they enact modernity there; they practice modern middle-class "being-in-Taos." Thus, modern colonization can be read in the lifecraft narratives of migrants. What are they doing in Taos? Why do they live there? What does Taos mean to them? The following observations are based on interviews with informants, the lives of people I know, and the lives of public people.

Modern Anglos generally migrate to Taos at significant turning points in their lives. Some come after a graduation, retirement, or other rite of passage built into the lifecycle of modern middle-class people. Others become disenchanted enough with life somewhere else or develop a desire for a different life and rearrange their lives to move to Taos. Most were looking to move somewhere and decided on Taos, which they imagined as a place of new possibilities, the site of a different and more content, more meaningful life. Some migrants tell of dreaming of Taos or having voices tell them that Taos is where they should be. Many migrants speak of "feeling at home" in Taos (often immediately on first arriving), an experience that tells them this is where they belong.

The ways in which migrants construe Taos, the meanings through which they understand and experience it as a place, are an important part of the cultural production of modernity in Taos. The most common meanings are "the land" and "the people." "The landscape," "the beautiful scenery," "the climate," "the weather," "the geography," "the land," "the beauty of it and the open space and the sunsets and the mountain and the color"—this is the language in which migrants typically evoke the experience of the natural environment. Words such as *landscape, scenery,* and *beauty* point to the significantly aesthetic experience of nature for modern migrants. Although most migrants I know engage in some outdoor activities (including "walking in the mountains," "hiking," "sleeping outside," "identifying plants and climbing cliffs," "getting water from a spring"), the distinct emphasis is usually on the visual

experience of the land—the land as landscape, environment as scenery, nature as gazed-upon thing: "People back home would say, 'Well, what are you
going to do in Taos?' and I told them I'm going to sit on the patio and watch
the scenery change"; "We like just sitting out here in the backyard looking at
the mountains and the weather and the birds." For many migrants, the visual
aspect of Taos as landscape undergirds a more distinctly felt experience of Taos
that evokes "inspiration" and "feeling at home," a deep felt "connection": "My
bones feel good being in this landscape"; "The land is really unique, and I bond
a lot with the land." As landscape, as spiritual inspiration, as a highly aesthetic
backdrop for everyday life, the natural environment forms a significant part
of modern migrant life in Taos: "I really just love the landscape. From anywhere you go it's just . . . everywhere around you is beautiful—mountains, the
gorge, the mesa. One-half of your world is in the sky; it feels very healthy, the
atmosphere of crystal clear air. And I live here because of that. I am enchanted
[laughs]." Meanings and experiences of nature are one of the sites of articulation between Taos's public culture and the lives of migrants there.

The "migrant social environment" is another significant cluster of meanings and experiences. This environment is evoked in three interlinked ways:
as "the people"—the kinds of people who move to Taos and become the
people that other migrants know; as "the community" formed by these
people; and as a "small-town" atmosphere in which such a community becomes possible and is fostered. Together these form a social context that
many migrants associate with the ability to construct an individual self and
meaningful life.

For the most part, Hispanos, Indians, and Anglos (especially migrants) live
in separate worlds. Although there are exceptions, extraordinary and mundane instances of border crossings, transcultural experiences and persons,
separation is instantiated in complex ways by individuals of every group.
Anglos form a superordinate, colonizing class, and consciously and not,
through their own practices and those of others, they form a significantly
separate social realm. Thus, it is not surprising that when migrants speak of
"the people," they are generally talking about the people who make up the
Anglo migrant community, the people like them. "The people" are characterized as "individual," "worldly," "educated," "friendly," "not afraid to pick
up and move," "supportive," "creative," and having "a commitment to self-
growth and development."

Formed by people there as a matter of "personal choice," the migrant community is "strictly individual," "socially horizontal . . . without any sense of
hierarchy": "You aren't judged by . . . any of those things that the city usually
sets up as restrictions." Informants speak of their experiences of "acceptance,"
"openness," and "freedom": "You can be who you are"; "You can transform

in any number of ways and no one's going to criticize you in any way." Multiple informants mention a general unbegrudging tolerance of loners: "The community gives me permission to be a hermit"; "You can be as private as you choose"; "One is allowed solitude, within." There is a long tradition among modern migrants of interpreting the Anglo migrant community as peculiarly composed of eccentric, self-sufficient, rugged individuals with a strong sense of autonomy and doing their lives themselves—"people that have come from all walks of life, but have sort of pitched it and . . . decided to try something new, something different," as one migrant described them to me. The encouragement of and value placed on creativity and "being an individual," the fact that "everyone here has a commitment to self-growth and development," is experienced by migrants as a supportive and stimulating atmosphere of "social freedom" to be as one feels. In this outpost away from the masses, one can be more truly "individual."

Another articulating aspect of the migrant social environment that people mention liking is the small-town character of life in Taos. "Being in a more familiar situation in terms of seeing people that you know more often," you "feel comfortable"—maybe you hug friends at the market and "have more . . . interpersonal relationships." Nevertheless, Taos is "sort of like a small town with big-town people"—again, meaning other migrants, for "it has a great deal of cultural advantage," as well as "complexity and sophistication," "something like a university town." In some ways the small-town characteristic of seeing people you know almost everywhere you go—the grocery store, the gas station, a movie—is decreasing as more and more people move to Taos and development sprawls. Nonetheless, if you and your friends have similar lifestyle habits—shop at the natural food co-op, patronize the coffee shops, attend classical music performances—then you will still see people you know on a regular basis. The migrant social environment—the kinds of people who move to Taos, the community those people form, and the small-town character of everyday interaction—is an important part of an everyday meaningful life for most migrants. The emphasis on "acceptance" and the value placed on "eccentricity" and "rugged individualism" gives people both a feeling of group belonging ("community") and a sense of personal freedom ("you can be who you are," "you can transform in any number of ways" without fear of derision). This dual sense of individual autonomy and membership in a larger community is particularly conducive to modern lifecraft. Migrants come to Taos and actively and passively participate in the construction of a community of migrants that articulates with the kinds of lives they want to live.

Taos's multicultural environment is another source of the unique experience of the area. This experience is one of co-present separation, physical proximity combined with social distance. Migrants narrate this situation in different ways, often focusing on the ambiguity of an "extremely stressful" "building block." In other words, migrants perceive multiethnic Taos as containing prejudice and mistrust on the one hand and the potential for understanding on the other. Some migrants describe aspects of the local Hispano community that they admire: family orientations, interpersonal courtesy and respect, and connections to the land. A few tie these together, seeing an inspirational example of a "simpler, more human" way of life, as one migrant told me. People glimpse these same qualities among the Pueblo people, but in a more obscure form. As Native Americans have come to assert more control over their cultural interactions with outsiders, Indianism, "the advocacy and emulation of Indian culture by non-Indians" (Rodríguez 1989, 91), has become a somewhat less prominent feature of migrant life now than in the art colony's early days, at least in its more extreme versions. Although the pueblo remains a powerful draw for many tourists and spiritually inclined migrants, when the latter discover that outsiders have no real access to Pueblo life and religion, most are content to "feel the power of their presence," as more than one informant expressed it, and decorate their homes and bodies with Indian or Indian-inspired arts and crafts. Some migrants mention liking Taos because "it's as close as you can get to the Third World without leaving the U.S.," "the furthest thing from America without leaving America." Others say that they "like being a minority." To a significant degree, these meanings seem to be aesthetic, part of having a dramatic set for everyday life tied to experiencing oneself as detached from "America," experiencing oneself as other and distinct in a way white middle-class Americans usually feel only on foreign vacations or in the kinds of neighborhoods they call ghettos. Unfortunately, these senses of cultural difference and an enclaved self serve to reproduce separation, which for some becomes an aesthetic resource in crafting an alternative self. Whether migrants understand the local social situation as one of colonization or not (most do not), the contrasts to modern Anglo culture provided by the Taos Pueblo and Hispano cultures (interpreted and experienced differently by different migrants) form a distinctive framework for migrant "being-in-Taos" and a significant part of an alternative life in Taos.

The human built environment, particularly the predominant rustic adobe look, adds to the everyday experience of alterity in Taos and ties the public culture to the lives of migrants. Some people live in the heart of the theme park, downtown near the plaza, which can take on the characteristics of an open-air museum—walking tours passing by, with people peering in windows and open doors or asking for restrooms. Even people who cannot afford to live downtown (where studio apartments rent for over $600 per month) often incorporate the adobe Southwest-style aesthetic into their lives and homes, from decorating their rented apartments with *ristras* and folk art to designing and building their own adobe or adobe-looking houses. People's homes, actual and desired, are frequent topics of conversation, and an adobe house is considered particularly desirable: they can be built with local materials; they insulate well and are cool in summer; and they have a distinct romantic, organic beauty that visually articulates with the natural environment. Owners of fancy, customized adobe homes sometimes give them evocative names such as "El Cielo Grande" (the big sky) and "Rancho Milagro" (miracle ranch), emphasizing the modern aesthetic-natural-spiritual experience of being in Taos. Almost everyone is fairly knowledgeable about construction techniques, and local bookstores have prominent home and architecture sections featuring books on historic adobe buildings and adobe construction and renovation techniques: *Taos Adobes, Adobe Architecture, Adobe: Remodeling and Fireplaces,* and *Adobe! Homes and Interiors of Taos, Santa Fe, and the Southwest,* to name just a few. Through their homes, people can tie their lives to place using historical forms (or at least styles—new building techniques are perfecting the adobe look using wood frames and other materials). They can make their personal space cohere with the image experience of the public space.

The character of everyday life for migrants in Taos is significantly framed and constituted through these experiences—the natural, social, multicultural, and built environments. They form a dramatic, aesthetic set in which modern individuals feel encouraged and able to craft lives and be individuals in storied and alternative ways. Thus migrants take up art or writing, find a personal-spiritual path, pursue a course of study for "growth," or explore new realms of experience. These are some of the ways migrants address the modern need to create a meaningful life using Taos as both content and background.

Maintaining a money-based livelihood is another main component of modern lifecraft: acquiring subsistence and other necessities of life through finding a place in the capitalist economy. In modern society acquiring money is the basic livelihood imperative. As in modern society generally, migrants practice livelihood in a variety of ways at a variety of economic levels. Importantly, however, many are able to do so in ways that promote the experience of an alternative life. General types of migrant livelihood strategy are translocal occupations, local investing, lifestyle capitalism, and the multitrack strategy of the unmoneyed majority. In different ways each of these strategies enables migrants to understand their lives as relatively autonomous, as more "individual" than "corporate."

Although life in Taos is not necessarily easy for many migrants, for most it is a place of contentedness, a place that is, as one told me, "absolutely congruent with my self." Migrants' modern lifecraft in Taos is characterized by a general sense of alterity. Several informants speak positively of being "off the grid of corporate life," of living an alternative temporality: they become more attentive to the seasons, more focused on "day-to-day things," "daily life," interpersonal relations and social interactions. For most migrants, the experience of alterity in everyday life is a crucial part of Taos as a site of self construction, a place where they can craft a meaningful self and life.

Posthippie Survivalism: Mike Reynolds's Earthship Homes and Communities

Through its history as a romantic colony, Taos developed a reputation as a place where adventurous modern people could be "rugged individuals" and "get back to the land," living eccentrically, self-sufficiently, and with less money. Descriptions of this lifestyle in the 1950s are recorded in Joan Love- less's memoir (1992) of the interlocked family lives of three weavers, art school graduates from the East Coast: building their own adobe homes, learning about the land, growing some food, perfecting a craft, and making a small livelihood doing it. This alternative-lifestyle theme was developed further in the late 1960s when several hippie communes were set up in the Taos area, which became "one of the regular stops on the hip circuit" (Melville 1972, 27). One of the best-known communes is still owned by some original mem- bers, who now run it as a posthippie bed and breakfast: "Throughout the EVOLUTION of New Buffalo from commune to bed and breakfast/retreat center, we have striven to maintain the ideals—community, brotherhood, universal responsibility—of the sixties" (promotional brochure). Today the most prominent alternative lifestyle in Taos is more individualist and prag- matic: "off-the-grid," self-built housing, particularly the "Earthship" de- signed by Taos migrant architect and contractor Mike Reynolds. Off-the-grid houses provide their own power (usually solar), their own water (well or rain), and their own sewage disposal. In this way one's home can be autono- mous from centralized public utility systems. There is a definite survivalist feeling associated with off-the-grid housing, the idea that one could continue to survive even if large-scale public organization began to break down.

In volume 1 of his Earthship trilogy, Reynolds makes clear the goal of the Earthship is to "evolve self-sufficient living units . . . independent vessels— to sail on the seas of tomorrow." Based on the master ideas of systems inte- gration and environmental interface or articulation, the Earthship design now allows for full self-sufficiency without even a well (rain water is caught on the roof and channeled into cisterns) or a septic tank (if you can live with the solar burning toilet). The current Earthship design is the result of years of trial-and-error experimentation in pursuit of an ecological house using recycled materials, mainly tires and aluminum cans. Several earlier, less successful prototypes lie clustered in a shallow valley west of town. Earthships start with a U-shaped "module" dug into a south-facing slope no larger than eighteen feet wide and twenty-six feet deep. The modules' earth walls are lined with stacked tires, each tire pounded full of dirt with sledgehammers. This basic structure is simply made but labor intensive. A ceiling/roof is framed with log beams and filled in with mortar and aluminum cans. The tire walls are plastered for an adobe look. The open side of the module, facing south, is covered with windows tilted in at an angle determined by latitude and, integrating with the sun, becomes the "greenhouse-hallway-heating duct," the home's source of solar energy. The side walls of this section are mortar and cans. Viewed from the outside, this windowed front is the primary architectural feature. An Earthship can extend from a single module to a string of several, and multiple stories can be added on a hill.

In some of his writings Reynolds presents a strikingly messianic view of his architectural designs, and more specifically of the knowledge and ways of thinking underlying those designs. He sees these conceptual tools as facilitating a fundamental "wizard"-inspired transformation into a more ecological, decentered way of life (Reynolds 1989, 1990). Volume 3 of Reynolds's Earthship series (1993) is titled *Evolution beyond Economics* and in part describes the founding of two of the three Earthship-only communities being developed, or "planted," by Reynolds in the Taos area. Reynolds rejects "modern approaches to community living [that] have tried to physically create the community" and proposes an alternative: "The Earthship concept (as presented in Volumes I, II, and III) is a method of creating a fertile soil from which a community can grow. We should not try to structure or build the community either physically, spiritually or emotionally any more than we should try to build a live tree. We can, however, create the ideal conditions from which a community can grow and flourish. We are makers of soil . . . all we need to do is create the proper psychic soil for a community." A "rich psychic soil" is related to "absence of survival stress" and a reduced need for money (1993, 140).

Reynolds goes on to describe his program for "planting" Earthship communities. It starts with an "initiator" ("the trick is for just one or two people to start it"), who buys a large piece of land, which is much cheaper in huge parcels, and files the property under a "land users association." This association then sells memberships that allow people to build an Earthship on an assigned "lodging site"—there is no sale of land. Membership cost is determined by the square footage of the Earthship you want to build and which "variable density area" you prefer (how far you want to be from your neighbors); your membership certificate specifically states where you will build and how big your Earthship can be. Membership prices in 1994 ranged from a few sites available for two dollars per square foot to a high of fifteen dollars per square foot; most memberships range from seven to eleven dollars per square foot. Thus, a membership for a site to build a medium-small 1,000-square-foot home in one of these "Greater World Communities" costs around $10,000, somewhat more than an average small plot of undeveloped land with no utilities this far from town. Although the "initiator" is "basically 'lord of the land' until the land is paid off [with new membership fees] and a board of directors takes over" (Reynolds 1993, 147), the communities are governed according to the Land Users Code, Articles of Association, and By-Laws published in volume 3 and available in the "Communities Information Packet." The corporate-constitutional framework laid out in these documents is surprisingly authoritarian, but the goal is to "provide a 'real life' setting for the research and development of architectural, mechanical, environmental, sociological, economic, spiritual and ecological ideas as put forth in the books by Michael Reynolds": "It is the opinion of this association that the current fundamental approach to living by modern society is at the root of all these problems [crime, drug abuse, ecology, energy, homelessness, child abuse, and war] and that the efforts of this association could shed light in the direction of change" (Greater World Land Users Association Articles of Association, article 3, A and B).

There is thus a clearly stated intent to "evolve beyond economics" and "explore new worlds" alternative to the hegemonic form of modern capitalist life. To build an Earthship at one of Reynolds's developments, however, to become a member of one of these communities, requires not only a commitment to "an adventure in living . . . [and] the evolution of humanity," as an information/sales packet says, but adherence to codes, articles, and bylaws and, even more to the point, money—money for the membership and then money to build your house. The prices of Earthships shown in volume 1 (1990) range from around $30,000 to around $150,000, and then there's actor Dennis Weaver's 7,000-square-foot Earthship in Colorado: $630,000. In other words, you still have to *buy* the chance to evolve—living like this, in an off-the-grid home, in this kind of community, remains, by definition, a commodity, a particular lifestyle available for purchase in a market of lifestyles. The fact that such a dramatically alternative lifestyle remains within the commodity logic of capitalism recalls the kinds of issues Lears (1994) discusses among turn-of-the-century "antimoderns." As an alternative within modernity rather than an alternative to modernity, off-the-grid Earthship living serves the expansion of capitalist modernity into new places and new realms of experience.

The Will to Alterity as Colonizing Contradiction

In Taos colonization by modernity, the taking and making over by and for modern people, is focused on constructing a commodified, aesthetic periphery, an outpost where people can have alternative experiences and craft alternative lives. In some straightforward ways, alterity can be found in Taos: different environments, different lifestyles, even different forms of temporality and senses of self—"you can transform in any number of ways." But these are clearly alternatives within rather than against capitalist modernity, serving to expand modernity into new geographic and conceptual territory. Even against the explicit intentions of some people, these alterity practices expand modernity into new territory, strengthening rather than subverting modernity by providing more possibilities within the cultural system. This is not necessarily a surprising finding, for it substantiates earlier studies (e.g., Lears 1994; Pratt 1992; Thomas 1994; Young 1990; Zukin 1989), but it is important for people concerned with social transformation because it casts doubt on the idea of a postcoloniality or a postmodernity generated by elite middle-class Americans. Even romantic-expressivist people who want to end coloniality, to transcend modernity, as do many Taos migrants and myself, inevitably extend that which they seek to counter. The will to alterity thus appears as a contradiction, an inconsistency between intent and execution.

Because of the complexity of cultural worlds, contradictions—in meanings, values, desires, and practices—are endemic in human life. They are particular to sociocultural forms, however, and even to particular locations within a form. Contradictions can be interesting in that they may produce activity or dynamics as people try to erase, work around, or ignore lacks of coherence; in this way contradictions can provide windows onto cultural change and reproduction. Developing the ideas of Marx, Giddens defines the primary contradiction of modern capitalism as "private appropriation versus socialized production" (Giddens 1979, 143). The modern will to alterity can be seen as a located instance of this primary contradiction: the "private," personal desire to be alternative found among some bourgeois people is constituted through and captured by the "socialized production" of sites and possibilities where that desire can be played out. The maintenance of this contradiction is the reproduction of modernity in an alternative mode.

Among migrants in Taos, the basic contradiction is the pursuit of an alternative lifecraft, a will to alterity, in the context of a modern capitalist colonization that displaces the traditional Hispano culture and poor people generally. A few migrants identify this contradiction, but the tendency is to throw up one's hands: "What can you do?"; "I have to make a living"; "This is where I can be happy." These occasional moments of felt contradiction and their elision, with subjects moving over or past them through rationalization or by contrasting themselves with more egregious examples of less-caring people, seem to be a significant if hardly noticed component of the (re)production of an alterity-oriented modern place such as Anglo Taos. Avoiding the issue allows colonization to continue.

One way to be in Taos and bypass this contradiction is to favor development and be less ambivalent about its effects on the local population. As growth in Taos increasingly emphasizes luxury resort development, these attitudes seem to characterize more migrants, going along with establishment views about the inevitability of "progress," taking things over and doing them better, in more rational ways. From this point of view, the local people should expect this to happen; indeed, they should be doing it themselves, "adapting." Although these migrants do not worry that their presence contributes to the displacement and marginalization of the local Hispano culture and population, the alterity-seeking contradiction manifests in a different way: one reason they choose to live in Taos is its still relatively small scale, and they realize that as more people like them move in, that quality dissipates and Taos becomes more like a suburb with a mountain. This is the "close the door behind me" contradiction—the desire for Taos to stay as it was when a migrant arrived.[4] An informant who works in a downtown book store told me: "One thing that does annoy me is when people come here and then they want to be the last one: 'Now that I'm here everyone else should stop coming.' I get that so much because people come into the shop to buy quad maps to see where their real estate is, you know. Almost all of them say that. Wanting to be the last person into paradise." Although sharing this desire, most migrants eschew "close the door behind me" as a valid position and instead throw up their hands, typically invoking the "inevitability" of "growth" (that is, tourism and migration-centered capitalist development). Thus migrants' movement into Taos is naturalized as part of an inevitable process, and individual agency in a colonization is obscured. At least a few people accept the contradiction, however, and admit wanting the doors closed after them ("slowed growth"). Finally, there are a very few people (the most profit-oriented entrepreneurs and real estate developers) who, judging from their public stances on issues such as airport expansion and zoning, seem to want Taos to become more like Santa Fe—more of an enclaved outpost for the rich and stylish, complete with acres and acres of well-removed trailer parks to house the Hispanos, Chihuahuences, and Spanish speakers from further south who fill the lowest-rung service jobs. This prodevelopment stance is unusual, but it seems worth noting that it does not produce the contradictions that subtly haunt more alterity-oriented migrants.

If middle-class people who seek alterity can overlook contradictions, can enact modernity while still experiencing a "way out," there does not seem to be much hope for them to move beyond colonization. Should we expect a clearly observable difference between one more advance of modern colonization and something really revolutionary and transcendent of modernity—a postmodernity, a postcolonialism? The twentieth-century modernization of Taos forms a live cultural test site for "postcolonial" questions about the commodification of alterity and the possibility of transcending modernity by employing modern practices in pursuit of modern values. Although these questions are not closed, the existing evidence does not look promising. As long as individuals can ignore or rationalize key contradictions that emerge in alter-modern lifecraft projects, the romantic-expressivist will to alterity seems likely to continue its role as an inadvertent colonizer for capitalist modernity rather than to form a serious alternative to it. Thus, while idealistic and adventurous middle-class migrants seek to transcend modernity out on the mesas west of town, capitalism accelerates its colonization of Taos and the displacement of the local Hispano culture.

Notes

This essay is based on dissertation research conducted with major funding from the National Science Foundation (Dissertation Improvement Grant 9318958) and small grants from the University of New Mexico's Department of Anthropology and Student Research Allocation Committee. At various times research was facilitated by the use of UNM's Southwest Hispanic Research Institute/Department of Anthropology Field Station in Taos. Thanks to UNM professors Sylvia Rodríguez, Louise Lamphere, Keith Basso, and Marta Weigle for support. Most of all I want to thank my friends in Taos, especially Frank DeLuca and Estevan Trujillo, and my many anonymous informants who were willing to open themselves up to me for the benefit of anthropology and one anthropologist's career.

1. Some migrants express the idea that they and other migrants remained outsiders, "long-term tourists," even after years in Taos.

2. L. Sue Greer (1990) discusses the politics of this process in the Jefferson National Forest in Virginia, specifically tying them to the state's role in fostering capital accumulation.

3. In a collection of essays on pueblo style and regional architecture, UNM philosophy professor Fred Sturm (1990, 21) writes that for any building built in the pueblo revival style, either it "conforms to what has been perceived through Anglo eyes to be 'typically Pueblo,' or there is an effort to utilize the 'traditional style' in a novel way that will add the stamp of the individual architect, or the consumer, in addition to the characteristics that are taken to be essential to the 'style.' Rather than constituting a modern development of an architectural style that reflects the Pueblo aesthetic, these buildings represent a sharp deviation from that style in order to reflect the radically different Anglo aesthetic." See Wilson (1990) for a history of pueblo revival style architecture in twentieth-century New Mexico.

4. This "close the door behind me" contradiction seems to be a personalized version of the economic-level contradiction between preservation and growth (the "golden goose syndrome") described by Rodríguez (1989, 89).

Works Cited

Babcock, Barbara. 1990. "'A New Mexican Rebecca': Imaging Pueblo Women." *Journal of the Southwest* 32:400–437.

———. 1994. "Mudwomen and Whitemen: A Meditation on Pueblo Potteries and the Politics of Representation." In *Discovered Country: Tourism and Survival in the American West*, ed. S. Norris, 180–95. Albuquerque, N.M: Stone Ladder.

Barrera, Mario. 1979. *Race and Class in the Southwest: A Theory of Racial Inequality*. South Bend, Ind.: University of Notre Dame Press.

Bodine, John J. 1968. "A Tri-Ethnic Trap: The Spanish Americans in Taos." In *Spanish-Speaking Peoples in the United States*, ed. June Helm, 145–54. Seattle: University of Washington Press.

Bourdieu, Pierre. 1984. *Distinction: A Social Critique of the Judgment of Taste*. Trans. Richard Nice. Cambridge, Mass.: Harvard University Press.

D'Emilio, Sandra, and Suzan Campbell. 1991. *Visions and Visionaries: The Art and Artists of the Santa Fe Railway*. Salt Lake City, Utah: Peregrine Smith Books.

Deutsch, Sarah. 1987. *No Separate Refuge: Culture, Class, and Gender on an Anglo-Hispanic Frontier in the American Southwest, 1880–1940*. New York: Oxford University Press.

Dorst, John. 1989. *The Written Suburb: An American Site, an Ethnographic Dilemma*. Philadelphia: University of Pennsylvania Press.

Ebright, Malcolm. 1994. *Land Grants and Lawsuits in Northern New Mexico*. Albuquerque: University of New Mexico Press.

Ewen, Stuart. 1976. *Captains of Consciousness: Advertising and the Social Roots of the Consumer Culture*. New York: McGraw-Hill.

Fanon, Frantz. 1963. *The Wretched of the Earth*. New York: Grove.

Giddens, Anthony. 1979. *Central Problems in Social Theory: Action, Structure, and Contradiction in Social Analysis*. Berkeley: University of California Press.

———. 1991. *Modernity and Self-Identity: Self and Society in the Late Modern Age*. Stanford, Calif.: Stanford University Press.

Greer, L. Sue. 1990. "The United States Forest Service and the Postwar Commodification of Outdoor Recreation." In *For Fun and Profit: The Transformation of Leisure into Consumption*, ed. R. Butsch, 152–70. Philadelphia: Temple University Press.

Hall, Thomas D. 1989. *Social Change in the Southwest, 1350–1880*. Lawrence: University Press of Kansas.

Harvey, David. 1989. *The Condition of Postmodernity: An Enquiry into the Origins of Cultural Change*. Oxford: Blackwell.

Jameson, Fredric. 1991. *Postmodernism; or, The Cultural Logic of Late Capitalism*. Durham, N.C.: Duke University Press.

Kellner, Douglas. 1992. "Popular Culture and the Construction of Postmodern Identities." In *Modernity and Identity*, ed. S. Lash and J. Friedman, 141–77. Oxford: Blackwell.

Kuroda, Etsuko. 1981. "Ethnicity and Ethnic Culture in Crisis: The Struggle for Existence of the Spanish Americans in Taos, New Mexico." In *Ethnicity and Its Identity in the U.S.A.: A Report of the Field Research in the U.S.A.* (1979), ed. Tsuneo Ayabe, 33–86. Ibaraki, Japan: University of Tsukuba.

Lears, T. J. Jackson. 1983. "From Salvation to Self-Realization: Advertising and the Therapeutic Roots of the Consumer Culture, 1880–1930." In *The Culture of Consumption: Critical Essays in American History, 1880–1980*, ed. R. W. Fox and T. J. Lears, 1–38. New York: Pantheon.

————. 1994 [1981]. *No Place of Grace: Antimodernism and the Transformation of American Culture, 1880–1920.* Chicago: University of Chicago Press.

Loveless, Joan. 1992. *Three Weavers.* Albuquerque: University of New Mexico Press.

Melville, Keith. 1972. *Communes in the Counter Culture: Origins, Theories, Styles of Life.* New York: Morrow Quill.

Mills, Caroline. 1993. "Myths and Meanings of Gentrification." In *Place/Culture/Representation,* ed. J. Duncan and D. Ley, 149–70. London: Routledge.

Pearson, Jim Berry. 1986. *The Red River-Twining Area: A New Mexico Mining History.* Albuquerque: University of New Mexico Press.

Pratt, Mary Louise. 1992. *Imperial Eyes: Travel Writing and Transculturation.* London: Routledge.

Reynolds, Michael E. 1989. *A Coming of Wizards: A Manual of Human Potential.* Taos, N.M.: High Mesa Foundation.

————. 1990. *Earthship,* vol. 1: *How to Build Your Own.* Taos, N.M.: Solar Survival.

————. 1993. *Earthship,* vol. 3: *Evolution beyond Economics.* Taos, N.M.: Solar Survival.

Rodríguez, Sylvia. 1987. "Land, Water, and Ethnic Identity in Taos." In *Land, Water, and Culture: New Perspectives on Hispanic Land Grants,* ed. C. Briggs and J. Van Ness, 313–403. Albuquerque: University of New Mexico Press.

————. 1989. "Art, Tourism, and Race Relations in Taos: Toward a Sociology of the Art Colony." *Journal of Anthropological Research* 45, no. 1:77–99.

————. 1990. "Ethnic Reconstruction in Contemporary Taos." *Journal of the Southwest* 32, no. 4:541–55.

————. 1994. "The Tourist Gaze, Gentrification, and the Commodification of Subjectivity in Taos." In *The Changing Images of the Southwest,* ed. R. Francaviglia and D. Narrett, 105–26. College Station: Texas A&M University Press.

Said, Edward W. 1978. *Orientalism.* London: Routledge.

————. 1993. *Culture and Imperialism.* New York: Vintage Books.

Sassen, Saskia. 1988. *The Mobility of Labor and Capital: A Study in International Investment and Labor Flow.* Cambridge: Cambridge University Press.

Sherman, John. 1990. *Taos: A Pictorial History.* Santa Fe, N.M.: William Gannon.

Sturm, Fred G. 1990. "Aesthetics of the Southwest." In *Pueblo Style and Regional Architecture,* ed. N. Markovich, W. Preiser, and F. Sturm, 11–22. New York: Van Nostrand Reinhold.

Thomas, Nicholas. 1994. *Colonialism's Culture: Anthropology, Travel, and Government.* Princeton, N.J.: Princeton University Press.

Weigle, Marta. 1989. "From Desert to Disney World: The Santa Fe Railway and the Fred Harvey Company Display the Indian Southwest." *Journal of Anthropological Research* 45, no 1:115–37.

————. 1992. "Exposition and Mediation: Mary Colter, Erna Fergusson, and the Santa Fe/Harvey Popularization of the Native Southwest, 1902–1940." *Frontiers: A Journal of Women Studies* 12, no. 3:117–50.

————. 1994a. "Selling the Southwest: Santa Fe InSites." In *Discovered Country: Tourism and Survival in the American West,* ed. S. Norris, 210–24. Albuquerque, N.M.: Stone Ladder.

————. 1994b. "On Coyotes and Crosses: That Which Is Wild and Wooden of the Twentieth-Century Southwest." In *The Changing Images of the Southwest,* ed. R. Francaviglia and D. Narrett, 72–104. College Station: Texas A&M University Press.

Willis, Susan. 1991. *A Primer for Daily Life.* London: Routledge.

Wilson, Chris. 1990. "New Mexico in the Tradition of Romantic Reaction." In *Pueblo Style and Regional Architecture,* ed. N. Markovich, W. Preiser, and F. Sturm, 175–94. New York: Van Nostrand Reinhold.

Young, Robert. 1990. *White Mythologies: Writing History and the West.* London: Routledge.

Zukin, Sharon. 1989. *Loft Living: Culture and Capital in Urban Change.* New Brunswick, N.J.: Rutgers University Press.

———. 1991. *Landscapes of Power: From Detroit to Disney World.* Berkeley: University of California Press.

10   Genocide 'n' Juice: Reading the Postcolonial Discourses in Hip-Hop Culture

Brij David Lunine

This essay looks at postcolonial theory and its applications to contemporary African American hip-hop culture in the United States. Hip-hop is such a densely layered phenomenon that many theoretical approaches apply to its analysis. Accordingly the questions that anticipate my inquiry are both phenomenological and theoretical. First, what are the connections between the culture of hip-hop and postcolonialism? Second, what does rap music have to do with postcolonial theory? Before I attempt to engage these questions, I will briefly examine postcolonial theory by considering the controversial issues pungently presented by Russell Jacoby in his article "Marginal Returns: The Trouble with Post-Colonial Theory" (1995). What follows is a short examination of the field of postcolonial studies by way of Jacoby and then a condensed look at the history of the hip-hop phenomenon and the ways in which postcolonial theory relates to contemporary hip-hop culture. The final part of this essay is a case study of a musical group that strikingly embodies hip-hop music's postcolonial dimension.

Postcolonial Studies: A Critical Overview

Jacoby's criticisms of postcolonial theory help us to define the field. He raises valid questions and issues that are useful in applying postcolonial theory to

American culture and history. By engaging his critique I will bring forth workable parts of postcolonial theory and demonstrate their viability for a specific case study within the culture of hip-hop. "While post-colonial studies claims to be subversive and profound, the politics tends to be banal; the language jargonized; the radical one-upmanship infantile; the self-obsession tiresome; and the theory bloated" (Jacoby 1995, 37). So ends Jacoby's rather bleak and ultimately discouraging polemic on postcolonial theory. If we are to believe Jacoby, postcolonial theory is so indeterminant that it does little more than open up new territory for Western academicians to "explore." Jacoby asserts, among other things, that postcolonial theory serves professors of English and literature who "face a crisis of dwindling material" by "open[ing] up new turf and allow[ing] the re-examination of old ground" (32). Jacoby's claims provide a useful, albeit negative, starting point from which to explore postcolonial studies' relevance for scholars interested in the history and cultures of the United States.

Jacoby's skillful indictment warrants our attention for several reasons. Although he constructs a rather scathing account, he does credit the intersection of Frantz Fanon's *Wretched of the Earth* and Michel Foucault's *Madness and Civilization* (both originally published in 1961) as undergirding the field. In these seminal authors we have a theorist of cultural and national liberation and a theorist of discourse and domination, respectively. Thus Jacoby identifies a broad theoretical foundation for postcolonial studies, one concerned with machinations of power, desire, and discourse as well as cultural and national liberation. This range of concerns is wide yet logical given the historical and intellectual contexts of the works of Foucault and Fanon. Significantly, language and its creation of the Other emerge as the ground on which Fanon and Foucault almost touch. Jacoby is comfortable with these beginnings of the postcolonial project. With the publication of Edward Said's *Orientalism* (1978), however, which "undoubtedly was the key book that launched post-colonial studies" (Jacoby 1995, 31), he starts to have some misgivings.

Said was instrumental in initiating the study of the discourse of Western hegemony in representations of the East. Jacoby cites issues of representation (which are symptomatic of postcolonial theory's engagement with poststructuralist literary theory) as the ground around which postcolonial theory continually walks in circles without ever getting anywhere. More recently *Orientalism* has been criticized for misrepresenting how representation works by oversimplifying the colonial reality of "East" and "West" into a Manichaean polarity. Indeed, the problem of self-representation is no less perplexing for postcolonial theorists than is that of representing the Other. In surveying issues of representation, Jacoby is never able to see past Gayatri

Spivak's "Can the Subaltern Speak?" (1988). Although space does not permit me to engage Jacoby's critique of Spivak, it suffices to say that Jacoby is unsympathetic to both the language and the spirit of current postcolonial discourses. He seems hostile to the idiom ("Spivak, like most post-colonial theorists, cannot write a sentence") and impatient with the degree of reflexivity necessitated by such critical self-conscious work (Jacoby 1995, 36). He is able to cite various pieces that he believes undercut the field with their internal bickering and accusations of imperial complicity.

Because the terrain of postcolonial theory is so wide and varied, Jacoby has his pick of examples that appear to corroborate his assertions of banal politics, jargonized prose, one-upmanship, self-obsession, and bloated theory. The pertinent question, however, concerns whether meaningful and useful issues are being rigorously debated within the space opened by postcolonial discourse. Internal strife may indicate something besides an area that holds no value other than advancing the careers of those who practice it. Rather, the degree of self-critical communication might signify a cumbersome but healthy and extremely comparative minded project that is, by its nature, always engaged in the politics and the ramifications of academic theory.

To be fair, one of Jacoby's more legitimate concerns can be summed up as follows: postcolonial theory spreads itself wide and thin across too much of the globe and too broad a period of history to permit sustained, in-depth analysis. Thus Jacoby is able to point out instances where lip service is paid to history even though greater specificity is warranted. Furthermore, he charges that such work is often judged on how it "fits into the field," a practice that "constitutes the most repressive academic inquiry" (Jacoby 1995, 33). He also identifies a pitfall of the field's interdisciplinary or transdisciplinary nature: "In breaking down intellectual compartments and expanding cultural terrain, the post-colonial theorists force old and new scholars to justify and rethink what they are doing. This is all to the good. However, a fracture, almost a hypocrisy, runs through the new field that sabotages its reach and promise. The post-colonial theorists are not only of decidedly mixed mind about their own academic place. They also challenge whether any knowledge of post-colonial society by outsiders is possible—and this leaves them exactly nowhere" (33). This problem is an epistemological one. It also is indicative of the debt owed to (or engagement of postcolonial theory with) the theoretical legacy outlined by Jacoby. In his account, "Marxism begat structuralism and post-structuralism; post-structuralism begat deconstructionism; deconstructionism begat post-modernism and they both gave rise to post-colonialism" (31). Chronological inaccuracies and simplifications aside, Jacoby identifies the theoretical history that has brought about this epistemological tension. He might also have included feminist criticism, psychoanalytic theory, culturalist material-ism, New Historicism, and materialist criticism in his reductive genealogy.

We must consider whether postcolonial studies incorporates a unified theo-retical position. In my opinion postcolonial criticism is concerned with the positions of the colonial subject and the postcolonial subject. It is concerned with identity, much of the time in the language of nationhood. It also exam-ines the representation of the postcolonial position in language and other forms of discourse. It asks questions about power, agency, and knowledge. Whether knowledge itself is subject to identity politics of the most basic type is one of the tough questions postcolonial discourse must consider. Never-theless, just because the process of knowledge acquisition is called into ques-tion and held up to self-scrutiny does not mean the field has deconstructed itself into a state of paralysis.

This high degree of self-reflexivity throughout postcolonial theory may well be a cumbersome but vigorous practice characteristic of an enterprise deeply affected by its theoretical history. In short, these various theoretical tensions can be healthy when they lead to important scholarship that cov-ers new ground in original ways, challenging existing paradigms not merely to do so but to complicate our understanding and clear space for further valuable and innovative work. In other words, to quote Bob Marley, half of the story has never been told. Not only has it not been properly told (in the West, at least), but we have not heard all the voices that tell these narratives of colonialism and postcolonialism, nor have we heard subalterns speak in their syncretic languages, which are, after all, part of colonialism's legacy. Furthermore, the philosophical question of knowledge of the postcolonial condition(s) deserves debate and exploration.

Unfortunately, once Jacoby encounters the topics of language, representa-tion, and epistemology, he sees the postcolonial terrain as running downhill. The landscape descends into issues of who can represent whom and schol-ars' allegations of others' various degrees of complicity. Jacoby is unable to see past these internal problems, many of which are due to postcolonial theory's historical ties to literary theory rather than any inherent logical flaw in the transdisciplinary field's formulation. His critique appears to be derived from his resistance to the poststructuralist and postmodernist moves within cul-tural theory.

Jacoby blames postcolonial critics for the disappearance of the transcen-dental signifier and the attack on universals instead of expanding his focus to include the many European and American intellectuals who espouse simi-lar antifoundationalist orientations. By positioning postcolonial studies at the center of controversial theory, he begs the following question: why place all the burden or blame on intellectuals (predominantly) of color when they are only one segment of the intellectual community? The crux of his argument rests on the disappearance of the ground from which to make generalizations. He cites the editors of Routledge's *Post-Colonial Studies Reader*, particularly their section devoted to the danger of "universality." The authors assert that "the myth of universality is thus a primary strategy of imperial control" (in Jacoby 1995, 35). Universality is attacked from all corners of academia, however, especially throughout the latter half of the previously mentioned theoretical genealogy.

Jacoby's response is a vigorous critique of this antiuniversal position and a rather convincing argument for the ability to generalize and to utilize universals. To summarize, he sees the "work of thought" as engaging generalizations and reworking them rather than "junking" them. He asserts that if all universals are suspect, truths are purely contingent and might as well be called myths. His argument is that postcolonial theory is so invested in a "new multiplicity" that theorists are unable to analyze and judge. Thus, "in virtually every field—anthropology, psychology, political thought—the principle that all humanity share certain qualities has marked an advance over the belief that 'civilized' and 'savage,' black and white, Bosnian Serb and Muslim, are different categories of people" (Jacoby 1995, 36). This leads Jacoby to state that "the undeveloped world needs a reaffirmation of universals, not a dismantling of them" (36).

Jacoby moves swiftly from the theoretical ground of criticism to the more concrete reality of politics. He posits one of democracy's basic rights as the right to adequate nutrition. Other obvious universals include human rights, literacy, and democratic voting. By and large these "universals" are not being contested in postcolonial studies. In my estimation, what postcolonial scholars contest is the history of the colonial and postcolonial subject, the ways of telling, knowing, and expressing the experience of colonialism and decolonization and what this history means now—the ontological reality of postcolonialism. Postcolonial theory examines modes of nationalism, liberation, and power and looks at the ways different forms of culture have wrestled with these phenomena throughout modern history. Moreover, postcolonial critics concern themselves with language, representation, and discourse within colonial and postcolonial cultures. There may not be room for Jacoby's universals, but the field does have both a history bound antagonistically with Europe's and a definable theoretical legacy tied to the West. In other words, I think *postcolonial* is a context-bound signifier, a practice more than discipline, unstable by nature but with a definite genealogy. Postcolonial theory does not allow for easy generalizations, nor does it embrace universals, but it does clear a space for those who, until rather recently, have been spoken for and represented in the West with no subject-hood, autonomy, or agency.

Postcolonial Theory and Hip-Hop Culture

My examination of Jacoby's critique shows how postcolonial theory is a precarious practice. The following discussion demonstrates how postcolonial theory can be applied to hip-hop culture. I attempt briefly to survey the wide terrain of hip-hop culture in the United States and then cut narrow and deep into the texts of one exceptional musical group. Although the culture of hip-hop—rap music, graffiti art, and break dancing—is viewed as a predominantly African American, urban phenomenon, my focus is on the history of current urban African diasporic practices in terms of their postcolonial elements. I want to explore the connections between rap music and postcolonialism in the themes of certain rap lyrics and, to a lesser extent, the musical practices in hip-hop culture. I will demonstrate the distinctive postcolonial component and aesthetic for both lyrics and music. Before doing this, however, I must qualify my discussion with the observation that the postcolonial dimension of rap music is inseparable from many other elements, including lyrical and rhetorical traditions in the blues, prison rhyme schemes, and "doing the dozens." Also essential to rap and hip-hop are the improvisational approaches in jazz, the rhythms of soul and funk, the more recent incorporation of rhythm 'n' blues, and gospel vocal techniques and harmonizations, as well as modern reggae and its predecessors, rocksteady and ska.

Almost any time the culture of hip-hop is considered in academia, a flood of references, histories, and explanations virtually overwhelms authors. In many cases academicians writing about hip-hop feel compelled to try to convey a comprehensive account of a subculture far too vast and intricate to be covered in one volume, not to mention a short essay. Moreover, many scholars working with hip-hop worry profoundly about their intended audience. Thus even such knowledgeable, brilliant critics as Tricia Rose, author of *Black Noise: Rap Music and Black Culture in Contemporary America* (1994), have to walk fine lines between too many allusions that only the initiated comprehend and didactic explanations that entail simplified, essentialized accounts (Potter 1994, 5). I will not presume to be addressing the initiated, nor will I enter into a history of all of hip-hop's various connections with postcolonialism. Instead I want to offer a rather compressed account of a few of the major connections hip-hop has with postcolonialism and postcolonial theory and then turn to focus on the work of a single group, the Coup, that peerlessly embodies the postcolonial impulse in rap music.

Looking beyond the problematic aspects considered by Jacoby, I hope we can see that the postcolonial project is ultimately concerned with the identity and agency of formerly colonized peoples. In the case of white settler colonies and the violently enforced diasporic experiences brought about by colonialism, the search for identity and the attainment of various types of political and social agency is even more difficult and therefore meaningful, a quest into recovery and redemption of formerly lost traditions and histories. Thus Frantz Fanon (1994, 37) characterizes the rediscovery of identity as often the object of "passionate research . . . directed by the secret hope of discovering beyond the misery of today, beyond self-contempt, resignation and abjuration, some very beautiful and splendid era whose existence rehabilitates us both in regard to ourselves and in regard to others."

This rehabilitative, passionate research has been at the heart of cultural practices such as rap music since its birth out of the dance-hall deejaying and toasting traditions. When we look at postcolonial phenomena, we see a history of cultural practices that in varying degrees address the lived conditions of the colonial and postcolonial experience. Paul Gilroy sketches an outline of this cultural history as it is played out in Jamaica, England, and the United States in his book "There Ain't No Black in the Union Jack" (1987). Gilroy describes the early history of Jamaican dance halls in the 1940s and 1950s, where the disc jockeys set up their own bass-heavy sound systems. Improvisation, spontaneity, and intimacy were highly valued in dance-hall culture. The oral quality of the deejay's introduction was emphasized over the content of the (imported) records, which are described as merely one element of the deejay's or MC's ("master of ceremonies'") performance. This important notion of recorded music as only one component of the performative process manifests itself in the practices of creating musical hip-hop tracks over which vocalists rap. This is illustrated in the history of Jamaican dance-hall practices, wherein as early as the 1960s deejays started removing labels from the records they were playing (Gilroy 1987, 192–93).

Gilroy (1987, 164) describes how "public performance of recorded music is primary in both reggae and soul variants of the culture. In both, records become raw material for spontaneous performances of cultural creation in which the DJ and the MC or toaster who introduces each disc or sequence of discs, emerge as the principal agents in dialogic rituals of active and celebratory consumption." He recounts how the "fledging" sound-system culture of urban Jamaica made its way to England during the 1950s. Gilroy's work follows the culture throughout the 1960s and 1970s as it changed with the political situation in Jamaica and the influence of Rastafarian religious ideology.

What emerges in Gilroy's artful description is a triangle of cultural communication between England, the United States, and Jamaica. Although the context of each "host" country greatly influenced the development of unique cultural expressions and forms, out of this transnational triangle of the African diaspora emerged a clearly evident aesthetic of performativity and spontaneity. Looking at the history of Jamaica, England, and the United States, one sees the postcolonial context of the cultural practices of the African diaspora. Throughout the diaspora people of African descent utilized musical technologies and improvised to create unique practices, traditions, and sounds that, in part, addressed their experiences as a colonized and subjugated people.

Rose's account of the birth of hip-hop picks up at this point of transnational cultural formation. She describes how a young Jamaican immigrant known as Kool DJ Herc, having moved to the South Bronx in 1967, set up his massive sound system for public consumption in New York City. His speakers were known as the "herculords." He is credited with developing the technique of spinning records backward to repeat desirable phrases. Herc, along with his contemporaries, also started using the beats between lyrics (breakbeats) to build new compositions. For Kool DJ Herc, his turntables were his instruments. Additionally, he and his peers, such as Afrika Bambaataa of the Zulu Nation, began emulating black radio deejay personalities and employing prison-type rhyming techniques. As these practices gained greater cultural currency and were more widely disseminated (mainly throughout the Bronx, Queens, and Harlem boroughs of New York City), hip-hop, as we know it, was born by the mid-1970s (Rose 1994, 34–41).

This compressed account obviously leaves out many of the conditions that aided hip-hop's formation. When focusing on cultural practices that can be placed in a postcolonial context, it is important to keep the general framework of postcolonial theory in tension with the specific example or manifestation under consideration. By doing this I hope to avoid the overgeneralization of which Jacoby warns. Specific socioeconomic conditions, for example, are among the many elements essential to understanding how and why hip-hop materialized. During the 1970s in the South Bronx, public policies were so disastrous they created a situation where residents had few means of expression other than graffiti art, break dancing, and rap music. As Rose describes:

> Hip hop culture emerged as a source for youth of alternative identity formation and social status in a community whose older support institutions had been all but demolished along with large sectors of its built environment. Alternative local identities were forged in fashion and language, street names, and most important, in establishing neighborhood crews or posses. Many hip hop fans, artists, musicians, and dancers continue to belong to an elaborate system of crews or posses. The crew, a local source of identity, group affiliation, and support system appears repeatedly in all of my interviews, and virtually all rap

lyrics and cassette dedications, music video performances, and media interviews with artists. Identity in hip hop is deeply rooted in the specific, the local experience, and one's attachment and status in a local group or alternative family. (1994, 34)

Rose's work foregrounds the role of the specific. Identity is often represented by locale and small-group affiliation. Nevertheless, in these very acts of recognizing and claiming specific identities, another phenomenological and theoretical postcolonial connection emerges in the narratives created by musicians.

In addition to noting the transnational triangle of musical practices and the "cross-pollination" of cultural forms, we can see narrative similarities that reflect the search for identity and agency in the most basic forms of self-empowerment. In his seminal study *Subculture: The Meaning of Style* (1979), Dick Hebdige describes how, in part because of Rastafarian ideology, the music of young Jamaican immigrants in England started to change from narratives of lone rebel archetypes to more group-oriented stories of rebellion. In hip-hop culture we see an opposite trend—an initial community-oriented approach that changes, at least in the "gangsta" genre of rap, to reflect the lone rebel archetype.

In *Spectacular Vernaculars: Hip-Hop and the Politics of Postmodernism*, Russell A. Potter (1995, 38) remarks that "what is less often noted is the strong similarity between the rhetorical and narrative conventions of ska and reggae with those of hip-hop. Of particular significance is the early 'rude boy' style, which glorified the angry, young, tough-living kids of West Kingston; there are striking similarities, both cultural and musical, between the 'rude boys' of ska and the 'gangstas' of hip-hop." The most visible representation of the "rude boy" for us in the United States is the lone gun-toting protagonist played by reggae star Jimmy Cliff in the film *The Harder They Come* (1972). Cliff's character moves to the city only to go down eventually in a blaze of gunfire. In story after story both rude boys and gangstas fight the law, each other, and the dominant society with a variety of outcomes. As Hebdige explains:

Reggae, and the forms which had proceeded it, had always alluded to these problems [of race and class] obliquely. Oppositional values had been mediated through a range of rebel archetypes: the rude boy, the gunfighter, the trickster, etc.—which remained firmly tied to the *particular* and tended to celebrate the *individual* status of revolt. With dub and heavy reggae, this rebellion was given a much wider currency: it was generalized and theorized. Thus, the rude boy hero immortalized in ska and rocksteady—the lone delinquent pitched hopelessly against an implacable authority—was supplanted as the central focus by the Rastafarian who broke the Law in more profound and subtle ways. (Hebdige 1979, 37)

In the short history of rap, conversely, we see a movement away from the initial engagement with more community-oriented narratives toward stories and images of the individual criminal comparable with those in early Jamaican ska, rocksteady, and reggae music. Although this trend does not apply to every genre of rap music, it is most evident in the emergence of the extremely successful gangsta rap style. How are the emphasis on and popularity of the individual indicative of a postcolonial consciousness? Again the work of Frantz Fanon reframes the folk culture and positions of these narratives in their postcolonial context:

> The people make use of certain episodes in the life of the community in order to hold themselves ready and keep alive their revolutionary zeal. For example, the gangster who holds up the police set on to track him down for days on end, or who dies in single combat after having killed four or five policemen . . . these types light the way for the people, form the blueprints for action and become heroes. Obviously, it's a waste of breath to say that such-and-such a hero is a thief, a scoundrel, or a reprobate. If the act for which he is prosecuted by the colonial authorities is an act exclusively directed against a colonialist person or colonialist property, the demarcation line is definite and manifest. The process of identification is automatic. (1994, 69)

In both early "rude boy" reggae and the current (although rapidly changing) genre of gangsta rap, we see narratives that are violent and confrontational. The creators of both forms provide a mythical example of revolt by portraying individual violence with which their audiences can identify and sympathize. Within the emergence of hip-hop one sees a preoccupation with both the individual and a racially constructed national identity that speaks to defining the self and a people in the postcolonial terms of race, nation, religion, and history. To be more exact, the gangsta genre of rap is preoccupied with the individual status of revolt, and the genre known as black nationalist, or "nation-conscious," rap is more concerned with group identity and mythical history. Both categories engage the postcolonial themes of individual and group identity. The concern with identity is seen throughout various rap styles and the short history of hip-hop.

The history of hip-hop is the history of the continuous production of texts, innovations, and the refinement of practices that address both individual and group identities. Much of rap music consistently analyzes the material, social, economic, and legal conditions. This analysis is prevalent in the earliest rap and subsequent early commercial successes. Songs such as Grand Master Flash and Furious Fire's single "The Message," featuring Melle Mel and voted best pop song of 1982 (Rose 1994), and KRS-One's song addressed to the police, "Who Protects Us from You?" (1989), lyrically analyze urban communities, crime, and police oppression in the terms of community rather than the lone rebel. In these works the texts speak to and define identity through their analysis of social conditions.

In hip-hop music's relatively short development, nationalism constituted a major theme before and during the emergence of the gangsta style. Given the history of African-Americans' forced removal within the colonial project, their relationship to other postcolonial people and nations deserves attention. In terms of postcolonial cultural production, Fanon's conception of the role of the native artist is applicable in qualifying and comparing the object of black nationalism for both Africa and its diaspora. In Fanon's discussion of national culture in the context of Africa, three different phases characterize the native intellectual's position and work. The third, which Fanon calls the "fighting phase," directly applies to many of the producers of hip-hop culture. The role of artists or native intellectuals in this phase is to awaken the people; thus they produce texts that fight, that are revolutionary and nationalistic.

Fanon identifies what might be termed a pitfall of authenticity, or lack of organic character, that many producers of hip-hop largely avoid:

> At the very moment when the native intellectual is anxiously trying to create a cultural work he fails to realize that he is utilizing techniques and language which are borrowed from the stranger in his country. He contents himself with stamping these instruments with a hall-mark which he wishes to be national, but which is strangely reminiscent of exoticism. The native intellectual who comes back to his people by way of cultural achievements behaves like a foreigner. Sometimes he has no hesitation in using dialect in order to show his will to be as near as possible to the people; but the ideas that he expresses and the preoccupations he is taken up with have no common yardstick to measure the real situation which the men and the women of his country know. (1994, 41)

Thus the consciousness of the native intellectual in this sense can be understood as altered in some manner; he or she no longer speaks from the subaltern position. Because of their historical circumstances, African American and other diasporic producers of culture can be seen not as foreigners returning with a nonindigenous language and cultural forms but as organic producers of culture utilizing a hybrid language that was originally an enforced but now is practiced as a mostly universal though adapted and regionalized code (e.g., different styles of Ebonics). Moreover, in their modes of expression they self-consciously utilize diasporic traditions and art forms, appropriating and vigorously reworking the dominant culture's language and texts.

It is one of the tasks of postcolonial theorists to define and analyze various diasporic phenomena. This endeavor includes the essential job of comparing and theorizing the role of the postcolonial cultural producer. Beyond the producer's role lies the cultural texts and the varied forms they take.

Jacoby's concerns about postcolonial critics' self-obsession and radical competition appear in this case to be overstated. The native intellectuals described by Fanon and the diasporic cultural producers I have described are self-reflexive without being solipsistic. Both intellectuals and cultural producers have to struggle with their position within their culture. They have to consider their own positionality while producing work to address and inspire their audiences. What is germane to my discussion is how we can move from a description of the history of the hip-hop phenomenon to a theorization of its origins and its contemporary characteristics.

Defined by the aesthetics of rupture, flow, and layering, hip-hop is working within certain African American urban cultures (Rose 1994, 21–61). Appropriating and subverting technology and language, hip-hop can be seen as a vernacular discourse that is *within* the people rather than outside, as Fanon describes. The (representational) distance Fanon identifies in the postcolonial context in Africa is collapsed for the most part within hip-hop culture. Hip-hop comes from inside certain segments of urban communities. The diversity reflected within its various genres mirrors differences in geographic locations and class affiliations, struggles over the meaning of gender and sexuality, and the racially heterogeneous composition of its producers. Rappers, by and large, have not been educated outside their communities or cultures, as their African counterparts may have been. They are operating within their own communities and producing cultural codes that synthesize and subvert both the language and the technology of the "colonizer." Their ideas and concerns are not derived from a foreign source. Instead of having "no common yardstick" to measure the "real situation," they are the men and women within their own communities producing work that is driven and shaped by the concerns of their existence.

Through Fanon's description we can see that although their historical contexts greatly differ, nation-conscious rappers work for the same liberatory and nationalistic goals that "native" intellectuals pursue. Of course, some African intellectuals bear the burden of a foreign education that distances them from their roots, whereas such separation is far less common in hip-hop culture. Nevertheless, the discourse surrounding nationalism within hip-hop includes comparable divisions in terms of qualifying the role of the organic, cultural intellectual.

Much of rap's engagement with nationalism takes one of two forms: either it is inspired by the Black Power movement of the 1960s and 1970s or it is concerned with a mythical conception of Africa. Jeffrey Louis Decker (1994, 100) theorizes these sources of inspiration as two distinct forms of nationalistic hip-hop: "nation time," Black Power–oriented rap best embodied by the group Public Enemy, and "nation place," typified in the Afrocentric works of groups such as Brand Nubian, the X-Clan, and Poor Righteous Teachers. I want to consider the work of one somewhat obscure group in terms of its articulation of yet another distinct form of cultural nationalism. I will demonstrate, by performing a fairly close reading, the extent to which this group's music speaks to an emerging, distinctly postcolonial conception of African American culture. Their music has affinities with nation time and place but is unique in its postcoloniality.

The Coup

The Coup broke out of Oakland with their 1993 album entitled *Kill My Landlord*. The album's cover features the three main members: Boots (Raymond Riley), E Roc (Eric Davis) and Pam the Funkstress (Pam Warren). The visual representation features a photo of the three members cramped into a small kitchen, stove in the background, with a clothesline above it. Boots, skillet in hand, E Roc, and Pam all stare directly into the camera with serious expressions. This image of the band in the kitchen is thus set apart from images on most other album covers. The three are wearing nondescript clothing signifying that they represent lower-class social and economic conditions. In other words, they are not dressed like gangstas or Black Panthers, and they are not wearing Afrocentric ga..b. What their image does, in combination with their unique sound and strong lyrics, is work to engage and redefine the nihilistic gangsta identity into a community-oriented, revolutionary, and, I hope ultimately to show, postcolonial one.

The album opens with the track "Dig-It," in which the first layer of crowd noise, yelling and cheering, underlies a superimposed heavy bass line (produced by a bass guitar, not a digital sample) and a snare-drum beat. The first line, "Presto, where's the communist manifesto?" sets the political and lyrically animated tone. Boots and E Roc exchange quick, dense rhymes that feature playful lyrics including "The slip of my Mao Tse-tung." There are also more meaningful puns, such as "We're all cooped up so feel the pain / From four hundred years of exploitation," which directly refers to the experience and history of colonial slavery. The music is bass heavy but does not employ the slow, eerie gangsta beats preferred by other West Coast groups. Rather, it is upbeat—slower than the average 109 beats per minute of early, hyperkinetic Public Enemy but far more rapid than the slow pounding bass lines of fellow Oakland gangsta-style rapper Too Short.

Although the lyrics are extremely dense, the more discernible lines and metaphors tend to be political. For example, the lines "Turn the shit over like Bush did a boat full of Haitians" and "Anesthesia provided by your local TV station" speak to a serious sense of systemic power and race relations. This is counterbalanced by the simple chorus, "Dig it!" which is repeated over

Pam's rhythmic scratching (produced with vinyl records and turntables). It merely urges the audience to listen to the music and pay attention to the message.

The Coup position themselves as musically innovative by using live bass lines, organs, piano, saxophone, flute, harmonica, keyboards, and eight background vocalists, as well as two featured guest groups. They define themselves as politically motivated and educated with lines such as "We won't get no calluses / Cause we're spittin' dialectical analysis" and references to Fanon that much of their audience might not catch: "I've been assumed since my native birth to the wretched of the earth." In addition, they link African American postcoloniality with Native American history when they cry "Free Geronimo!" and "Fuck Columbus!" All this is stated within the first few minutes of the recording. Moreover, they participate in the requisite tradition Rose mentions, geographically situating themselves and their community by asking rhetorically, "The origin of the flow? / Oakland California 94610"—a playful mention of their postal code and possible parody of the television program *Beverly Hills 90210*.

One could perform an extensive analysis of the lyrical text alone, not to mention the layers of music. Instead of attempting such a comprehensive reading of the music and lyrics, I want to focus on just a few of the postcolonial and identity-defining elements of their first album in order to read the ideological components and pedagogical audience-engaging strategies.

The second song on the album, "Not Yet Free," speaks on several levels by addressing the concept of freedom in different contexts. The overt historical and political connotations of living under conditions that continue to deny true freedom to many segments of the population indicate how the legacy of slavery still afflicts us today. Lines such as "I'm 21 / So I've reached my life expectancy" are powerful comments on American society. Additionally, the lyric "I've got a mirror in my pocket / And I practice looking hard" is an obvious critique of gangsta posturing that links the hardness associated with the gangsta image to its wider historical meanings of survival. "Not Yet Free" is a poetic and systemic analysis featuring Boots. His metaphoric commentary covers religion, the police, and most powerfully, his role in our economic system:

> Capitalism is like a spider
> The web is getting tighter
> I'm strugglin' like a fighter . . .
>
> just when I think I'm free
> It seems to me the spider steps.
> This web is made of money,
> made of greed, made of me
> Oh what I have become in a parasite economy

These lyrics are set apart by the music, which slows down to draw attention to this verse. The next segment of the song describes the current stereotypes of black men and women and asks, "What can we do to change this?" At a corresponding point many rap songs introduce a more spontaneous "freestyle" section. Here, when E Roc asks about freestyle, Boots replies that it is impossible because the society is not yet free. The song concludes with what are commonly known as "shoutouts." Usually this is a group-identification ritual of naming friends, various groups, and other prominent people whom the artists wish to recognize publicly. This hip-hop practice is inverted, however; against the sounds of a gun being loaded and between gunshots, Boots and E Roc name the enemies of the black community in "shot-outs." These enemies include Pete Wilson, George Bush, Bill Clinton, H. Ross Perot, the Oakland Police Department, the Los Angeles Police Department, skinheads, and prominent black figures such as Tom Bradley and David Dinkins, all characterized as "sellout motherfuckers." The section includes reference in the form of a quotation from gangsta Ice Cube directed at these enemies: "Be true to the game." This segment powerfully evokes Fanon's emphasis on the fragility of identity and the rigorous qualifications for racialized, indigenous leadership.

A commentary on hair care and redefining what "good" hair is follows in the third song, "Fuck a Perm." The short, seemingly simple song works to indicate the patriarchal and racist standards of beauty in the dominant society while forcefully rejecting them in favor of a more Afrocentric aesthetic. This is as close as the Coup come to any type of Afrocentrism. The next song—"The Coup"—begins with a ringing telephone and a call from reporter Dick Doolittle asking Boots to comment on the "tragic riots in Los Angeles." Boots replies that it was not a riot; it was a rebellion. He then asks, "Tragic for who?" After the reporter's short description of the rebellion as chaos, Boots counters that it was not chaos but progress. When asked whether this is his comment, he says no—a dial tone immediately follows in a complete disavowal of the media as an accurate voice for African Americans. Here Boots's reaction has affinities with both the violent, individuated image of the gangsta and Gilroy's reading of the riots of the summer of 1981 and the autumn of 1985 in Britain's inner cities. In a section entitled "Disruptive Protest and the Symbolism of Community," he describes how "disorderly protests reflect the experiences of participants and by conveying antagonism against the world as it is, they can be shown to embody a view of how participants would like it to be. This relates directly to the concerns of the social movement around 'race.' . . . In order to appreciate the political character of these protests, it is however, essential to grasp the manner in which the symbolism of disorder has come to dominate its instrumental aspects" (Gilroy 1987, 237).

Obviously the differences are great, yet both Gilroy's and Boots's readings of rioting and the socially constructed meanings around what riots represent and to whom they represent it speak to a racially nationalistic, visionary element in these riots, protests, and rebellions. The fourth song reconceives the riots in Oakland and beyond as organized rebellion. A fantasized, idealistic, revolutionary vision imagines economic redistribution. The narrative provides an ongoing critical commentary on education, government aid, crime, and other urban social phenomena. Additionally, self-references (to other songs on the album) are prominent when they state, "The song 'I Ain't the Nigga' is the constitution." The beat is fast with a prominent piano, as E Roc describes the revolution spreading through Oakland across to San Francisco and beyond. The line "Everybody is out of jail / But nobody's out on bail" describes mass escape from overincarceration. A "new meaning to police brutality" is also described in this conceptual, social inversion. The chorus—"All we need is satisfaction / We want more than just a fraction"—is sung in harmony by several female vocalists over the scratched, repeated lines "Things ain't never gonna be the same." The female vocalists continue with the lyrics "And we come to the conclusion / Revolution is the solution."

These first four songs paint a clear picture of the Coup as being vehemently nationalistic and unafraid to criticize their peers. The songs also depict them as being analytical artists whose self-examination is conscious of the interrelated social positionality of race, class, and gender constructs. They identify and critique the political, social, and even linguistic representational factors of oppression. Their major targets are postindustrial capitalism, the police (specific cases are referenced in the fifth song, "I Know You," which is directly addressed to the police; significantly, the police are referred to as "tools of colonialism"), substandard education (which they contrast to liberating education), imprisonment, intraracial divisions, and self-destructive behavior. All this is done with skillful rhymes and a talented female deejay—a true rarity in an industry where production is dominated by males (Rose 1994).

Such songs as "Last Blunt" forcefully but playfully criticize marijuana usage, which is drastically on the rise among young African Americans. The song condemns the use of marijuana in several contexts, from the personal to the historical and racial. It opens with inhaling, coughing, and then a sample of Ernie from *Sesame Street* asking, "Do you know what's green?" The lyrics go on to detail how tough it is to grow up when role models all smoke "weed." They emphasize the difficulty of quitting, the unsatisfying experience of making love while stoned, and the effect that the lack of motivation resulting from marijuana use has on finding a job—not to mention that it causes the narrator to "put the revolution off until tomorrow." The psychological function of marijuana use is insightfully portrayed in the line "I can't quit / Cause then I might have to deal with some real shit." The "Chronic" (slang for potent marijuana and the title of Dr. Dre's multimillion selling gangsta rap album) is said to be "moronic." The lines "We're not getting fucked up, we're just getting fucked—shit out of luck . . . the ganja is jailer . . . take some Ex-Lax / It's mental constipation . . . Ain't no revolution gonna come from the blunted" wittily and forcefully reiterate this very unpopular position over a smooth groove of an organ, piano, female chorus, and Pam's talented mixes. The larger significance can be seen when the situation is analyzed with the historical comparison to the British promulgation of opium in China, which positions drug users in this instance as colonized peoples. By criticizing and directly engaging one of the most prevalent themes in gangsta rap—marijuana and actual fetishization—the Coup deconstructs even somewhat benign drug usage as a subtle factor of oppression in their search for a reconstructed postcolonial, drug-free identity.

The Coup also provide a strong commentary on the power of language and its ability to represent. The song "I Ain't the Nigga" is probably the best example of their linguistically analytical quest for a progressive identity. It evaluates rap music's common usage of the term *Nigga* and bravely analyzes its significance within hip-hop by equating its use with that of the word *bitch*, condemning the prevalence of both terms:

> Nigga is a word we use today,
> Ya say, it don't mean the same if you spell it with an "a"
> But that's argument that makes me itch,
> I twitch, if I took the "t" out would I still be bich?

> There's a fact that when I know that my skin is brown,
> And never ever will I put another brother down.
> So I make the mental move and massacre the word,
> Cause when I hear it, it gets me straight stirred.

> I ain't the one. I ain't the nigga.

> Identify yourself as a part of being conscious.
> If I call myself a gangsta then I'll rob ya with a gat [gun].
> If I call myself a brother than ya know I got your back.
> If I call myself oppressed than I'm clear where I'm at.
> But if I call myself a nigga what the fuck is that?
> . . . Don't be the one. Don't be the nigga.

I have examined several of the Coup's songs in the order they appear on their first album to give a sense of the lyrical, ideological density throughout the record's thirteen songs. The group continually produces analytically playful rhymes that emphasize the postcolonial themes of identity, race, nationhood, language and representation, disruptive protest, and challenge to the dominant political, economic, and social order. Furthermore, just as Fanon's native intellectual attempts to engage his or her people on their own terms and in their own idiom, the Coup attempt the same level of interaction, especially in their second album, *Genocide & Juice* (1994).

The Coup's second album was named in reference to gangsta rapper Snoop Doggy Dogg's multiplatinum song "Gin 'n' Juice." Whereas Snoop sang of "Rollin' down the street smokin' indo [marijuana]/ Sippin' on gin 'n' juice / With my mind on my money and money on mind," the Coup continued to address individuality and community in terms of crime and other pressing social issues by signifying on Snoop's work. On the second album the gangsta image is foregrounded. Although addressing other issues, such as the rate of illegitimate childbirth and incarceration, the group focuses more squarely on the incredibly popular gangsta image and stereotype. One of the featured songs, "Fat Cats, Bigga Fish," is narrated from the first person, in the style of many gangsta rhymes. After robbing a "motherfucka in a tweed suit" (as opposed to another resident of the same neighborhood), the protagonist sneaks into a dinner party to continue his crimes. Here the narrator overhears various conversations by "the power elite." The song continues by describing how urban land developers and politicians use the fear of gangs to manipulate the media and create a moral panic in order to open space for profiteering gentrification. The song closes with the prophetic verse that recontextualizes the lone rebel in a larger, socioeconomic setting of which Rose might approve:

> That's when I step back to contemplate what few know
> sat down to wrestle with my thoughts like a sumo.
> Ain't no one player that could beat this lunacy.
> Ain't no hustler on the street could do a whole community. . . .
> I'm getting hustled,
> only knowing half the game . . .
>   ("Fat Cats, Bigga Fish," 1994)

In terms of Stuart Hall's conception of cultural identity and diaspora, the Coup's musical and lyrical representations function as a part of the process of identity formation within cultural production (Hall 1994, 392–93). Instead of drawing on a conception of identity as an already accomplished fact or origin, as in the Afrocentric conception, the Coup problematize the semantics and assumptions in other hip-hop artists' work as well as within American society at large. Their critical approach undermines much of the authority and authenticity to which the gangsta genre (in particular) lays claim. By reconceptualizing the role of language and what it signifies in terms of intraracial violence, the Coup make a strong, racially unifying statement. Their conception of identity is rooted in race, economic conditions, language, and place, more than in any explicit mythic conception of the past. As my discussion of postcolonial theory demonstrates, these issues form the crux of postcolonial critical discourse. Essentially, the postcolonial discourse in the African diaspora is marked by the priority of defining individual and group identity as the starting point from which to proceed.

The Coup's narratives of revolution certainly contain a view of shared culture. They also speak directly to the "sort of collective 'one true self' . . . . hiding inside the many other" selves that Hall identifies as the first of two ways of thinking about cultural identity. This "true self" is viewed within the history of the United States, specifically from the position of urban African Americans. The Coup's sociohistorical positioning, however, seems more accurately described in Hall's second conception of cultural identity:

> Cultural identity . . . is a matter of "becoming" as well as "being." It belongs to the future as much as to the past. It is not something which already exists, transcending place, time, history, and culture. Cultural identities come from somewhere, have histories. But, like everything which is historical, they undergo constant transformation. Far from being externally fixed in some essentialized past, they are subjected to the continuous "play" of history, culture and power. Far from being grounded in a mere "recovery" of the past, which is waiting to be found, and which, when found, will secure our sense of ourselves into eternity, identities are the names we give to the different ways we are positioned by, and position ourselves within, the narratives of the past. (1994, 394)

The Coup are positioning themselves as cultural workers, agitators, and revolutionaries. Their work is guided more by an analysis of the present and a radical vision of the future than by a reexploration into the suppressed histories of the recent or mythical past. They introduce, rethink, criticize, and attempt to play off of and subvert the extremely popular gangsta image, transforming it into an image of a qualitatively different type of rebel. Thus the identity they are constructing is dialogic in its engagement with the audience and various texts. Taking the images of the present, the group semiotically and semantically plays with them to invert and affect their political significance. The Coup are postcolonial, organic cultural workers who, through their various critiques, have highly informed visionary ideas of the way our society could transform. Nonetheless, they seem to have been dragged into the individual level of identity formation in their attempt to engage the gangsta image on their second album.

Conclusion

My goal for this discussion of the Coup and their music has been to provide an example of the postcolonial dimension of hip-hop's musical practices and lyrical content. I want to reiterate how both the history of the musical practices in hip-hop and the lyrical themes, be they cultural nationalism or lone gangstas, reflect a logical outgrowth of the history of their predominantly African American producers. Hip-hop itself is one example of cultural forms that express the history of colonialism and a postcolonial consciousness and aesthetic. Despite Jacoby's assessment, postcolonial theory provides a valuable framework for examining historical and current phenomena. Postcolonial theory, as varied as it may be, provides a helpful set of tools for analysis, comparison, and (re)contextualization. It enables us look around and make sense of the world in a different fashion. Although fraught with the internal contradictions and argumentation Jacoby describes, postcolonial studies is a useful constellation of theoretical and historical perspectives that considers ways of seeing, representing, knowing, interpreting, connecting, and comparing various colonial and postcolonial experiences. Without a postcolonial perspective important connections, comparisons, and analyses could not be made.

My discussion has shown one way in which the analysis of postcolonialism in America adds depth to our understanding of the rich and varied African American experience. A postcolonial reading of hip-hop is only one dimension of this history. When we include postcolonial theory in our analyses of American culture, we can start to consider how postcolonial studies resonates with other facets of the American experience. Such comparisons enabled by a postcolonial practice might consider the experiences of Asian, Latino, and Native American peoples. Although postcolonial studies may be too unwieldy for Jacoby, it provides an essential practice for scholars wishing to analyze the history of colonialism and its legacy.

Note

All lyrics from the Coup's songs are quoted by permission of Raymond Riley (Boots).

Works Cited

Decker, Jefferey Louis. 1994. "The State of Rap: Time and Place in Hip Hop Nationalism." In *Microphone Fiends: Youth Music and Youth Culture,* ed. Andrew Ross and Tricia Rose, 99–121. New York: Routledge.

Fanon, Frantz. 1994. "On National Culture." In *Colonial Discourse and Post-Colonial Theory: A Reader,* ed. Patrick Williams and Laura Chrisman, 36–52. New York: Columbia University Press.

Foucault, Michel. 1961. *Madness and Civilization: A History of Insanity in the Age of Reason.* New York: Vintage Books.

Gilroy, Paul. 1987. *"There Ain't No Black in the Union Jack": The Cultural Politics of Race and Nation.* Chicago: University of Chicago Press.

Hall, Stuart. 1994. "Cultural Identity and Diaspora." In *Colonial Discourse and Post-*

Colonial Theory: A Reader, ed. Patrick Williams and Laura Chrisman, 392–403. New York: Columbia University Press.

Hebdige, Dick. 1979. *Subculture: The Meaning of Style.* London: Routledge.

Jacoby, Russell. 1995. "Marginal Returns: The Trouble with Post-Colonial Theory." *Lingua Franca* 5 (Sept.–Oct.): 30–37.

Potter, Russell A. 1994. "Black Modernisms/Black Postmodernisms." Review of Rose, *Black Noise. Postmodern Culture* 5, no. 1 (Sept. 1994). Electronic journal; available at <www.iath.virginia.edu/pmc>.

———. 1995. *Spectacular Vernaculars: Hip-Hop and the Politics of Postmodernism.* Albany: State University of New York Press.

Rose, Tricia. 1994. *Black Noise: Rap Music and Black Culture in Contemporary America.* Hanover, N.H.: University Press of New England/Wesleyan University Press.

Said, Edward. 1978. *Orientalism.* New York: Vintage Books.

Spivak, Gayatri Chakravorty. 1988. "Can the Subaltern Speak?" In *Marxism and the Interpretation of Culture,* ed. Cary Nelson and Lawrence Grossberg, 271–313. Urbana: University of Illinois Press.

11   The Imperial Dynamic in the Study of Religion: Neocolonial Practices in an American Discipline

Russell T. McCutcheon

Prologue: Just What Is the Postcolonial Study of Religion?

Because religion is generally presumed to involve deeply personal, uncontestable emotions, experiences, and insights of otherworldly origin, it is easy to understand why many scholars steer clear of adopting a historical, critical approach to studying religious practices as part of the cultural world. Although earlier generations of social scientists often considered religious beliefs, practices, and institutions to be false and delusory cultural survivals, mere superstitions, or even protoscientific efforts to account for, and thereby control, aspects of the natural world, a number of contemporary Western scholars have adopted a far more empathetic (sometimes even sympathetic) attitude when describing and understanding the religious beliefs and behaviors of others— let alone ourselves. Whereas the openly condescending ethnographies of late nineteenth- and early twentieth-century scholars have only recently been historicized and placed within their proper colonialist context, in the academic study of religion there seems to be a widely operating consensus that recent moves toward empathetic or reflexive scholarship are, at least in part, capable of righting the imperialist wrongs of the past by allowing the people whom we study to "speak for themselves." For some, then, the postcolonial study of religion is a concerted effort to recover indigenous meanings that have been distorted and subverted by a century of Euro-American exploitation; it is an attempt to drop "our" preconceived classifications and definitions in an effort to allow "their" voices to be heard.

This essay is a critical study of the roots of this consensus as they were articulated in American-based scholarship dating from the 1950s; as will be argued throughout, because of the novel manner in which this discourse reproduces the dehistoricization and idealization associated with much early scholarship, a large portion of the modern study of religion is better understood not as a *post-* but rather a *neo*colonial practice. In other words, whereas an earlier generation used such categories as "primitive," "heathen," "pagan," and "savage" to essentialize, categorize, and control diverse populations, this new empathetic form of scholarship is based on the presumption that its methods can allow the researcher to understand the deep, unmediated, and common experiences that span the human community; accordingly, the very categories "private experience" and, more specifically, "religious experience" have become new tools useful in the homogenization and management of cultural difference—both of which are key ingredients in imposing social, economic, and political structures from without.

This new brand of sympathetic scholarship reproduces old tendencies by portraying the Other as a neutral screen onto which researchers are able to project and read their own emotions. In the words of the feminist scholar of religion Marsha Hewitt, although it is one thing to learn something about the human condition from the study of other cultures, it is

> something quite different to focus on our own experience in such a way that we mine other worlds for our own benefit. To put the matter bluntly: to what extent are researchers appropriating the spiritual wealth of other peoples, thereby annexing their worlds to the researchers' own? Efforts to deconstruct the colonializing tendencies in anthropological, ethnographic, and comparative-religious research are in danger of recolonializing other cultures precisely by means of our excessive preoccupation with ourselves and our experiences. . . . In an age as obsessed with therapeutic solutions to private and community problems as ours is, one needs to ask if our interest in other cultures and their religious practices is not motivated to a large extent by our own relentless search for yet another "therapy" that is more exotic and therefore perhaps more effective than what is available to us in our own context. (1994, 289)

This emphasis on the private, experiential nature of religion, coupled with the presumably therapeutic ability of the researcher to reexperience what his or her data describe, constitutes the heart of neocolonial practice. Taking the Other as a blank page on which is written our own supposedly universal desires is, in my reading, the height of ethnocentrism—a strategy common in neocolonial discourses. Although we may no longer be mining others' lands for transportable raw materials, we are still in fact mining their cultural systems for portable values.

Rather than presume religious discourses to be about essentially private and otherworldly matters—for my argument is that the rhetoric of privatization is *precisely* what needs to be challenged—I follow the work of the University of Chicago scholar Bruce Lincoln in conceptualizing religion as a mechanism that authorizes a variety of social practices; it is "that discourse whose defining characteristic is its desire to speak of things eternal and transcendent with an authority equally transcendent and eternal" (1996, 225). Based on this strictly historicist understanding of religious practice as social activity, this essay, then, is an attempt to lay a new foundation for a postcolonial study of religion; it is a consistent effort to understand the modern, liberal discourse on religion as it has developed in the United States as but one mechanism employed in the ongoing business of nation building.

In the Beginning . . . : Skeletons in Our Closet

The origins of a coherent effort to study religion in a nonreligious manner— once termed *Religionswissenschaft,* comparative religion, the history of religions, the science of religion, the academic study of religion, or simply religious studies—lie in a complex of events that coalesced in mid-nineteenth-century Europe. In the reports that early explorers, traders, and missionaries carried back to Europe, scholars found tales and practices remarkably similar to those that European and North American Christians had for centuries presumed to be unique to themselves alone. Stories of cosmic creations and cataclysmic destructions, of earth-altering floods, mischievous snakes, and disguised saviors, all made their way back to Europe. Such apparent similarities quickly led scholars to rethink a number of commonly accepted and even fundamental notions; for instance, the results of translating and comparing ancient Sanskrit to other languages severely undermined the belief that Hebrew was the oldest human language. As part of this rethinking, scholars were challenged, first, to develop a means for comparing the assortment of human practices and, second, to devise theories capable of explaining the results of their comparisons.

Although the basis of the comparative method had been developing for centuries—it dates back at least to the ancient Greeks' thoughts on the gods of their neighbors—the two names that generally come to mind as the acknowledged founders of comparative religion are the German-born Oxford philologist F. Max Müller (1823–1900) and the Dutch scholar of ancient Egyptian and Mesopotamian religion and culture Cornelius P. Tiele (1830–1902). A number of histories of the field have been written (several notable ones in the past seventy-five years), but few have taken seriously the observation that the intellectual traditions that produced both these scholars, as well as the discipline they helped to found, rose to prominence at precisely the same time as the colonial worlds they inhabited were reaching, or had just past, their zenith. Simply put, scholars of religion have yet to address the relations between European expansionism and the rise of their own discipline. Even fewer scholars have recognized that after its initial but brief gains in the pre–World War I American university,[1] the academic study of religion (then often called the history of religions) was successfully reborn just as the United States' worldwide political, economic, and military dominance was being tested in Korea and Vietnam. Simply put, if the European origins of the field might be linked to a number of colonial practices, then its rebirth in America might be linked to a number of neocolonial practices.

The widely accepted story of the American field's rebirth is in large part derived from an aside in the 1963 U.S. Supreme Court judgment on school prayer (*Abington School District v. the Schempp Family*), where the majority decision stated that, although confessional instruction in publicly funded schools is unconstitutional, one's "education is not complete without a study of comparative religion or the history of religion and its relationship to the advancement of civilization." Although the school prayer decision is only tangentially related to teaching the academic study of religion in state schools, historians have, in the opinion of the noted Chicago scholar of religion Jonathan Z. Smith (1995, 411), made of this judicial aside a virtual cosmogony for the discipline, repeatedly retelling it as the authoritative account of the discipline's mythical origins.

As Smith's own research has made all too apparent, however, stories of "how things came to be" are intimately related to claims concerning "how things *ought* to be," making cosmogonies among society's most politically loaded, socially efficacious tales. Take, for instance, the ancient Hindu tale of how a cosmic being named Purusha was sacrificed to produce everything from the universe itself to ritualized chants and even animals. The tale goes on to narrate how the social classes arose from this sacrifice, explaining that whereas ritual specialists (*brahmins*) arose from the mouth and the warrior class (*kshatriyas*) arose from the arms of Purusha, servants (*shudras*) predictably originated from its lowest extremities. That the *brahmins* are the group who told and eventually wrote down this tale suggests the powerful role cosmogonies play in legitimizing the distribution of power and privilege. Such tales of origin are loaded, then, precisely because such unrecognized, even disguised, normative claims often function to suppress oppositional accounts that support alternative patterns and social associations. When it comes to our own tales concerning the rebirth of the study of religion in America, postcolonial criticism provides us with a means for constructing an alternative reading that inquires not simply into *whether* and *how* religion could be studied in state universities but precisely *why* this debate arose in the late 1950s and early 1960s. Simply put, we now have at our disposal tools to inquire into the sociorhetorical factors that constructed the thinkable conditions for defining, describing, and understanding the religions of both ourselves and other people in the first place. Not only do we now have a way to see the skeletons that may be in our own closet, but we have a means for finding the closet in which they have remained hidden.

Idealism, Colonialism, and Religion

As already suggested, the field's history has generally been written only in the light of the increasingly apparent clash between the emerging comparative methodology, associated with the work of both Müller (1893) and Tiele (1897, 1899), and the work of their contemporaries who were content simply to evaluate the worth and truth of "non-Christian" religions. The origins of the academic study of religion, or so say our accepted histories, is to be found in the startling shift away from using descriptive accounts of other peoples' religious habits and beliefs as a means for more effective European missionary activities toward using them as the basis for a nonevaluative, comparative science of religion. Through the use of the newly devised nonevaluative, comparative method, then, historical religions or religious traditions (in the plural) were studied to learn about what was widely presumed to be a fundamentally human characteristic (religion in the singular), termed by some a religious a priori and by others religious consciousness. As important as it is to acknowledge the clear advances of such nonevaluative, comparative work, it is equally important to recognize that the field has been greatly influenced by a brand of suspect philosophical idealism. Much as the study of religion is often limited to matters of faith and creed, as opposed to practice and institution, the historical origins of the field itself are generally traced to a clash in belief systems manifest in mid- to late nineteenth-century Europe rather than to any number of wider contextual factors that characterized this period. In a nutshell, the idealism characteristic of the field obscures these materialist factors.

In their widespread commitment to this idealist thesis, scholars have generally ignored a number of other scales of analysis—among them, the various materialist scales such as politics and economics—that might also assist in explaining the rise and success of the study of religion at a precise point in history. As already indicated, no one has yet explored in detail the relations between the development of the comparative study of religion with the manner in which an increasingly sophisticated colonial bureaucracy and state-sponsored civil service were at the same time replacing the previous stage of expansionist economics. This earlier stage was characterized by private commercial enterprise and originally represented by such organizations as the English East India Company (founded 1599), the Vereenigde Oost-Indische Compagnie (Dutch East India Company, founded 1602 and bankrupt in 1799), and the Netherlands Trading Company (founded 1824). Simply put, as yet we have not investigated the links between the early scholar of religion's efforts to label, sort, catalog, and compare an apparently distinct set of human beliefs, actions, and institutions, on the one hand, and the kind of mid-nineteenth- and early twentieth-century bureaucratic, economic, and political activity that brought about a new phase of expansion first for Europe and then for America, on the other.

There are a number of alternative and largely unexplored lenses through which this history can be reconceived. Take, for example, the case of Müller and the East India Company. Müller's four-volume English translation of the massive Hindu text known as the *Rig Veda* ("hymns" or "chants of praise") is to this day heralded as an immensely important early development in philology and comparative religion. Nevertheless, when we learn such things as the fact that the publication of this translation (which ran from 1849 to 1862) was financed by the East India Company—one of the primary arms in the development of British colonial rule—and that this translation has been widely recognized as a step in revitalizing the Hindu tradition itself at this time (by making available in English translation this extensive collection of ancient Sanskrit texts), we can plainly see the often occluded relations between imperial politics, economics, scholarship, *and* the effects of this complex set of related practices on indigenous self-understandings. Furthermore, when we take into account that the East India Company's role in financing Müller's translation is noted, but only in passing, by Eric Sharpe in his widely read and generally authoritative history of the field (Sharpe 1986), we are led to inquire why material relations and influences occupy such a marginal and incidental place in our histories.

As David Chidester asks in his ground-breaking study of colonialism and the history of comparative religion in southern Africa, "What kind of narrative leaves out all the dramatic tension, human conflict, or human comedy that makes for a good story?" (1996b, xiii). His answer: only official histories, "internal to the development of a set of European academic disciplines. As a result, the real story remains to be told." Contrary to the official history, the brand of postcolonial criticism to which I subscribe presumes from the outset that the origins of the study of religion, like all products of the European Enlightenment, took place in both an intellectual and sociopolitical context of conquest. Furthermore, it argues that by marginalizing or outright ignoring the contextual and material relations that have shaped scholarship on religion, histories of the field themselves are implicated in this dynamic network of overlapping and competing material interests. This is as true in the case of the field's nineteenth-century origins as it is in its 1960s rebirth in America.

The Imperial Dynamic in the Study of Religion

What specifically links all this with postcolonial critique is the fact that the study of religion, conceived by many scholars in the field as an institutionally and methodologically distinct, unique, and autonomous pursuit—in a word, sui generis—participates in a far wider geopolitical discourse that functions to minimize the historical specificity of human agents and populations through the manner in which these agents and populations are represented in scholarship. In other words, in its very conception of religion as utterly removed from all issues of power and privilege (by viewing them as sui generis, scholars presume religion, religious experiences, and institutions to be self-caused and not the result of historical and material factors), the regnant discourse in the study of religion lies precisely where neocolonial strategies of control and domination intersect with the politics of representation. As David Spurr (1993) has convincingly argued in the case of travel writings that date from the colonial period, such techniques as idealization, dehistoricization, and aestheticization are essential rhetorical, textual, and ideological strategies of imperial rule. As I will demonstrate, these same techniques were the primary means by which many American scholars constructed "religion" and made of it an item of intellectual discourse. Accordingly, to borrow a term from Edward Said, the discourse on sui generis religion, like the media he critiques in *Culture and Imperialism* (1993), is but one more instance of the modern "imperial dynamic."

That the study of other people's religions attracted the interest of scholars as well as geopolitical, economic powers should, then, come as no surprise. As the scholar of religion and politics Gustavo Benavides (1995, 162) has recently noted, "That many of these scholars [in the European colonial period] dealt with religion is not surprising, since 'religion' is the name given to those practices and presuppositions which, infinitely malleable both by insiders and outsiders, articulate a culture's, or perhaps just an elite's, unspoken understanding of itself." Given the utter dominance, from the colonial to the modern era, of definitions that construe religion in terms of personalistic experiences and various states of individual consciousness, Benavides's observation is correct. Religion understood as the sum total of an individual's scruples, a private feeling, or one's ultimate concern is an ideal rhetorical and ideological tool.

Examples of this dominant tradition include the highly influential writings of the German romantic and pietist theologian Friedrich Schleiermacher

(1768–1834); the Kantian "religious a priori" of the early twentieth-century successor to this tradition, Rudolf Otto (1869–1937); or even the influential writings of the Christian theologian Paul Tillich (1886–1965). Because religion is conceptualized as an essentially subjective, unspoken intuition concerning unseen forces and feelings, the scholar of this supposedly mysterious force has no need for interpersonal argumentation in its interpretation and study. The description and study of private religion, much like the study of aesthetic feelings and poetic impulses, is a powerful means for reducing complexity into simplicity, heterogeneity into homogeneity, materiality into ideality, actions into thoughts, and society into individuality. Accordingly, in their efforts to prevent a mechanistic reduction of these supposedly fundamental religious feelings at the hands of the Freudian psychologist, the Durkheimian sociologist, or the Marxist economist, scholars of religion have ironically constructed a highly abstract, ahistorical tool that can be effectively used to reduce complex human beliefs, practices, and institutions to matters of relevance only to isolated, privatized thinking minds.

A complex system of such rhetorical and ideological strategies for controlling the production of knowledge through the representation of people and events was developed to serve the European, and later American, centers of trade and political decision making in their moves to govern more effectively and thereby control and determine not only their own populations but also the inhabitants, natural resources, and economies of distant lands. Such representations ensured that, above all, the inhabitants of distant lands were not confronted or portrayed as human beings embedded within complexly integrated social, historical, and intellectual contexts. As long as such rhetoric goes unchallenged by members of either the possessed society or the imperial nation, the control of material and intellectual production, and therefore the benefits and powers that result from such production, remains in the hands of those who do the possessing—that is, those who do much of the consuming.

The study of religion provides a useful site for linking all these diverse issues, from the imperial dynamic to the politics of representation and even the potential for postcolonial opposition. Although there are no doubt many reasons this field was reborn in the United States, the intriguing problem in need of closer examination lies in discovering the possible relations between the discourse's dehistoricizing strategies and the needs of the growing, worldwide American hegemony. One of the primary means by which the study of religion was reestablished in America was through the oft-heard claim that because religion is unique and autonomous (i.e., sui generis), its study deserved to be housed in a methodologically unique and institutionally autonomous setting. Although such claims can be found in the writings of a large number of European and North American scholars, it seems to have been only in America that such strategies were explicitly linked to the intellectual and institutional justification for the field. Therefore, we may be able see the history of the discourse on sui generis religion as a case study in the changing fortunes of the imperial dynamic. Whereas essentialist, dehistoricizing practices once defined the field, it seems clear that the future successes of the study of religion are linked more to cross-disciplinary cooperation and theoretically based scholarship than to definitive interpretations of the seeming transparent "native's" point of view.

To explore these interrelated issues requires at least three steps. First, we must demonstrate that the regnant discourse on sui generis religion is ideological inasmuch as it is a discourse whose sociopolitical authority is gained only by disguising its own material, social, and political history or trace. This ideological aspect is precisely where the imperial dynamic can be seen to exist. Second, because many American departments of religion have found their most effective justification for institutional autonomy in terms of such intellectually and politically problematic notions as that of sui generis religion, it will be necessary to argue that their continued existence in the postcolonial university seems highly unlikely. In other words, we must demonstrate that such essentialist constructs as sui generis religion, and the institutional structures it sanctions, are destabilized by critical reading techniques. Third, given the requirements of our work as carried out in the context of the postcolonial university, we need to argue that nontotalizing research on religion—where religion is conceived as a theoretical construct and not an essential aspect of human experience—can provide the study of religion with a more secure and defensible identity within the academy.

In broad outline, then, such an analysis is both diagnostic and prescriptive. In its diagnostic aspect it moves within a cross-disciplinary setting, applying the methods of such critics as Terry Eagleton, Fredric Jameson, Michel Foucault, Michel de Certeau, Edward Said, and others to an analysis of the study of religion as it has developed in America. To this end, I identify the ways in which the scholarship of three leading and representative scholars of religion in America, Mircea Eliade, Huston Smith, and Joseph Kitagawa, rely on and help to foster conditions conducive to the domination of distant populations. In its prescriptive aspect, my recommendations coincide with historian Arthur McCalla's claim that "the dream of a unified, autonomous study of religions must be dropped in favor of an interdisciplinary model" (McCalla 1994, 435). Space restrictions, however, require that I limit the discussion to several facets of the first, diagnostic, aspect of the argument and leave more detailed prescriptive recommendations for another day.

Ideology and Sui Generis Religion

What I am terming the discourse on sui generis religion has three primary aspects: (1) Religion is understood as essentially personalistic, experiential, and underivable from other aspects of human life such as society, politics, and economics. (2) Because of this autonomy and unique status, the field must use special descriptive and hermeneutic methods that can somehow access the supposedly deep aspects of devotees' so-called privatized religious experiences. (3) As a result of both (1) and (2), the unique ways of studying this supposedly distinct aspect of human consciousness preclude all efforts to explain the phenomenon; moreover, these interpretive methods need to be housed in autonomous departmental settings so as to protect the datum of the study of religion (the sacred, power, the *mysterium tremendum,* the religious a priori) from the kinds of supposed misreadings that result from studying it—explaining it—in such contexts as psychology or sociology departments. In a word, when religion is declared to be sui generis, as it has been by a surprisingly large number of scholars in the field, it is understood by them to be utterly *irreducible.* Accordingly, the issue of reductionism is one of the most important theoretical *and* political debates in the history of the field (see Proudfoot 1985; Idinopulos and Yonan 1994).

We find no clearer articulation of this discourse than in the words of the Romanian expatriate and famous University of Chicago historian of religions Mircea Eliade (1907–86), its foremost twentieth-century representative:

> Although the historical conditions are extremely important in a religious phenomenon (for every human datum is in the last analysis a historical datum), they do not wholly exhaust it. . . . All these dreams, myths, and nostalgias . . . cannot be exhausted by a psychological [or, we might add, any other form of naturalistic or social scientific] explanation; there is always a kernel that remains refractory to explanation, and this indefinable, irreducible element perhaps reveals the situation of man in the cosmos, a situation that, we shall never tire of repeating, is not solely "historical." (1964, xiv)

Based on this indefensible a priori assertion—even intuition—that there is (1) a transhistorical "kernel" constituting a unified essence of all religious experiences that (2) cannot be causally explained with the tools of psychology, sociology, and so on, Eliade went on to delineate the sociopolitical program he termed the "new humanism," founded on what he labeled the "creative hermeneutic." Simply put, if only scholars of sui generis religion have descriptive and interpretive accesses to the deep, essential character of all religious experiences (for such scholars are, in his opinion, the only ones who study religion *as* religion), then only they are in the position to make authorized, normative claims, since their basis for these claims has not been adversely affected by such historical contingencies as politics. For Eliade, this hermeneutic, like the practice of yoga or shamanism, is considered creative inasmuch as it is a "spiritual technique" that can change and even save not only the scholar but society at large: "a good history of religions book ought to produce in the reader an action of *awakening*" (Eliade 1984, 62).

Practitioners of the discourse on sui generis religion thus conceive it as personally and socially salvific.[2] Accordingly, this discourse implies three additional claims: (1) their data provide scholars of religion access to previously lost or disguised meanings and values; (2) these scholars continually reveal, apply, and disseminate these values in their work and lives; and (3) based on the historical and social autonomy of their datum, such scholars and their social judgments and pronouncements necessarily possess sociocultural authority and privilege.

This discourse is ideological inasmuch as these claims to sociocultural and political authority are based on putatively self-evident and nonhistorical insights and intuitions into what we can describe only as the real nature of things. I use the term *ideology* here not simply to designate a worldview or in a much harsher fashion to imply the notion of false consciousness. Rather, I use it to designate those systems of thought and action that, intentionally or not, fail to recognize their own context and historicity. To be ideological is to disguise the trace of one's ideas and actions and to represent them as sui generis. Within our context in the public university and the assumptions or rules that ground interpersonal, rational discourse, no thoughts, actions, insights, or even guesses—whether good ones or not—can be attributed the kind of absolute autonomy and authority that Eliade claimed for the historian of religions.

Clearly, we as scholars routinely set up analytic systems to construct "data" that can be, for a time and for our own good reasons, abstracted from otherwise complex sociopolitical and historical contexts; otherwise, given the complexity of observable human actions and institutions, scholarship would be impossible. Accordingly, we scholars employ various analytic, categorical tools of our own making to engage in comparison and study. Nevertheless, to fail to acknowledge the extraintellectual motivations and implications of the processes of abstraction and analysis, to fail to recognize that a representation is not necessarily to be equated with a presentation, and, as Jonathan Z. Smith has reminded us, that "map is not territory," and then to use such a failure as the basis for claiming sociocultural authority is to fall into the trap of ideology. It is precisely this trap into which Eliade's scholarship falls. It is also the trap into which much mid-twentieth-century American scholarship on religion falls as well.

Huston Smith and the Rhetoric of Tradition

We may find no better example of the ideological nature of some mid-twentieth-century American scholarship on religion than in the introductory world religions textbook by Huston Smith (b. 1919) entitled *The Religions of Man* (1958)—a book that has continuously been in print since its first edition, has been translated into several languages, remains a standard introductory text throughout much of the field, and is now available in a slightly revised edition with a new title, *The World's Religions* (1991).[3] Consider the chapter on Confucianism, which provides an example of the significant role such ideological categories as "tradition" can play in this type of scholarship. At this point in his chapter, Smith seems to be attempting to communicate to his American readers the role tradition plays in their own lives and how this differs from its role in the Chinese setting he is describing. Smith writes:

> Modern life has moved so far from the tradition-bound life of tribal societies as to make it difficult for us to realize how completely it is possible for mores to be in control. There are not many areas in which custom continues to reach into our lives to dictate our behavior, but dress and attire remains one of them. Guidelines are weakening even here, but it is still pretty much the case that if a corporation executive were to forget his necktie, he would have trouble getting through the day. . . . His associates would regard him out of the corners of their eyes as—well, different. And this is not a comfortable way to be seen, which is what gives custom its power. Someone has ventured that in a woman's certitude that she is wearing precisely the right thing for the occasion, there is a peace that religion can neither give nor take away. (1991, 161)

Although tribal behavior is, in his words, dictated by what Smith earlier characterized as nonrational tradition,[4] the modern lives of his readers conform merely to such apparently minor customs or guidelines as those of fashion and beauty (apparently more so in the case of women, making this passage one of the primary sites where Smith's androcentrism is all too evident). Smith concludes:

> If we generalize to all areas of life this power of tradition, which we now seldom feel outside matters of attire, we shall have a picture of the tradition-oriented life of tribal societies. . . . [In the case of Confucianism] China had reached a new point in its social evolution, a point marked by the large number of individuals in the full sense of the word. Self-conscious rather than group-conscious, these individuals had ceased to think of themselves primarily in the first person plural and were thinking in the first person singular. Reason was replacing social convention, and self-interest outdistancing the expectations of the group. . . . Individualism and self-consciousness are con-

tagious. Once they appear, they spread like epidemic or wildfire. Unreflective solidarity is a thing of the past. (1991, 162–63)

Smith's text sets up a number of polarities, all of which assist "the Chinese" irresistibly to progress—or better, evolve—toward the liberal 1950s American ideal of individual freedom, rationality, and self-consciousness. In all this, and in spite of his apparent efforts to convince readers that the first-person singular is the most important pronoun, Smith's text is concerned to portray a "them" in opposition to an "us." His text manufactures his American reader's identity by means of a different and exotic Other that is determined by mysterious and nonrational forces his readers can only just begin to fathom. We are told that we are free whereas they are controlled; it is the reader's duty not only to understand what controls them but to witness and even prompt their social evolution, to ensure that the contagion of freedom spreads.

This rhetoric of tradition and progress is not simply part of a minor trend in the study of religion at this historical juncture; it is a particularly apt example of the intimate relations between political power and academic discourse that are made possible when the study of religion is presumed to be isolated from issues of power and privilege. In the preface to the earlier edition of his book, Smith betrays these relations quite candidly in his remarks on the motivations for understanding other religions:

> The motives that impel us toward world understanding may be several. Recently I was taxied by bomber to the Air Command and Staff College at the Maxwell Air Force Base outside Montgomery, Alabama, to lecture to a thousand selected officers on the religions of other peoples. I have never had students more eager to learn. What was their motivation? Individually I am sure it went beyond this in many cases, but as a unit they were concerned because someday they were likely to be dealing with the peoples they were studying as allies, antagonists, or subjects of military occupation. Under such circumstances it would be crucial for them to predict their behavior, conquer them if worse came to worst, and control them during the aftermath or reconstruction. This is one reason for coming to know people. It may be a necessary reason; certainly we have no right to disdain it as long as we ask the military to do the job we set before it. (1958, 7–8)

The imperial dynamic identified by Said is evident once again: American society is "impelled" to understand so that, when necessary, it can occupy, conquer, and control more effectively. For Smith, the world is divided between those who possess and those who are possessed, and the study of religion mediates between these two groups, ensuring their demarcation through the euphemism of "understanding," an activity more accurately read as the practice of domination. The knowledge brought about through the comparative study of religions (for example, the distinctions between the tradition-bound tribe and modernity) is therefore an effective tool to ensure that one group remains the possessors. Such an imperialist discourse, with its totalizing rhetoric, gives new meaning to the passage immediately preceding the one just quoted, where Smith remarks, in a rather Eliadean fashion, that in the future the "classic ruts between native and foreign, barbarian and Greek, East and West, will be softened if not effaced. Instead of crude and boastful contrasts there will be borrowings and exchange, mutual help, cross-fertilization that leads sometimes to good strong hybrids but for the most part simply enriches the species in question and continues its vigor" (1991, 7). It seems apparent, however, that Smith is completely unaware of just how "crude and boastful" his contrast between tradition-bound and free societies is, let alone his earlier distinction between men and women with respect to "proper" attire. If anything, his own rhetoric of tradition and progress is just as unthinking as that which he critiques, making his own claims implicitly based on the very unreflective solidarity he identifies in "tribal" societies. The cross-fertilization that he envisions for those who engage in the study of religion comes at the expense of the cultural, economic, and political autonomy of the Other, the raw data for "our" enrichment.

Accordingly, the themes of mutual cooperation and the development of a totalized, global culture are undermined by Smith's ever-present imperial and ideological discourse. If anything, these examples lend much momentum to deepening these seemingly minuscule ruts, to use Smith's term, that have led to the domination of entire societies. Such expressions as "world understanding" and references to such abstract constructions as "global" or "universalizing cultures" therefore function as euphemisms for domination—a domination that ultimately involves no blame, for "we" are passive, having been "impelled" by the faceless forces of social progress to take such courses of action.

Joseph Kitagawa and the Rhetoric of Family

A potent example of the neocolonial nature of this era in American scholarship on religion is found in the manner in which Joseph Kitagawa (d. 1992), a scholar of Japanese religions and colleague of Eliade, deploys the rhetoric of the "West" and the "family." No doubt readers familiar with Roland Barthes's *Mythologies* (1973), in particular his essay that identifies the homogenizing and ideological nature of an art exhibit entitled The Great Family of Man, will see that my critique is indebted to Barthes's critical readings of authorized cultural products.

Kitagawa employs these two highly loaded terms in his preface to the *En-*

cyclopedia of Religion (Eliade 1987) as a means to identify the nineteenth-century attitudes of the "European family of nations" toward their colonial "charges," all in an effort to distance the "mental worlds" of the new encyclopedia from those of previous reference works in the field. He writes:

> It was doubtless true that politically, socially, culturally, religiously, economically, and militarily, the power of the Western colonial nations reached its zenith during the nineteenth century, and that the most important events of the modern world occurred through the impetus and initiative of the West . . . ; and furthermore, although World War I undeniably weakened the unity and cohesiveness of the European family of nations, a persistent carryover of the vitality of the Western powers, Western civilization, and Western learning remained even in Asia and Africa until the end of World War II. (Kitagawa 1987, xiv)

Kitagawa then goes on to remark that from the viewpoint of "many non-Western peoples, the year 1945 marked a significant line of demarcation between two worlds of experience. In their eyes, the Western colonial powers—even when they meant well—had acted in the manner of parents who refuse to allow their children to grow up by making all the important decisions for them. The years after World War II witnessed not only the emergence of many new and inexperienced nations but, more important, a redefinition on a global scale of the dignity, value, and freedom of human beings, including non-Western peoples" (ibid.). These two passages are highly problematic for a variety of reasons, most of which revolve around Kitagawa's efforts to isolate a number of historic events from the contemporary world situation, ensuring that sociopolitical conflict remains far removed from modern scholarship. In particular, his rhetoric of the family glosses over and ignores not only significant discontinuities among the European nations themselves but also the very nature of colonialism. Kitagawa not only favorably compares colonial nations to benevolent parents rearing immature children but asserts that this is indeed how the ruled populations saw and see themselves. Moreover, his text blatantly subscribes to a long-standing social-evolutionary misconception that yet dominates many governments' foreign policies, that is, the idea that so-called underdeveloped and immature non-Western nations require moral and economic guidance and, at times, discipline—all of which is broadly generalized as "aid." It is as if the problem with colonialism, from this point of view, is not so much that it ever occurred but rather that the European nations were over- or underprotective and miscalculated the point at which their progeny should "leave the nest." Based on such an interpretation, surely the political instability and physical violence that have plagued many formerly colonized nations in the last several decades could be downplayed and explained away as the result of the premature departure rather than as a result of the colonial presence in the first place.

Like Huston Smith, Kitagawa's implicit judgment that the West was simply well meaning is linked to his thoughts on its almost contagious social and cultural "vitality," for after all, it was the West that had the "initiative" to bring about "the most important events of the modern world." No doubt there are good grounds for questioning whether such events as the two twentieth-century European wars for territory and resources, which spilled throughout the colonized world, were indeed important (we could describe them more accurately as horrendous). Indeed, the "new and inexperienced nations" formed at the close of World War II in many cases resulted from bargaining among the victors as they fought over the spoils. Furthermore, these nations were hardly inexperienced; rather, they were the remnants of older national, social, and ethnic groupings divided in ways convenient to the needs of such nations as Britain, the United States, and the Soviet Union. The various current upheavals among portions of what was formerly known as eastern Europe speak little to what Kitagawa understands as the supposed redefinition of dignity and value—a virtual repetition of the rhetoric of the "New World Order"—that somehow came about after 1945.

Related to his interest in distinguishing the era of the new encyclopedia from that of its predecessors, Kitagawa ensures that the association of Western power, civilization, and learning—a formula rather similar to talk of the military-industrial-educational complex—is limited in its application to the effects of the European nations in the nineteenth century, which Kitagawa believes to have lasted until 1945. For Kitagawa, issues of power and national domination are therefore essentially historic and European and not to be confused with the supposedly new global situation, which has made the pre-1945 East-West division obsolete. Kitagawa strategically limits the discourse on the sociopolitical to a pre-1945 world, effectively silencing any debate on such matters as the ways that post-1945 relations between America and the Soviet Union and wars such as those in Korea, Vietnam, and Central America have shaped not only people's perceptions of themselves and their living conditions but also the efforts of historians of religions to study one facet of these people's complex lives. Instead, as Eliade has phrased it time and again, various peoples (e.g., Asians) simply and mysteriously "reentered our history."

Unfortunately, the differences so necessary for Kitagawa to establish the authority of the new American encyclopedia over the previous generation's scholarship result from his circumscribed and incomplete reading of the changes in the world that occurred after 1945. One of the primary changes on the geopolitical stage during this period was the decline of the European colonial powers' global influence, which resulted in the gradual disintegration and redistribution of their accumulated land wealth during and following World War II. According to Kitagawa, however, the new global order is evidenced today not by such a redistribution of political and military clout but by the role non-Western scholars have begun to play in "the global effort to develop more adequate interpretive schemes for apprehending the entire religious experience of humankind, past and present, prehistorical to modern" (Kitagawa 1987, xiv). An alternative reading would instead cite as one of the more significant changes in the post-1945 world the rapid and often violent rise of both the United States and the former Soviet Union to world hegemony, followed by the eventual confirmation in the 1990s that capitalism had indeed become the controlling economic paradigm for the modern world. Because of the manner in which religion and scholarship on religion are presumed to rise above material as well as sociopolitical issues, however, these readings are entirely absent from Kitagawa's account.

A tactical counterreading of Kitagawa's inclusive global order would therefore suggest that the new order actually constitutes a startling enhancement and powerful legitimation of the hegemony of idealist and conservative discourses on the stage of world politics. Not only are contemporary writers in Europe and America interested in using "non-Western" peoples as sources of supposedly essential and ahistorical religious insights, but now scholars from these assorted societies have been trained in and influenced by the regnant ideology, causing them to become fully involved in what we can identify as the effort to idealize themselves and their own populations, thereby effectively minimizing their own ethnic, national, and historical contexts and particularities. For example, even though his concerns were rather different from my own, the research of the Swedish scholar David Westerlund has convincingly demonstrated that the study of African religion as carried out by African scholars is uniformly idealist. He writes that "as a rule, these scholars have an idealist view of religion and regard it as a phenomenon *sui generis*" (1985, 87). Presuming that hegemonic systems function to reproduce themselves by means of a population's internalization of such strategies of control, Westerlund's findings suggest that the scholarship in formerly colonized and ruled societies may, ironically perhaps, perpetuate the same dehistoricization that characterized and constrained them during the colonial era. Given a materialistic scale of analysis, what such scholars as Kitagawa, Smith, and Eliade celebrate as the universalizing of assorted methods to understand deep and socially salvific experiences and insights turns out to be the reformulation of assorted populations as their own jailers.

Therefore, the mid-twentieth-century transformations applauded by these three American-based scholars of religion actually constitute a startling confirmation of the degree to which the modern hegemony has attained cultural, social, and political transparency. The ironically provincial nature of this supposedly global new world, evidenced in its ability to minimize the complex lives of human beings via a discourse limited to matters purely of the mind is also found in Eliade's and Huston Smith's highly questionable efforts to establish a universal culture where, in Eliade's words from his own preface to the encyclopedia, "for the first time in history we recognize today not only the unity of human races but also the spiritual values and cultural significance of their religious creations" (Eliade 1987, 1:ix). That this unity is based on a highly abstract, idealized type is not acknowledged whatsoever.

Ethnocentrism and the Discourse on Sui Generis Religion

For my current purposes, what is most important is to link the construction of this idealized type to the practice of ethnocentrism, itself one of the central strategies operating within various neocolonial representative practices. Although I have already shown the ethnocentric nature of Smith's earlier scholarship, as well as of Kitagawa's, it will help to return to the work of Eliade, for in the recent history of the study of religion there is no more explicit example of the attempt to subsume the Other by the strategies of appropriation and domestication. As already argued, in Eliade's program supposedly ahistorical and purely religious myths, rituals, and symbols of the Other—known as the politically and socially autonomous *Homo religiosus*—were collected, cataloged, and eventually interpreted so as to be used by Western, secular people to revitalize Western culture. This is nothing other than the new humanism; however, that the new humanism is a deeply ethnocentric practice continues to pass unrecognized.

Take, for example, the following representative passage from Eliade's journal, 22 October 1959:

> I see the history of religions as a total discipline. I understand now that the encounters, facilitated by depth psychology, with the stranger within, with that which is foreign, exotic, archaic in ourselves, on the one hand—and, on the other, the appearance of Asia and of the exotic or "primitive" groups in history—are cultural moments which find their ultimate meaning only from the perspective of the history of religions. The hermeneutic necessary for the revelation of the meanings and the messages hidden in myths, rites, symbols, will also help us to understand both depth psychology and the historical age into which we are entering and in which we will be not only surrounded but also dominated by the "foreigner," the non-Occidentals. It will be possible to decipher the "Unconscious," as well as the "Non-Western World," through the hermeneutic of the history of religions. (1989, 69–70)

This most troubling passage concisely summarizes Eliade's overall project as it appears in his many scholarly and personal writings. On one level, the quoted passage can be read to present a powerful program for a hermeneutic of the recovery of meaning, and many commentators focus their interpretive efforts almost exclusively on this level.[5] If, however, one problematizes such things as the self-evidence of this supposedly archaic, deep meaning or the motives and implications of writing on such generalities as "non-Occidentals" or the exotic, as well as the supposedly universal applicability of his findings, then such comments can be read in different ways as well.

Reading such passages in this alternative and tactical fashion provides an explicit example of the power that comes from appropriating and domesticating the Other—what Hewitt meant by her comments regarding "appropriating the spiritual wealth of other peoples." In this case, the concern is over the Other of one's own unconscious, accessible thanks to Freud's insights, and the Other of the "Orient," accessible thanks to the work of nineteenth- and twentieth-century anthropologists, missionaries, traders, and soldiers. The point that must be emphasized in this counterreading of Eliade's text is that because the foreigner inside (the unconscious, the savage within), as well as the foreigner outside (the non-Occidental), is exotic, foreign, archaic, and unknown, it needs to be defined and contained; both are in need of domestication through interpretation and understanding precisely because they both threaten to "dominate" us. What is perhaps most disturbing about Eliade's remarkably ethnocentric project is the fact that few commentators and critics have identified it as such.

The new humanism is ethnocentric not simply because it presumes that *their* means are valuable inasmuch as they are useful in serving *our* ends but also because it presumes that *our* ends are to be equated with *everyone's*. Clearly, ethnocentrism is not the fact of having a culture but the assumption that one's own culture and the sociopolitical goals relevant to one's own culture are by definition everyone's—a presumption crucial to neocolonial systems of representation. To be ethnocentric is to presume that the Other is transparent to one's advances and to obscure the fact that the recovery of meaning so important to the project undertaken by Eliade and others is the aim primarily of European- and American-based scholars; others may not share it. Simply put, to study cultures is not itself ethnocentric, for as Roy Wagner (1981, 16) has noted, "the study of culture is in fact *our* culture." As David Hoy has remarked, however: "The difficulty with ethnocentrism is not so much that we see the world through our own self-understanding, but instead *that we expect every other self-understanding to converge with ours*" (1991, 78, emphasis added; see also Hoy 1978).[6] It is precisely through deploying the infinitely malleable notion of sui generis religion that scholars continue to disguise the ethnocentric implications of their universalizing and dehistoricizing claims.

The Representation of "Self-Immolations" and Sociopolitical Autonomy

Although I have concentrated on the work of several representative scholars of religion in discussing the neocolonialism of the modern discourse on sui generis religion as it has developed in the United States, this essentialist, ideological, ethnocentric, and neocolonialist discourse can be documented at virtually every imaginable site in the modern study of religion. One site where such a critique comes into sharpest focus is the case of the scholarly and media representations of the first of the so-called self-immolations of a Vietnamese Buddhist monk in 1963. The point in examining this one discursive site in particular is not to offer the definitive or final reading of the significance, meaning, and motivations of the event but rather to demonstrate that by marginalizing historical and material analysis, the discourse on sui generis religion not only authorizes itself and its own self-understanding but is implicated in a complex web of specific sociopolitical and even geopolitical issues.

The often occluded relations among power, imperial politics, and the specific portrayals of religious issues are perhaps no more apparent than in the case of the interpretations that American media and intellectuals gave to the much publicized actions of several Vietnamese Buddhists who, beginning in mid-June of 1963, died by publicly setting themselves on fire. The first of several such deaths occurred in Saigon on 11 June 1963 and was widely reported in American newspapers the following day, although the *New York Times,* along with many other newspapers, declined to print Malcolm Browne's famous—or rather, infamous—Associated Press photograph of the lone monk burning (Moeller 1989, 404). (Indeed, this one photograph is one of the two or three most powerful and memorable photographic images from the Vietnam War.) In the first such death, the monk, seventy-three-year-old Thich Quang Duc, sat at a busy downtown intersection and had gasoline poured over him by a fellow monk. As a large crowd of Buddhists and reporters watched, Quang Duc lit a match and, over the course of a few moments, burned to death while seated in the lotus position.

Despite the fact that this event took place during a busy news week when the U.S. civil rights movement was reaching a peak (with the enrollment of the first two black students at the University of Alabama and, early on 12 June, the murder of the civil rights leader Medgar Evers in Mississippi), as the week progressed the American media covered Quang Duc's death and the demonstrations associated with his funeral in increasing detail. The *New York Times* initially reported the death on 12 June with a small article accompanied only by a photograph of a nearby protest that prevented a fire truck from reaching the scene; the story was briefly summarized and updated on page 5 the next day and then ran as the lead on page 1 on 14 June 1963, accompanied by the following headline: "U.S. Warns South Vietnam on Demands of Buddhists: [South Vietnamese President] Diem is told he faces censure if he fails to satisfy religious grievances, many of which are called just." The story, no longer simply concerned with describing the actions of an apparently lone Buddhist monk, was now concerned with the official U.S. reaction and remained on page 1 for the following days. It was reported in greater detail in the Sunday edition (16 June 1963) and was mentioned for the first time in an editorial column on 17 June 1963, one week after it occurred. By the autumn of that year the images of protesting or burning monks had appeared in a number of popular magazines, most notably *Life* (June, August, September, and November issues).

Despite the wide coverage this event received in newspapers and the popular press, at that time it received relatively little treatment by scholars of religion.[7] Apart from a few brief descriptions of these events in an assortment of books on world religions in general, only one detailed article was published at that time, written by Jan Yün-Hua (1965) and appearing in the University of Chicago periodical *History of Religions*. It was concerned with examining the medieval Chinese Buddhist precedents for Quang Duc's death, a death that quickly came to be interpreted in the media as an instance of self-immolation, or self-sacrifice, aimed at protesting the religious persecution of the Buddhists in South Vietnam by the politically and militarily powerful Vietnamese Roman Catholics.

According to such accounts, the origin of the protests and, eventually, Quang Duc's death, was a previous demonstration on 8 May 1963 where government troops aggressively broke up a Buddhist gathering in the old imperial city of Hue: a demonstration for, among other things, the right to fly the Buddhist flag along with the national flag. The government, however, took no responsibility for the nine Buddhists who died in the ensuing violence, blaming their deaths instead on communists. Over the following weeks this denial fueled outrage for what the Buddhists considered to be the unusually violent actions of the government troops at Hue, culminating, according to this interpretation, in Quang Duc's sacrificial death.

Given that interpreters generally acknowledged the event to have been a sacrifice, an essentially religious issue, it is no surprise that Jan's central concern is to determine whether such an action could be considered Buddhist, given the religion's usually strict rules against killing in general and suicide in particular. As Jan (1965, 243) puts it, these actions "posed a serious problem of academic interest, namely, what is the place of religious suicide in religious history and what is its justification?" The reader is told that the monks' motivations were "spiritual" and that such self-inflicted deaths were "religious suicides" because "self-immolation signifies something deeper than merely the legal concept of suicide or the physical action of self-destruction" (ibid.). Given that the event is self-evidently religious (an interpretation based on an unsupported assumption), the question of greatest interest has to do not as much with its possible political origins or overtones as with the question of "whether such a violent action is justifiable according to religious doctrine" (ibid.). It seems clear that for this historian of religions, the action can be properly understood—and eventually justified—only once it is placed in the context of texts written by Buddhist specialists from the fifth-century C.E. onward. Jan's concern, then, is to determine whether these actions were justifiable (something that is not properly the concern of scholars of religion) based exclusively on devotee accounts, some of which were written over one thousand years before the Vietnam War.

After surveying such early texts, the article concludes that self-inflicted death is indeed justifiable within the Buddhist tradition. Basing his argument on changing Chinese Buddhist interpretations of self-inflicted suffering and death, Jan (1965, 265) finds a "more concrete emphasis upon the practical action needed to actualize the spiritual aim." Accordingly, these actions are undertaken largely by elite devotees, inspired by scriptures (255), as a means to demonstrate great selflessness, the paradigms of which are to be found in stories and legends concerned with acts of unbounded compassion and mercy. The closest Jan comes to offering a political reading of any of these reported deaths is that the "politico-religious reasons" for some scriptural instances of self-immolation are "protest against the political oppression and persecution of their religion" (252). Even when political concerns are entertained, they are tightly bound to essentially religious issues.

In terms of the dominance of the discourse on sui generis religion, this article constitutes a fine example of the way an interpretive framework can effectively manage, control, and domesticate an event. Relying exclusively on authoritative Chinese Buddhist texts and, through the use of these texts, interpreting such acts exclusively in terms of insider doctrines and beliefs (e.g., self-immolation, much like an extreme renunciant's abstention from food until dying, could be an example of disdain for the body in favor of the life of the mind and wisdom), rather than in terms of their sociopolitical and historical context, the article prompts its readers to see in these deaths acts that refer only to a distinct set of beliefs foreign to the non-Buddhist. When politics is acknowledged to be a factor, moreover, it is portrayed as essentially oppressive to a self-evidently pure realm of religious motivation and action. In other words, such articles reinforce the assumption that religion is the victim of politics because the former is a priori known to be pure and true. In addition, precisely because the action and belief systems were foreign and exotic to the vast majority of Americans who read about the event in newspapers while having their morning coffee back in 1963, these actions needed to be mediated and managed by trained textual specialists who could utilize the authoritative texts of elite devotees to interpret the essential meaning and motivation of such actions.

The message of such an article, then, is that this act can be fully understood only if it is placed within the context of ancient Buddhist documents and precedents rather than in the context of contemporary geopolitical debates. Further, it conveys the message that the ancient occurrences of such deaths can themselves be fully understood only from the point of view of the intellectual devotees of the time (i.e., Buddhist historians). That the changing geopolitical landscape of Southeast Asia in the early 1960s might assist in this interpretation is not entertained whatsoever. Based on the ways in which such representations insulate these human practices from issues of power and conflict, matters are just as Spurr (1993, 36) has noted: the Vietnam War was fought not simply in the fields but in the media and in scholarship as well.

New Directions for the Postcolonial Study of Religion: "There Is No Data of Religion"

Although there is probably no one reason explaining why the study of religion arose just when and as it did, either originally in Europe or later in America, it should now be clear that the particular collection of methods that coalesced into the field's regnant tradition were highly conducive to legitimizing and maintaining specific distributions of power and privilege. On the individual level, this power was that of the authorized researcher capable of discerning the essential nature not just of religious practices but of human nature itself. On the social level, this power was focused on institutionalizing a set of discursive practices within publicly funded education. On the geopolitical level, this power manufactured isolated, dehistoricized, and more manageable human beings, removed from their context and reduced to their ostensibly essential nature. Although scholars of religion have by no means been the primary or sole representatives of colonial empires, the manner in which their analytical construct, sui generis religion, authorizes a field of scholarship *while at the same time* manufacturing more manageable, transparent populations clearly indicates that the study of religion has been deeply implicated in supporting, rather than challenging, the colonial legacy.

The discourse on sui generis religion is based on an ideological process similar to one that Said has identified in the European novel, a process whereby an imagined community (to borrow a phrase from Benedict Anderson) is not only constructed as entirely accessible to the European or American specialist but also taken by these outsiders to be real and not dependent on their own pre-operative theories, methodologies, and sociocultural interests. Although this discourse first rose to prominence in the academy precisely as the ascendant global hegemony of the United States was being tested and applied in Vietnam, it continues to dominate the study of religion (if nothing else, the continued presence of Huston Smith's textbook in classrooms attests to this). It is not the only discourse currently available to scholars, however—this essay should make it apparent that an oppositional discourse is alive and well in the field. Just as Spurr (1993, 184–85) has noted, "the very nature of [a regnant] discourse as a framework involves principles of limitation and exclusion and therefore creates the possibility for alternative ways of speaking." To end this essay, then, I need to return to what was introduced in the prologue and describe briefly just what constitutes an alternative way of speaking of the postcolonial study of religion.

The historian Sam Preus (1987) has chronicled an alternative, naturalistic tradition used to define and study religion, a tradition that stretches back several hundred years through such writers as David Hume, Émile Durkheim, and Sigmund Freud. In its current form, this tradition fully recognizes that "religion" is an analytical construct of the scholar's making, a second-order category that must not be confused with the scholar's first-order description of the insiders' accounts of their own experiences and behavior. Jonathan Z. Smith is perhaps the best-known contemporary representative of this alternative discourse, notably when he writes that "while there is a staggering amount of data . . . that might be characterized in one culture or another, by one criterion or another, as religious—*there is no data of religion*. Religion is solely the creation of the scholar's study. It is created for the scholar's analytic purposes by his imaginative acts of comparison and generalization. Religion has no independent existence apart from the academy" (Smith 1982, xi). In other words, religion is not a natural category; instead, it is the product of scholarly theories concerning how and why human being organize their individual and social lives and interactions. Given a researcher's interests, context, motivations, and expectations, it may or may not be a useful analytical tool. For those of us schooled in the European, Christian tradition, where the category "religion" has an apparently self-evident meaning and usage (most often referring to belief in a deity), J. Z. Smith's comments appear to be counterintuitive. For those of us who understand the relations between intellectual thought and sociopolitical action, however, his comments suggest that the notion of religion is a tool that, depending on how it is defined and deployed, will have very real, practical consequences.

Most recently, the postcolonial study of religion took a giant leap forward with the publication of David Chidester's compelling history of nineteenth-century colonialism and comparative religion in southern Africa (1996a, 1996b). Relying on a theoretical framework derived from, among others, Foucault and Said, Chidester takes seriously the tactical advantages to be gained by studying and then re-presenting what Benavides characterized earlier as "those practices and presuppositions which [are] infinitely malleable both by insiders and outsiders." In his own words, he develops a "critical analysis of the emergence of the conceptual categories of *religion* and *religions* on the colonial frontier" (Chidester 1996b, 1). Chidester's work is an excellent example of the way in which the postcolonial study of religion will increasingly focus on the deployment of such key cognitive categories as religion, myth, ritual, scripture, and symbol. Appropriately enough, Chidester focuses his critique on earlier European practices; that such a critique is just as applicable to the contemporary American discipline should by now be more than clear.

Given the recognition of this link between scholarly interests, sociopolitical context, and the constructed nature of religion, the naturalist discourse works toward effective postcolonial opposition by detailing a genealogy of categories, understanding them not simply as being conceptual but also as accomplishing, at a variety of sites, the strategic representation necessary to colonial rule. Instead of viewing religion as a natural category or brute fact, the naturalist or historicist tradition acknowledges it to be something of the scholar's own making, a material product with specific cognitive, social, and political implications. In fact, a key component in the colonial rule studied by Chidester was the portrayal of indigenous peoples as *not* having religion whatsoever. Accordingly, practicing this alternative discourse will allow us to chart the rise and decline of sui generis religion and other dehistoricizing rhetorical practices and connect them with such sociopolitical factors as the changing fortunes of the imperial dynamic.

Therefore, recognizing the constructed and inevitably tactical nature of religion, like all the other analytic tools scholars employ in the definition, study, and comparison of human practices and beliefs (I have in mind culture, economics, literature, text, gender, etc.), is the starting point of not only a postmodern but also a postcolonial study of religion capable of deconstructing dominant readings of the field's origins and autonomy.[8] No longer are scholars of religion simply presumed to be wise cultural pluralists intent on saving humanity through the recovery of ostensibly archaic, deep insights and feelings, for the ideologically loaded nature of such potent oversimplifications is now painfully apparent. Resistance to the regnant discourse, and with it resistance to conceiving of scholarship as sociopolitically autonomous and completely overlapping with insider claims and experiences, arises precisely from within the alternative, naturalist approach to studying human culture. The direction of the postcolonial, oppositional study of religion, then, is as others have informed us: it lies in the direction of methodological pluralism rather than methodological exclusivism and entails multidisciplinary cooperation that fully recognizes the theoretically bound and culturally entrenched nature of all human practices—which by definition also includes the scholarly study of such practices.

Notes

Portions of this essay are based on work published in greater detail in McCutcheon 1997c and appear here by permission of Oxford University Press. The analysis of ethnocentrism in the section "Ethnocentricism and the Discourse on Sui Generis Religion" is based on research found in McCutcheon 2000.

1. See Shepard 1991 for an account of the early twentieth-century rise and fall of comparative religion in the United States.

2. Especially since Ivan Strenski's (1987) critique of Eliade's early relations with fascist politics and politicians in pre–World War II Romania and, as Strenski argues, its eventual influence on his later scholarship on myths and rituals, as well as on the field as a whole, considerable work has gone into what we can term the Eliade affair (the Heidegger and de Man affairs come to mind as analogous cases). For a survey of the scholarship on the relations between Eliade's biography and his work in the history of religions, see McCutcheon 1993 and forthcoming. For a thorough, though much more sympathetic, reading of the Eliadean corpus, see Rennie 1996.

3. Interestingly, Smith, like the Jungian scholar of mythology Joseph Campbell (d. 1987), has relatively recently figured in a series of PBS interviews with the journalist Bill Moyers. The fact that politically conservative scholars of religion, myth, and ritual seem to be the only ones widely known by the reading public is itself worth analysis.

4. "Patterns [in tribal societies] simply take shape over centuries, during which generations fumble their way toward satisfying mores and away from destructive ones. Once the patterns becomes [sic] established . . . they are transmitted from generation to generation unthinkingly. As the Romans would say, they are passed on to the young cum lacte, 'with the mother's milk'" (Smith 1991, 161).

5. For two useful examples of such sympathetic scholarship, see the work of Carl Olson (1992) and David Cave (1993). For an insightful critique of Olson's implicit depoliticization of both Eliade the man and Eliade the scholar, see Murphy 1994, 386–89.

6. I must thank Tim Murphy of the University of California at Santa Cruz for bringing Hoy's insightful work to my attention.

7. Most recently, Charles Orzech (1994) and several of the essays in a collection edited by Kenneth Kraft (1992) address the topic of the "self-immolations"—Orzech's essay doing so most explicitly. The critique to be developed here is equally applicable to these more

recent instances of the discourse on sui generis religion. See McCutcheon 1997c for a detailed critique.

8. For other examples of this critique, see McCutcheon 1997a, 1997b, and 1997d.

Works Cited

Barthes, Roland. 1973. *Mythologies.* Trans. Annette Lavers. London: Paladin.

Benavides, Gustavo. 1995. "Giuseppe Tucci, or Buddhism in the Age of Fascism." In *Curators of the Buddha: The Study of Buddhism under Colonialism,* ed. Donald S. Lopez, 161–96. Chicago: University of Chicago Press.

Cave, David. 1993. *Mircea Eliade's Vision for a New Humanism.* New York: Oxford University Press.

Chidester, David. 1996a. "Anchoring Religion in the World: A Southern African History of Comparative Religion." *Religion* 26:141–60.

———. 1996b. *Savage Systems: Colonialism and Comparative Religion in Southern Africa.* Charlottesville: University Press of Virginia.

Eliade, Mircea. 1964. *Shamanism: Archaic Techniques of Ecstasy.* Princeton, N.J.: Princeton University Press.

———. 1984. *The Quest: History and Meaning in Religion.* Chicago: University of Chicago Press.

———. 1989. *Journal II: 1957–1969.* Trans. Fred H. Johnson. Chicago: University of Chicago Press.

———, ed. 1987. *Encyclopedia of Religion.* 16 vols. New York: Macmillan.

Hewitt, Marsha Aileen. 1994. "Reflexivity and Experience in the Study of Religion." *Method and Theory in the Study of Religion* 6, no. 3:285–90.

Hoy, David. 1978. *The Critical Circle: Literature, History, and Philosophical Hermeneutics.* Berkeley: University of California Press.

———. 1991. "Is Hermeneutics Ethnocentric?" In *The Interpretive Turn: Philosophy, Science, Culture,* ed. David Hiley, James Bohman, and Richard Shusterman, 155–75. Ithaca, N.Y.: Cornell University Press.

Idinopulos, Thomas, and Edward A. Yonan, eds. 1994. *Religion and Reductionism: Essays on Eliade, Segal, and the Challenge of the Social Sciences for the Study of Religion.* Leiden, the Netherlands: Brill.

Jan Yün-Hua. 1965. "Buddhist Self-Immolation in Medieval China." *History of Religions* 4:243–68.

Kitagawa, Joseph. 1987. Foreword. In *Encyclopedia of Religion,* 16 vols., ed. Mircea Eliade, 1:xiii–xvi. New York: Macmillan.

Kraft, Kenneth, ed. 1992. *Inner Peace, World Peace: Essays on Buddhism and Nonviolence.* Albany: State University of New York Press.

Lincoln, Bruce. 1996. "Theses on Method." *Method and Theory in the Study of Religion* 8:225–27.

McCalla, Arthur. 1994. "When Is History Not History?" *Historical Reflections* 20:435–52.

McCutcheon, Russell T. 1993. "The Myth of the Apolitical Scholar: The Life and Works of Mircea Eliade." *Queen's Quarterly* 100, no. 3:642–63.

———. 1997a. "A Default of Critical Intelligence? The Scholar of Religion as Public Intellectual." *Journal of the American Academy of Religion* 65, no. 2:443–68.

———. 1997b. "The Economics of Spiritual Luxury: The Glittering Lobby and the Parliament of Religions." *Journal of Contemporary Religion* 13, no. 4:51–64.

———. 1997c. *Manufacturing Religion: The Discourse on Sui Generis Religion and the Politics of Nostalgia.* New York: Oxford University Press.

———. 1997d. "'My Theory of the Brontosaurus': Postmodernism and 'Theory' of Religion." *Studies in Religion: Sciences Religieuses* 26, no. 1:3–23.

———. 2000. "'We're All Stuck Somewhere': Taming Ethnocentrism and Trans-Cultural Understandings." *Critics, Not Caretakers: Redescribing the Public Study of Religion.* Albany: State University of New York Press.

———. Forthcoming. "Methods, Theories, and the Terrors of History: Closing the Eliadean Era with Some Dignity." In *Mircea Eliade: Paradigms and Problems,* ed. Bryan Rennie. Albany: State University of New York Press.

Moeller, Susan. 1989. *Shooting War: Photography and the American Experience in Combat.* New York: Basic Books.

Müller, F. Max. 1893. *Lectures on the Science of Religion.* New York: Scribner's.

Murphy, Tim. 1994. "Review of Carl Olson, *The Theology and Philosophy of Eliade.*" *Method and Theory in the Study of Religion* 6:382–89.

Olson, Carl. 1992. *The Theology and Philosophy of Eliade: A Search for the Centre.* Houndmills, Basingstoke, U.K.: Macmillan.

Orzech, Charles D. 1994. "'Provoked Suicide' and the Victim's Behavior." In *Curing Violence,* ed. Mark I. Wallace and Theophus H. Smith, 137–60. Sonoma, Calif.: Polebridge.

Preus, J. Samuel. 1987. *Explaining Religion: Criticism and Theory from Bodin to Freud.* New Haven, Conn.: Yale University Press.

Proudfoot, Wayne. 1985. *Religious Experience.* Berkeley: University of California Press.

Rennie, Bryan S. 1996. *Reconstructing Eliade: Making Sense of Religion.* Albany: State University of New York Press.

Said, Edward W. 1993. *Culture and Imperialism.* New York: Knopf.

Sharpe, Eric J. 1986. *Comparative Religion: A History.* La Salle, Ill.: Open Court.

Shepard, Robert S. 1991. *God's People in the Ivory Tower: Religion in the Early American University.* Brooklyn, N.Y.: Carlson.

Smith, Huston. 1958. *The Religions of Man.* New York: Harper and Row.

———. 1991. *The World's Religions.* San Francisco: HarperCollins.

Smith, Jonathan Z. 1982. *Imagining Religion: From Babylon to Jonestown.* Chicago: University of Chicago Press.

———. 1995. "Religious Studies: Whither (Wither) and Why?" *Method and Theory in the Study of Religion* 7:407–13.

Spurr, David. 1993. *The Rhetoric of Empire: Colonial Discourse in Journalism, Travel Writing, and Imperial Administration.* Durham, N.C.: Duke University Press.

Strenski, Ivan. 1987. *Four Theories of Myth in the Twentieth Century: Cassirer, Eliade, Lévi-Strauss, and Malinowski.* Iowa City: University of Iowa Press.

Tiele, Cornelius P. 1897. *Elements of a Science of Religion.* Vol. 1: *Morphological.* Edinburgh: William Blackwood and Sons.

———. 1899. *Elements of a Science of Religion.* Vol. 2: *Ontological.* Edinburgh: William Blackwood and Sons.

Wagner, Roy. 1981. *The Invention of Culture.* Chicago: University of Chicago Press.

Westerlund, David. 1985. *African Religion in African Scholarship.* Stockholm: Almqvist and Wiksell.

12 Postcolonial Encounters: Narrative Constructions of Devils Tower National Monument

John Dorst

Those who have seen Stephen Spielberg's 1977 film *Close Encounters of the Third Kind* may recall that its plot turns on the idea that a number of seemingly ordinary citizens have been mysteriously implanted with visions of the remarkable landscape feature known as Devils Tower (fig. 12.1). Standing on the northwest edge of the Black Hills, this massive rock formation, pleated with immense vertical columns of granite, rises abruptly some 1,200 feet above the floor of the Belle Fourche River valley in northeastern Wyoming. Although not previously aware of the tower's existence, a few key characters in the film respond to a mysterious inner compulsion to make their way there, where as it turns out, the first official contact with alien beings is to take place.

Two moments in *Close Encounters* are particularly significant for my purposes here. Although we see numerous replicas, images, and television views of Devils Tower, it is only near the end of the film that the characters experience the landmark directly. The hero and his companion, having made their way to Wyoming, drive their car up to a barbed-wire roadblock. For a moment we see them through the windshield gaping open-mouthed at something above and behind the camera position. They leap from the car and scramble up a dirt embankment to another wire barrier. As they do so, the

Figure 12.1. Devils Tower

camera ascends vertically to reveal in the middle distance the uncanny mono-lith of the tower. The camera movement gives the impression that this im-mense object is emerging from the ground right before the viewer's eyes. That this is a major moment of revelation, a kind of monumental, ceremonial unveiling, is underscored by the soundtrack, which crescendos to symphonic climax as the tower comes fully into view. Most likely unintentionally, the cinematically produced impression that the tower suddenly rises up from the ground echoes a number of traditional Native American narratives from several Plains tribes. These accounts report just such an emergence, explained as resulting from supernatural agency.

The other moment to which I want to call attention also comes near the conclusion of the film. The hero has, against the best efforts of the authori-ties, managed to scramble over the rockfall at the base of the tower to discover a scientific and military installation set up to receive the alien visitors. The climax comes with the arrival of the techno-sublime mother ship, which hovers silently over and dwarfs the tower. Prior to that stunning arrival, how-ever, an advanced guard of scout ships descends, presumably to survey the site. They first become visible as distant moving lights in the night sky. For the

briefest moment, seven of these lights come together above the tower and organize themselves into a formation identical to the constellation Ursa Major, the Great Bear, more commonly known as the Big Dipper.

Whereas the visual trick of the tower's vertical emergence is no doubt an inadvertent echo of Plains Indian associations, this brief celestial tableau is perhaps the filmmaker's conscious acknowledgment, however indirect and obscure, of Native American traditions. In *The Way to Rainy Mountain,* N. Scott Momaday recounts a tale explaining the appearance of Tsoa ai, "Tree Rock," as the formation is known to Kiowa tradition. The brother of seven sisters is mysteriously transformed into a bear. He pursues his siblings, who seek refuge on top of a large tree stump. The tree rises miraculously, lifting the seven sisters all the way to the sky, where they become the stars of the Big Dipper. The immense stump is scored by the clawing of the bear, giving Tree Rock its distinctive appearance (recounted in Gunderson 1988, 32–35).

Other Plains tribes (Arapaho, Cheyenne, and Lakota) have traditional narratives with similar core elements, though of course with many variations and degrees of elaboration (e.g., Pleiades instead of Ursa Major, rising rock rather than tree stump, chthonic bear rather than transformed sibling). In the historical period, the most common Plains Indian name for the formation is "Bear's Lodge," a designation that appears on early maps made by Euro-Americans.

I dwell on these scenes from a mass-culture text because they lend themselves to a parabolic reading. They may be understood as small gaps where postcolonial relations peek through, gaps that I will attempt to widen in this essay. Those decidedly marginal moments in the film where an alternative narrative presence might be dimly perceived mark Devils Tower, however evanescently, as a site of cultural contestation. We might take them as examples of those aporias where a text glancingly acknowledges its own instability. A dominant message of the film is that "we" need not fear the power of mysterious alien forces (with racial difference encoded in the classic mass-cultural symbol of beings from another world) because they will turn out to be benign and even luminously godlike. The barely visible and perhaps even accidental traces of a Native American narrative presence at this site introduces a potential disruption, if only because the small incursion of a "real world" cultural element implies the existence of something outside the film's symbolic space. Read for those moments where its gears slip slightly, the film points us toward Devils Tower/Bear's Lodge as a place of postcolonial encounter.[1]

By taking this site as our critical landing pad, examining both earlier and recent developments there, we can gain some understanding of how several vectors of power converge on this unusual feature of high plains geomorphology. In particular, I am interested in how the tower has been constructed as an element of landscape through its various narrative incarnations and through the larger management of narrative resources. A great many narratives come together to "make" Devils Tower, not all of them mutually compatible or equally recognized in the dominant construction of this site. Many of them are, I believe, stories about seeing, and that will be my focus here. By looking at the "narratives of looking" that swirl around the tower like its turbulent winds, we can gain some purchase on the issues of access and ownership in a postcolonial context.

It has not gone unremarked that the modern Euro-American colonial project as a whole is deeply invested in the fundamental rearrangement of visual regimes that occurred during the nineteenth century. Timothy Mitchell (1988), for example, has convincingly demonstrated how the colonization of Egypt depended on the visual reordering of the colonial object, both conceptually and materially, so that it conformed to the protocols of coherent commodity display. Early colonialism, in other words, had as one of its main conditions of possibility an ideological way of seeing perhaps best exemplified by the grand nineteenth-century international exhibitions, beginning with London's Crystal Palace (1851), and other cultural or commercial institutions (e.g., department stores, museums, theaters, and zoos) devoted to a distanced mode of visuality according to which the whole world takes on the quality of representative display. To colonize was to occupy a position from which the colonial object could be seen coherently as an artifact available for appropriation.

To anticipate my argument, I believe the current conflict over Bear's Lodge/ Devils Tower needs to be placed in the context of this colonial (and postcolonial) visuality. Historically, the Native American claim on this site, as symbolized by its narrative traditions, has largely been contained through the simple and familiar colonial mechanisms of selective deafness and trivialization. In recent years Indian voices have become more insistent in their call for some form of reappropriation. As a result, new forms of containment have come into play.

I will take as a premise that whoever establishes and controls the definitive *view,* literal and metaphorical, of the site occupies thereby the position of cultural ownership. Access to that vantage point will be strictly policed. In the postcolonial context this policing is less likely to take the heavy-handed form of coercive suppression than to rely on subtle incorporation through the liberal discourse of inclusiveness and balance. Although in recent years subaltern voices have reached the threshold of audibility at Devils Tower, we can see them undergoing this process of incorporation. It is on the ground of narratives of seeing that these postcolonial cultural politics are currently being played out.

* * *

First let me say a few general words about this site and its history. Devils Tower is a national monument; in fact, it is the first place so designated, approved by the presidential decree of Theodore Roosevelt in 1906 under the terms of the Federal Antiquities Act passed in June of that year. That act provides for the preservation of "historic landmarks, historic and prehistoric structures, and other objects of historic or scientific interest that are situated upon the lands owned or controlled by the Government of the United States." Important for my purposes here is the addition that the president "may reserve as part thereof parcels of land, the limits of which in all cases shall be confined to the smallest area compatible with the proper care and management of the objects to be protected."

As early as 1892 a local and state effort was underway to keep Devils Tower and the surrounding landscape out of private hands. An area of more than sixty square miles was placed under the category of forest reserve by the General Land Office. At about the same time, Wyoming political leaders set about proposing the formation of a Devils Tower national park, to encompass somewhat more than eighteen square miles. Both arrangements included not only the tower but also a group of related geological formations of the same type known as the Little Missouri Buttes. The national monument established in 1906 encompasses less than two square miles of territory, just enough to include the tower and an infrastructure for maintenance and access. Under national monument designation, Devils Tower is managed by the National Park Service (Mattison 1973).

I mention this history because it reveals a kind of narrative act being played out both on the ground itself and at the level of a national discourse of preservation. National monument designation is the primal act of framing that establishes the tower as an object for certain kinds of narrative. Not to put too fine a point on it, it establishes the tower as an object for spectatorship, as a tightly framed and, metaphorically speaking, elevated artifact to be viewed from close proximity, but with a kind of detachment. In support of this I point out that the larger geological feature of which the tower is a part is excluded from the site. The Little Missouri Buttes are just as significant geologically, but they do not share the tower's visual drama, its coherent "viewability," the real reason for its preservation. The positioning of the monument's visitors' cen-

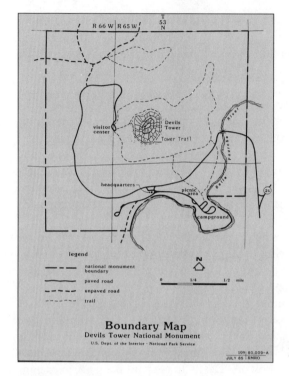

Figure 12.2. Map of Devils
Tower National Monument

ter and the system of roadways and hiking trails construct the tower as a series of imposing circumference views and surprising revelations, all focused
tightly on the isolated artifact (fig. 12.2). One might well read the unveiling
scene in *Close Encounters* as a kind of extreme or paradigm text for this mode
of viewing, awestruck wonder at the revelation of an uncanny object, but the
act of viewing taking place from behind a barrier.

The three narrative constructions most prominent at Devils Tower today
are functions of this visual protocol. Embodied in the visitors' center exhib-
its, National Park Service (NPS) brochures, tourist iconography (e.g., sets of
slides, postcards, and posters), and NPS staff interpretive programs, these
three narratives might be characterized as the story of formation, the story
of emergence, and the story of ascent. All three participate in the common
project of constructing this site as the object of a certain species of looking,
the mode that is consistent with the way the landscape is framed through
national monument designation and that I am tempted to call "touristic."

I will not dwell here on the first of these three dominant stories, the story
of formation, which is the account of the tower's geological history, other

than to mention its three basic scenes, these being the episodes of slow sedimentation, violent intrusion from below, and extended revelation through the forces of erosion. Over eons ancient seas laid down strata of sedimentary rock. Between 60 and 70 million years ago, violent igneous forces deep beneath the earth's surface—forces associated in the popular mind, however playfully, with infernal agency[2]—pushed material nearly through the earth's crust before expending their energy. They left their trace in the form of congealed and striated fingers of rock wedged into cracks formed near the earth's surface by the violent assault from below. The final act involves the gentle but powerful agencies of moving wind and water, which slowly peeled away the surface sedimentary layers, finally to reveal the hard igneous core that is the tower as we now see it (Robinson n.d.).

This account of Devils Tower geology constitutes an explanatory mythology, a kind of popular-science narrative, and another tale of unveiling, though somewhat different in construction from that moment in Spielberg's film. In any case, its import is as a narrative of spectatorship, a story about how this artifact became visible and why it looks as it does. Its visual drama, framed by the national monument boundary lines, is the displayed residue of an agonistic drama of formation in which endogenic and exogenic forces fought each other. This pop-science narrative of formation is historically important because it provides the basic alibi for federal preservation.

The second narrative formally endorsed and presented at the site has its source in the Native American cultures of the northern plains. Far from allowing it access as a fully alternative voice, however, the interpretive management of this narrative component is a textbook example of the trivialization that colonial conditions often impose on indigenous cultures. Relegated to the categories of the quaint, the picturesque, and the historically remote, these elements are safely cached as residual.

More than twenty tribal groups have had some historical association with Bear's Lodge (Hanson and Chirinos 1991), and a number of origin myths have been recorded. One of them, a Cheyenne tale, has taken on something like official status, largely through its prominent display at the visitors' center and its representation in postcard and poster form. This one tale, or more accurately its reduction to a postcard image, has come to stand for an immensely complex and long-standing history of American Indian involvement, materially and ideologically, with Bear's Lodge and the surrounding region. This is a truncation perhaps even more radical than the geological one accomplished by the narrow designation of the site boundaries.

In cursory outline, the Cheyenne story is about seven brothers, the eldest of whom has his wife stolen by a giant bear, a holy being. The youngest brother, who possesses powerful medicine and who has certain traits that perhaps associate him with the Cheyenne culture hero Sweet Medicine, uses super- natural means to recover the stolen woman. She and all the brothers flee the pursuing bear. To rescue his relatives, the hero sings a song four times, caus- ing the small rock he always carries with him to grow into the huge stone edifice of Bear's Lodge. The chthonic bear leaps higher and higher, leaving his claw marks on the rock walls. On his fourth try the hero kills the bear with the last of four arrows the brothers have made. He whistles for four eagles, each of which carries two of the humans safely to the ground. The coda to the story has the brothers killing all the other bears in the area except two. These are warned to leave the people alone, and as emblem of their mastery, the humans cut off the bears' long ears and tails, giving them the appearance we recognize today.

Needless to say, this narrative is much more than a mere explanation of the rock's appearance. I will not presume to offer an interpretation of the story, but some of its symbolic resonance may be intuited if we know even a little bit about traditional Cheyenne cosmology. For example, Cheyenne tra- dition orders the world in four layers. The bottom-most of these is "Deep Earth," which extends downward from the point where the roots of grow- ing things end. It is associated with burrowing and digging animals, includ- ing the bear (the hero of the story rescues his brother's wife by transform- ing into a gopher and burrowing into the great bear's underground lair). This realm is also associated with the female principle, balancing the maleness of the top-most layer, the "Blue Sky Space." Deserts, cliffs, rock faces, and waste places in general are perceived in this worldview as Deep Earth's projections into the layer of the world inhabited by humans, the layer of living and grow- ing things (Surface Dome). The Bear's Lodge formation is perhaps especially loaded with significance because it not only connects Deep Earth with the human sphere but extends through the latter into the next higher zone of the Cheyenne cosmos, the "Nearer Sky Space," which is the domain of clouds, birds, and high places (Moore 1974, 142–86).

Even this cursory account of a few elements of Cheyenne worldview sug- gests some of the symbolic richness of the Bear's Lodge story. This narrative of emergence, however, is positioned in the official discourse of Devils Tower as a kind of picturesque counterpart, or quaint alternative, to the scientific narrative of origins. In fact, the "official" image of the giant bear clawing at the tower[3] is included as one slide in a packaged set otherwise made up of cross-section representations of the stages of the tower's geological formation.

Positioned thus—that is, trivialized virtually to the status of cartoon— the Cheyenne tale, emblematic of all Native American presence, becomes an-

Figure 12.3. The Creation of Bear's
Lodge

other easily consumable story about the tower's appearance, both in the
sense of its first emergence and in the sense of the way it appears to us today. The iconography of the definitive poster identifies and freezes the moment of the bear's clawing as the climax of the narrative (fig. 12.3). Of para-
mount importance in this narrative construction is, once again, the tower's
visual interest.

The third official narrative line, the story of ascent, is the dominant one
in the current construction of Devils Tower. At first glance it might seem to
run contrary to the two other stories I have just identified, since it is a narrative about direct encounter with the tower through the act of climbing it
rather than a narrative expression of distanced spectatorship. I will suggest
in a moment why I think it is the master narrative of spectatorship.

One of the earliest commentaries on the tower by a Euro-American comes
from Henry Newton, the geological assistant on an 1875 military expedition
to the region: "Its remarkable structure, its symmetry, and its prominence
make it an unfailing object of wonder. . . . It is a great remarkable obelisk of
Trinh, with a columnar structure, giving it a vertically striated appearance, and
it rises 625 feet almost perpendicular, from its base. Its summit is so entirely

inaccessible that the energetic explorer, to whom the ascent of an ordinary difficult crag is but a pleasant pastime, standing at its base could only look upward in despair of ever planting his feet on the top" (quoted in Mattison 1973, 6). From the beginning of colonial encounters with this object, the goal of getting to its top was taken for granted.

Henry Newton's despair was answered eighteen years later by William Rogers, a local rancher. On the Fourth of July in 1893, the year of Chicago's great Columbian Exposition,[4] Rogers made the official inaugural ascent of the tower. He did so before an assembled throng of spectators numbering, by conservative estimates, at least a thousand—and this at a time when there were no good roads into the area and one had to ford the Belle Fourche River numerous times to reach the site.

The ascent was accomplished by means of a makeshift ladder laboriously constructed by Rogers and two other local residents bent on promoting Devils Tower and the region for economic purposes. At no small risk, they pounded two-and-one-half-foot pegs into a continuous crack running to within two hundred feet of the top. To the protruding ends of the pegs they nailed strips of wood to give some stability. A local artist sewed and painted a seven-by-twelve-foot American flag, and a group from Deadwood, South Dakota, provided Rogers with a handmade Uncle Sam suit to wear for his climb. In the grand nineteenth-century tradition of vernacular patriotic celebration and entrepreneurship, the event was widely publicized and served as the centerpiece of a gala Fourth of July celebration, the tower already having been used for some years as a site for Independence Day observance.

Rogers made the exhibition climb without mishap and unfurled his flag on the large flagpole waiting there to receive it. (Obviously a number of people had already climbed the rock in completing the ladder and making other preparations.) The violent winds that swirl around the tower tore the flag loose later in the day, and it floated down onto the dancefloor that had been constructed for the festivities. The event's promoters cut up the flag on the spot and sold the pieces for souvenirs (Gunderson 1988, 73–83).

What I have called the story of ascent is in fact a series of small narratives or implied narratives that together constitute a cumulative tale. The Rogers ascent is merely the first in a series of "first" climbs or otherwise notable ascents: first solo ascent by a woman (Rogers's wife in 1895, again on the Fourth of July), ascent by world-renowned "human fly" Babe White in 1927, first ascent (1937) by a team using alpine climbing methods and equipment rather than previously fixed aids, first alpine ascent by a woman, and so on. Perhaps the most notable event of this sort, exclusive of Rogers's original climb, was the unauthorized 1941 parachute jump onto the top of the tower by daredevil George Hopkins. This stunt was particularly notable because the rope by which Hopkins was supposed to descend did not land on the tower with him, leaving him stranded for six days on the barren summit. His ordeal was front-page news nationwide (Gunderson 1988, 84–91).

It should be obvious that these official narratives of ascent are, individually and collectively, just as much involved in constructing Devils Tower as a viewable artifact as are the other two narrative formations I have identified. In this case, though, the focus of the spectacle is human conquest—mastery of the tower. These early climbs were for the most part media events, or at least newsworthy special occurrences. As such, they invested the tower with a new load of visual interest, remade it, so to speak, as an even more exciting spectacle. One might say they constitute part of a modern apparatus for making the tower visible to a mass audience through the magnifying powers of commerce and information technologies, and in this they are continuous with the reproductions of the tower in tourist artifacts. Along this line of thinking, *Close Encounters* might be seen as a culmination of the mutually reinforcing narrative strands that construct the tower as an object for spectatorial viewing.

* * *

The three narrative constructions I have isolated have until recently worked well to make Devils Tower a "coherent" artifact, one that fits neatly with public assumptions and expectations about federally preserved sites and with a certain mode of viewing appropriate to the western landscape, not to mention its consistency with a century of colonialist visuality in general. Through seemingly innocent and "natural" ways of framing the tower, these narratives also participate in the long history of expulsion and containment of indigenous peoples. By 1990, however, one begins to see a significant disruption of the heretofore smoothly running narrative machine, the kind of disruption I am inclined to associate with distinctly postcolonial conditions of cultural production.

One source of this disruption appears to grow naturally out of the previously discussed narrative thread of ascent, whereas a second source might be understood as a return of cultural voices repressed both by the tight framing of the site and by the narrative element of emergence. That both these new cultural forces began to make themselves felt at about the same time, the early to mid-1980s, suggests that they are not entirely independent factors.

In 1950 two people climbed Devils Tower; in 1960, 104; in 1970, a little over 200. By 1980, however, the figure was approaching 2,000, and in 1990 it was well over 5,000. Since 1992 the tower has had more than 6,000 climbers each

year.[5] Another change has occurred as well. Through 1980 the majority of
these climbers were making it to the top of the tower. In no year since that
time has the number of summit climbers exceeded the number who do not
reach the top, and the ratio of nonsummit to summit climbers has grown
dramatically (National Park Service 1995, xii).

What all this means is that Devils Tower has been reconstructed, since
roughly 1980, as one of the premier recreational rock-climbing sites in the NPS
system. Not surprisingly, the official interpretive program at the tower incorporated this development as if it were merely a continuation of the well-
established ascent narrative. Among other things, the parking area now includes a special kiosk display that reproduces a segment of the tower at full
scale and explains the methods, equipment, and types of rock climbing. The
brightly clad climbers who scramble up the tower daily in the summer months
are presented as an element of the spectacle. Watching the climbers was
identified in a recent NPS-commissioned study as the favorite activity of the
national monument's visitors (Hanson and Moore 1993, 66).

The second complicating development can be dated roughly to 1984, when
there was a public revival of the use of Bear's Lodge as a sacred ceremonial
site by various Native American peoples. Since that time prayer vigils, vision
quests, and most important, the Sundance have been practiced again near
the base of Bear's Lodge.[6]

These two major developments since 1980 present significant problems for
the efficient narrative operations of the site. For one thing, the Indian emergence story frozen in the icon of the giant clawing bear depends on positioning Indians as inhabitants of an absolute past, members of defunct cultures
that have left their trace at the site only in the form of picturesque mythologies that can be incorporated, through a process of radical selectivity, into
the dominant spectatorial program. To have people coming into the site and
cutting trees for the Sundance or leaving prayer bundles at the base of the
tower is a kind of implicit embarrassment to the established narrative arrangements.

The development of rock climbing as a mass sport, though seemingly as-
similable, is also problematic. This mode of ascent is entirely different from
that embodied in the historical narrative. Although they are watched by visitors, the contemporary climbers do not think of themselves as part of the
display. For many, the eminently watchable act of getting to the top is not a
goal. Negotiating a difficult pitch, perfecting a crack or corner technique, or
exploring a new route are some of the nonspectatorial activities they pursue.
The element of dare deviltry that made many of the earlier climbs enhancements or magnifications of the tower as a display is largely missing from the

activities of the rock climbers. For many of them, moreover, the classic tourists at the site, the spectators, are merely nuisances, as evidenced by such things as the genre of "comic tourist encounter" stories shared among climbers.

The apparently greatest disruption to the site's narrative tranquility, however, is the fact that these two "new" presences in many respects directly conflict with one another. For the tribal peoples who see Bear's Lodge as a sacred site, the presence of large numbers of climbers assaulting its sides, many of them pounding in pitons or using permanently fixed bolts and sometimes leaving equipment, trash, and smudges of chalk, is more than an affront to religious sensibilities. It is literally destructive of spiritual power, not to mention damaging to the spiritual health of those doing the climbing. Some of the climbers, on the other hand, insist that their claim on the site is just as strong as that of Native American peoples. In fact, some argue that their climbing itself has a profoundly spiritual dimension.

This is just to begin to get at the current complexities that have disrupted what has become a significantly contested site. We might fairly see the dilemma as a sudden explosion of narratives, far too many and too various for the U.S. Park Service to incorporate into the established narrative construction of the tower as a set of frozen, detached views or unique spectacles of ascent. For one thing, the narratives of both the climbers and the spiritual practitioners involve active engagement with the site in ways that are not inherently spectatorial. From the participants' perspective, the most significant activities of each group are hardly even visible to an outside audience, much less structured for mass spectatorship. Most spiritual engagement is literally hidden from spectatorial view or is by nature undetectable to sight. Oddly similar, many of the practices of modern rock climbing, its meaningful technical accomplishments, occur at a scale too small to be the object of nonparticipant spectatorship. Climbing of this sort is a private, small-group activity, though carried out on the very public face of the tower.

The cultural forces currently at play around the site of Devils Tower/Bear's Lodge, at least the ones of concern to me here, may be summarized as follows: a well-established program involving procedures of framing and a coherent narrative apparatus has, up until quite recently, constructed the tower primarily as an object of detached spectatorship. As a result, this construction closed out (or incorporated through trivialization) the preexisting indigenous presence. In recent years the active revival of Native American claims on the site as a sacred place and, less directly, the rise of a recreational subculture dependent on the physical properties of the tower have disrupted the smooth operation of the dominant ideology. These "new" cultural factors have certain structural elements in common, but most important, nei-

ther fits neatly into the established program of mass spectatorship that has
governed this site since well before its official establishment as a national
monument. Abstract similarities notwithstanding, however, Native American religious practices and rock climbers' recreational activity are widely
perceived, especially by Native Americans, as conflicting uses of the site.

* * *

Although at first glance it may seem that this conflict is the major source
of the current cultural disruption, I will conclude by suggesting that, perhaps
paradoxically, it is precisely through the incorporation of this conflict that
the larger spectatorial program preserves its hegemonic place. To put it another way, the postcolonial conditions of possible disruption, particularly the
revival of Native American voices with the potential of reclaiming the site,
are in the process of being displaced into a new containing narrative—a story
of conflict and resolution, the hero of which is bureaucratic procedure and
"balanced" management.

Native American religious practitioners and rock climbers each make up
only about 1 percent of the over 400,000 visitors who come to the tower in a
year. Their conflict, however, currently occupies a central position in the
cultural production of this site. It is the main subtext of the Final Climbing
Management Plan (FCMP) recently completed by National Park Service
personnel and put into practice for the first time in the summer of 1995. More
than three years in preparation, this plan is a virtual textbook of bureaucratic
procedures for conflict resolution. Among its more explicit guiding principles
are enlistment of the fullest possible public participation; identification and
representation of all relevant interest groups in the planning process; maintenance of communication; search for compromise between conflicting interests; and devotion to middle-of-the-road solutions, rejecting all "extreme"
positions.

This more or less overt ideology of liberal and rational management floats
above a host of less directly acknowledged assumptions and procedures.
Among these are the definition of all factors, including social and cultural
ones, as "resources" subject to rational management; perception of the planning process as an attempt to balance the concerns of discrete, homogeneous
"interest groups"; strict delimitation of the "relevant" management issue so
that the more radical proposals or critiques can be ruled outside the scope
of the process (i.e., little tolerance for emergent elements); and an unquestioned acceptance of positivist premises that privilege resource quantification,
"objective" scientific inquiry, and narrow definition of goals.

The application of these premises and procedures has resulted in a plan that purports to reflect a consideration of all the points of view expressed during the lengthy scoping process and to constitute a balanced proposal for use. Implemented for the first time in the summer of 1995, the centerpiece of the climbing plan is a request that rock climbers voluntarily refrain from climbing during the month of June. The period around the summer solstice is particularly important to Plains tribes, it being the time of the Sundance ceremony. The plan also prohibits any new climbing bolts, the permanent anchors drilled into the rock face, whose use is deemed most harmful to the tower itself and most offensive to Native American religious principles. Finally, the interpretive program at the site will be expanded to help educate the public about the history of Native American presence at the tower.

In an official press release the National Park Service declared the implemented plan a success in its first year—with the voluntary climbing moratorium being widely observed. At this writing it appears that tensions between climbers and Native American have lessened, the principle of voluntarism being a key factor (*High Country News* 16 Oct. 1995). In news reports some tribal members have expressed the opinion that there is more value to the respect shown by the active choice not to climb than would be the case if climbing had been simply prohibited. Although there is still considerable ambivalence, climbers also seem willing to accept the ban if they are given the chance to "make their own decisions."

So why not simply accept what may be shaping up as a "happy ending" to this conflict? As I have already implied, this planning process has, in the name of balanced management, served the interests of containment and incorporation. For one thing, it provides the mechanism for discounting certain voices. In some of the public meetings, for example, individuals expressed the view that the site's sacred significance should take precedence and all climbing should cease. This view became positioned in the planning document as one of the extreme ends of a spectrum of management options, which meant that it would be dismissed automatically. The opposite extreme was the view that climbing should have no restrictions of any kind. Placing these two positions at opposite ends of a spectrum of six possibilities makes them seem like equivalent and equally unreasonable options. This kind of flattening, in which Native American cultures and a recreational subculture are reduced to equivalence as "interest groups," is characteristic of the discursive operations of the plan as a whole.

Perhaps most important, the NPS plan implicitly portrays itself as a major departure from past practices in that it is the first substantial effort to make clear to visitors the importance of Native American cultures, both historically and in current practice. What this means practically is that Native American cultural performances (e.g., drumming and dancing, craft demonstration) will be incorporated into the official Park Service interpretive program, which up to now has been dominated by the geological and climbing histories.[7] Although certainly a kind of improvement, the addition of these isolated Native American cultural elements is not inconsistent with the larger and thoroughly taken-for-granted premise, the assumption that spectatorship is the real business of national monuments. The greatest likelihood is that such performances will serve merely as a new addition to the visual interest of the site, with the tower as their backdrop. Somehow vaguely related to the issue of sacred significance, these fragmentary cultural displays are likely to function as the symbolic stand-in for (and deflection from) deeper political questions that cannot really be confronted in the highly managed venue of mass spectatorship. Questions a propos of a postcolonial context—questions about cultural ownership and control, about reappropriation, about rights of access and use—are thoroughly out of bounds.

As a final bit of evidence for this, consider the sense of floating anxiety that seems to surround the controversial issue of the monument's name. The review process for the climbing management plan elicited several suggestions that the site be officially renamed Bear's Lodge. Even this symbolic act of reclaiming is profoundly threatening to some, perhaps most of all to the well-established way of seeing the western landscape as a series of interesting views rather than as a humanly inhabited, constructed, and contested terrain.

One larger lesson we find confirmed in the case of Devils Tower/Bear's Lodge is that the postcolonial scenario of resistance and reclamation, of rights claims and repatriation, is rarely if ever straightforward. One of the directions it takes is toward subtle containment through a mechanism we might call spectatorial conflict. Deeply seated and perhaps ultimately unresolvable cultural dilemmas—Euro-American conceptions of public lands versus Native American conceptions of sacred landscape, for example—become displaced onto localized, definable conflicts—in this case, between recreational rock climbers and tribal religious practitioners—that can be "managed," if not completely resolved. Even more to the point, however, such conflicts as this one can be constructed as "watchable," as themselves objects of spectatorship. The management of cultural conflict over Devils Tower becomes one more episode in a long history of the politics of display at this site. As a mechanism of postcolonial containment, this regime of managed spectatorial display is even more effective than the Close Encounters fantasy of a powerful threat from elsewhere that evaporates in the reassuring glow of angelic aliens.

Notes

1. There is much more to be said about this film's place in terms of its postcolonial positioning. For one thing, Spielberg has acknowledged the influence of John Ford's classic Western film *The Searchers*, where Indians constitute a hostile, alien Other that has spirited away white women. The theme of compulsion to pursue an alien force, in this case for revenge, drives the plot of Ford's film. In *Close Encounters* Spielberg plays a complex game of liberal reinscription and displacement that bears examination in terms of postcolonial containment.

2. The origin of the name *Devils Tower* is something of a mystery and no doubt involves multiple factors. One of these might be the nineteenth-century penchant for perceiving elements of the western landscape either in paradisiacal or in infernal terms.

3. The original of this image is a painting that hangs above the fireplace in the visitors' center. It is reproduced in poster format and as a postcard.

4. William Henry Jackson's photographs of Devils Tower were displayed in the Wyoming exhibit at this great fair. It was in this form that the tower first became know to the general American public (Gunderson 1988, 107).

5. These are National Park Service estimates based on registration cards submitted by climbers. The nature of this registration system may lead to some exaggeration of actual climber numbers (Hanson and Moore 1993, 64).

6. Perhaps the inaugural date of these developments should be pushed back to 1981. Like several other sacred sites in the Black Hills, Devils Tower was "occupied" in that year by members of the American Indian Movement who maintained a camp for several months on the grounds of the national monument. The encampment was subjected to a number of acts of harassment. Since 1984 the Sundance has been performed with the permission and cooperation of the National Park Service, under the mandate of the American Indian Religious Freedom Act (AIRFA) of 1978. Currently Lakota groups from the Pine Ridge Reservation appear to be the most active religious practitioners at Devils Tower (Hanson and Moore 1993, 8–10). It is quite possible that Native American religious observances have been continuous at this site, though performed secretly until 1984.

7. A first effort at cultural programming occurred in 1995. It included an eclectic range of presentations and performances, a living history depiction of Theodore Roosevelt, an American Indian flutist, Indian dancing and crafts, cowboy poetry, an explanation of sweat lodges, and a classical guitar performance. An estimated 900 visitors attended these programs (*Casper Star-Tribune* 17 Dec. 1995).

Works Cited

U.S. National Park Service, Rocky Mountain Region, Department of the Interior. 1995. "Final Climbing Management Plan/Finding of No Significant Impact."

Gunderson, Mary Alice. 1988. *Devils Tower: Stories in Stone.* Glendo, Wyo.: High Plains.

Hanson, Jeffery R., and David Moore. 1993. "Ritual and Recreational Perception and Use at Devils Tower National Monument: An Applied Ethnographic Study." Unpublished study conducted for the National Park Service, Rocky Mountain Region.

Hanson, Jeffery R., and Sally Chirinos. 1991. "Ethnographic Overview and Assessment of Devils Tower National Monument." Unpublished study conducted for the National Park Service, Rocky Mountain Region.

Mattison, Ray H. 1973. *Devils Tower National Monument—A History*. Devils Tower Natural History Association.

Mitchell, Timothy. 1988. *Colonising Egypt*. Cambridge: Cambridge University Press.

Moore, John Hartwell. 1974. "A Study of Religious Symbolism among the Cheyenne Indians." Ph.D. diss., New York University.

Robinson, Charles S. n.d. *Geology of Devils Tower National Monument Wyoming*. Washington, D.C.: United States Department of the Interior.

13   Postscript: Exhibiting Hawai'i

David Prochaska

University of Illinois
at Urbana-Champaign

Department of History
College of Liberal Arts and Sciences
309 Gregory Hall, MC-466
810 South Wright Street
Urbana, IL 61801

1 February 2000

Dr. Maarten van de Guchte, Associate Director
Cummer Museum of Art and Gardens
829 Riverside Avenue
Jacksonville, FL 32204

Dear Maarten:

Following up on our recent telephone conversation, I am enclosing the formal exhibition proposal with illustrations for the traveling exhibition Hawai'i: Postcards of Exoticism, Exoticism of Postcards, which I am curating. After opening in fall 2000, the exhibit will be available for loan early in 2001. Designed for four small rooms or gallery areas, the exhibit does not require extensive space. A 125-page paperback exhibition catalog consisting of an introductory and critical essay by myself plus reproductions of the cards and a checklist will accompany the exhibit. Currently I am developing an interactive, Web-based CD-ROM version of the exhibition that visitors will be able to view on computer monitors placed at several locations in the exhibition galleries. I hope you will consider adding the exhibit to your exhibition schedule for the Cummer Museum of Art and Gardens.

Although the attached proposal describes the exhibit in detail, I would like to underscore a number of points here. Whereas museum exhibitions of Hawaiiana mostly emphasize the past over the present, and chiefs over commoners, this exhibition takes a revisionist approach. Hawai'i is not generally considered a settler colony in popular American discourse; Hawaiian picture postcards, produced primarily for tourist consumption, are not generally viewed as exoticist imagery produced in a colonial situation. By putting on view such exoticist images of Hawai'i, by demonstrating the formal photographic practices used in constructing Hawai'i as exotic, and by showing implicitly how they are analogous to colonial and postcolonial practices elsewhere, this exhibition contends that terms and categories such as *colonial, postcolonial, internal colonialism,* and *settler colonialism* are in fact applicable to Hawai'i. The exhibition stages these issues through formal museological and visual practices, which in turn grow out of current critical and art historical theory.

Although trafficking between "high" and "low" art is a sine qua non of twentieth-century art and art history, such quintessentially popular genres as picture postcards are rarely, if ever, displayed in art museums. Through careful selection of a wide number of striking images, this exhibition does just that. As such, the exhibition adds a strong voice to the ongoing colloquy concerning the porous nature of "high" and "low" art. It does so through the presentation of a distinctive, readily identifiable genre of objects—postcards—that aims to elicit the reaction, "Why didn't someone think of this before?"

The exhibit is innovative not only in regard to the objects it displays but in the way it displays them. Instead of implicitly representing an identifiable art historical approach, as most exhibitions do, this exhibit problematizes contemporary currents in art history and critical theory by explicitly staging them for the museumgoer. Just as the now middle-aged "new art history" challenged the hegemony of the art object per se (and its associated discourses of artist, oeuvre, career, and connoisseurship) and broadened the scope of art history to encompass the contexts in which art objects are produced and circulated (audience, reception), so too does the exhibit embody such newer approaches by explicitly presenting the three-part nexus of production, image, and reception in the first three exhibition rooms. To further underscore the contingent nature of art historical interpretations, the fourth room self-reflexively stages the exhibition in the form of a museum within the museum. As you are well aware, such underlying display practices are themselves innovative and by no means common in museology.

At the same time, the postcards on display are intrinsically interesting both in formal aesthetic terms and as documents (in the late nineteenth- and early twentieth-century sense of the term). Not simply picture postcards of Hawai'i, the cards selected for display exemplify the construction of Hawai'i as exotic. The formal photographic practices seen here thus echo analogous practices—more often textual than visual—discussed extensively in postcolonial studies, and often in terms of orientalism. Therefore, the cultural work that this exhibition of exoticist Hawaiian postcards performs is twofold: first, to expand the discussion of orientalism to exoticism more generally and, second, to shift the usual register of debate from the textual to the visual. Additionally, such visual images perform the political work of questioning the status of Hawai'i vis-à-vis the continental United States—is it a state or colony? A colony or postcolony?

The attached exhibit proposal develops these and other points in a discussion organized around the postcard images themselves. Taken together with the proposal, these remarks will, I hope, convey to you a sufficiently detailed picture of the exhibition so that you will be able to consider it for the Cumer Museum of Art and Gardens. If you have any questions, or if I can supply any additional information, please do not hesitate to contact me.

Sincerely yours,

David Prochaska
Associate Professor

HAWAI'I: POSTCARDS OF EXOTICISM, EXOTICISM OF POSTCARDS

CONTENTS

INTRODUCTION

This exhibition scrutinizes the colonialist construction of Hawai'i as exotic exemplified in picture postcards and related images. In staging the construction of exoticist Hawaiian postcard images in a museum space, the exhibition draws extensively on contemporary discussions concerning representation, art and artifact, the gaze, and high and low art.

Colonial and postcolonial terms and categories are not generally applied to Hawai'i in systematic, analytically rigorous ways, although Hawai'i is commonly glossed as "exotic" in popular discourse. Rather than critically interrogate such exoticizing moves, however, most studies and museum exhibitions are content to reproduce exoticist terms and categories. In Hawai'i and elsewhere museum exhibitions emphasize the past over the present, chiefs (*ali'i*) over commoners (*maka'ainana*), and royal lifestyle over the material culture of the Hawaiians. Often encountered in written texts on Hawai'i, such uncritical use of exoticist categories is even more prevalent in works concerning visual culture. Thus, studies of Hawaiian photography—and non-Western photography generally—consist primarily of surveys and monographs on individual photographers. Similarly, studies of Hawaiian postcards, and postcards more generally, consist overwhelmingly of coffee-table compilations often fueled by imperialist nostalgia. Even after the "new art history," very few theoretically informed studies of Hawaiian and other non-Western photographies exist.

This exhibition exemplifies newer critical approaches in its organization and installation. The exhibition is divided into four rooms or areas that focus on the following four themes: postcard production, imagery, reception, and construction of the exhibition. Within each gallery area the visitor's gaze is directed to a number of focal points. Using as an organizing principle the nexus of production, imagery, and reception, the exhibition moves away from a focus on images per se to demonstrate visually the ways exoticist postcard imagery is constructed. A further innovative feature is the fourth gallery area—laid out as a museum within the museum—which constitutes a metacommentary on the exhibition the visitor has just seen. Such an installation recalls and extends such museum shows as Art/Artifact (Center for African Art) and especially Mining the Museum (Maryland Historical Society).

The design and layout of the accompanying exhibition catalog mimic the "look" of an early twentieth-century postcard album. The catalog essay is organized visually. In other words, the text is driven by reproductions of postcards and other images so that the images become the "text." Thus, the written text amplifies and complements the images rather than vice versa.

ROOM I: PRODUCTION

The overall space of this installation area creates the interior of a postcard publishing plant with vertical panels separating the printing presses from the retouching studio. Large-scale photomurals picture such a plant in cutaway sections. A photo blowup depicts a press printing postcards, and ambient printing press noises recorded on a tape loop are audible to visitors standing directly beneath an overhead speaker. For the retouching studio, stools, drafting tables, brushes, and paints are used. A photo blowup of retouchers at work clearly shows that primarily women performed this work.

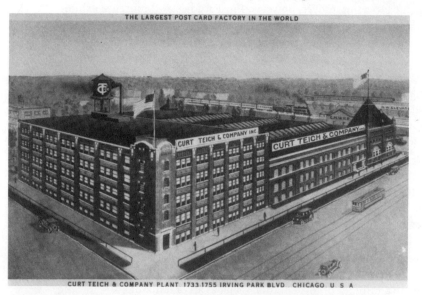

Figure 13.1. "The Largest Post Card Factory in the World," advertising postcard for Teich Company "used by salesmen to let customers know when to expect a sales call" (Teich postcard, A91552, 1922, reproduced in *Image File* 8 [1995]: 10). Courtesy of the Lake County (IL) Museum, Curt Teich Postcard Archives.

Focal Point I.I: A Job Folder

Job folders from the Teich Company, one of the largest U.S. postcard publishers, document the creation of Hawaiian postcards step by step from the initial order through photo retouching and blue monochrome proof to final color postcard. The contents of two job folders arranged on the wall and in a glass case, along with descriptive labels, show stages of production of two postcards.

Figure 13.2. "Hula Maids and Poi Pounder," original black-and-white photograph (Teich archives). The job folder for "Hula Maids and Poi Pounder" includes the order form plus various artwork. The order form informs us that Teich postcard 1B-H649 was ordered 24 April 1941 by the Patten Co. in Honolulu. An initial run of 50,000 cards was printed. The original black-and-white photo was supplied by the customer. Note the cropping that was done to produce the final card. Courtesy of the Lake County (IL) Museum, Curt Teich Postcard Archives.

Figure 13.3. "Hula Maids and Poi Pounder," proof (Teich archives). This version would have been sent to the customer for final approval. Courtesy of the Lake County (IL) Museum, Curt Teich Postcard Archives.

Figure 13.4. "Hula Maids and Poi Pounder," final postcard (Teich archives). The colors of the final card were stipulated on the order form: "Color Description: Girls' skirts are green and their blouses are yellow." Courtesy of the Lake County (IL) Museum, Curt Teich Postcard Archives.

Focal Point I.2: A Geographical Index

Geographical indexes from the Teich Company served primarily as the photographer-salesperson's order book in Hawai'i. They list the retailer ordering the cards, the cards ordered, the number ordered, the date, and whether the card was reprinted. Sample pages from geographical indexes combined with the postcards referred to map cities and towns, such as Honolulu and Hilo, where the retailers were located.

Figure 13.5. "Honolulu Tom Boy, Honolulu, T. H." (Teich color postcard, ca. 1905). The page from the geographical indexes that includes "Honolulu Tom Boy" is the fifth of thirty-four pages for Honolulu. The geographical index tells us that Weinberg, another postcard publisher, placed the order and that "Honolulu Tom Boy" was one of twelve cards ordered. The index also gives the card number, A9200, which falls within a numbering schema used by Teich in the first decade of the twentieth century. Courtesy of the Lake County (IL) Museum, Curt Teich Postcard Archives.

Focal Point 1.3: A Postcard Catalog of
Colonial Hawai'i

This focal point consists of sample pages of a computerized check-list of Hawaiian postcards produced by the Teich Archives, along with the cards indexed. For other postcard publishers, the only way to reconstruct all the postcards produced is by searching in public collections and among private collectors, an extremely time-consuming, painstaking, and hit-or-miss process. For Teich Hawaiian postcards, however, we have copies for all 1,582.

Figure 13.6. "Royal Hawaiian Hotel, Waikiki, T. H." (2B-H892, 1942, Teich archives). This card appears on the seventh of sixty-four pages of a computer list of all 1,582 Hawai'i cards produced by Teich. For each card the Teich production number is given (here, 2B-H892), the major and minor subject is identified (hotels), the location is specified (e.g., Waikiki or Hawaii), and a computer record number assigned (102225). Courtesy of the Lake County (IL) Museum, Curt Teich Postcard Archives.

Focal Point 1.4: Altered Images

Comparing the same or slightly altered photograph in different contexts provides telling clues about the way that postcards helped to construct Hawai'i as "exotic." In the late nineteenth and early twentieth centuries, when photographers were typically considered artisans rather than artists, with the result that their work was rarely copyrighted, photographs were frequently purchased, retouched, and reissued as postcards. Certain alterations were more common than others, such as elimination of ethnic details, in keeping with the tendency to render Hawai'i "exotic."

Figure 13.7. J. J. Williams color photo (signed color photograph, "Williams Honolulu," Teich archives). On the back the structure is referred to as a "chicken coop." Courtesy of the Lake County (IL) Museum, Curt Teich Postcard Archives.

Figure 13.8. "Old Hawaiian Grass Hut" (6A-H475, 1936, Teich Archives) Teich changed the "chicken coop" to a "grass hut," according to Teich production order no. 60001, dated 27 March 1936. The card was produced for the Patten Co., which was based in Honolulu and which also supplied Williams's original photograph. Significantly, the Teich order also includes the following instructions for retouching and airbrushing: "Eliminate figure of man, also pig pen in background. Suggest that you put in a poinciana tree in place of the pig pen and move the grass shack a little further over towards the right." Courtesy of the Lake County (IL) Museum, Curt Teich Postcard Archives.

OLD HAWAIIAN GRASS HUT

Focal Point 1.5: Individuals and Generic Types

In conformity with older visual genres, postcards usually caption people as representative of generic types rather than as named individuals. Sometimes, however, researchers can recover the identity of these "generic" individuals, as is the case here.

Figure 13.9. "Hula Maids." Kodak Hula Show performers identified left to right: "Tiny" Akeo, unknown, David ———, Hannah Atwood, Ruby Notley, Ida, Naone, Helen Alama, Tootsie Notley, Helen Smith, Smabo Auna. Little girl is Fran Xavier (postcard, Visual Collections, Bishop Museum, Honolulu; identifications by Bishop Museum). Courtesy of the Bishop Museum.

ROOM 2: IMAGERY

The second exhibition room is the single largest installation space, but it should not be so large as to overshadow the others. The centerpiece of this area is a darkened room within a room in which slides of postcards are continuously projected on the walls.

Focal Point 2.1: Postcarding the World of Hawai'i

During the so-called golden age of picture postcards, running from 1900 to 1920, the sheer number and diversity of postcards produced suggest a more or less conscious attempt to create a comprehensive archive or visual encyclopedia of the world. To convey the sensation of this "postcarding" of the world, of this image saturation, the visitor enters a darkened hexagonal room on whose walls six slide projectors continuously screen sets of postcard images from Hawai'i reflecting different genres (views, scenes, and types), locales (Waikiki, Diamond Head, Oahu, the "neighbor islands"), and themes (hotels and tourists, surfing and beachboys, Hawaiian chant and ukelele, and boat day [the day when a ship arrived or departed] and cruise liners).

Figure 13.10. "Surf Riding, Honolulu, T. H." (Teich color postcard, ca. 1905). Courtesy of the Lake County (IL) Museum, Curt Teich Postcard Archives.

Figure 13.11. "A Native Feast or Luau, Honolulu" (Teich color postcard, 30T, ca. 1904). Courtesy of the Lake County (IL) Museum, Curt Teich Postcard Archives.

Figure 13.12. "Moana Hotel, [W]aikiki, Honolulu" (Teich color postcard, 96T, ca. 1913). Courtesy of the Lake County (IL) Museum, Curt Teich Postcard Archives.

Figure 13.13. Hawaiian woman with leis (color postcard, reproduced in Brown, *Hawaii Recalls,* 105). Courtesy of the DeSoto Brown Collection.

Figure 13.15. "Pa'u Rider" (Teich color postcard, ca. 1905). Courtesy of the Lake County (IL) Museum, Curt Teich Postcard Archives.

Figure 13.14. "Aloha Hawaiian Islands" (cover, Teich postcard booklet, 1935). Courtesy of the Lake County (IL) Museum, Curt Teich Postcard Archives.

Focal Point 2.2: Continental U.S.
Postcard Producers

Arrangements on surrounding walls or rectangular-shaped "kiosks" in the middle of the room explore additional aspects of postcard imagery in greater detail. Postcards not of Hawai'i but of the mainland that draw on comparable exoticist tropes—"the tropics" or the "South Seas"—underscore the use of similar pictorial strategies in different places to produce similar exoticist effects.

Figure 13.16. "The Tropics, Hotel Phillips, Kansas City, Mo." (color postcard, reproduced in Barry Zaid, *Wish You Were Here: A Tour of America's Great Hotels during the Golden Age of the Picture* [New York: Crown, 1990], 89).

Focal Point 2.3: Local Hawaiian Postcard Producers

Besides being produced by continental American firms, postcards were made locally in Hawai'i by both "haole" (whites) and ethnic Asian photographers. Often local photographers catered to specific local communities and ethnic groups and produced a range of photographs, from postcards to wedding album photos. Different ethnic Asian photographers— for example, On Char, Morito Koga, and Tai Sing Loo—catered to different ethnic Asian communities, such as the Japanese, Chinese, or Filipinos. Some postcards were produced or hand tinted in Japan. Yet there was considerable contact in this cultural contact zone. Asian photographers learned photography from whites, and some were employed in white photography studios. White photographers—for example, J. J. Williams and Ray Jerome Baker—catered as well to Asian communities.

Figure 13.17. "Japanese Grass House, Hilo, Hawaii. Cane in Blossom, Wainaku" (color postcard, mailed 1909 [Bishop Museum]). Courtesy of the Bishop Museum.

Focal Point 2.4: Tropes

To say "Hawai'i" is to say stereotypes, tropes. Although exoticist stereotypes are reproduced over and over, and although by definition stereotypes appear unchanging, they do have a history—they come and go—and they vary over time. Displays here show repetitiveness as well as variation by juxtaposing postcards alongside other images ranging from the so-called contact period to the present. For example, hula in Hawai'i has a much more complex history than is apparent from its stereotyped representation on picture postcards. Postcards of hula girls can be juxtaposed with images drawn from historical and anthropological works. At the same time the extent of the hula stereotype can be conveyed by displaying hula girls in other visual media—travel posters, movie stills, Hawaiian shirts, Matson liner placemats, and sheet music covers. A second trope illustrated here is leis and lei sellers.

Figure 13.18. "Flower Girls, Honolulu" (Teich color postcard, 76T, ca. 1904). Courtesy of the Lake County (IL) Museum, Curt Teich Postcard Archives.

Figure 13.19. John Webber, *A Girl of Atooi, Sandwich Islands* (1778) (reproduced in Forbes, *Encounters with Paradise,* 30). Webber (1752–98) was the official artist on Captain James Cook's third voyage, 1776–80. Private collection; courtesy of the Honolulu Academy of Arts.

Figure 13.20. Herb Kawainui Kane, *Lei Sellers* (collection of the Chart House, Inc.; reproduced in Kane, *Voyagers* [Bellevue, Wash.: WhaleSong, 1991], 154).

Focal Point 2.5: Other Genres

Hawaiian postcard images exemplify more genres than can be displayed in this exhibition. Two additional ones included here are postcards of national expositions and humorous postcards employing gigantism. Hawaiian pavilions at national expositions, such as the 1915 Panama-Pacific International Exposition in San Francisco, represent aspects of Hawai'i that were represented in turn on postcards. Included, moreover, are several artifacts that re-create the space of such expositions. Humorous postcards popular especially between 1905 and 1915 utilized gigantism as a pictorial conceit, such as depicting pineapples bigger than people.

Figure 13.21. "Panama-Pacific International Exposition, San Francisco, 1915: 1903. The Hawaiian Pavilion" (R54270, 1915, Teich Archives). Courtesy of the Lake County (IL) Museum, Curt Teich Postcard Archives.

ROOM 3: RECEPTION

The overall space creates the interior of an early twentieth-century American upper-middle-class sitting or drawing room. A large photomural of such an interior on the wall and various objects and furnishings suggest the range of exoticist visual culture common at the time. An easy chair, table, and postcard album ready for viewing dominate the scene. Also included are a stereoscope and stereographs, exoticist Hawaiian sheet music on the piano, and an exoticist memento from the 1915 Panama-Pacific exposition on a coffee table. Through a ceiling speaker over the piano viewers can hear a continuous tape of nineteenth- and early twentieth-century exoticist classical compositions (Rimsky-Korsakov, Saint-Saëns).

Figure 13.22. On the Beach at Waikiki; or The Golden Hula (1915; reproduced in Elizabeth Tatar, *Strains of Change: The Impact of Tourism in Hawaiian Music* [Honolulu: Bishop Museum Press, 1987], 8). Courtesy of the Bishop Museum.

Focal Point 3.1: Postcard Messages

This focal point displays postcard messages. A message written by a sender on a postcard appropriates the card from the producer; mailing it puts it into circulation between a sender and a sendee. Levels of appropriation range widely: no message, a signature over the image, an *X* marking the hotel room where the tourist stayed, a lengthy message, "all-over" cards (i.e., cards written "all over"), and postcard sequences in which the message carries over from one card to another to form a continuous narrative. One of the most striking characteristics of messages is how often they have nothing to do with the postcard image. All too frequently cards express casual racism toward the people and places depicted.

Figure 13.23. "Japanese Grass House, Hilo, Hawaii. Cane in Blossom, Wainaku" (color postcard, front, mailed 1909 [Bishop Museum]). Courtesy of the Bishop Museum.

Figure 13.24. "Japanese Grass House, Hilo, Hawaii Cane in Blossom, Wainaku" (color postcard, back, mailed 1909 [Bishop Museum]). "To Master J. Ross McConkey, Honolulu: 'Hello Brother, how are you enjoying yourself? I know what you enjoy are the Moving Pictures, don't you. How is Tom & the girls? Give them my love & keep some for my little doctor. With love from your friend Agnes.'" The message on the back has nothing to do with the image on the front. Courtesy of the Bishop Museum.

Focal Point 3.2: Postcard Albums

The preferred way of organizing and preserving postcards in the early twentieth century was in an album. The different kinds of cards collected and juxtapositions of themes and genres provide valuable insights into the ways in which a contemporary audience viewed and appropriated postcards. Here albums placed under glass are opened at appropriate pages.

Figure 13.25. Bryan postcard album, p. 6 (Bishop Museum). The handwritten text for the photo on the left reads: "Leis. When you come to us across the world of waters, / We're a lei a-waiting just for you; / Pansies from a little cottage garden, / Violets still glist'ning with the dew; / Tokens true are they of our Aloha -/ Emblems of a welcome from our heart; / If you'll wear one for a while, joy will walk / with you a mile, / That's the magic of a lei—Hawaii's art." The text under the upper right photo reads: "The coin divers / They dive / and thrive / On submerged wealth." Courtesy of the Bishop Museum.

Figure 13.26. Bryan postcard album, p. 71 (Bishop Museum). The handwritten text reads: "Ancient Hawaiians had innumerable objects of wor[ship] . . . air, sea, and earth were filled with invisible beings . . . Every manifestation of nature had its living spiritual consciousness. The volcano, thunder, the winds, meteors, big and little fishes, lava flows, flowers and trees, all had a worshipful significance. They were either the work or actual embodiment of spirits, good or bad. Some deities haunted particular localities; some presided over different occupations. There were family gods, and spirits of the departed. The four great gods were Kane, Kanaba, Ku and Lono, who were supposed to have existed from the beginning. They were given a home above the clouds and credited with occasional visits to earth in human form. The most powerful was Kane, father of men and founder of the world, less malicious than the other deities. Kanaba was Kane's younger brother. Ku was feared as a malevolent being delighting in suffering. Lono had a separate order of priests. He was especially invoked for rain. Divinities became multiplied; the various attributes of the four gods became separate persons. There were many gods of different localities. Pele, the goddess of volcanoes, and her numerous family, formed a class of deities by themselves." Courtesy of the Bishop Museum.

Focal Point 3.3: Same Image, Different Contexts

Tracking the same photograph in different publications—with different titles and different explanatory text—provides telling clues regarding intended audience and reception. Here the same photograph circulates in different publications and formats, including postcards, but the contexts in which they circulate are different, so that the audience responds differently.

Figure 13.27. Roy Jerome Baker, "Hawaiian Woman Washing Clothes in Stream near Paia, Maui, 1912." With details concerning place and date, this photograph conveys to the viewer a sense of a document (reproduced in Baker, *Hawaiian Yesterdays,* 20). Courtesy of Mutual Publishing.

Figure 13.28. "Hawaiian Wash Day" (postcard version of photo in fig. 13.27). "Real Photo Card by Baker. Mauna Kea Galleries, Hilo, Hawai'i. $20–30" (reproduced in Blackburn, *Hawaiiana,* 64). Note the difference in caption. Here the same image is viewed in terms of its exchange value as a commodity. Courtesy of Mark Blackburn.

Focal Point 4: Postcards and Tourism

Connections between postcards and tourism are displayed here. For many, Hawai'i is synonymous with tourism. Retail stores, such as the Hawaii and South Seas Curio Company, sold postcards along with other tourist items as souvenirs of Hawai'i. To advertise their cruise ships, Matson Lines used not only postcards but also murals, menu mats, calendars, tourist brochures, baggage labels, and ticket envelopes.

Figure 13.29. Advertising postcard, Hawaii and South Seas Curio Co., mailed ca. 1914 (Bishop Museum). Courtesy of the Bishop Museum.

Figure 13.30. "225. The Island Curio Co. Honolulu, Hawaiian Islands. Oldest, largest and most complete curio store" (advertising postcard, Hawaii and South Seas Curio Co. [reproduced in Blackburn, *Hawaiiana,* 225]). Courtesy of Mark Blackburn.

ROOM 4: CONSTRUCTING "HAWAI'I: POSTCARDS OF EXOTICISM, EXOTICISM OF POSTCARDS"

The final installation space consists of a museum within the museum. Life-size photo blowups on the walls depict museum staff "behind the scenes" preparing the exhibition that the visitor has just seen. The fourth room thus serves as a coda to or commentary on the first three rooms. By self-reflexively staging the exhibition the museum visitor has just viewed, the room stresses the contingent nature of the art historical perspective and museological practices that inform the exhibition. Thus, the exhibition presents multiple perspectives on Hawaiian postcards with the aim of letting museum visitors make up their own minds.

Focal Point 4.1: What We Don't Know

The contingent nature of the exhibition is emphasized through visual displays of what we know and what we do not know. What is striking about postcards is not how much but how little we know. Generally, all we have are the cards themselves. What we do not know—the names of most postcard photographers, the dates of production, the number produced, or, when there is only a catalog number, what the card looked like—is suggested here through a series of blank photographs on the wall, each bearing the name of a photographer of whom we lack a portrait.

Figure 13.31. "Hawaiian Grass House" (postcard [Bishop Museum]). Courtesy of the Bishop Museum.

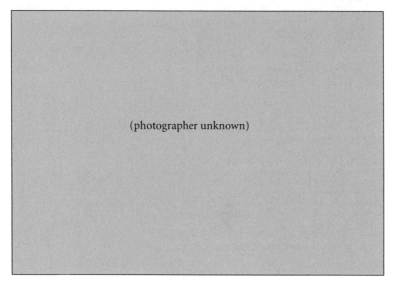

Figure 13.32. "Hawaiian Grass House."

Focal Point 4.2: Deltiology and Deltiologists

What we do know about postcards is pictured here: dealers' business cards, postcard exposition posters, recent book republications of old postcards, and sample pages from price guides. These materials clearly suggest the extent to which the study of postcards (deltiology) is driven not by art historians and museum professionals but by amateur and professional deltiologists and collectors.

Figure 13.33. "Mark Blackburn is the owner of Mauna Kea Galleries in Hilo, Hawai'i" (inside back cover, Black-burn, *Hawaiiana*). Courtesy of Mark Blackburn.

Mark Blackburn is the owner of Mauna Kea Galleries in Hilo, Hawai'i, specializing in items like those illustrated in this book, along with fine paintings, rare books, and artifacts from the romantic past of Hawai'i and Polynesia. Originally from southern California, Mark has a successful import business in Lancaster, Pennsylvania. He has been under the spell of the Pacific islands for over twenty years while actively collecting and dealing in Hawaiian and Polynesian art and artifacts. He can be contacted at the Mauna Kea Galleries, 276 Keawe Street, Hilo, Hawai'i 96720. Telephone 808-969-1184. Fax 808-969-4827.

Focal Point 4.3: But Is It Art?

Since postcards are not generally considered art, they are not usually displayed in museums. Different postcards elicit different responses to the question "But is it art?" some of which are staged here. For those inclined to view postcards as art, certain postcard images can be emphasized. In addition, the view of many contemporaries that such images constitute factual documents or a visual record is also presented. Influenced by the traffic between "high" and "low" culture in twentieth-century art, this exhibition expands the more common art historical emphasis on images per se to encompass their production and reception as well.

Figure 13.34. Hawaiian woman with lauhala for mat weaving, Pukoo, Molokai (Baker photo, 1912; reproduced in Baker, *Hawaiian Yesterdays*, 17). Courtesy of Mutual Publishing.

Figure 13.35. Capitol Building (former Iolani Palace) (Teich color postcard, mailed 1934; reproduced in Edler and Koplin, *26 Postcards of Early Hawaii*, 9). Courtesy of the Lake County (IL) Museum, Curt Teich Postcard Archives.

✳ ✳ ✳ ✳ ✳ ✳ ✳ ✳ ✳ ✳ ✳ ✳ ✳ ✳ ✳ ✳ ✳ ✳

After viewing the various perspectives on postcards presented here, the museum visitor is invited to record his or her comments on the exhibition in a notebook at the exit.

BIBLIOGRAPHIC NOTE

Space limitations prohibit more than a brief bibliographic note. (For a longer In-
ter-net version of this essay, with extensive bibliography and many color
illustrations, go to <http://www.history.uiuc.edu/collecta/Prochaska/Hawaii.html>.)
For background on colonial Hawai'i, see Patrick Kirch and Marshall Sahlins,
Anahulu: The Anthropology of History in the Kingdom of Hawaii, 2 vols. (Chicago:
University of Chicago Press, 1992); Patrick Kirch, *Feathered Gods and Fishhooks*
(Honolulu: University of Hawaii Press, 1985); Marshall Sahlins, *Islands of History*
(Chicago: University of Chicago Press, 1985); Sahlins, *How "Natives" Think: About
Captain Cook, for Example* (Chicago: University of Chicago Press, 1995); Gananath
Obeyesekere, *The Apotheosis of Captain Cook: European Mythmaking in the Pacific*
(Princeton, N.J.: Princeton University Press, 1992); Valeno Valeri, *Kingship and
Sacrifice* (Chicago: University of Chicago Press, 1985); David Malo, *Hawaiian An-
tiquities* (Honolulu: Bishop Museum Press, 1951); John Papa I'i, *Fragments of Ha-
waiian History* (Honolulu: Bishop Museum Press, 1983); Ralph Kuykendall, *The Ha-
waiian Kingdom,* 3 vols. (Honolulu: University of Hawaii Press, 1938–1967); Eleanor
C. Nordyke, *The Peopling of Hawai'i,* 2d ed. (Honolulu: University of Hawaii Press,
1989); Elizabeth Buck, *Paradise Remade: The Politics of Culture and History in
Hawai'i* (Philadelphia: Temple University Press, 1993); and Elvi Whittaker, *The
Mainland Haole: The White Experience in Hawaii* (New York: Columbia University Press, 1986). On separatist political movements in Hawai'i, see Michael Kioni
Dudley and Keoni Kealoha Agard, *A Call for Hawaiian Sovereignty;* Robert H. Mast
and Anne B. Mast, *Autobiography of Protest in Hawaii* (Honolulu: University of
Hawaii Press, 1996); and Noel J. Kent, *Hawaii: Islands under the Influence* (Hono-
lulu: University of Hawaii Press, 1993).

On recent discussions of issues including art and artifact, the gaze, high and low
art, and the nexus of production, imagery, and reception, see Lucien Taylor, ed.,
Visualizing Theory (New York: Routledge, 1994); Martin Jay, *Downcast Eyes: The
Denigration of Vision in Twentieth-Century French Thought* (Berkeley: University
of California Press, 1993); Jonathan Crary, *Techniques of the Observer* (Cambridge,
Mass.: MIT Press); Norman Bryson, *Vision and Painting: The Logic of the Gaze*
(New Haven, Conn.: Yale University Press, 1983); W. J. T. Mitchell, "The Pictorial
Turn," *Picture Theory,* 11–34 (Chicago: University of Chicago Press, 1994); Nelson
Goodman, *Languages of Art* (New York: Bobbs-Merrill, 1968); Laura Mulvey, *Vi-
sual and Other Pleasures* (Bloomington: Indiana University Press, 1989); Linda
Nochlin, "The Imaginary Orient," *The Politics of Vision,* 33–59 (New York: Harper
and Row, 1989); Carol Squiers, ed., *The Critical Image* (Seattle: Bay, 1990), esp. the
essays by Christian Metz and Griselda Pollock; and David Prochaska, "Art of
Colonialism, Colonialism of Art: The *Description de l'Egypte* (1809–1828)," *L'Esprit
Créateur* 34 (1994): 69–91.

On European and North American photography, see Rosalind Krauss, "Photography's Discursive Spaces," *The Originality of the Avant-Garde and Other Modernist Myths*, 131–50 (Cambridge, Mass.: MIT Press, 1985); Rosalind Krauss and Jane Livingston, *L'Amour fou: Photography and Surrealism* (New York: Abbeville, 1985); Abigail Solomon-Godeau, *Photography at the Dock* (Minneapolis: University of Minnesota Press, 1991); Allan Sekula, "The Body and the Archive," *October*, no. 39 (1986): 3–64; and Sekula, "The Traffic in Photographs," *Art Journal* 41 (1981): 15–25. Surveys of photography in Hawai'i or in which photographs figure prominently include Joseph Feher, *Hawai'i: A Pictorial History* (Honolulu: Bishop Museum Press, 1969); Jean Abramson, *Photographers of Old Hawaii* (Honolulu: Island Heritage, 1976); Palani Vaughan, *Na Leo I Ka Makani, Voices on the Wind: Historic Photographs of Hawaiians of Yesteryear* (Honolulu: Mutual, 1987); Joseph G. Mullins, *Hawaiian Journey* (Honolulu: Mutual, 1978); E. B. Scott, *The Saga of the Sandwich Islands* (Crystal Bay, Lake Tahoe, Nev.: Sierra-Tahoe, 1968); Gail Bartholomew, *Maui Remembers: A Local History* (Honolulu: Mutual, 1994); DeSoto Brown, *Aloha Waikiki: 100 Years of Pictures from Hawaii's Most Famous Beach* (Honolulu: Editions Limited, 1985); Grady Timmons, *Waikiki Beachboy* (Honolulu: Editions Limited, 1989). On painting in Hawai'i, see David W. Forbes, *Encounters with Paradise: Visions of Hawaii and Its People, 1778–1941* (Honolulu: Honolulu Academy of Arts, 1992). Monographs on photographers in Hawai'i include Ray Jerome Baker, *Hawaiian Yesterdays: Historical Photographs* (Honolulu: Mutual, 1982); Lynn Ann Davis, *A Photographer in the Kingdom: Christian J. Hedemann's Early Images of Hawai'i* (Honolulu: Bishop Museum Press, 1988); and Davis, *Na Pa'i Ki'i: The Photographers in the Hawaiian Islands, 1845–1900* (Honolulu: Bishop Museum Press, 1980). Works that reproduce Hawaiian postcards or in which postcards are featured include Jack Edler and Edith Koplin, *26 Postcards of Early Hawaii* (Honolulu: Maile, 1989); Timmons, *Waikiki Beachboy;* and DeSoto Brown, *Hawaii Recalls: Selling Romance to America, Nostalgic Images of the Hawaiian Islands (1910–1950)* (Honolulu: Editions Limited, 1982).

Among analytic, theoretically informed studies of non-Western photography, see Christopher Pinney, *Camera Indica: The Social Life of Indian Photographs* (Chicago: University of Chicago Press, 1997); Deborah Poole, *Vision, Race, and Modernity: A Visual Economy of the Andean Image World* (Princeton, N.J.: Princeton University Press, 1997); Abigail Solomon-Godeau, "A Photographer in Jerusalem, 1855: Auguste Salzmann and His Times," *October*, no. 18 (1981): 91–107; Elizabeth Edwards, ed., *Anthropology and Photography, 1860–1920* (New Haven, Conn.: Yale University Press, 1992), esp. the essays by Pinney and Faris; Frederick Bohrer, *A New Antiquity: Assyria, Exoticism, and Reception* (forthcoming); Malek Alloula, *The Colonial Harem* (Minneapolis: University of Minnesota Press, 1986); David Prochaska, "The Archive of 'L'Algérie imaginaire,'" *History and Anthropol-*

ogy 4 (1990): 373–420; Prochaska, "Fantasia of the *Photothèque:* French Postcard Views of Colonial Senegal," *African Arts* 24 (1991): 40–47; and Prochaska, "Telling Photos," in *Orientalism and History,* ed. Edmund Burke III and David Prochaska (forthcoming).

Two innovative museum installations are Susan Vogel, *Art/Artifact: African Art in Anthropology Collections,* exh. cat. (New York: Center for African Art, 1988); and Lisa G. Corrin, *Mining the Museum: An Installation by Fred Wilson,* exh. cat. (New York: New Press, 1994). Less innovative but closer thematically to the exhibition proposed here is Antonin Sevruguin and the Persian Image, curated by Frederick N. Bohrer and scheduled to open at the Arthur M. Sackler/Freer Gallery of Art in September 1999. On museum representations of Hawaiians generally, see Adrienne L. Kaeppler, "*Ali'i* and *Maka'ainana:* The Representation of Hawaiians in Museums at Home and Abroad," in *Museums and Communities,* ed. Ivan Karp, Christine Mullen Kreamer, and Steven D. Lavine, 458–75 (Washington, D.C.: Smithsonian Institution Press, 1992).

On the constructed nature of postcard images, see Prochaska, "*L'Algérie imaginaire*" and "Fantasia of the *Photothèque*"; and Virginia Lee-Webb, "Manipulated Images: European Photographs of Pacific Peoples," in *Prehistories of the Future: The Primitivist Project and the Culture of Modernism,* ed. Elazar Barkan and Ronald Bush, 175–201 (Stanford, Calif.: Stanford University Press, 1995). On collecting, including postcard collecting, see John Elsner and Roger Cardinal, eds., *The Cultures of Collecting* (Cambridge, Mass.: Harvard University Press, 1994); and James Clifford, "On Collecting Art and Culture," *The Predicament of Culture,* 215–51 (Cambridge, Mass.: Harvard University Press, 1988).

Postcards and photographs by photographers active in Hawaii are located primarily in the Hawaii State Archives and the Bishop Museum, both in Honolulu. These repositories, especially the Bishop Museum, also contain a certain amount of manuscript information on the photographers On Char, Morito Koga, Tai Sing Loo, J. J. Williams, Ray Jerome Baker, and others. On Baker, see in addition Baker, *Hawaiian Yesterdays.* For information on the Curt Teich Postcard Archives, see their periodical, *Image File.*

Contributors

Rachel Buff, an assistant professor of history at Bowling Green State University, is the author of *CALLING HOME: Im/Migration, Race, and Popular Memory in Caribbean Brooklyn and Native American Minneapolis, 1945–1992*. She is working on a cultural history of illegal immigration.

Laura E. Donaldson is of Scots-Irish and Cherokee descent and teaches English, women's studies, and American Indian/native studies at the University of Iowa. She is the author of *Decolonizing Feminisms: Race, Gender, and Empire-Building* and two books-in-progress, *The Skin of God: American Indian Writing as Colonial Technology and Postcolonial Appropriation* and *Signs of Orpah: Biblical Reading in the Contact Zone*.

John Dorst is a professor of American studies at the University of Wyoming and the author of the highly regarded ethnography *The Written Suburb*. He has recently completed *Looking West*, on the discourse of visual experience in the American West and its relations to museums, living history, and other display environments in the region.

Elena Glasberg is an assistant professor of liberal studies at California State University at Los Angeles. She is the author of the textbook *Literature and Gender* and is completing an interdisciplinary study of the symbolic and literal mappings of Antarctica as part of a broader reconsideration of the intersections of postcolonial theory and American studies.

C. Richard King, an assistant professor of anthropology at Drake University, is the author of *Colonial Discoures, Collective Memories, and the Exhibtion of Native American Cultures and Histories in the Contemporary United States*. He is researching the history and significance of Native American mascots, devoting particular attention to race, identity, and resistance.

Brij David Lunine is a doctoral candidate in American studies at the University of New Mexico. His dissertation offers an ethnographic account of adolescent identity formation and the uses of popular culture in south Berkeley, California.

Donna Kay Maeda is an associate professor of religious studies at Occidental College in Los Angeles. Her work in the area of social ethics examines the use of the language of rights to articulate claims about justice. She is writing an article that considers intersections of legal and religious discourses in productions of racial and cultural difference in the United States.

Arthur Martin, a writer and teacher living in northern Georgia, has a Ph.D. degree in anthropology from the University of New Mexico. His dissertation, "Enchantment and Colonization," analyzes the culture of modernity among twentieth-century Anglo migrants in Taos, New Mexico.

Russell T. McCutcheon, an assistant professor of religious studies at Southwest Missouri State University, is the author of *Manufacturing Religion: The Discourse on "Sui Generis" Religion and the Politics of Nostalgia* and a coeditor of *Dictionary of Religion, Society, and Culture.* He is also the editor of the journal *Method and Theory in the Study of Religion.*

Susie O'Brien is an assistant professor at McMaster University in Hamilton, Ontario, where she teaches courses in postcolonial literatures and popular culture. Her current research focuses on relationships between postcolonial culture and the environment.

David Prochaska is an associate professor of history at the University of Illinois at Urbana-Champaign. The author of *Making Algeria French: Colonialism in Bone, 1870–1920,* among other works, he specializes in comparative colonial history and postcolonial studies. His current research focuses on colonial photography.

E. San Juan Jr. is the chair of and a professor in the Department of Comparative American Cultures at Washington State University. He has published extensively on race and ethnic relations, cultural studies, comparative literature, and historical materialism, including *Hegemony and Strategies of Transgression, The Philippine Temptation, From Exile to Diaspora,* and *Beyond Postcolonial Theory* and is completing a book entitled *The Racial Imaginary.*

Jenny Sharpe teaches English at the University of California at Los Angeles and is the author of *Allegories of Empire: The Figure of the Woman in the Colonial Text.*

Jon Stratton is a senior lecturer in cultural studies at Curtin University of Technology in Perth, Western Australia. He has published widely in the area of cultural studies and is the author of three books, including *Writing Sites: A Genealogy of the Postmodern World* and *The Desirable Body: Cultural Fetishism and the Erotics of Consumption.*

Index

Typeset in 10.5/12.5 Adobe Minion
with Gill Sans display
Composed by Celia Shapland
for the University of Illinois Press
Manufactured by Data Reproductions Corporation

University of Illinois Press
1325 South Oak Street
Champaign, IL 61820-6903
www.press.uillinois.edu